Vanja Hamzić is Senior Lecturer in Legal History and Legal Anthropology at the School of Oriental and African Studies (SOAS), University of London. He has held numerous prestigious research positions, including the residential membership in the School of Social Science of the Institute for Advanced Study at Princeton. His main body of work interrogates historical and present-day formations of gender and sexuality in various Islamicate societies of South Asia, Southeast Asia and West Africa. He is co-author, with Ziba Mir-Hosseini, of *Control and Sexuality: The Revival of Zina Laws in Muslim Contexts* (2010).

'Human rights law speaks volumes to Islamic law on behalf of sexual minorities in the Muslim world, but this book, based on extensive fieldwork in Lahore, Pakistan, turns the tables. It plumbs Islamic Law as a source for understanding, celebrating, protecting, and learning from sexually diverse and gender-variant Muslims today and historically – and for enriching a human rights vocabulary on sexual diversity that pales by comparison with Vanja Hamzić's rich ethnography and his genealogy of treasured sexual minorities in Islamic law from the early *umma* to the never-quite-post colonial present.'

— Janet Halley, Royall Professor of Law, Harvard Law School

'Vanja Hamzić's book is one of those rare endeavours that gather up disparate worlds of human action to present a synthesis that jolts us out of our accustomed ways of thinking. Undertaking a masterful journey through history, law, and ethnography this book reflects on gender and sexual diversity in the Muslim world – both past and present. How does the salvational agency of the law discipline this diversity as it reorients subjectivities and lifeworlds? How do we square sexual and gender difference with equality? These are some of the probing questions this book cogently asks.'

— Saba Mahmood, Professor of Anthropology, University of California at Berkeley

SEXUAL AND GENDER DIVERSITY IN THE MUSLIM WORLD

History, Law and Vernacular Knowledge

VANJA HAMZIĆ

I.B. TAURIS

LONDON • NEW YORK • OXFORD • NEW DELHI • SYDNEY

I.B. TAURIS
Bloomsbury Publishing Plc
50 Bedford Square, London, WC1B 3DP, UK
1385 Broadway, New York, NY 10018, USA

BLOOMSBURY, I.B. TAURIS and the I.B. Tauris logo
are trademarks of Bloomsbury Publishing Plc

First published 2016
Paperback edition first published 2019

ISBN: HB: 978-1-7845-3332-8
PB: 978-1-7883-1508-1
ePDF: 978-0-8577-2818-0
eBook: 978-0-8577-2883-8

Series: Library of Islamic South Asia 1

Typeset in Garamond Three by OKS Prepress Services, Chennai, India

To find out more about our authors and books visit
www.bloomsbury.com and sign up for our newsletters.

To Safet

CONTENTS

Acknowledgements   x

Introduction   1

Subjectivities and Subjects of Analysis   3
The Concept, Scope and Structure of the Book   5
How to Read and 'Interrupt' with this Book   7

1. A Critique of Terminological Conundrums   11

Law and Identity   12
Human Rights   14
Sexual Rights   18
Sexual Orientation and Gender Identity   23
Muslims and Sexual/Gender Taxonomies   31

2. Sexual and Gender Diversity in International Human
    Rights Law and Its Originatory Milieux   34

Criminalisation and Decriminalisation: A Discursive Genealogy   37
    Desexualising the Human: Stoic Legacies and Early
    Christian Anxieties   38
    Reviving the Ancient: Sexuality and Gender in the
    Context of Church Reform   42
    Buggery and Its Afterlives: From Royal Opportunism
    to Republican Deceit   48

Sexuality, Gender and Diversity in (a Post-Colonial)
International Law   53
   The Rise of 'Sexual Orientation' and 'Gender Identity' in
   International Human Rights Law   56
   The Brave New Millennium: From Brazilian Resolution
   to Yogyakarta Principles   59
   The (Muslim) Opposition and (Some) Discontents:
   The Sexuality and Gender of a Body Politic   68
Empire of Law and Subjectivity   77

3. Sexual and Gender Diversity in Islamic Law and the
   Muslim World   80

Dynamics of Desire: Towards an Interruptive History
of Islamic Law   86
   On Indeterminacy and Form(ul)ation: From Early Umma
   to Eponymous Fuqaha'   87
   The First Interlude: Hudud *and* Liwat *in Classical* Fiqh 100
   The Second Interlude: Siyasa *and* Liwat *in the Great*
   Seljuk Empire   102
   Some 'Post-Classical' Dilemmas: Mamluk and Ottoman
   (Re-)Visions of a Muslim Self   108
   The Third Interlude: Khuddam/Aghawat *in the*
   Interstices of Law   121
Islamic Law in (Post-)Colonial Macrocosm: Modernity
and Its Others   123
   Hybrids and Capitulations: Reforms in 'British' India
   and in Late Ottoman State   125
   European and Muslim Modernism: On Futility of Resistance
   from a Nation State   129
   From Feminist to Sexual/Gender-Pluralist Hermeneutics:
   Islamic Law in Post-Modern Futurity   134
Interruptive Pasts of Discursive Legalities   137

4. Muslim Sexual and Gender Diversity in Contemporary
   Pakistan   141

Law and Society in Pakistan and Punjab   144
   Formal Judicial System of Pakistan   147

Constitutional Law: Fundamental Rights and Case 63/09 148
The Punjabi Paradigm: Social as Legal Ethos 151
Sexually Diverse and Gender-Variant Muslims: Toward
un Pèlerinage Inclusif 153
The *Khwajasara* Tropes 156
  Origins, Kinship and Sociality 159
  Spirituality 164
  Law, Politics and Society: Limitless Solidarity, Limited
  Co-operation 166
The Circuits of Class and Knowledge: 'Why Don't We Go
Across the Canal?' 169
  Selfhood, Communality and Communicability 170
  Spirituality 175
  Law, Politics and Society: Between Our Niyyat *and Their Agenda* 176
Lessons in the Vernacular: How to Dismantle an
Epistemic Bomb 179
  The Spectacle of Intervention 180
  Domestic Law 182
  International Law 184
  Human Rights: A Quest for Greater Happiness 186
  Whither Islamic Law (in Punjab/Pakistan)? 187
Towards Epistemological Primacy of Vernacular Knowledge 188

Conclusion 190

Co-Histories in the Making 190
Insurrectionary Vernacular Knowledge 193
Towards the Praxis of Human Rights? 194
Towards the Praxis of Islamic Law? 196

Notes 198
Bibliography 286
Index 322

ACKNOWLEDGEMENTS

Writing this book has been a labour of love and struggle, in which countless acts of kindness, advice and support have sustained me and critically shaped my work. I have tremendous gratitude for my family, friends and colleagues, scattered around the world. While I cannot name all of you here, I hope that you know how profoundly you have enriched my life and the pages that are about to unfold.

The book is primarily based on my doctoral thesis at King's College London, University of London, submitted in 2012 CE. This project was supervised by Robert Wintemute and Penny Green, of School of Law, King's College London. Rob, your wisdom, intellectual rigour and constant encouragement have made my doctoral journey an enjoyable and multiply rewarding experience. Not only were you my enthusiastic mentor in all the stages this work has gone through; teaching with you a Human Rights Law module at King's gave me an invaluable opportunity to further develop my insights into some of the key concepts of this book, through lively conversations with our students. And, above all, you were my friend, someone I could always rely on, someone who always had time and some good advice to offer for this research. Penny, I have benefited enormously from your engaging feedback, inspiration and patience. Your unreserved support and kindness have followed me since the beginning of my doctoral studies, to the extent that I have never experienced before in an academic setting. So, Rob and Penny, I owe you both the greatest debt of thanks. I am also grateful to other colleagues and friends at King's for turning our school into an oasis of learning, especially to Maleiha Malik, whose early engagement with my thesis has given it some of its critical orientations.

Beyond the walls of my doctoral alma mater, my foremost academic advisor and a true friend was Janet Halley, of Harvard Law School. Janet, I cannot express my gratitude enough for your invaluable insights, friendship and support. To you and your scholarship I owe the gift of critique. Our cordial and inspiring encounters have made Harvard's critical legal landscapes my second intellectual home. For that I am also grateful to other wonderful 'crits', gravitating around the Institute for Global Law and Policy (IGLP) at Harvard Law School. Our invigorating exchange is reflected in this work.

My thesis was meticulously examined by Susan Marks, of London School of Economics and Political Science, and 'Amr Shalakany, of the American University in Cairo. Their comments were immensely instructive in turning my doctoral work into this book. Without their critique and support, I would not have been able to articulate some nuances intrinsic to this study. Susan and 'Amr, I am so grateful for your guidance. This book's making was, of course, a stylistic exercise, too. Genevieve Painter's candid comments helped me gradually abandon some of my less palatable 'doctoral' stylistic traits. Thanks, Genevieve, for all your help.

I acknowledge the generous institutional support to this project. My doctoral studies at King's were made possible through a three-year studentship, awarded by the School of Law. My ethnographic work in Pakistan, especially in 2011 CE, was partly sponsored by the University of London Central Research Fund, while my archival research in Egypt, in 2012 CE, was funded by the Centre of European Law at King's College London. My other archival work and ability to obtain sometimes very difficult to find and expensive literature was mainly dependent upon a series of grants provided by the Santander/Doha fund administered by the IGLP and Harvard Law School. To all of them I would like to extend my sincere gratitude.

Additionally, I am thankful to my colleagues at the School of Oriental and African Studies (SOAS), University of London, where I presently work, for allowing this research to take precedence over some of my other duties, especially in the final stage of writing the book. That this work is published in the present form is mainly thanks to the enthusiasm and support with which the I.B.Tauris editor Azmina Siddique has welcomed it, for which I am deeply grateful. My thanks are also due for the remarkable professionalism of David Campbell and other members of the I.B.Tauris crew; what a joy to publish this book with them!

I am, however, particularly and incalculably indebted to my numerous friends and interlocutors in Pakistan and India, for bringing this book to life. Thank you for your welcome, your guidance, your trust and your limitless kindness. Out of respect for those of you who wish to stay anonymous, I refrain from giving out any names, but my deepest admiration and gratitude goes to each and every one of you. I hope that this book will be of some help in your valiant uphill struggle.

Finally, Safet Hadžimuhamedović has given this work those most precious, ineffable dimensions. So, Safet, this is for you.

INTRODUCTION

The late afternoon mist engulfs Lahore and, with it, the light and noise from the street outside. We are sitting at Neeli's modest home, surrounded by her *sari*-clad companions. Her eyes command my full attention. And then, in a somewhat solemn voice, she begins to recount:

> Mainandi was the first; there were many others afterwards, but we remember her. Mainandi used to work in a Mughal royal court. One day, one of the women of the royal court got pregnant, so it was necessary to find out how did that happen. Mainandi used to work at the court, but she was born *khwajasara*, so she didn't have the male organ, she had something of the size of an almond. So, when one of the women got pregnant, it was necessary to find out who had impregnated her. So, the men were lined up, including Mainandi, and they started stripping them down naked. Mainandi was really scared, for this was the first time that everyone in the palace would know that she was born *khwajasara*. When the time came for Mainandi to strip, she was so ashamed of being recognised as *khwajasara*, that she left the beloved palace and started wandering the streets. She asked the Mughal emperor, 'Oh, what will become of me?' And he replied, 'I give you the authority to beg; go wherever you want'. That's where the tradition of begging started.
>
> Anyway, so, Mainandi was walking as she was begging, and a *zenana* came up to her. *Zenana* asked, 'What are you doing?' She replied that she was given authority to beg, because of the way she

was born. And she showed her genitals to the *zenana*. *Zenana* went home and took a sugarcane, which has a peel over it. And the peel is really sharp. So, she used it to cut off her male organ. And the next day she went to Mainandi and said, 'I'm exactly like you now'. But Mainandi was shocked and cried, 'Oh, what things start happening in this world!' So, Mainandi prayed to Allah that she would be buried alive. As she prayed, the earth opened up and she started falling inside the earth. And, as she was going in, she told the *zenana*, 'Use oil and water on your wounds, and you will be fine'.[1]

This book is about those who followed in the footsteps of Mainandi and about many other sexually diverse and gender-variant Muslims. The book follows their own footsteps, in literature, oral traditions, vernacular histories and cultural memory. But it is also about finding and understanding their *place* between the dominant discursive iterations of international human rights law and Islamic law.

In the history of today, the legal concepts of sexual orientation and gender identity are increasingly seen as strictly forbidden grounds of discrimination in international law. Yet, according to some Muslim-majority governments, such concepts explicitly 'contradict the tenets of Islam' and can, thus, 'be considered as a direct insult to the 1.2 billion Muslims around the world'.[2] Through a comparative historical analysis, this book interrogates both of these claims, in order to examine their veracity as well as to comprehend why and how they came about. I argue that the principal historical environment of international human rights law is European legal and social ethos, with its intricate ideological baggage, while pre-modern Muslim polities traditionally housed the key developments in and of Islamic law. This book, therefore, looks into those two specific legal, social and religious environments in order to recount their complex relationship with human sexual and gender diversity. These parallel genealogies are, then, juxtaposed with a brief ethnographic study of the lifeworlds of sexually diverse and gender-variant Muslims in contemporary Pakistan, where discourses of Islamic law and human rights law meet and produce peculiar *localised* narratives.

The central idea pursued in this book is that Muslim sexually diverse and gender-variant subjectivities are not merely the inert subjects of the dominant discourses of international human rights law and Islamic law, but rather the resilient and skilful participants in their iteration, contestation and localisation, which can involve a variety of disruptive, counter-hegemonic practices. The book also shows that a closer look into the histories of the two dominant discourses reveals the potential for a more harmonious relationship between them, one in which sexual and gender difference is no longer seen as an 'insult' but, rather, an intrinsic element of human selfhood.

Subjectivities and Subjects of Analysis

While the number of comparative academic analyses of international human rights law and Islamic law has seen a steady increase,[3] they either choose not to address the question of sexual and gender diversity *at all*,[4] or they give it a passing, apologetic commentary. The latter is, for example, the case in Mashood A. Baderin's widely influential study *International Human Rights and Islamic Law*, which asserts that '[h]omosexuality is generally seen to be strongly against the moral fabric and sensibilities of Islamic society and is prohibited morally and legally under Islamic law'.[5] This is, claims Baderin, one of those 'moral questions' that warrant the margin of appreciation similar to that in the European Court of Human Rights:[6] a leeway from otherwise enforceable principles of international human rights law that would allow the Muslim-majority states to do as they see fit with their sexually diverse and gender-variant citizens.[7] This may come as a surprise, especially because the general tenor of this and other similar studies is largely uncritical of international human rights law, which is presented as a model system, in conformity with which the contemporary versions of Islamic law should generally be remoulded. Excluding sexual and gender plurality from this paramount course may, then, be understood as a balancing act, a 'necessary' sacrifice at the altar of inter-governmental 'human rights' co-operation in Muslim-majority contexts.

Aside from still indeterminate and unbecoming comparative academic discourses on Islamic law and international human rights law, the literature that focuses on sexually diverse and gender-variant Muslims discusses only 'the law in context'. Islamic law is seen and dealt with as integral to the Muslim self, while human rights are rarely, if ever, mentioned. The relevant studies include historical,[8] literary,[9] theological,[10] anthropological and sociological[11] critique, often by scholars whose personal identification with the subject matter gives these accounts an activist edge.[12] This literature generally sees 'Islamic law [a]s a derivative act tied ultimately to the interpretations and extractions of the jurists and legal scholars'.[13] Seeking to sunder a Gordian knot, this literature aims to rescue Islamic law from the legal elites, past and present, by means, *inter alia*, of its own 'queer-friendly Islamic hermeneutics'.[14] While significant, these academic interventions are not necessarily 'law-friendly' in a sense that they, by and large, fail to showcase how the distinctly *legal* narratives on sexuality and gender had managed to prevail in the great majority of pre-modern Muslim polities and, arguably, resurface in the wake of Muslim-majority nation states.

How, then, can the 'common grounds' and disparities between international human rights law and Islamic law be more productively analysed? Where and how can sexually diverse and gender-variant *subjects* be located *and* approached? Who are they? When and how did they come about? Does the law – whether of Islamic, European, international or domestic provenance – *matter* to them, or it is 'just there'?[15] If it does, how do they perceive it and use it in their specific social and political environment? Moreover, what can both historical and present-day discourses about sexuality and gender that affect sexually diverse and gender-variant Muslims tell us about the *law* itself; that is, about its structures and mechanics, about its social performativity and its capacity for change?

This book has an ambitious task in seeking to offer potential answers to these and many other related questions. If the *subjectivity* of human beings is understood as their *personal* interpretations of their experiences (consisting of emotional, intellectual, spiritual, cultural, gender/sexual and – one could also add – historical, political and legal perceptions of *themselves*, and of the world that surrounds them), then the main protagonists of this book are those Muslim *subjectivities* whose lifeworlds – the individual realms of experience and desire – transgress the heteronormative boundaries of their society at large. Although, as we shall see, these subjectivities sometimes go by a variety of vernacular and/or globalised taxonomies, in this book I do not attempt to confer upon them any universal identitary lexeme or episteme. That is because they themselves are, more often than not, exceptionally careful not to be 'called names' that they do not feel entirely comfortable with. Furthermore, however important, their sexual and gender experience is only a segment of their negotiation and understanding of themselves, which cannot be artificially extrapolated outside the domain in which other experiences and desires form equally significant iterations of their selfhood. For this reason, certain discursive practices of Islamic law and human rights may have an affective value, too; that is, they can matter *personally*, on an individual, subjective level, as part of one's sense of self.

In light of the affective capacity of both Islamic law and human rights, this book benefits, in particular, from the insights of the school of thought known as legal Realism, which aphoristically proposed, in 1881 CE, that '[t]he life of the law has not been logic; it has been experience'.[16] This chiefly jurisprudential experience,[17] the Realists assert, had gradually gone *beyond* the skilfully dogmatised pragmatic considerations of the past,[18] thereby creating large gaps between the 'law in books' and the 'law in action'.[19] Central to the later elaborations of these claims was a proposal, put forward in 1979 CE, that 'legal action' of sorts *also* takes place outside the formal realm of the law – that is, *in its shadow*[20] – via an intricate web of everyday bargaining practices. The Realist view of law is, thus, not confined to legal statutes and treatises, or to their formal mechanisms of implementation; instead, 'law [is] in flux'[21] precisely because it is based on human agency on various societal levels, including those that may not be readily apparent or acceptable to the 'official' legists. When dealing with Islamic law and international human rights law, then, this book *also* takes an interest in their historical and contemporary *shadows*. As we shall soon find out, these shadows are bursting with (legal) life.

The Concept, Scope and Structure of the Book

This book rests upon three interrelated premises. First, I propose that a critical, comparative look into the historical trajectories of international human rights law and Islamic law can unearth hitherto uncharted legal and social landscapes, in which what passes today as 'the law' on sexual and gender diversity, in either Muslim or human rights milieux, is given a much-needed *contextual* interpretation. The interpretative signposts come from jurisprudence, but also from the politics, theology and sociology of law.

Second, if this comparative historical exercise is to include 'the shadow of the law' as well, it needs to develop a critical approach both to *how* legal historiographies are told and to *what* sources and materials they encompass. The problem is not only in the hegemonic deployments of 'European' knowledge and worldviews, commonly centred in Enlightenment thought, permeating academic research; the difficulty also lies in escaping from the ideas advanced by legal studies as to *where* one can *seek* and *locate* the law (of the present and of the past). This book thus embraces chiefly anthropological approaches to legal research, including explorations of cultural memory and vernacular narratives about the law – phenomena well below the radar of legal studies. Related to this is the question of the approach to history *as such*: its periodisation; its obfuscation of 'non-normative' sexual/gendered subjectivities; its ideological colourisation of people and events; in short, its limited capacity to listen and to tell. This book seeks to overcome those misgivings by inventing, in due course, its own, 'interruptive' narrative voice.

Third and lastly, it is posited that, whatever one can discover in a general historical study of international human rights law and Islamic law, those findings need to be tested on the ground. In other words, a material locale, with its idiosyncratic social and legal landscape, offers an all-important litmus test of broader theoretical claims. In this case, then, a critical legal ethnographic analysis is pursued, based largely on my fieldwork, in 2011 CE, on the gender-variant and sexually diverse Muslims of Lahore, Punjab and Pakistan. Neither that specific research, nor this book in general, pretends, however, to convey a 'totalistic' narrative of sexual and gender difference in *any* and *every* Muslim locale. The same caveat applies to my explorations of the general discursive practices of international human rights law and Islamic law. Their aim is, rather, to offer a limited contribution to the ongoing academic and societal debates on gender, sexuality, law and human rights, especially in Muslim contexts.

The tale of the book that is about to unfold is woven around three major quests, each with a specific geographical and temporal scope. The first one explores the discursive practices and legal landscapes that arguably have coalesced, over the past two millennia and only after dramatic seismic moves, into what is today seen in international law as the dominant position on sexual and gender diversity. The second quest follows Islamic law: from its inception, in the seventh-century CE Hijaz,[22] through its iterations and developments in the centres of Muslim medieval thought (including historical 'visits' to Damascus,

Baghdad, Cairo and Istanbul), until its modern and post-modern incarnations. The goal is to provide a closer look into the Islamic legal and social ethos, as it relates to sexual and gender plurality. Finally, the third pursuit begins in Lahore and stays within the Indian subcontinent; this story begins with the *imponderabilia*[23] largely associated with the region's Mughal past, but its main protagonists are the contemporary gender-variant and sexually diverse Pakistani Muslims, with their vernacular experience of Islamic, international and municipal law, and of human rights.

The structure of the book is as follows: Chapter 2 offers a brief discussion of the meanings and scopes of the key notions used in this study. Chapter 3 examines the historical and contemporary domain of international human rights law. It recounts a discursive genealogy of criminalisation and decriminalisation of gender-variance and certain same-sex sexual practices, and it then moves on to discuss gender/sexual plurality in post-colonial international law. Chapter 4 turns to the Islamic legal tradition and its philosophical, historical and socio-political perspectives on sexual and gender diversity. After a detailed account of the early Muslim polities, it also considers the relevant laws and their political and cultural milieux in Muslim colonial and post-colonial societies. Chapters 3 and 4, then, can be read in parallel with one another, and thus compared and contrasted. In Chapter 5, the high seas of international human rights law and Islamic law meet in a single, contemporary locale: that of the Islamic Republic of Pakistan and, more specifically and intimately, its cultural capital, the ancient city of Lahore, with its numerous sexually diverse and gender-variant subjectivities and their exhilarating legal narratives. Finally, Chapter 6 hosts some concise concluding remarks.

How to Read and 'Interrupt' with this Book

In so far as the relevant historical and contemporary literature is concerned, this book pursues an interdisciplinary theoretical approach mindful, in the first place, of the value of *critique*[24] and of those *critical* studies of law, gender and sexuality that are based on, or at least take account of, vernacular systems of knowledge. Those include, but they are by no means limited to, the various post-colonial, Marxist, feminist and legal Realist insights. Also, whenever possible, the preference is given to primary historical sources, although their secondary *critical* explorations are not dismissed. But such multiplicity and hierarchy of sources does not guarantee, in and of itself, the unseating of *hegemonic pasts*. In fact, the very categories of 'time' and 'context' are often susceptible of historical determinism that seeks to preserve the normativities of the present by means of an overbearing, seemingly *orthodox* past. That there are parallel and multiple pasts and presents, sometimes providing utterly disparate views of public or social 'order', is beside the point here; what matters is *how* to approach and critically intervene into the continuous reproduction of such hierarchical trajectories of both 'time' and 'context'.

Historical analyses pursued in this book – particularly those relating to Islamic law and the Muslim world – seek to avoid *linear* portrayals of the past. Instead, an 'interruptive' method is developed, which allows for looking into historical narratives from various temporal and cultural contexts, thus challenging the mainstream, non-vernacular period-isations and generalisations of certain long-lasting historical phenom-ena. This method relies especially on *interludes* – the detailed explorations of a certain topic from a specific cultural angle – strategically deployed within the main narrative to balance its potentially 'totalising' effects. The idea is, quite simply, to interrupt the central storyline with shorter and more specific narrations, which by revealing how a particular historical community has dealt with certain issues can help us see those issues as developing in *multiple*, sometimes even incommensurable contexts, rather than through an imagined, general linear progression. Legal studies are, arguably, especially prone to crude historical generalisations; this book is careful to avoid this unhelpful disciplinary predicament.

The empirical segment of this book, presented in Chapter 5, is a critical ethnography of law and society in Lahore and, by extension, in Punjab and Pakistan, focusing on the lifeworlds of sexually diverse and gender-variant Muslims.[25] Since an ethnographic research 'acquires knowledge of the social world from intimate familiarity with it',[26] the fieldwork for this book relies primarily on the process of 'participant observation', a qualitative anthropological method that involves, *inter alia*, unstructured or semi-structured individual and group interviews[27] as well as records of 'everyday life'. In this book, it is also complimented with an examination of the collected oral traditions and recordings of other iterations of cultural memory in Lahori daily life. The empiricist character of this methodological orientation is emphasised by aiming to present the 'primary data of sufficient quantity and depth to allow them to be reinterpreted from a theoretical perspective different from the one that produced them'.[28] It is geared towards establishing a rapport with the participants[29] and towards understanding 'the world as it is known to those who dwell therein',[30] in order to account for what Clifford Geertz has dubbed 'local knowledge'[31] and what Boaventura de Sousa Santos has referred to as 'vernacular epistemology'.[32] It is in this – less geographical than intimate or relational and by no means state- or polity-bound – sense that 'the Muslim World' of this book should be primarily understood and appreciated. It is a world of lifeworlds and worldviews, with no finite borders yet with plenty of locales, and the knowledge systems constitutive thereof.

Being a *critical* ethnography, the empirical part of this book is, methodologically, also 'an ethnography of ethnography',[33] which examines this approach *itself* whilst pursuing it and which rigorously positions the researcher in the field, as both an outsider to the dynamics of *localised* cultural/social exchange[34] and as at least a temporary *participant* in that process. It is, however, also acknowledged that 'ethnography is especially well-suited to handle the methodological challenges associated with distinguishing practices, identities and hegemonic structures of gender and sexuality'.[35] For instance, due to their focus on 'local knowledge', ethnographic accounts are less likely to reproduce 'the power structures of colonialism by subsuming non-Western configurations of personhood into Western constructs of sexuality and gender'.[36] In this book, that quality is particularly emphasised by applying the method of *ethnographic analogy*, which looks for clues of the past in the practices of living communities and contemporary human subject positions.[37] This is not to essentialise the vernacular identitary tropes and practices, past and present, but, again, to provide for an epistemological approach that does not depend on the dominant, mostly global northern, systems of knowledge (production). Furthermore, as explained in some detail in Chapter 5, this work was shaped by various ethical considerations, including those of the security and, where requested, anonymity of my interlocutors in Pakistan.

The terms, phrases and quotations from the languages that do not use the Latin alphabet are Romanised in this book in accordance with the most widely used styles of transliteration, but diacritical marks of those styles are omitted, save in the case of Sanskrit, and except (‘) and (’) for *'ayn* and *hamza* in Arabic. Furthermore, the words and sentences in Greek and Russian are reproduced in their original alphabets, whilst diacritics of those languages that are nowadays commonly written in Latin alphabet, such as Turkish or Bosnian, are not left out. The non-English terms are always italicised, save for the proper nouns.

Finally, a word about calendars. The book uses, wherever appropriate, a dual system of dating, with the Gregorian dates (marked CE or BCE) usually preceding the dates from the Hijri calendar (marked AH). While this is a standard practice in studies of Islam, it is *also* pursued here in order to remind the reader of the multiple perceptions of time that inform this work, and with them, of multiple perspectives on the historical and present-day human *self*.

CHAPTER 1

A CRITIQUE OF
TERMINOLOGICAL
CONUNDRUMS

Prior to an analysis of sexual and gender diversity in international human rights law and Islamic law and their relevance to the lifeworlds of sexually diverse and gender-variant Muslims, it might be salient to critically introduce a number of underlying discourses on human self-identification and rights. These discourses remain the site of fierce contestations across academic disciplines and social institutions, and more often than not, direct and frame the way sexual and gender diversity is thought and taught, especially in the legal domain. My primary intent here is to problematise the meaning and the scope of notions such as 'human rights', 'sexual rights', 'sexual orientation' and 'gender identity', as well as some identitary scripts of sexual and gender difference. That these notions and scripts form *a* language, or often – *the* language, in which one's knowledge about the self and the other is related, contested or preserved, is apparent to any contemporary scholar of gender and sexuality; what is sometimes less readily visible is the limited capacity of this language to account for ambiguities, imponderabilia and other-than-common senses of one's sexual/gender selfhood and any public claims, including those framed as one's *rights*, attached to them.

For example, in the case of 'human rights', the seemingly perennial disagreement between the universalist and cultural relativist camps[1] is relevant in regards to the so-called international human rights legal *standards* on sexual orientation and gender identity. States that incline to cultural relativist interpretations of human rights may seek to justify the violations of those standards by claiming that human rights to sexual and gender plurality conflict with their particular 'culture'. In a similar vein, the clashing essentialist and constructionist discourses on the origins and universal validity of the notions of 'sexual orientation' and 'gender identity' have been instrumental in discussions about the identity politics around sexual and gender diversity.[2] But, can the language of standards suffice in an ontic dilemma that individuals and communities sometimes face when forced to choose, in private as well as in public domains, between multiple facets of 'what it means to be themselves'?

Let us, then, first query (if somewhat rhetorically) what law has to do with human identities, and *vice versa*, what it means to be someone in law. This trajectory reveals, of necessity, that law 'can "make up" people'[3] and that identities, orientations and proclivities remain the domain of legal intervention *par excellence*. We can then proceed with a brief critical assessment of human rights, sexual rights, sexual orientation, gender identity and some taxonomies relevant for sexually diverse and gender-variant Muslims. When interrogating sexual orientation and gender identity, a focus on the definitions of these notions offered in the *Yogyakarta Principles on the Application of International Human Rights Law in relation to Sexual Orientation and Gender Identity* (Yogyakarta Principles)[4] is in order, especially since they have arguably come to occupy a rather exceptional place in the language and 'instruments' of international law. Finally, a brief ontological and epistemological insight into the world of meanings and designations constructed around sexually diverse and gender-variant Muslims should reveal some of the most dramatic social, political and legal clashes of discourses, including those of (anti-)Orientalism[5] and (post-/anti-)colonialism.

Law and Identity

The Lebanese-French author Amin Maalouf relates that a life spent writing has taught him to be wary of words: 'Those that seem clearest are often the most treacherous. "Identity" is one of those false friends'.[6] For him, identity resembles a *panther*: 'Why "panther"? Because a panther kills if you persecute it and kills if you leave it alone, and the worst thing you can do is to leave it alone after you've wounded it. But also because a panther can be tamed'.[7] Indeed, one can observe on a daily basis the unrelenting attempts by states, religious elites and other power centres to tame this perfidious notion and thus exert some control over those aspects of human self-defining that they deem *dangerous*. It is precisely this imaginary danger that propels persecution and sanctions against those who 'differ'; that is, who identify *outside* the prescribed, socially and politically fixed notions of the self.

Identities are perceived as exceptionally powerful (and dangerous) because they 'provide what we might call scripts: narratives that people can use in shaping their life plans and in telling their life stories'.[8] Yet the mere existence of certain 'mainstream' scripts does not *ipso facto* guarantee that the power structures they perpetuate will remain unchallenged. In the continuous process of self-constitution, human beings 'tend to prioritize different forms of "community" as spaces of self-accomplishment, no matter if the community is real or imaginary, self-selected or simply imposed'.[9] Identities migrate, develop and transform, thereby inevitably remoulding the communities they inform. The dominant scripts – the identities prescribed by ruling elites – need to be constantly reiterated to sustain themselves.

Unsurprisingly, the imposition of the dominant identity-construing narratives is commonly facilitated by law. Critical legal studies have disclosed and widely debated *juridical* and *disciplinary* powers of law, whereby '[j]uridical power refers to the enforcement of forms of behaviour and *disciplinary* power refers to the normalizing, production and colonization of forms of identity'.[10] Legal rhetoric and stipulations are therefore employed not only to *classify* the behaviours that are either permissible or prohibited but also to *identify* the *types* of people under the rule of law. This inevitably means that, as Sara Ahmed argues, 'to become a subject *under* the law one is made subject *to* the law that decides what forms lives must take in order to count as lives "worth living"'.[11] Such 'quality judgment' necessitates an enquiry of primarily moral(ising) nature in which human identities, orientations and proclivities are negotiated and categorised in order to support the dominant value system.

Given this powerful and problematic role of law in human lives, it is understandable why the tenets of identity politics as well as their critiques are so often framed in legal terms. As much as it can be the principal site of systemic oppression of certain 'outlawed' identities, the judicial realm seems to be perceived, at least by some, as a *tour de force* of positive social changes. This seemingly ambiguous role of law and legality is perhaps best reflected in the paradox of human rights.

Human Rights

The idea of human rights has been explained, *inter alia*, as a two-part claim: first, it proposes that human beings are 'special' because they possess an 'inherent dignity' and they are endowed with 'equal and inalienable rights';[12] second, because they are 'special', 'certain choices should be made and certain other choices rejected; in particular, certain things ought not to be done to any human being and certain other things ought to be done for every human being'.[13] These choices are generally categorised as rights in international law and universally promoted and protected via the international human rights system.

International law has thus become 'the official language of human rights, quite distinct from customary or even constitutional rights regimes'.[14] As such, it has dramatically reformed the international legal domain: what had been known as a 'gentle civiliser of nations'[15] had, seemingly, gradually evolved into an international mechanism for the protection of the individual both *by* and *from* the State.[16] Yet, 'rights language' as epitomised in international law is a paradox. On the one hand, its avowed legal strength derives from an articulated ambition to be binding *erga omnes,* thus cutting across the political, cultural and religious differences of the today's world. On the other hand, this purported *lingua franca* is a product of continuous negotiations and political compromises, the most insidious of which are dealt under the ideological banner of neo-liberalism.[17]

It is beyond the scope of this book to engage with numerous historical and contemporary critiques of human rights. But, even if it is taken for granted that the concept of human rights is an indispensible socio-legal reality, there are at least three underlying discourses that need to be critically examined, since they are continuously deployed in the heated *pro et contra* debates on sexual and gender pluralism. The three discourses concern (1) the origins of human rights; (2) the human rights debate between cultural relativist and universalist camps; and (3) the critique of human rights as an 'anti-emancipatory' project.

Despite the fact that '[m]odern human rights law derives primarily from Western philosophical thought dealing with the relationship between those who govern and those who are governed',[18] human rights as an ethico-legal concept can well be traced into antiquity. Most notable examples include the Neo-Sumerian Code of Ur-Nammu (*c.* 2050 BCE);[19] the Buddhism-inspired edicts promulgated by Aśoka the Great (304–232 BCE), an Indian emperor of the Maurya Dynasty;[20] the philosophical works of Socrates, Plato and Aristotle on φυσικόν δίκαιον (natural justice/right);[21] as well as numerous human rights reforms enacted by the Prophet Muhammad[22] and his four immediate successors, who established the first Muslim caliphate (632–61 CE).[23]

Yet, the variety of historical and present-day social justice claims pronounced via the 'rights language', and their wide geopolitical distribution, do not make that discourse immune to neo-imperialist ideological usurpations that serve the political and class elites. As Gayatri Chakravorty Spivak has observed, the 'idea of human rights [. . .] may carry within itself the agenda of a kind of social Darwinism – the fittest must shoulder the burden of righting the wrongs of the unfit – and the possibility of an alibi [. . .] for economic, military, and political intervention'.[24] The narrative of the 'fittest' providing for the 'unfit' resuscitates the colonial vision of Euro-American supremacy, cloaked in the veneer of an illusionary model of human rights. Cunningly informed by what is indeed *a kind of*[25] social Darwinism, this narrative is duly preached to the 'underdeveloped' societies of the global south by the new local classist elites, which now include many domestic non-governmental organisations (NGOs). As Spivak explains, this emerging elite representing the 'fittest', 'although physically based in the South [. . .], is generally also out of the touch with the mindset – a combination of episteme and ethical discourse – of the rural poor below the NGO level'.[26] This malicious phenomenon renders *subaltern*[27] all those below the exclusivist reach of certain civil society structures formally devoted to the promotion and protection of human rights. The post-colonial critique of human rights[28] is, therefore, an apt mechanism for disclosing and resisting the exploitative narratives and deployments of the 'rights language', especially in the 'developing' post-colonies of the world.

In a similar vein, universalist and relativist stands on rights are often defended as two opposing and mutually exclusive epistemological categories[29] – two distinct parallel 'truths' about human nature – in the language of human rights. Universalist claims are based on the assumption of universal human nature,[30] since we are all *'born* free and equal in dignity and rights'.[31] This notion legitimises the purported task of international human rights law to uphold the moral universality of human rights[32] and transcend all culturally relative claims – the assumptions that rights and their interpretations vary from culture to culture. Cultural relativism is based upon the conviction that no 'pre-social rights can exist, [. . .] because all values are socially constructed'.[33] Universalism further asserts that universal human rights have proven to be the only 'refuge of the individual' in their moral, legal, political and even cultural resistance against the oppression of state and society.[34] The cultural relativist response is that the 'individuated' approach to human communities and their socio-cultural systems is an instance of 'cultural imperialism'.[35] Despite the attempts to reconcile these opposing views,[36] it appears that the debate has reached an impasse.[37]

Some Muslim scholars and statespersons are particularly prone to condone cultural relativist positions on human rights. In doing so, they have elucidated a number of competing and conceptually problematic claims, including (1) that 'true' human rights can be fully realised solely within the ambit of (the contemporary state-sanctioned) Islamic law; (2) that human rights must be rejected *tout court*; (3) that human rights are incompatible with the 'proper' Muslim *Weltanschauung* and (4) that human rights are notoriously 'anti-religious'.[38] These assertions permeate almost every discussion on the implementation of international human rights standards within Muslim communities, regardless of whether these communities are located in Muslim-majority or Muslim-minority states. Apart from particular socio-political reasons,[39] they are largely informed by an anthropomorphised and ahistoricised vision of Islam as *a culture* (or, indeed, *the Culture*) to which all Muslims somehow belong. This simplistic narrative deliberately neglects the astonishing diversity of cultures in which the various Muslim communities are found. As Talal Asad aptly observes, '[i]t is too often forgotten that "the world of Islam" is a concept for organizing historical narratives, not the name for a self-contained collective agent'.[40]

Analogous to 'the world of Islam' is the discursive tradition that constitutes 'the world of human rights'. Amongst the myriad historical narratives that constitute this tradition, the narrative on the agency of the human rights 'claimant' is particularly remarkable. The global ascendancy of human rights has prompted an enquiry into the effects of their implementation on individuals and communities deemed 'vulnerable', due to their underprivileged social status. Feminist scholars have demonstrated how identity politics designed to protect and 'advance' members of 'vulnerable' social groups is observable of a type of Nietzschean *slave morality*, in which the oppressed feel morally right and politically righteous only because they are disadvantaged.[41] In Nietzsche's view, the subject of oppression is prone to develop *ressentiment* – a form of self-destructive passivity that denounces resistance and 'power' as morally inacceptable.[42] Wendy Brown has criticised the discourse of human rights as particularly susceptible to this 'triumph of the weak as weak', which in effect obliterates the agency of those deemed 'vulnerable', thereby leading to their further marginalisation.[43]

From this perspective, then, a human rights framework can only succeed if it is conceived as an introspective insurrectionary project, which empowers human beings *qua* human beings to self-realisation. As such, it seems irreconcilable with hard-line identity politics prescribing what exactly it means to belong to a certain social group. As it becomes apparent later on in this book, one ought to be wary of the crude and 'victimising' generalisations often employed by the language of human rights. If the idea of human rights carries, indeed, an emancipatory potential, its 'disruptive' ability to overcome the boundaries of socially imposed roles and definitions must be put to a test. Related to this is Judith Butler's optimistic observation that

> human rights is always in the process of subjecting the human to redefinition and renegotiation. It mobilizes the human in the service of rights, but also rewrites the human and rearticulates the human when it comes up against the cultural limits of its working conception of the human, as it does and must.[44]

Continuously calling into question what it means to be human causes, as it were, an acute societal 'identity crisis', which munificently enables oppressed forms of self-definition to flourish and gain the momentum. Such a conception of human rights carries, it seems, a promise to rectify the consequences of *ressentiment* in the victims of the dominant human rights discursive practices. But it requires, in turn, both the individual and the collective agency of the human to work on – and *undo*, to the extent possible – human rights' mainstream ideological baggage. The trouble is, then, that, for some, this might just prove too laborious a task.

Sexual Rights

By way of definition, sexual human rights refer to the physical and mental integrity of the individual in determining and exercising their sexuality in both the private and public spheres, free from coercion, discrimination and violence.[45] These rights are limited[46] by the principles of consent,[47] age of consent[48] and the degree of bodily and mental harm.[49]

Human sexuality is a complex phenomenon, 'integral to an entire matrix of social, economic, cultural, and relational forces'.[50] On the one hand, it is perceived as a *private* matter, shielded by various societal taboos and what Michel Foucault would call 'mutisms',[51] designed to not only maintain dominant moral narratives but also to provide a certain amount of 'breathing space' for intimacy and experimentation. On the other hand, sexuality *publicly* and 'so pervasively links the human being to other people and events, to a past, a culture and a tradition, be these links harmonious or troubled'.[52] Since sexuality encompasses both the intimate and the public social spheres, it is often related to numerous human rights, safeguarding, *inter alia*, the right to privacy; equality and freedom from discrimination; freedom from arbitrary arrest; asylum rights; the right to life, liberty and security of person; the right to education; labour rights; access to information; the right to health; freedom from torture and other inhumane or degrading treatment; and the right to peaceful assembly and association.[53] Or, as Paul Hunt once famously declared, the dominant liberal discourse on sexual rights wants us to believe 'that the correct understanding of fundamental human rights principles, as well as existing human rights norms, leads ineluctably to the recognition of sexual rights as human rights'.[54]

However, since their considerably late introduction to the United Nations (UN) human rights fora in the mid 1990s CE,[55] sexuality and sexual rights remain the site of fierce contestation. States have employed various moral and cultural arguments to justify their reluctance to address human rights violations related to sexuality. The amount of energy invested in the attempts to sweep these issues back under the carpet showcases how control of human sexuality still figures among the prime instruments of the state's will to power.[56] Despite these opposing agendas, sexuality has become an unavoidable aspect of the UN human rights language. While initially all sexual rights have been contested *per se*, more recent developments indicate that it is no longer an issue whether human rights will engage with sexuality, but rather 'on what terms, for whom, for what purposes, about which aspects of sexuality, and with what limits'.[57]

While sexual rights can no longer be ignored, numerous challenges related to their concept and content remain to be systematically tackled. Those challenges include, and are subsequently given some thought in this chapter, the following *problématique*: the question of the sex/gender divide and its impact on sexual/gender human rights policies; the problem of the scope of sexual rights; the issue of sexual equality *versus* sexual diversity; and some potentially surprising dimensions of the comparative analysis of sexual and religious rights. All these quandaries are also related to the concepts of sexual orientation and gender identity, which arguably form an integral part of the broader sexual rights spectrum.

A stark conceptual division between the term 'sex', posited as a biological substratum based on the genetic, hormonal, anatomical and psychic conditions of one's body, and the term 'gender', defined as a set of behavioural and social meanings affixed to sex, has long reigned supreme in the academic literature as well as in the human rights policies related to sexuality and gender.[58] One of the consequences of this theoretical divide has been a reductive and depreciatory conception of sexuality as a strictly bodily matter, a mere drive bereft of major social implications.[59] This view has given wings, *inter alia*, to the assertions that sexuality has nothing to do with human rights and that sexual rights are but the product of powerful lobby groups.[60]

However, as many scholars of sexuality (and gender) have aptly demonstrated, sexuality, sex and gender may be separate phenomena, but they are mutually dependent and, *as such*, constantly negotiated in the society.[61] Accordingly, while the distinction between, for instance, sexual behaviour (one's sexual acts), sexual orientation or desire (pertinent to one's object choice or fantasy) and sexual identity (which may or may not coincide with desire or behaviour) may be salient,[62] the related social and political claims, including those figured as human rights, should so be framed as to address all of these aspects and their social implications. The 'incalculable choreographies' of gender and sexual variance[63] across the world's distinct societies call for approaches sensitive to the ambiguities and intersectionalities that their performance entails.

While the advocates of sexual rights agree that free expression of one's sexuality needs to be safeguarded by reference to a number of human rights, cutting across both private and public life, there is still no consensus as to the exact scope of sexual rights and their legally cognisable definitions. Some notable efforts, such as the 1995 CE Charter on Sexual and Reproductive Rights produced by the International Planned Parenthood Federation,[64] have suffered from serious flaws, including an inability to cover some important aspects of sexual rights and the lack of international support.

Furthermore, as previously noted, there is insufficient clarity in the explanatory systems devised to defend sexual rights from the relentless attacks orchestrated by their powerful opponents. What exactly is being protected: a status, an identity, a behaviour, a public presentation, a public role or all of them put together?[65] Also, what is meant by, for instance, the right to privacy in relation to sexuality?[66] That is, to what extent should the State be allowed to penetrate and regulate the private sphere, in order, for example, to provide an effective protection from domestic violence? Related to this, of course, is the *problématique* of whether and where to draw the line between the public and the private, especially in the societies – such as the majority of those designated, for various reasons, as 'Muslim' – where such boundaries have somewhat idiosyncratic historical and social contexts. Being the 'newest kid on the block'[67] of the international human rights 'neighbourhood', sexual rights still lack the solid framework necessary to remove or at least diminish the confusion described above.

This situation is widely exploited by the opposition camps, which permeate international human rights fora, to persistently deny the existence or relevance of undesirable notions, social groups and practices pertinent to gender and sexuality, such as 'sexual orientation', 'gender identity', 'sex workers', 'sexual rights for women', etc., thereby maintaining their systemic marginalisation.[68] Conceptual confusion is also exploited to wrongly blame the proponents of sexual rights of 'ushering in the social normalisation and possibly the legitimisation of many deplorable acts, including paedophilia'.[69] Although often disguised as moral concerns, the assertions and actions of the opposition camps are chiefly of a political nature, since the patriarchal system they strive to preserve is primarily employed to legitimise the present ruling elites. In turn, as one author concludes, 'any effort to clarify and deepen conceptual understanding of sexual rights as human rights is a deeply political project [. . .] both because of the importance and sensitivity of sexuality and sexual issues, and because this work will help to refashion the relationship between individuals and the state'.[70]

Some theoretical work on this subject has already moved beyond the conventional human rights frameworks. For instance, 'with its mobile combinations of the political, the economic, the social, the legal and the ethical, *citizenship* seemed to be a neat concept for articulating (and agitating) the field of sexual politics generally'.[71] Accordingly, the concepts of *sexual citizenship* or even *intimate citizenship* have been proposed as the most apposite niches for sexual rights mainstreaming. Sexual citizenship has been understood, *inter alia*, as a tripartite claim to rights related to sexual acts, rights related to identity (i.e. self-definitions based on one's sexuality) and rights concerning (intimate, sexual) relationships.[72] Intimate citizenship has been put forward as a more complex claim involving ten 'zones of intimacy', enumerated as self, relationships, gender, sexuality, family, body, emotional life, senses, identity and spirituality.[73] Although these concepts have been criticised for their markedly political focus grounded in the liberal tradition (which arguably limits their universal application and creates potential for abuse),[74] they are sometimes thought to be of some salience as a point of departure for framing sexual rights claims of groups such as sexually diverse and gender-variant Muslims because they recognise and elaborate both acts and identities related to one's expression of sexuality, as well as – extraordinarily enough – their spiritual dimension. But, as shown in Chapter 5 of this book, when such concepts are used in practice, they often attest to the rights claimant's primary, even exclusive, reliance on the domestic legal system and the state-sanctioned practice of Islamic law. That citizenship cannot be disentangled from the concept of the State is, in this scenario, both an opportunity (for further political action) and a serious limitation (insofar as it restricts the rights claimant's political imagination).

Another notable feature of the discursive deployments of sexual rights is their relation to gender equality, often presumed as a peremptory desideratum of any gender- and sexuality-related legal claims. There is, however, a well-developed stream of feminist critique of the concept of equality as applied to gender.[75] It argues, in a nutshell, that gender equality – as formally pronounced in human rights discourses – is thwarted by structural inequalities of power, resulting in continuous marginalisation of women. That is because the prime model of equality uses as its reference point or 'comparator' the white, global northern, middle-class, able-bodied, educated and heterosexual man, according to whose needs and entitlements all other claims must be tailored. Gender diversity is therefore proposed as an alternative concept that draws attention to differences both *among* and *within* genders and emphasises the ways in which genders are intersectionally shaped by the social categories of race, ethnicity, sexuality, class, age and disability.[76] Similar disparities of power permeate the domain of sexuality and sexual rights. It has been observed, for example, that the 'three realms of sin (religion), sickness (medicine), and crime (law) have historically worked to reinforce one another, producing structural sexual inequality'.[77] Yet the attempts to redress this inequality – promulgated, in particular, by identity politics – have been too prone to model their claims in accordance with their own compartmentalised visions of human rights, thus once again 'losing out in the intersections'.[78]

Finally, due to a long history of clashes and schisms between them, sexuality and religion are often posited as two incompatible, even incommensurable aspects of human existence. In the same vein, the social justice movements established to advance religious or sexual rights are habitually found on different sides in human rights fora, arguing against each other's presence and agenda.[79] Ironically, however, the nature and the content of their human rights claims are astonishingly similar.

For example, in her analysis of Article 18 of the International Covenant on Civil and Political Rights[80] and its further elaboration and development in the Declaration on the Elimination of All Forms of Intolerance and of Discrimination Based on Religion or Belief,[81] the prominent scholar of sexuality, Alice M. Miller, has found these claims:

the absolute right to have (or not have) an identity, (2) the recognition of a relationship between the individual and the community, (3) the acceptance of public and private aspects of practice, (4) a discussion of the scope of activities that are accepted as manifestations of religion and (5) the limited ability to restrict manifestation.[82]

Their striking similarity with sexual rights claims is obvious. Apart from providing a basis for possible re-thinking of the inimical relationship between the two sets of human rights claims, this similarity suggests that there is little, if any, difference in the implied nature of state responsibility to protect and promote these particular aspects of human rights. How, then, can these conceptual links be further examined?

In order to facilitate the dialogue between sexual and religious rights, it seems instrumental to revisit, once again, the question of the authenticity of human rights. Out of the wellspring of concurring theories, a notable study proposes that 'we cannot, in defending human rights, eschew a metaphysical view of the human person and that, if we do, our position becomes self-defeating'.[83] Apparently, that is so because the idea of human rights involves the *belief* in the *sacredness* of the human being.[84] If this faith is replaced solely with the vague idea of some moral law that inheres within us *sui generis*, what we are left with is undeniable rational *uncertainty* about its existence and tenets, thereby reducing the meaning of human rights discourse to an arbitrary set of pragmatic dicta.[85] Yet if the sacredness of the human being is understood as transcendent of 'both individual conscience and the state',[86] it provides a firm albeit necessarily metaphysical ground for moral viability and cross-cultural applicability of human rights norms. Once so conceived, human rights seem to be morally and teleologically bound to address the *totality* of human experience, including its interrelated sexual and spiritual dimensions.

Sexual Orientation and Gender Identity

As I demonstrate in Chapter 3 of this book, concepts of sexual orientation and gender identity have gained considerable weight in international human rights law. In the proceeding analysis, I endeavour, first, to provide a working definition of these two notions and then to engage at some length with their critique, primarily revolving around the queries relating to various aspects of their ontology.

Much like all other aspects of human sexual and gender expression, the notions of sexual orientation and gender identity are not easily and definitely ascertainable. There have been numerous competing attempts to precisely capture their gist, informed by different disciplinary and theoretical approaches.[87] Historically, the concept of sexual orientation was first widely discussed in psychological and biomedical literature.[88] It is present in (anti-discrimination) law as of the 1970s CE[89] and sociologically problematised since the early 1980s CE.[90] Similarly, the concept of gender identity was first discussed as a medical phenomenon,[91] and then widely explored in the emerging inter-disciplinary academic field of transgender studies as of the early 1990s CE.[92] Geopolitically, both notions originate in what is neatly called the global north, yet arguably their usage and relevance span wide across its borders.[93] To be sure, although it is not described in those exact terms, the sexual and gender variance that the notions of sexual orientation and gender identity attempt to denote is found across the world and throughout history.[94]

Let us, then, briefly consider the definitions of the notions of sexual orientation and gender identity as articulated in the Yogyakarta Principles,[95] which are analysed in greater detail in the subsequent chapter. Not only have these definitions received the widest recognition in international human rights law,[96] they also seem to succeed (as the ensuing analysis demonstrates) in overcoming the majority of theoretical conundrums associated with the notions of sexual orientation and gender identity. The Yogyakarta Principles define *sexual orientation* as

> each person's capacity for profound emotional, affectional and sexual attraction to, and intimate and sexual relations with, individuals of a different gender or the same gender or more than one gender;

and *gender identity* as

> each person's deeply felt internal and individual experience of gender, which may or may not correspond with the sex assigned at

birth, including the personal sense of the body (which may involve, if freely chosen, modification of bodily appearance or function by medical, surgical or other means) and other expressions of gender, including dress, speech and mannerisms[.][97]

Importantly, sexual orientation is here determined in relation to personal *capacity* for *attraction* to and *relationship* with individual(s) on the ground of their *gender*. Thus, this (a) *attraction* may or may not involve (b) *conduct*; while any reference to (c) *identity* is avoided. Such an attraction is not only sexual but also *emotional* and *affectional*. The genders to which this attraction is directed are *not binary* (male-female); there are more than two of them and their exact number is not specified. Consequently, the *number* of possible sexual orientations is also unspecified. Also, there is no reference as to whether this capacity is *mutable* or not, nor *how* exactly it comes into being.

Gender identity is described as a personal *experience* of (a) *gender* and (b) the *body*, which is either in congruence or not with the sex *assigned* at birth (or, in the case of the majority of intersex people, in an early postnatal stage of their life). If this bodily *and* gender-based *relationship* with the assigned sex is unsatisfactory, a person can freely make or request various adjustments to their physical appearance *by the means* and *to the extent* of their choice. This indicates, *inter alia*, that surgical intervention and/or hormonal treatment (and/or, indeed, other means of *transition*) may involve, if desired, only partial so-called 'sex reassignment'. Finally, gender identity is defined as *inclusive* of gender expression(s). Again, no reference is made as to *mutability* or *origin* of gender identity. All these elements of the Yogyakarta definitions are of exceptional importance for the subsequent discussion of the challenges related to the concepts of sexual orientation and gender identity.

The debate across the academic disciplines and policy think tanks about sexual orientation and gender identity has a markedly *ontic* character, and is typically composed of four quintessential steps. First, there is (1) the question of whether these two concepts should be adopted at all, i.e. to what extent are they relevant for human sexuality and the sense of gender? For those who adopt them, the next question is, patently, (2) their *raison d'être*. Further discussion focuses on (3) the exact meaning of the two phenomena and (4) whether the conditions they describe are somehow mutable, either by force or by choice.

(1) *Existence.* The scholars who question the existence of either of the two concepts generally maintain that the term *sexuality* 'implies autonomy and fluidity'[98] and as such better describes various conditions of human sexual and gender expression. *Sexual autonomy* is proposed as an alternative concept because it is deliberative, conduct-oriented and expressive.[99] These models are chiefly proposed out of a desire to challenge the concept of *identity*, often attached to the notions of sexual orientation and gender identity, because of its potential to exclude, by obliterating all those whose particular performance[100] of gender and sexuality does not necessarily respond to the common identity labels attached to it (e.g. women who have sex with women yet who do not consider themselves lesbian or bisexual). However, the exclusivist use of identity labels has also been squarely rejected by the proponents of the notions of sexual orientation and gender identity.[101] In fact, as suggested by the definitions from the Yogyakarta Principles expounded above, the concepts of sexual orientation – as the capacity to *attraction/relationship* – and gender identity – as a gender-bodily *experience* – require no notion of identity at all. The absence of identity from the definitions of sexual orientation and gender identity does not imply that individual or group self-identification on the basis of these two phenomena is wrong *per se.* Rather, while accepting (or, perhaps, simply being indifferent to) that an individual may *choose* to invent, accede to or reject social categories associated with the notions of sexual orientation and gender identity, these notions are neatly held *separate* from such social intervention, thereby reaffirming their overall relevance. In this sense, these notions, indeed, seem indispensible in addressing specific questions of sexuality and gender that are related to attraction, intimate relationships and performativity of gender.

(2) *Origins.* On this point, there is an age-old disagreement between the two prominent theoretical camps, the so-called *essentialists* and the *constructionists.*[102] In the essentialists' view, espoused in particular in relation to sexual orientation and by proponents of identity politics concerned with sexuality, the phenomena in question are *inborn*, caused by genetic, hormonal and/or other biological reasons. In this sense, they are 'essential to personhood'.[103] On the contrary, constructionists maintain that both sexual orientation and gender identity are socially constructed and that as such they 'do not always translate into an innate psychobiological identity'.[104] This latter view is the mainstay of queer

theory, an analytical movement that has been polemically described as 'keenly focused on the exposure and demystification of essentialised *ontologies* of gender and sexual identity'.[105] This school of thought is largely informed by critical studies of sexuality and power[106] and the feminist critique construed thereupon.[107] Essentialism has been criticised, *inter alia*, for the lack of scientific evidence of the biological causes of sexual orientation or gender identity,[108] for the marginalisation of persons who fall outside of prescribed identity boxes based on their gender and sexuality[109] and for maintaining the heterosexuality *versus* homosexuality dichotomy upon which much of systemic societal oppression has been constructed.[110] In turn, constructionism has been deemed unfit to respond to political realities affecting 'non-heterosexual' and gender-variant persons across the world,[111] in particular because of its failure to acknowledge some 'permanent fixtures' of sexual desire[112] and/or gender expression across times and cultures.[113] Ultimately, therefore, neither the essentialist nor the constructionist camps can alone give a definite answer to what causes sexual orientation and/or gender identity.[114]

Despite the absence of epistemological proof, the constructionist explanatory system still seems more convincing, for (at least) the following reason: the biological determinism upon which essentialism is based misrepresents the elements of the human psycho-physiological system as somehow isolated from their pertinent environments. Genes, hormones and living beings as a whole 'can only develop in interdependent, interactive relationship with other living things'.[115] In short, even if it is taken for granted that there are certain biological predispositions in relation to human sexual orientation and gender identity (as believed by the essentialists), it is inevitable to conclude that these two phenomena will also be conditioned, at least to some extent, by the social system in which they are bound to operate. This necessarily makes the essentialists' argument critically less 'essentialist'.

This ultimately inconclusive discussion is altogether avoided in the definitions of sexual orientation and gender identity proposed by the Yogyakarta Principles, which makes them even more apposite for a variety of academic, legal and socio-political contexts.

(3) *Meaning*. Across the numerous attempts to capture the notions of sexual orientation and gender identity, there appear several recurring

issues that warrant closer consideration. These issues are related to both the concept and the content of sexual orientation and gender identity, as well as to their intrinsically social ramifications.

In the case of sexual orientation, as Robert Wintemute summarises, it may refer 'to (a) the direction of the person's *attraction*, (b) the direction of their *conduct* (taken as a whole), the direction of a *specific instance* of their *conduct*, or (d) their *"identity"'*.[116] As I have already demonstrated in this chapter, out of these four constitutive ingredients, the notion of *identity* is problematic because of its exclusionary use.[117] This is probably the reason why it has not been made part of the Yogyakarta Principles' definition. Instead, this definition includes an often forgotten *capacity* for *intimate* and *sexual relations* as one of the foundational aspects of sexual orientation. This capacity, as well as actual *conduct*, is obviously socially conditioned. It is only the constitutional *attraction* of sexual, emotional and affectional nature that does not require *prima facie* a social interplay with other human beings. This means that sexual orientation is not 'merely a directional metaphor drawn from magnetism and navigation',[118] but a set of interrelated capacities spanning both intimate and public aspects of one's sexual expression. Another dilemma is as to *what exactly* a person is sexually oriented. Historically, it has been understood that 'one's sexual orientation is defined by the *sex* (*same* or *other*) of the people to whom one is emotionally and sexually attracted'.[119] Studies of gender,[120] however, have revealed that one is far more likely to be oriented towards the other person's *gender*, including (but not being limited to) their specific bodily characteristics. Furthermore, the idea of *sameness* (*homo*-sexual) and *otherness* (*hetero*-sexual) of the object choice of one's desire needs to be contested. As Sara Ahmed explains, 'women desiring women does not mean that they desire the same: sameness as well as difference is invented as fantasy'.[121] This fantasy crudely generalises all women as 'the same' and thereby supports the argument often used against 'same-sex' relationships imputing that they are 'inevitably narcissistic' and that they 'deny difference'.[122] It follows that terms such as 'homosexuality' and 'heterosexuality' are but limited pseudo-medical signifiers unfit to capture the interplay of sameness and difference in one's sexual orientation. This does not mean that one cannot be attracted to persons of specific gender that may be *nominally* identical to and/or different from their own, but that there are serious discursive limitations in the pseudo-medical notions used to describe such sexual orientation. Here the relational, social aspects of human sexuality become all the more important.

The discussion around the meaning of gender identity typically focuses on the two fundamental manifestations of this phenomenon that have been strategically merged within a single definition in the Yogyakarta Principles: (a) the personal *experience* of one's gender *and* the body in relation to one's *sex* and (b) the *expression* of that experience in its various forms, such as 'dress, speech and mannerisms'.[123] The *experience* of gender is understood as foundational of either a specific *identity* or an *identification*, the latter of which signifies an ongoing and ultimately incompletable mission of 'articulation' of one's social identity.[124] While gender experience posited as *identity* presupposes certain categorical dispositions in which it may be inscribed (e.g. transgender, male, female), gender *identification* emphasises gender liminality[125] and ultimately seeks to destabilise all social categories built upon the experience of gender.[126] It is, however, hard to imagine that an endeavour to radically de-categorise gender experience *per se* can be (politically and socially) successful in any foreseeable future. Therefore, the scholars and activists of gender predominantly opt for *identity* as an adequate signifier of this phenomenon, though often with a 'de-essentialising' caveat denoting the fluidity of one's performance of gender.[127] This performance, commonly described as *gender expression*, has long been referred to in queer and transgender theory as a phenomenon separate from (and more diffuse than) gender identity.[128] If, however, it is subsumed into the definition of gender identity, as in the Yogyakarta Principles, gender expression becomes the desired destabiliser of the concept of gender identity because it allows for liminal and 'non-categorical' performances of gender to be recognised as fundamental to one's gender experience.

(4) *Mutability.* The question of mutability of one's sexual orientation and/or gender identity comes up in a variety of social contexts, from the oppressive demands to 'heterosexualise' nonconforming sexualities[129] or to outlaw gender transitions,[130] to the firsthand experiences of some transsexual persons whose sexual orientation has changed after undergoing certain medico-surgical interventions.[131] Once again, the fluidity and complexity of human sexuality and gender experience exclude possibility of an easy and definite answer. It seems, nevertheless, that both sexual orientation and gender identity, although developed and negotiated across one's lifetime, are generally impervious to interventions intended to

change them.[132] Furthermore, even constructionist views – which see these notions as mutable *because* they are, arguably, socially constructed – do not naively maintain that they are a simple matter of choice.[133] Rather, they are understood as resultant of the constant (both conscious and subconscious) process of 'articulation' of sexuality and gender in a variety of intimate and social environments. As such, sexual orientation and gender identity are independent yet mutually influential,[134] prevalently resilient to both voluntary and involuntary external interventions aiming at curtailing their directions, span and float. It does not follow, however, that they cannot be personally 'played with' to some extent (e.g. positively 'subverted'[135] or negatively 'downplayed'[136] in relation to their environment). But the impact of such play varies from person to person and seems rarely (if ever) sufficient to exert an overall control over these complex phenomena.

This chapter has so far endeavoured to define and discuss sexual orientation and gender identity in general terms, applicable across the disciplinary lenses or varying socio-political contexts. At this point, however, it is necessary to single out and briefly reflect upon the specific issue that maliciously inhibits the majority of conversations around these two notions. This issue has been labelled *heteronormativity* because it refers to an idealised and institutionalised vision of heterosexuality as the supreme norm of intimacy, sexual expression and even the 'way of being in the world'.[137] In its most drastic instances, this pervasive ideological construct, fuelled by patriarchal systems across the world's cultures and polities, 'naturalises' heterosexuality[138] through strict social compulsion[139] and terror.[140] Consequently, all other forms of sexual and gender expression are proscribed and misrepresented as 'subaltern, insidious disease, deviance and danger'.[141] This is the premise of the binary 'natural *versus* unnatural' discourse on gender and sexuality, operationalised as the stranglehold of institutionalised heteronormativity to maintain what has been called *heteromorality*,[142] i.e. moral codes entrenched in the assumption of heterosexuality as the moral and social imperative. What is more, both heternormativity and heteromorality have recently been joined by the comparatively oppressive 'mirror phenomena' of *homonormativity* and *homomorality*, which tend to ideologically employ and 'naturalise' homosexuality as a political conduit *par excellence* of neo-liberal normativity and legality, thereby crudely universalising the 'homosexual subject' in the service of global capitalism. As will become apparent in the subsequent chapters of this book, these phenomena often operate in tandem and are doubly perilous for sexually diverse and gender-variant communities.

Muslims and Sexual/Gender Taxonomies

The self-identified Muslims, from across historical and present-day Muslim communities, whose sexual and gender experience and desire challenge heteronormativity, are not given any common identitary denominator in this book. Notwithstanding the fact that many contemporary sexually diverse and gender-variant Muslims have *nominally* adopted the identity categories such as *lesbian, gay, bisexual* and *transgender* (LGBT) as reflective of their sexual/gender experience, and the concomitant claims that *queer* 'persists as the only term successfully encapsulating an intersection between non-normative sexualities and gender expressions',[143] the principal protagonists of this book are not called 'LGBT Muslims' or even 'queer Muslims'. At least three reasons support this stance. First, as studies have shown,[144] when appropriated in various cultural contexts across the world, the LGBT categories often come to mean something distinctively *different* from place to place, and are no longer reducible to a single definition.[145] Second, these categories do not fully resonate with *traditional* sexually pluralistic and gender-variant communities, still very much alive and present within Muslim societies. Examples include the gender-variant Muslim *waria* in Indonesia,[146] Muslim *mak nyah* and *pak nyah* in Malaysia,[147] the *hijra (khwajasara)* and *zenana* individuals who identify as Muslims in Pakistan, Bangladesh and India[148] and *khanith* in Oman.[149] Third, there is a remarkable number of Muslims whose sexuality and gender challenge heteronormativity but who do not subscribe to any particular identity categories.[150] Thus, even within the morphological ambits of the term *queer*, which simultaneously signals an identity and the resistance to or critique of the identities as such (thereby acknowledging their ultimate fluidity), such persons cannot or do not want to find their *niche*. Because human gender and sexuality have been, and still are, 'productively imprecise'[151] in delineating their *nominal* boundaries, the recent globalised taxonomies are abandoned in the present work, thereby reaffirming the prerogative of sexually diverse and gender-variant Muslims to negotiate and articulate their sexual and gender *self* in their own terms.

Apart from their diverse sexual orientations and gender identities, the principal protagonists of this book are self-described Muslims. As such, they share a number of important underlying discourses relevant to all Muslims. As I attempt to demonstrate later on in some detail,[152] many of these discourses are exceptionally influential in shaping the dominant Muslim considerations of sexuality and gender. The discourses include, for example, Orientalism and colonialism, as well as the reaction of the oppressed epitomised in Muslim nationalism and modernism, upon which the remaining (yet deeply problematic) geopolitical, cultural and religious dichotomy of the 'East' and the 'West' has been conceptualised. Further complicated by the emergence of globalisation, this dichotomy has been instrumental, on the one hand, in asserting heteronormativity across Muslim-majority polities and, on the other hand, in maintaining the deeply degrading 'Muslim legal subject' of international law.[153]

In both linguistic and theological terms, *Islam* is but the Call to *submit* oneself to God, the Most Gracious, the Most Merciful.[154] *Muslims* are those who answer this Call by accepting that there is no god but God, and that Muhammad is the Messenger of God,[155] as revealed in the Qur'an. Muslims are, therefore, those who engage in various *hermeneutics* in order to make sense of God's will as expounded in Qur'anic verses, in the example of Muhammad's life and sayings, as well as in the signs embedded in one's daily life. The simplicity of this *credo* is overwhelming. Yet there is a major confusion about what Islam *is* or *can be* and, consequently, what counts as an *Islamic* matter and what as a *Muslim* one.

Islam is, strictly speaking, an ideal, omniscient signifier. It does not speak in tongue, even though the Qur'an is God's transcendent voice *par excellence*. Islam, much like the Qur'an, requires interpretation, in the first instance by those who call themselves Muslims. It is through human supplication that the divine will becomes apparent. Thus, the attempts to anthropomorphise Islam in the constructs such as 'Islamic culture', 'Islam says [...]' or 'the Qur'an says [...]' must be resisted, since they are 'fundamentally and prejudicially flawed from the start'.[156] There can only be Muslim cultures and human interpretations of Islam and the Qur'an.

This semantic distinction is important, *inter alia*, because of its effect upon sexually diverse and gender-variant Muslims, who are often ostracised precisely 'in the name of Islam'. These Muslims – *qua* Muslims – share an indubitable right with the rest of the *umma* (community) to engage in the hermeneutics of Islam. The vast diversity of Muslim exegetical traditions demonstrates an inherent *plurality* in Muslim spiritual and social experience. It has been referred to in the Qur'an as God's will, 'in which there are signs for those who know'.[157] Perhaps sexually diverse and gender-variant Muslims are uniquely positioned to decipher those signs as they relate to sexual and gender plurality. Only if they are properly located *within* the discourse on pluralistic Muslim religious, social, cultural, sexual and gender experience, can such Muslims negotiate their integrity and diversity within the larger *umma*.

CHAPTER 2

SEXUAL AND GENDER DIVERSITY IN INTERNATIONAL HUMAN RIGHTS LAW AND ITS ORIGINATORY MILIEUX

Writing in 1950 CE, Sir Hersch Lauterpacht forcefully argued that '[f]undamental human rights are rights superior to the law of the sovereign State [and should, hence, lead to the] consequent recognition of the individual human being as a subject of international law'.[1] The rise of the individual, not only as a subject of domestic but also international law, was predetermined to challenge the stark statist vision of international relations and their legal *modus operandi*, and to open up this system to profound transformations.[2] Crucially, the individual, bestowed with sets of internationally agreed *moral* and *legal* rights,[3] was to ascend above the competing interests of the sovereign states both in their domestic and international legal affairs, or, indeed, *mutatis mutandis*, to become their primary and inextricable interest. Hailed as a 'most astonishing development in world history',[4] human rights law thus entered hostile international waters back in Lauterpacht's time and gradually established itself, in the decades to follow, as their significant part. Though still an *enfant terrible* of sorts in governmental and inter-governmental dealings, it figures as the strongest proprietor and regulator of human rights claims, their catalyst *par excellence* en route to political and social recognition.

However, the elevated position of international human rights law does not come without a price. The scene it entered and immersed itself in remains deeply tainted with the historical and present-day horrors of imperialism, warfare, political opportunism and manipulation. Depending on the delicate balance between the elitist interests of powerful states, and primarily *moral* (and, consequently, political and legal) weight of the oppressed population's demands, international law has historically figured both as a promise and as a damnation of most pressing justice claims. The troubled history of decolonisation and subsequent 'development strategies', which promote the rule of international law to protect the exploitative interests of foreign investors, offers one such narrative.[5] Is international law *still* there to gently 'civilise' the nations[6] in accordance with the age-old notorious imperial practice, or is it, indeed, there to decolonise and democratise them? Faced with such continuous and tiresome ambiguity of international governance, 'the profession of international law has [. . .] been bogged down in fruitless and repetitive forms of thinking about the international world; bureaucratic étatism on the one hand, imperial or nostalgic humanism on the other'.[7] Some authors are, thus, highly pessimistic of the prospect for radical change of international law *as such*,[8] not least because it has arguably become a 'wasteland' for any alternative theoretical solutions.[9]

Being an integral part of international law, human rights law is in constant danger of misuse, misappropriation and ideological control akin to those befalling other realms of international governance. Examples of dangerous conditionality of international human rights law as a sub-discipline of international law abound. Antony Anghie, for instance, describes how the ascendance of this sub-discipline 'coincided' with the processes of decolonisation, suggesting that *at least then* its *raison d'être* was partly grounded in the former colonisers' aspirations to significantly condition the character of sovereignty of the emergent global southern states.[10] For similar reasons, the recent military operations of the United States and its allies in Iraq and Afghanistan have been ironically branded *Human Rights Wars*.[11] These occurrences expose an acute and deep-running fragility of the United Nations justice system, meted out, *inter alia*, via conduits of international human rights law. Yet they also signal that law on human rights in its international form(s) represents a perennially contested field, in which human interests, power relations and mores compete against (or, indeed, at times combine to create) a seemingly neutral and universal legal norm.

Although seemingly indispensible for contemporary social justice claims, international human rights law is not an ahistorical, sanitised, safe space. Its handling warrants caution.

My purpose here is to critically interrogate the precarious domain of international human rights law and its originatory milieux – the ancient and medieval European legal and social ethea – as they relate to the notions of sexual orientation and gender identity. My first step is to examine, in some detail, the roots of criminalisation of (some) same-sex sexual relations and gender transgressions. While these matters have traditionally been dealt with on a domestic level – i.e. by means of criminal and family law – they have come about as a result of larger, supra-national discourses. In a similar vein, the subsequent moves towards decriminalisation of same-sex sexual activities and gender identity-related reforms have had region-specific geopolitical contours, including various important developments in international (or regional) human rights law. From the examination of the root causes of sexual and gender 'criminalities', I move to a brief historical analysis of the ascendance of sexual orientation and gender identity in international human rights law and the various related international fora. I showcase how these concepts, despite virulent opposition, have gradually acquired a firm and wide recognition in the relevant domains of international law and the international human rights system. I conclude, however, with some important caveats relating to this particular international legal and political arena, which suggest that the imminent danger of political misuse of the two concepts, including by means of international human rights law, should not be overlooked.

While it is impossible and, ultimately, undesirable to offer a 'finite' *legal* solution to human sexual and gender diversity, international human rights law remains an all-important site for countering the violence and oppression so often associated with state and non-state regulation of this phenomenon. It is, however, a site of violence itself, where strong politically motivated currents intersect and clash, sometimes at the dire expense of the distant rights-holder. The long road that the notions of sexual orientation and gender identity have travelled through this volatile environment, from negligence to protection, thus calls for a close examination; an examination that, of necessity, cuts deep into the historical tissue of the European selfhood and legality.

Criminalisation and Decriminalisation: A Discursive Genealogy

The idea of asserting legal control over human sexuality and sexual/ gender diversity, including by means of criminal law and its antecedents, runs wide and deep in the history of humankind, so much so that its origins cannot be ascribed to any *particular* ancient, medieval or contemporary society, *sui generis*. Early examples include the laws of Hammurabi (*c.*1772 BCE), Eshnunna (*c.*1900 BCE) and the Hittites (*c.*1650−1100 BCE), all of which prescribed extremely harsh penalties for adultery.[12] It is, however, often posited that the ancient Greco-Roman and Judeo-Christian moral and legal systems, whether taken separately or as combined in subsequent historical reinterpretations, stand out as particularly cruel matrices for stigmatisation and suppression of human sexual/gender plurality.[13] Greco-Roman views on gender and sexuality had retained, at least, an exceptional philosophical diversity (e.g. significant differences between, and within, various classical Greek schools of thoughts on the matter) and, thus, had informed and shaped the societies in which the law on sexual/gender offences, if at all existent, had been more or less loosely applied.[14] In contrast, both the ecclesiastical (canonical) and municipal European medieval laws had eventually spurred most brutal and systemic persecutions of sexual/gender transgressions, on an apparently *unparalleled* scale:

> It can hardly be argued that these horrors were a necessary stage in the development of civilized societies. In China and Japan the philosophical wisdom of Confucianism and the religious teaching of Buddhism did not foster them. Indeed, China was more tolerant than ancient Rome, lacking that empire's deep-seated fear of male effeminacy; and Japan, in its Samurai code, produced an ethos remarkably akin to that of classical Greece.[15]

These historical precepts are important for this book for various reasons. First, owing much to the world-spanning and long-lasting European colonial project, the moral and legal legacy of pre-modern Christendom has been given an uncanny afterlife in as much as the colonising states have forced their laws and morality across the 'New World'. Hence the legal developments in European imperial states, as of the fifteenth century CE, have had more or less a direct impact on their colonies and beyond. Nowhere, perhaps, is the depth of these encroachments as readily evident as in the surviving colonial criminal laws against sexual and gender diversity, even if – as in the case of Pakistan – they have been covered with a novel religio-cultural veneer.[16] Second, as elucidated in considerable detail in Chapter 4 of this book, whether in the process of a direct colonial administration or via influences achieved, *inter alia*, by means of international law, the then mainstream European sexual/gender propriety, much more than any other alien social ethos, has gradually remoulded the general Muslim views on sexual/gender diversity. It is, *ipso facto*, important to understand where this all-pervading propriety came from, as well as to be able to compare and contrast it with concomitant developments in the Islamic legal tradition. Third and lastly, the enduring influence of this particular ethos on the making of and power relations within the domain of international law,[17] together with a partly derivative and complementary discourse propounded by the Organisation of Islamic Co-operation (OIC), remain the strongest opponents of the recognition of the notions of sexual orientation and gender identity in international human rights law (or in any comparable municipal legal framework). It is, therefore, necessary in an analysis of the root causes of criminalisation of sexual/gender diversity to pay special attention to the rise and fall of a predominantly late medieval Christian concept[18] of gender and sexuality and their regulation.

Desexualising the Human: Stoic Legacies and Early Christian Anxieties

Utter contempt for human sexuality, as a social and theological stance, had slowly become a defining feature of European medieval mores. Intersected with gender, class, political and cultural struggles and vehemently opposed, not only by the illiterate masses, but by their feudal rulers as well, it had taken an entire millennium for this discourse to assert its absolute dominance and, more specifically, its doctrinal purity (i.e. its 'Christianness'). The wealth of multidisciplinary research into early and medieval Christian constructs of sex and gender reveals at least two major sources of an ideological desexualisation and the subsequent religious and municipal criminalisation of various forms of sexual/gender diversity: (1) an 'anti-corporeal' exegesis of early Judaic and Christian religious texts and laws on the matter and (2) the revival of selected ancient Greek philosophical treatises on sex and gender and re-enactment of the old Roman laws on control of sexuality.[19] These sources had been coupled with peculiar concepts of the human body in medieval European medicine and, invariably, a sheer political opportunism (exercised both by clerical and non-clerical elites) to exert an enduring and all-encompassing societal control.

As the first major source of an 'anti-corporeal' view of human existence, medieval scholars had sought to narrowly reinterpret the Old Testament's complex and often rather detailed depictions of sexual life as relating, almost exclusively, to various (legal) prohibitions.[20] For the specific interest of this book, most pertinent are the stipulations of Mosaic law as collected in the Pentateuch; in particular:

> If a man also lie with mankind, as he lieth with a woman, both of them have committed an abomination: they shall surely be put to death; their blood [shall be] upon them.[21]
>
> Thou shalt not lie with mankind, as with womankind: it [is] abomination.[22]
>
> The woman shall not wear that which pertaineth unto a man, neither shall a man put on a woman's garment: for all that do so [are] abomination unto the LORD thy God.[23]

These injunctions, however, had rarely been given special attention; instead, they had been invoked to corroborate, together with other Biblical gender/sexuality-related prohibitions, an increasingly popular scholastic view that human sexuality altogether was, in the words of Sir Thomas Browne (1605–82 CE), 'an odd and unworthy piece of folly'.[24] One of the early Christian exegetes, Origen (c.185–254 CE), believed that Adam and Eve had introduced death into the human lifeworlds by committing 'the first sexual sin' (disobeying God's command not to eat the forbidden fruit and thus becoming aware of their nakedness): 'Only a cessation of sexual activity in the world would bring about life without death. Thus so long as people [...] have sex, they will also die'.[25] Importantly, though, women, rather than men, were to be principally blamed for such 'carnal corruption'. Origen wrote, with obvious contempt: 'There are some women, though not all of them [...], who are indiscriminate slaves to lust, like animals they rut without discretion'.[26] Salvation and spiritual progress of humankind thus largely depended on a steadfast struggle against such lowly *feminine* impediments.

Unsurprisingly, then, rampant patriarchal misogyny and phobia are often attributed to a wide range of both early and patristic Christian thought.[27] Epistles of St Paul the Apostle (c.5–67 CE),[28] written before the four Gospels,[29] represent the earliest examples of 'a furry[,] reckless of grammar and logic',[30] with which the apostle scorns, *inter alia*, those who 'dishonour their own bodies between themselves'.[31] In one such rant, women who 'change the natural use into that which is against nature' and 'men with men working that which is unseemly' are described as '[b]eing filled with all unrighteousness, fornication, wickedness, covetousness, maliciousness'. They are 'full of envy, murder, debate, deceit [and] malignity'. They are 'whisperers, [b]ackbiters, haters of God, despiteful, proud, boasters, inventors of all evil things [and] disobedient to parents'. They are '[w]ithout understanding, covenantbreakers, without natural affection, implacable [and] unmerciful'. Quite simply, 'they which commit such things are worthy of death'.[32] In other letters, Paul reveals that much of his contempt for sexual and gender 'transgressors' comes from his deep-seated belief in men's supremacy over women[33] and his disdain with 'all things feminine' in men.[34] For femininity *as such*, that 'deceitful' and 'prone to sin' trait needs to be constrained at all times.[35]

Paul's letters stand in remarkable contrast with the marginal concern with sexual issues that the writers of four canonical Gospels attributed to Jesus.[36] In this respect, the Pauline teachings, especially their patristic interpretations, seem to be conceptually closer to some non-Christian Greek moral doctrines than to the distinctively less prohibitive ethos of the Gospels. Sexual restraint or even total sexual abstinence has figured as a prominent tenet particularly of some Stoic philosophers.[37] Although it is not known how familiar Paul himself was with Stoicism,[38] his 'anticorporeal' views of Christian morality[39] curiously reflect the leading Stoic teachings of the time on sexuality. Seneca (c.4 BCE–65 CE), for example, warned that sexual pleasure – as a form of incontinence (ἀκρασία) – is detrimental for human reason and a barrier to the 'higher love'.[40] 'Unchaste behaviour' for him was 'the plague of our time', which could be countered primarily by self-restraint.[41] Seneca claimed his reasoning corresponded with the laws and processes occurring *in nature*;[42] hence, human deviations were, *mutatis mutandis*, crimes against nature. Such views gradually became popular well beyond the Stoic circles, as a moral standard of the Greco-Roman intellectual elite competing against libertine and – what some thought – plebeian sexual mores.

It is perhaps primarily in this fashion – as an aristocratic virtue – that Pauline gender and sexual morality entered the first Christian imperial courts. Already under Constantine (272–337 CE), '[a]dultery became a public crime, and heinous cases became punishable by death'.[43] Strict separation of the genders and social classes was thought to reduce sexual misbehaviour because, as St Cæsarius of Arles (*c.*470–542 CE) preached, the lower a woman's class, the higher chances she stood to be sexually corrupt.[44] The Synod of Gangra, held in 340 CE, forbade members of either gender to wear clothes peculiar to the other, even if they cross-dressed for strictly religious purposes.[45] Under Justinian (483–565 CE), *Lex Iulia de adulteriis coercendis* – an old Roman law on sexual mores introduced in 17 BCE by Augustus (63 BCE–14 CE) – was invoked in support of the prohibition of men's 'abominable lust with [other] men', which was now an offence punishable by death.[46] Yet, despite Justinian's explicit claim,[47] the *lex Iulia* only punished those guilty of *stuprum* (fornication) or *adulterium* (adultery) with property confiscation and relegation, and largely ignored sexual relations between upper-class men and lower-class women.[48] It seems, rather, that the criminalisation of male same-sex sexual acts came from Justinian's strong personal disapproval of them. 'Because of such offences', he wrote angrily, 'famine, earthquakes and pestilence occur'.[49] Apart from establishing a link (however non-existent) with the old Roman law, Justinian also sought to imbue these novel legal injunctions with divine authority, by reference to the Biblical account of the demise of the city of Sodom: an exegesis already developed by the influential patristic scholar, St Augustine of Hippo (354–430 CE).[50]

Although quintessential for the late medieval and early modern conceptions of 'sexual crimes', these theological and legal interventions did not accrue a considerable laic or ecclesiastic base for much of the first Christian millennium. The majority of the canonical sources before the eleventh century CE paid only passing attention (if any) to gender and sexual matters.[51] Instead, as of the sixth century CE onwards, a literary genre aimed at basic moral education of the Christian populace – the penitentials – rose to the task of regulating gender and sexual mores. These handbooks of penance, written by and for confessors in need of practical advice on how to deal with sinners who wished to make peace with God and the Church, provided an indiscriminately grim view of all things sexual, which were always regarded as sinful. Their primary intention was, however, to regulate the believer's private life, rather than to order public space. Hence, their overall influence remained conjectural.[52] It is not before the dramatic split of the Western and Eastern Church in 1054 CE, known as the Great Schism, and the surrounding social, political and theological reforms that both cleric and municipal authorities have realised how powerful a discourse on gender and sexuality can be. One must, therefore, turn to this troublesome and complex period to see the Pauline and Justinian sex/gender politics finally erupting into a full-fledged dogmatic shift, informing both canon and civil law.

Reviving the Ancient: Sexuality and Gender in the Context of Church Reform

The eleventh-century CE schism between the Eastern and Western Church marked the commencement of rapid theological, social and political changes across Europe, which have eventually led to a period of all-encompassing reformation, known as 'the renaissance of the twelfth century'.[53] One of the most important facets peculiar to this time was an unprecedented wave of urbanisation:

> As urban business activity grew along with the town populations, further changes in social structure were bound to follow – and so they did. Bourgeois townsmen were, by and large, legally free, not bound to the soil, as were many of their contemporaries in rural areas. Townsmen in the prosperous urban centers sought, and most of them sooner or later obtained, rights of self-governance: they made laws and created courts to enforce them, they levied taxes and chose officials to collect and disburse them, they raised armed forces and allied with other towns for mutual defense.[54]

The burgeoning urban population, with an increasingly independent social status, demanded literacy and schooling that had been previously accorded almost exclusively to clergy and high aristocracy. Their academic interests varied and intersected with those of clerical students, so much so that the studies of law, medicine, philosophy and theology flourished and significantly expanded both in size and scope. One of the most significant turns and, indeed, a paradigm shift, involved the study and teaching of Roman law, as compiled centuries ago in Justinian's *Corpus iuris civilis*.[55] The voracious thirst for Roman legal thought and, *mutatis mutandis*, Justinian's own jurisprudence, which had sought to give the ancient Roman law a novel *Christian* interpretation, 'arguably had a more profound, extensive, and lasting impact on European life and society than any other facet of the twelfth-century intellectual renewal'.[56] Just as Justinian had envisioned an ambitious *renovatio imperii* by means of a substantial remake of the contemporary Christian legal thought (and practice) to the image of the olden civil law of the (non-Christian) Roman emperors, the emerging scholars, jurists and lawgivers began developing a distinctly expansionist, intrusive and powerful Romano-Christian jurisprudence.

The legal reformers were particularly bent on the renewal of canon law, which they thought must govern a true Christian society. A stream of voluminous canonical compilations was developed to respond to the exigencies of this task. The compilations often included a dismal outlook on human sexuality[57] – a discourse permeating the old Stoic, Pauline and Justinian treatises that was now given a new *legal* sense. For gender traits and sexual mores were no longer to be governed primarily by the penitentials and the ritual of private confession; they were to become one of the chief tools in making and breaking of political power and social control. Arguably, one of the key catalysts of this sudden rise in legal regulation of gender and sexuality had been the reformers' determination to prohibit clerical marriage as a canonical crime – a long-time goal eventually achieved by the Lateran decrees of 1123 and 1139 CE.[58] Doctrinally, the sordid delights of the bedchamber were seen as incompatible with the sacred office of the priesthood. Even more importantly, however, celibacy was a cheaper, more dedicated and more easily controllable lifestyle, which gave the Church an exceptional administrative and social impetus.

The successful campaign against clerical marriage made the reformers aware of the powers hidden in sexual/gender legal discourses. Canonical criminalisation and public punishment of all kinds of gender/sexual transgression became thus an increasingly viable means of social control, capable of instilling both fear and respect in the unruly masses. The vice of 'sodomy' in particular, as an ambiguous form of 'deviance from normalcy' involving at times both different-sex and same-sex acts as well as sex with animals, became an exemplary sin warranting – arguably for the first time – a canonical punishment. In 1179 CE, in an attempt to revive the harsh Justinian stance on the matter, the Third Lateran Council adopted a canon addressing 'that incontinence which is against nature': clergy found guilty of this nameless sin were either to leave the sacred order or to suffer an indefinite solitary confinement; laics were to be excommunicated and relinquished of any public post.[59] Soon after the canon was adopted, the reformers stepped up their campaign against this *peccatum mutum* – the sin so horrid that it needed to remain *silent* for even hearing about it could cause contamination.[60] In 1187 or shortly after, Peter Cantor of Paris (*c.* 1125–97 CE) published his *Verbum abbreviatum*, a practical moral guide for the clergy that 'provided for a new generation of scholars the most complete compilation of the arguments in favor of active condemnation of sodomy'.[61] According to the Dominican rendition of his *magnum opus*, Peter Cantor proposed – relying, supposedly, on an account of St Jerome (*c.* 347–420 CE) – that Christ himself had postponed repeatedly his incarnation, unwilling to enter into a human nature defiled by 'unnatural vice'. Hence, on the night of Christ's birth, *all sodomites died*, for 'it was fitting that the enemies of nature could not endure the advent and splendour of the author of nature himself' ('Iustum erat, ut auctore naturæ nascente morerentur hostes naturæ, non valentes sustinere adventum et splendorem ipsus').[62]

The reformers contended that the peculiar nature of 'unnatural sin' was that, although more prevalent amongst men, it somehow *originated* in the 'natural' weakness and sinfulness of women. One of the earliest 'specialists' in all sins of gender and sexuality, St Peter Damian (*c.* 1007– 72 CE), wrote in his infamous *Liber Gomorrhianus*, published in 1049 CE, that the true, demonic nature of sodomy is quintessentially *feminine*, and gave *her* vivid description:

> This utterly diseased Queen of Sodom renders him who obeys the laws of her tyranny infamous to men and odious to God. She mobilises him in the militia of the evil spirit and forces him to fight unspeakable wars against God. She detaches the unhappy soul from the company of the angels and, depriving it of its

excellence, takes it captive under her domineering yoke. She strips her knights of the armour of virtue, exposing them to be pierced by the spears of every vice. She humiliates her slave in the church and *condemns him in court*; she defiles him in secret and dishonours him in public; she gnaws at this conscience like a worm and consumes his flesh like fire.[63]

The apocalyptic image of a she-devil signals the writer's intention to salvage masculinity, as the perfect form of human gendered existence, from lowly and contagious femininity in which all sins, including that of sodomy, originate and abide. This patriarchal quest aptly illustrates the dominant ethos of the eleventh- and twelfth-century CE ecclesiastic and social reforms – the period which some feminist medievalist scholars describe as key to the construction of European notions of gender.[64]

Another important aspect of the increasingly legalistic reformist discourse on sodomy was that – apart from being an intrinsically feminine and 'unspeakable vice' (*vitium nefandum*) – it was a *foreign* disease. Cardinal Jacques de Vitry (*c.*1166–1240 CE), for instance, claimed that the Prophet Muhammad had personally introduced sodomy to the Arabs as a means to defile the pure souls of Christian men.[65] Similarly, sodomy was often linked with heresy, especially that of the Cathars, known for their theological rebuttal of marriage.[66] These descriptions were particularly salient for the reform's larger imperialistic goal – to mobilise and prepare Christian boys and men for the Crusades[67] – that ultimate outpour of the precarious militant theopolitical masculinity of the time. In these machinations, canon law seemed increasingly fit to homogenise and discipline an ever-growing number of men in the service (military and otherwise) of the Church and its numerous subsidiary units.

These turbulent changes encountered widespread but by and large futile resistance. In times when the reform movement was yet to coalesce, the court of the Norman king William II of England (*c.*1056–1100), for example, was notorious for its open defiance of the new sexual/gender mores. In keeping with his ancestral tradition, the king despised the English and their culture but even more so he vehemently opposed the intrusions of the Church in what he thought were his sovereign affairs. He made his court a fashionable refuge to poets, musicians and libertine intellectuals, as well as those that his enemies called 'parasites': alluding to immorality and prostitution they thought these individuals had openly indulged in. The Benedictine historian, William of Malmesbury (c.1095–1143 CE), writing some 25 years after the king's death, made sure that his defiant court is remembered as an utterly abominable place. 'It was in those days', he warned, 'that the fashion for flowing locks, luxurious clothes, the wearing of shoes with curved points was launched: to rival women in soft living, to mince with foppish gestures and to flaunt naked flesh, was the example set to young men'.[68] Some five years later, he gave an even more frightening account of 'soft living' at the late William's court:

> In times such as these, wanton seduction walked abroad with impunity, and sodomitic lust foully corrupted effeminates destined to the fires of Hell; adultery openly defiled the marriage bed. [...] In those days effeminates ruled the world, unrestrainedly pursued their revels, and foul catamites, doomed to burn in Hell, subjected themselves to the filth of sodomy; [...] they ridiculed the exhortations of priests, and persisted in their barbarous behaviour and dress.[69]

During his reign, William II cared little for the repeated complaints he was receiving from the clergy. Instead, he adamantly claimed 'that questions pertaining to sodomy, dress, hairstyles, incestuous marriages and the like were under the purview of the King, not the Church'.[70] Yet the aristocratic resistance across Europe was soon politically throttled. Eventually, the reformists succeeded in imposing a rigid model of *chivalry* as the dominant upper-class male subject position, constructed upon the stringent new sexual and gender mores. Sodomy remained an elusive gender/sexual sin,[71] albeit with a novel political power.

While the newly invented punishments for the convicted sodomites under canon law were harsh, the penalties for the same offence under municipal law became even harsher. They figured as an exaggerated reflexion of the ecclesiastical reforms, designed for essentially the same purposes: to exert control over an increasingly self-sufficient urbanised populace. It is in the municipal laws across Europe, as of the late thirteenth century CE onwards (i.e. over a century after the canonical criminalisation of 'unnatural vice' by the Third Lateran Council), that capital punishment for sodomy was reinvented, hundreds of years after the last such attempt by the Byzantine emperor Justinian:

> The Bologna statutes of 1288 [CE] replaced the earlier fine levied for homosexual [sic] offenses with death by burning; thirteenth-century Portuguese practice, adapted from the *Fuero real* of Alfonso the Wise, prescribed castration for male homosexuals [sic], followed (three days later) by hanging by the legs until death; Siena also prescribed hanging, but 'by the virile members', while the customs of Tortosa prescribed the death penalty without specifying the means.[72]

Western Christendom was now ripe with bloodthirsty gender/sex laws, while 'sodomy' joined the regular set of buzzwords used in malevolent political intrigues (along with 'heresy', 'witchcraft' and other more accustomed terms and concepts):

> The charge of sodomy became a more or less routine ingredient of political and social invective just when secular penalties for homosexual [sic] practices were becoming markedly more savage. The Knights Templars were suppressed, in part for practicing sodomy; William of Nogaret included sodomy among the numerous other vices that he ascribed to Pope Boniface VIII and to Bishop Guichard of Troyes; the sodomy charges preferred by King James II of Aragon against Count Alvaro of Urgel were a potent weapon in a political vendetta; if these charges also had some foundation in fact, that was a convenient coincidence.[73]

The effects of the ill-reputed Queen of Sodom's[74] entrance into the legal and political mainstream of the late medieval Europe were nonetheless ambiguous. The 'unspeakable' gender and sexual transgressions apparently did not diminish,[75] although they were less visible in an increasingly morally saturated public space. The furore and gore of 'the renaissance of the twelfth century' was soon met with culturally tumultuous yet socially broad-minded age of Renaissance (fourteenth to seventeenth century CE), in which both Church and the urban masses underwent profound moral and political changes. Yet the uncanny legacy of the bleak last phase of the Middle Ages survived in dusty chronicles and in the rising stream of the Machiavellian politics of the perennially precarious European ruling classes. When the Renaissance vigour eventually entered its late, critical phase, sodomy laws surfaced yet again in some struggling municipal legal environments to attempt another round of their political *danse macabre*.

Buggery and its Afterlives: From Royal Opportunism to Republican Deceit

The second coming of the concept of sodomy as a capital offence occurred truly as a surprise, due to its timing as well as its utterly unexpected location. It happened in the sixteenth-century CE England, the island kingdom traditionally at odds with ecclesiastical wrangling which had somehow been spared any prior municipal legal 'sodomite-hunts' akin to those of continental Europe. Even the lesser punishments prescribed by canon law had almost never been imposed in practice.[76] Hence, when it was passed in 1533 CE by the parliament of Henry VIII, it was clear that the Buggery Act[77] was a product of purely political concerns.

The act provided as follows:

Le Roy le vault

Forasmuch as there is not yet sufficient and condign Punishment appointed and limited by the due Course of the Laws of this Realm for the detestable and abominable Vice of Buggery *committed with Mankind or Beast* [. . .] it may be enacted [. . .] that the same Offence be from henceforth adjudged *Felony* and that such an Order and Form of Process therein to be used against the Offenders as in Cases of Felony at the Common law. And that the Offenders being herof convict by verdict Confession or outlawry shall *suffer such Pains of Death and Losses and Penalties of their Goods, Chattels, Debts, Lands, Tenements and Hereditaments as Felons do* according to the Common Laws of this Realm. [. . .] And that no Person offending in any such Offence shall be admitted to his Clergy, and that Justices of the Peace shall have Power and Authority within the limits of their Commissions and Jurisdictions to hear and determine the said Offence, as they do in the Cases of other Felonies.[78]

Subsequent interpretation established that the offence of 'buggery' is committed if the accused male person has engaged specifically in *anal sex* with either men, women or animals, while sexual relations between women (or, presumably, between women and animals) were exempt from it.[79] These were, however, mere formalities. The crux of the new law was that *all material possessions* ('their Goods, Chattels, Debts, Lands, Tenements and Hereditaments') of the convicted offender were subject to expropriation, under the pretext of a sexual offence.

Around the time of enactment of the Buggery Act, the rift between Henry VIII (1491–1547 CE) and the Church reached its peak. In 1533 CE, Henry formally stripped of her title his first wife and married Anne Boleyn (*c.*1505–36 CE), despite papal disapproval. Only a year after, Parliament passed the first Act of Supremacy,[80] which declared that the king is 'the Only Supreme Head in Earth of the Church of England, called Anglicans Ecclesia', and that the English crown shall enjoy 'all Honours, Dignities, Pre-eminences, Jurisdictions, Privileges, Authorities, Immunities, Profits and Commodities to the said Dignity'. The Buggery Act was but one in a series of statutes, prepared by the king's legal counsel (and, later, chief minister) Thomas Cromwell (1485–1540 CE) between 1532 and 1536 CE, which were specifically designed to deprive the clergy of their powers and possessions.[81] If charges of buggery could be brought against them, the wealth of the priests, in particular the members of the monastic orders who still enjoyed a wide popular support, could easily be pillaged by the king's loyalists. A decade later, in private correspondence with the Scottish regent, Henry proposed a similar solution for the resistant Scottish monasteries. He advised the regent to send a commissioner to 'examine all the religious of their conversation [meaning *acts*, including sexual acts] and behaviour in their livings, whereby if it be well handled, he shall get knowledge of all their abominations', which would then allow his compatriots to seize their lands and possessions 'to their great profit and honour'.[82] The advice was based on the success of one such campaign in England, only two years after the Buggery Act was passed:

In 1535 [CE] Cromwell sent agents to make formal 'visitations' of England's monasteries to determine their assets, uncover superstitions, and report on sexual misconduct. The monks were subjected to much rough bullying by the rapacious visitors in order to elicit confessions. As a result, the documents they produced, called the *Comperta* (or 'Disclosures'), caused sensation.

[. . .] In 175 entries we find over 180 monks designated as 'sodomites'.[83]

Some of the condemned monks were designated as 'sodomites *per voluntarias pollutiones*',[84] meaning that masturbation (or 'voluntary pollution') was also understood as a type of sodomy. The process of intimidation and public imprecation of the monastic communities finally culminated in the second Act of Dissolution of 1539 CE,[85] by which all remaining Catholic monasteries and houses were forcefully disbanded.

When Henry's Catholic daughter Mary (1516–58 CE) succeeded to the throne in 1553 CE, the new parliament repealed most of Cromwell's statutes, including the Buggery Act. The act, was, however, restored under Queen Elizabeth I (1533–1603 CE), presumably not due to a particular Protestant doctrine but a scandal involving a high-ranking Spanish scholar which 'seems to have reminded the authorities of the deficiency in English law'.[86] 'Sithence which Repeal so had and made [in 1553 CE], divers evil-disposed Persons have been the more bold to commit the said most horrible and detestable Vice of Buggery', claimed the new statute and thenceforth revived the Buggery Act 'in full Force, Strength and Effect for ever'.[87]

The Elizabethan statute had a very long life, indeed, yet until the mid-eighteenth century CE it was rarely enforced.[88] In the eighteenth and nineteenth century CE, however, hundreds of people were executed on charges of buggery. In 1828 CE, the statute of 1563 CE was revoked by a consolidating act, but it retained the death penalty.[89] In 1861 CE, the capital punishment was substituted with life sentence or, in some instances, imprisonment of at least ten years.[90] In 1885 CE, buggery was supplemented by a novel offence of 'gross indecency' between male persons.[91] In 1956 CE, the Sexual Offences Act united the two categories as 'unnatural offences'.[92] The statute survived until 1967 CE, when same-sex sexual relations between consenting male adults in private were finally decriminalised in England and Wales on the recommendation of the Wolfenden Committee.[93] It was, however, only in 2003 CE that the categories of buggery and gross indecency were completely removed from English criminal law.[94]

In some other parts of Europe, however, sodomy laws and their repeals followed a very different timeline.[95] Perhaps most notably, in 1791 CE republican France, the new *Code pénal de la Révolution* made no mention of same-sex relations in private, thus ending forever a long era of dreadful punishments that infamously included *les bûchers de Sodome* ('the pyres of Sodom') upon which the culprits were burnt to death.[96] This early act of decriminalisation is nowadays often recounted with a sense of pride in the Enlightenment era's social transformations. It seems, however, that what really occurred was a change in the understanding of the concept of *crime* (whereby ecclesiastical insights no longer played an all-decisive role), rather than in the largely negative social outlook towards sexual and gender difference. A notable intellectual of the era, Nicolas de Condorcet (1743–94 CE), penned perhaps the most accurate summary of the actual reasons guiding the legal change:

> Sodomy, when there is no violence, cannot fall within the scope of the criminal law. It does not violate the rights of any other man. It has only an indirect influence on the good order of society, like drunkenness, or the love of gambling. It is a low, disgusting vice whose proper punishment is scorn. The penalty of fire is atrocious [...], [for] we must not forget to remark that it is to superstition that we owe the barbarous use of this punishment.[97]

Public contempt for sodomy was characteristic of the age: an abusive vocabulary permeated the works of Voltaire, Montesquieu, Marat, Diderot and other leading minds of the Enlightenment, thus channelling a common French ethos which, centuries before, had already construed this 'vile deed' as a foreign (*le vice ultramountain*) and upper-class vice (*le beau vice*).[98] Yet drastic public punishments were no longer fit for the 'Age of the Reason'. Instead, controlling gender and sexual diversity was to employ more covert measures. Napoleon Bonaparte (1769–1821 CE) himself believed that in his ever-expanding empire 'the law should [not] concern itself with these offenses. Nature has seen to it that [sodomites] are not frequent. The scandal of legal proceedings *would only tend to multiply them*'.[99] The old logic of the *peccatum mutum* – a sin *kept* silent so that it remains suppressed – seems to inform this 'enlightened' turn. The law deemed too public, Napoleon wryly suggested that '[i]t would be better to give the proceedings [against sodomites] another direction'.[100] Hence, the new Napoleonic Code of 1810 CE made no attempt to reinstate sodomy laws. They were instead replaced with administrative measures, which granted the police independent powers to detain or internally displace the individuals suspected of 'being' or 'acting like' sodomites. This deliberate 'regulatory' intimidation 'remained the routine in France for almost two centuries. The special department set up by the police in Paris to control [sodomites] was not abolished until 1981 [CE]'.[101]

Historical developments around the buggery laws in Britain and decriminalisation of sodomy laws in France epitomise two distinct yet not entirely dissimilar approaches to sexual and gender diversity that the European legal traditions have generally assumed. On the one hand, in Britain and its colonies, harsh criminal provisions were retained and propagated in the hope of achieving public deterrence through the sheer force of law. In France and its colonies, on the other hand, public compliance with the dominant sexual/gender norms was regulated via administrative measures duly implemented by the police, largely outside the courtrooms and other public domains of the law. Despite the ascendance of the 'Age of Reason', both of these approaches remained saturated with the (overt or covert) medieval ideas of Christian masculinity and 'redemptory mission', which made them part and parcel of European 'civilising' projects across the globe. Both also retained an utter disdain towards perceived sexual/gender transgressions. For what had been deemed the 'unspeakable vice' (*vitium nefandum*) remained an essentially *ordre public* offence, whereby to utter the 'unspeakable' meant to break the societal peace, to stir *apparently* still waters.

By the mid-twentieth century CE, this pretence was no longer tenable. Europe and the rest of the world were to advance into yet another renaissance, this time dubbed a 'sexual revolution', and the repressive gender/sexual *ordre public* was soon to be challenged precisely from its alterity, the conceptual space enshrined in 'the right to respect for *private* life'.[102] Yet the legacies of the British and French epitomes of the twelfth-century CE European normative view of human gender and sexuality lingered on. Their complexity was exceptional and their consequences immense.

The remainder of this chapter attempts to unpack and situate some of those legacies in relation to international human rights law and the ongoing legal and political mêlée for the universal recognition of the notions of 'sexual orientation' and 'gender identity'.

Sexuality, Gender and Diversity in (a Post-Colonial) International Law*

This section introduces the entry of sexual orientation and gender identity as *legal categories* into international law from the perspective of *post-colonial* sex/gender politics. While there are, indeed, many avenues from which these issues could have been explored, I find it important to trace the particularly *colonial* legacies of the paradigmatically *bloc-based* divide which advocate for sexual/gender diversity before the United Nations currently faces. Whereas greater (totalising) narratives of 'Christian', 'Muslim', 'liberal' and 'conservative' axioms on this matter still tend to be used to justify certain policy positions, they are effectively deployed within and by the clusters of states steeped in peculiar (post-)colonial histories and contexts. I posit that these geopolitical groupings operate along the former colonial fault lines *more* than along their contemporary ideological divergences. This obviously does not apply to all cases,[103] but it does concern so-called 'Western' – 'Muslim' relations to a large extent. As this book attempts to describe in relation to sexual/gender diversity, these imagined political poles are far more entangled in a *shared* (inter-)imperial heritage and the logic of (neo-liberal) political economy than their ruling elites are willing to admit, so much so that 'Orients' within the 'Occident' and 'Occidents' within the 'Orient' always already coexist in a dynamic (yet precarious) symbiosis. It is through such perturbations and metamorphoses that a medieval Christian concept of gender and sexuality, refashioned through the later European imperial projects, could have been proclaimed as 'traditionally Islamic' in a twentieth-century post-colonial Muslim-majority Asian or African nation state. And it is due to the very same phenomenon that this fallacy has been often taken for granted in the 'West'.

On a purely legal plane, the consequences of colonial exportation of the British and French models of state control over sexual/gender diversity have been markedly different. British colonial legislators endeavoured to entrench the criminal concepts of 'buggery' and 'gross indecency' in all their overseas dominions,[104] accompanied by a stark binary outlook of human genders. Wherever a greater diversity in sexual and gender expression was encountered, it was frowned upon and suppressed, by law as well as by other means of social control.

In the vast lands of the British Raj, for example, where sexual/gender plurality was traditionally abundant and by and large socially acceptable, the colonial administration invested enormous efforts in categorising, according to their own views, such variance. Thus, the term 'eunuch' was seen fit to encapsulate all gender transgressions from the rigid male/female divide, thereby deliberately neglecting the long and complex histories of the local gender-variant subjectivities.[105] In so doing,

> not only did [the British colonial invention of 'eunuch'] construct a category of personhood, but it also defined this figure under the governing gaze of law: the constructed entity was defined by its legal sanction. Since eunuchs were defined mostly in terms of exclusion, their treatment as a legal category was based on notions of containment and control.[106]

In the French dominions, the 'governing gaze of law' was largely absent, yet the colonial administrators dully applied Napoleon's approach in regulating sexual/gender life by means of police interventions. This meant, however, that the first 'sodomy laws' appeared only after the independence of some of the former French colonies, where such legislation was passed relying on the pretext of 'local traditions'. But a number of other states that wrestled their independence from France decided not to invent such laws. In sum, in the 1960s CE, when the process of decolonisation reached its full swing, three distinct trends emerged amongst the newly independent nation states.

The first trend already became visible in the late 1940s CE, epitomised in the 1947 CE Partition of British India into the sovereign states of the Dominion of Pakistan (later the Islamic Republic of Pakistan) and the Union of India (later Republic of India). Both states simply retained ('domesticated') the relevant colonial criminal provisions.[107] This model came to be a preferred choice of former British colonies.[108] Although rarely applied in practice, the continued existence of discriminatory statutes was to ensure that heteronormativity, politically restyled both as a 'traditional' and 'modern' value, remained forcefully preserved under pain of criminal punishment. In this process, Victorian laws and social mores were given a new ('African', 'Muslim', 'Asian', etc.) veneer.[109]

The second trend, prevalent amongst some former French colonies, was to criminalise certain expressions of sexual-gender diversity upon their independence. By far the most prominent measure was to outlaw same-sex sexual acts, due to perceived incongruence with Muslim legal traditions.[110] The new laws were scarcely applied, but had the same public function as the comparable legislation of the former British colonies.

The third trend was that of the countries – notably *all* on the African continent – that in their entire history as independent states have *never* had 'sodomy laws'. Those are Benin, Burkina Faso, Central African Republic, Chad, Republic of the Congo (Congo-Brazzaville), Côte d'Ivoire, Democratic Republic of Congo, Gabon, Madagascar, Mali, Niger and Rwanda. All, save one,[111] of these countries won their independence from France. The appeal of politically opportune narratives of 'Muslim' or 'African' values, so readily explored in connection with criminal provisions against same-sex sexual intimacy in the neighbouring countries, somehow has never coalesced into a powerful social discourse in these states, regardless of their geopolitical position and religious make-up. Not only is the majority of the population of some of these states Muslim, their governments are often also at the forefront of the Muslim bloc-politics in the United Nations.[112] Their continuous resistance to the criminalisation of same-sex sexual acts thus formidably defies the argument that *all* Muslim states consider such acts as a serious criminal offence.

The three trends in post-colonial legal politics demonstrate the inescapable complexity of the encounter of an aetiologically European idea of 'buggery'/'sodomy' laws with other cultural, social and legal traditions. The resulting local, national, regional and transnational narratives, competing vehemently against each other, were, however, still conveniently kept outside the domain of international law. No State or international organisation was, simply, ready to intervene. Inter-state interests and relations were occupied with other matters, and so were the majority of human rights advocates before the UN.

By the mid-1970s CE, however, the first significant breakthroughs were made towards social recognition of sexual and gender difference.[113] With supra-national human rights treaties already in place,[114] it did not take long before the first cases, civil society coalitions and political initiatives entered the rocky terrain of international human rights law.

The Rise of 'Sexual Orientation' and 'Gender Identity' in International Human Rights Law

In the 1980s CE, as a result of a broadly felt post-'sexual revolution' societal flux, gender and sexuality slowly became a *debatable subject* in international affairs. Challenging the ageing Victorian construct in which the mere public examination of these matters would almost already constitute an 'outrage on decency' – a conception carefully imbedded and universally reproduced in the unwritten codes of conduct in diplomatic and international legal circles – the global 'society of states' became a forum for deliberation of previously 'unspeakable' subjects, such as sexual and reproductive rights.[115]

These operations have demanded a specific *discursive intervention*. Ever since its inception, 'international law imagined itself in terms of progressive, or pedigree history'.[116] Although the social Darwinist arrogance of its European and North American 'founding fathers' was, indeed, systematically challenged by the processes of decolonisation and 'third bloc' and 'Third World' ideas such as the Non-Aligned Movement,[117] the proleptic structure of international law could not be entirely circumvented. Hence, the language of sexual rights was to uncomfortably embrace the universalising, trans-cultural mission and to insist upon impoverished, 'global' models of *the woman* and *the man* and their inherent rights, to which humanity *tout court* should aspire. This was, primarily, a bargaining strategy, based on a vision akin to that of American legal Realism, in which (international) law was seen 'as a means to social ends and not as an end in itself'.[118] Law was an apt tool, so much so that misgivings about it could be temporarily disregarded or even welcomed – as in the above case – for the sake of transnational social reforms. An 'entire matrix of social, economic, cultural, and relational forces', integral to human gender and sexual experience,[119] was set aside for a much later socio-legal articulation.

In legal documents and activist policy papers alike, produced in the 1980s CE, sexual diversity was given a set of agreed denominators all originating in the global north, where 'heterosexuality' was contrasted with 'homosexuality' (and, by and large only nominally, by 'bisexuality') and linked to specific terms-of-art: 'straight', 'lesbian' and 'gay'. By the end of the decade, the 'transsexual' legal subject entered the frame, thus creating the ubiquitous acronym LGBT. Gender as a term distinct from sex was still poorly understood, or at least seen as unfit for the ongoing transnational legal battles.

At the United Nations (UN) level, the principal sites of sexual rights polemics and activism were four world conferences on women: in Mexico City in 1975 CE, in Copenhagen in 1980 CE, in Nairobi in 1985 CE and in Beijing in 1995 CE.[120] A lesbian caucus was formed at the Mexico City conference, along with various lesbian workshops. The visible presence of lesbian activists, which continued at all subsequent conferences, resulted, *inter alia*, in the first statement of a government delegation in support of lesbian rights in Nairobi and in an address delivered at the Main Committee plenary session in Beijing.[121] Paragraph 96 of the Beijing Platform for Action, the main policy document of the 1995 CE world conference, recognised women's sexual and reproductive rights, albeit without the suggested references to their sexual orientation.[122] Sexual rights, primarily associated with women, were now irrevocably present at the global stage, with other UN social conferences[123] and international criminal courts[124] significantly contributing to the legal cognisance of their transnational discourse.

In Europe, important developments occurred primarily at the level of the Council of Europe. In 1981 CE, its Parliamentary Assembly adopted Recommendation No. 924, calling on member states to decriminalise same-sex sexual activities between consenting adults and equalise the age of consent for all sexual partners, irrespective of their sexual orientation. Violence and discrimination in employment against gays and lesbians, as well as custody and visitation restrictions against homosexual parents, were also condemned. Eight years later, in its Recommendation No. 1117, the Assembly asked its member states to combat discrimination against transsexuals and legalise sex reassignment surgeries and name changes.[125]

It was, however, through the jurisprudence of the European Court of Human Rights (ECtHR), under the European Convention on Human Rights (ECHR),[126] binding on all member states of the Council of Europe, that the most significant legal changes were achieved. First came the landmark decision in the 1981 CE case of *Dudgeon* v *United Kingdom*, when the ECtHR ruled that criminalisation of same-sex sexual conduct amongst consenting adults violated the right to respect for private life, protected by Article 8 of the ECHR.[127] This was a swan song to all relics of 'sodomy laws' in the Council of Europe member states, as confirmed in the 1988 CE decision in *Norris* v *Ireland*[128] and the final 1993 CE case on the matter of *Modinos* v *Cyprus*.[129] Following the lead of the Parliamentary Assembly of the Council of Europe, the ECtHR ruled, in 1992 CE, that Article 8 of the ECHR also protects the transsexuals' right to change sex on their birth certificate.[130]

Privacy thus became the first niche in human rights law from which sexual difference could be claimed and protected. Adorning a multitude of human rights treaties,[131] this concept ensured the starting bargaining position, in which the lawful existence of the sexually diverse legal subject could be acknowledged, albeit only if their sexual and relational life was kept safely outside the public domain. After all, as the ECtHR stated in the *Dudgeon* judgment, '"[d]ecriminalisation" [on the grounds of privacy] does not imply approval'; hence, 'some sectors of the population [should not] draw misguided conclusions'.[132] The right to privacy of the sexually diverse legal subject was a right to a silent existence on the fringes of the dominant social order, a right to a tolerated but abject life. Yet it signalled a new era in the struggle for sexual rights that in the 1990s CE inevitably spilled over to the UN treaty bodies, and beyond.

In 1994 CE, the Human Rights Committee, the UN treaty body under the International Covenant on Civil and Political Rights (ICCPR),[133] decided in *Toonen* v *Australia*[134] that 'a criminal prohibition on same-sex sexual activity, even if unenforced, constituted an unreasonable interference with Mr Toonen's privacy'.[135] It went on to conclude that 'the reference to "sex" in articles 2, paragraph 1, and 26 [of the ICCPR] is to be taken as including sexual orientation'.[136] Some states, including Mr Toonen's,[137] complied with this interpretation; others argued, in defiance, that this UN treaty body had gone astray from the ICCPR drafters' vision of human civil and political rights, thereby causing 'uncertainty' in interpretation and application of international legal standards.[138] Such an open resistance was made possible due to the problematic nature of the UN Human Rights Committee's decisions – which are arguably binding *de jure* yet very difficult to implement, given the lack of substantial enforcement mechanisms, and thereby often non-binding *de facto*. The Committee has since reiterated its position that the prohibition of discrimination based on sexual orientation is implicitly contained in the ICCPR,[139] but the objecting states still refuse to endorse it.

Other UN treaty bodies have opted for a 'softer' legal approach, confining their opposition to human rights violations based on the victim's perceived or actual sexual orientation to their General Comments and Concluding Observations.[140] It was not until 2009 CE that one such commentary mentioned gender identity as well.[141] The various Special Procedures of the former UN Commission on Human Rights and the incumbent UN Human Rights Council have gradually joined them, thereby creating a powerful unison of independent UN human rights experts against discrimination on the grounds of sexual orientation and gender identity. 'It can never be acceptable', proclaimed the then UN High Commissioner for Human Rights, Navanethem Pillay, 'to deprive certain individuals of their rights, indeed to impose criminal sanctions on those individuals, not because they have inflicted harm on others or pose a threat to the well-being of others, but simply for being who they are, for *being born* with a particular sexual orientation or gender identity'.[142] By accentuating the natural cause of these phenomena, Pillay undoubtedly intended to challenge the oppositional narrative of universally imposed yet artificially created 'new' sexual/ gender rights, otherwise supposedly non-existent in cultures and histories of the specific regions of the world. Yet she also foreclosed the alternative, non-essentialist views of human sexual and gender diversity. If the non-heteronormative legal subject were to assume a protected position in international law, any volatility and fluidity of their identitary script had to be downplayed. Their 'certainty', as a type of 'normalcy' conferred upon the comparable heterosexual subject of the law, had to be firmly asserted.

The Brave New Millennium: From Brazilian Resolution to Yogyakarta Principles

At the dawn of a new millennium, the supra-national legal and political scene was ripe for a substantial makeover. Sexual and gender rights became a prominent feature of the international human rights jurisprudence, expanding well beyond their initial privacy niche. The new regional and transnational coalitions of non-governmental organisations from across the world took on the task of advocating for sexual and gender diversity, with some – like the Geneva-based ARC International – being specifically formed and equipped to facilitate it.[143] Over the first decade of the new millennium, the novel global impetus propelled the notions of sexual orientation and gender identity as the foremost concepts of international human rights law relating to sexual and gender diversity. Yet it also created 'an extraordinarily fractious space',[144] reflecting with striking accuracy the geopolitical, ideological and cultural divisions in today's societies. Not only did the emerging global activism draw out internal discordances, it also provoked a series of strategic multilateral alliances of right-wing governments and ultra-conservative religious organisations determined to stop it. The world was at war, it seemed, and it was changing faster than ever before.

In the geopolitical region of the Council of Europe, which following the demise of the Eastern bloc exploded into a huge territory comprising 47 member states, significant gains were being made. In *Smith and Grady* v *United Kingdom*[145] and *Lustig-Prean and Beckett* v *United Kingdom*,[146] the ECtHR ruled that a ban on military recruitment of lesbian and gay individuals is in violation of the ECHR. It also recognised, in the case of *Salgueiro da Silva Mouta* v *Portugal*,[147] that sexual orientation is a prohibited ground of discrimination, while deciding that the refusal to grant parental rights to a father on this basis could not be tolerated. In 2003 CE, the ECtHR compared the difference in treatment on the basis of one's sexual orientation with that of 'race, origin or colour' and ruled expressly against the unequal age of consent between same-sex and different-sex consenting sexual partners.[148] In the same year, it also outlawed the difference in treatment relating to housing rights on the ground of sexual orientation of unmarried cohabitating partners.[149] Further, in 2008 CE, the different treatment of a single lesbian woman in relation to her eligibility to be considered as a potential adoptive parent was also found to be in breach of the ECHR.[150] In 2010 CE, in *Schalk and Kopf* v *Austria*, while stopping short of recognising a right to same-sex marriage, the ECtHR affirmed, *obiter dictum*, that same-sex relationships fall within the ambit of 'family life', protected by Article 8 of the ECHR.[151]

After a series of unsuccessful applications,[152] the ECtHR finally recognised, in the 2002 CE case of *I* v *United Kingdom*, the need for 'legal certainty, foreseeability and equality before the law' of post-operative transsexual persons.[153] In that same year, in *Goodwin* v *United Kingdom*, it granted those of them sexually oriented towards the gender that is different from their post-reassignment gender a right to marry.[154] In *Van*

Kück v *Germany*, the ECtHR upheld a male-to-female transsexual's 'freedom to define herself as a female person'[155] and in *L* v *Lithuania* it called for the transsexual applicant's gender identity to be duly recognised as 'his true identity'.[156] These developments occurred, as argued by the ECtHR in its *Goodwin* judgement, so that transsexual persons could 'live in dignity and worth in accordance with the sexual identity chosen by them at great personal cost'.[157] Yet, with the continuous reliance of the European judges on so-called 'medical considerations', which maintain that gender variance is caused by 'gender identity disorder' and therefore in need of cure, correction, re-binarisation,[158] one cannot help but wonder whether *Goodwin* and the subsequent judgements are really a 'good win' for gender-variant individuals[159] or a more sinister, heteronormative legal curative procedure.[160]

The ECtHR has also moved to protect the right to freedom of assembly, guaranteed by Article 11 of the ECHR, in connection with public protests and Pride marches of LGBT groups, which had been banned in Poland[161] and Russia.[162] This signalled that the European public sphere could no longer be lawfully 'protected' from various expressions of sexual and gender diversity, including political activism. Russian authorities, however, have so far declined to comply. Moreover, the country's three local legislatures – that of Ryazan, Kostroma and Arkhangelsk Regions – adopted by-laws prohibiting 'propaganda of homosexuality among minors' under pain of a fine.[163] A similar law, banning 'propaganda of homosexuality, bisexuality, transgenderism and paedophilia', took effect in March 2012 CE in Saint Petersburg.[164] Thus, the prejudice of the 'predatory nature' of same-sex oriented men, still deep-seated in Russian society, helps the state and local authority maintain control over the (heteronormative) public sphere, in defiance of broader European legal developments. Such open resistance is, however, surprisingly rare. In general, the substantial jurisprudential changes relating to sexual and gender diversity introduced by the ECtHR and other organs of the Council of Europe have led to significant domestic legislative reforms across Europe.

In the Americas, the Organisation of American States (OAS) General Assembly has repeatedly and unanimously called for freedom from discrimination on the basis of sexual orientation and gender identity.[165] The Inter-American Convention against All Forms of Discrimination and Intolerance expressly ('sexual orientation') or impliedly ('gender and sexual identity') mentions these concepts.[166] In its recent landmark case of *Atala Riffo y niñas* v *Chile* (*Atala Riffo and daughters* v *Chile*), the Inter-American Court of Human Rights also affirmed that 'sexual orientation and gender identity are protected categories under the [1969 CE American Convention of Human Rights]'.[167] This interpretation confirms the intention of the OAS judicial organs 'to turn attentions to all the areas of discriminatory human behaviour, including those which have so far been ignored or neglected at international level'.[168] However, only a few cases concerning sexual and gender diversity have so far reached these bodies.[169] In spite of still scarce case law, the OAS judicial organs are resolute in their condemnation of violence and discrimination on the grounds of gender identity and sexual orientation.[170] It remains to be seen how far they will be willing to extend their support in potentially more controversial cases, such as one currently pending before the Inter-American Commission on Human Rights that challenges Jamaican 'sodomy laws', inherited from the country's former colonial administrators.[171]

The most dramatic events, however, have occurred on the UN plane. In 2000 CE, the former UN Commission on Human Rights passed a resolution on extrajudicial, summary and arbitrary executions, which for the first time included references to sexual orientation. Resolutions on the same topic were since passed on an annual basis, with concepts relating to sexual and gender rights becoming increasingly prominent each coming year. Since 2002 CE, the UN resolutions on the death penalty have also urged states to abolish capital punishment for sexual relations between consenting adults of any sex/gender.[172] These moves have arguably prepared the ground for a global advocacy, spearheaded by ARC International at the UN human rights fora, with a long-term goal of securing a UN document specifically recognising rights to sexual and gender diversity.

In 2003 CE, the Brazilian delegation to the former UN Commission on Human Rights presented a groundbreaking resolution on human rights and sexual orientation, which was immediately met with stark and vocal opposition predominantly from the delegations associated with the Organisation of Islamic Co-operation (OIC).[173] Due to their pressure, the resolution was eventually dropped. However, civil society organising around this resolution has led to powerful joint statements on behalf of numerous UN member states, including: *Statement Made by*

New Zealand on behalf of 32 States;[174] *Norwegian Joint Statement on Human Rights Violations based on Sexual Orientation and Gender Identity*;[175] the 2006 CE *Finnish Joint Statement on Sexual Orientation, on behalf of the European Union, Accession and Related Countries*; *Argentinean Statement on behalf of Ten Latin American States* and the 2008 CE *Slovenian Joint Statement on behalf of the European Union*.[176] Many of these statements have been co-signed by Turkey, Albania, Bosnia and Herzegovina and other counties with significant Muslim population, which enjoy either full membership or observer status at the OIC.

In December 2008 CE – 60 years after the Universal Declaration of Human Rights was adopted[177] – Argentina presented before the UN General Assembly, on behalf of 66 states, a historic statement on human rights, sexual orientation and gender identity.[178] The statement calls upon all states and relevant international human rights mechanisms 'to commit to promote and protect the human rights of all persons, regardless of sexual orientation or gender identity' and urges states: (1) 'to take all measures, in particular legislative and administrative, to ensure that sexual orientation or gender identity may under no circumstances be the basis for criminal penalties, in particular executions, arrests or detention'; (2) to end impunity for human rights violations based on these grounds; and (3) to remove obstacles and ensure appropriate protection for human rights defenders who work on issues related to sexual orientation and gender identity.[179] The OIC launched a counter-statement, delivered by Syria on behalf of 57 states.[180] It declined to acknowledge sexual orientation and gender identity as grounds of discrimination in international law and warned that the introduction of these categories might lead to 'the legitimisation of many deplorable acts, including paedophilia'.[181] The OIC's intention beyond this response was to demonstrate that there is a substantial rift (mostly) between the Muslim-majority states and others on this matter, but some of its important member states, such as Turkey, Kyrgyzstan and Uzbekistan, decided not to support it. On 21 March 2011 CE, a new *Joint Statement on Sexual Orientation and Gender Identity* was delivered at the 16th session of the UN Human Rights Council by Colombia, this time on behalf of 85 states.[182] Pakistan, representing the OIC, and Nigeria, speaking for the African Group, once again made counter-statements denying the notions of sexual orientation and gender identity a place in international human rights law.[183] The battle was now clearly

raging between the governments determined to preserve heteronormativity at any cost, including human lives, under the guise of religious or
regional 'values', and a growing number of states ready to acknowledge,
at least formally, human sexual/gender plurality.

The highest UN officials were by now ready to speak up. In a
televised message for an inter-governmental panel, convened by Brazil
and South Africa at the UN Human Rights Council in Geneva to
specifically address violence and discrimination based on gender identity
and sexual orientation, the UN Secretary-General, Ban Ki-moon,
proclaimed:

> To those who are lesbian, gay, bisexual or transgender, let me say:
> You are not alone. Your struggle for an end to violence and
> discrimination is a shared struggle. Any attack on you is an attack
> on the universal values the United Nations and I have sworn to
> defend and uphold. Today, I stand with you [. . .] and I call upon
> all countries and people to stand with you, too.[184]

At the same event, the then UN High Commissioner for Human Rights,
Navanethem Pillay, presented her groundbreaking report documenting
discriminatory laws and practices and acts of violence against individuals
based on their actual or perceived sexual orientation or gender
identity, published in December 2011 CE.[185] But, is there a uniform
understanding of what these concepts mean across the different cultures,
histories and legal jargons of the world?

An expert group convened in Yogyakarta, Indonesia, from 6 to 9
November 2006 CE, set out to answer this question. It came up with the
*Yogyakarta Principles on the Application of International Human Rights Law
in Relation to Sexual Orientation and Gender Identity* (the Yogyakarta
Principles), which were officially launched on 26 March 2007 CE in
Geneva, at a side event of the UN Human Rights Council.[186] The
Yogyakarta Principles were negotiated and agreed upon by 29 experts.
About half of them were either past or then still serving UN Special
Procedures or members of UN treaty bodies, including the former High
Commissioner for Human rights, Mary Robinson. The other half was
made up of distinguished judges, scholars and activists from across the
world, including several Muslim-majority states.[187] After much
deliberation, the signatories agreed on a common definition of both

sexual orientation[188] and gender identity,[189] and sought to catalogue the forms of violence, discrimination and human rights violations based on these notions.[190] They also endeavoured to establish how the existing standards of international law apply to these human rights violations and to ascertain the scope and nature of state responsibility to uphold those standards.[191]

The 29 Principles agreed in Yogyakarta address, *inter alia*, universality of rights, equality and non-discrimination and recognition before the law, as well as numerous individual civil, political, social, economic and cultural rights. The emphasis is, however, placed on civil and political human rights, in line with the dominant trend in international human rights law. These include, via Principle 21, the right to freedom of thought, conscience and religion. Accountability and effective remedies for violations of these rights are also briefly addressed. In most of cases, the Yogyakarta Principles endeavour to directly reflect the provisions of international human rights conventions, although some also seek to highlight non-treaty-based human rights standards, such as countering impunity for human rights violations.[192]

The right to freedom of thought, conscience and religion – a firmly established concept in international human rights law – is interpreted in the Yogyakarta Principles as including state responsibility to guarantee this right to everyone, regardless of their sexual orientation and/or gender identity, even when its enjoyment by some members of society appears to contravene mainstream religious and other beliefs. This is in line with the UN Human Rights Committee's authoritative interpretation of this right,[193] as well as with the jurisprudence of the ECtHR.[194] An appalling state practice of continuous persecution of their religious minorities may, indeed, particularly concern human sexual and gender diversity. State regimes around the globe have failed to protect not only those whose beliefs and practices have differed from the official norms, but also those who have been castigated as incongruent or even harmful to their religious and other communities, for the simple fact of their sexual/gender divergence from the dominant social norms. Sexually and gender-variant Muslims face particularly severe discrimination, since their allegiance to either the mainstream or a minority Muslim community is often denied, including by the State, as an oxymoron.[195] Relying on established international human rights law,[196] the Yogyakarta Principle 21 seeks to remedy this situation by reasserting state responsibility to protect individuals and communities targeted by the damning majoritarian credos.

The UN treaty bodies and Special Procedures have shown a univocal support for the Yogyakarta Principles, thereby reaffirming their importance in international legal affairs.[197] The response from certain sections of the academy has, however, been less favourable, accusing the Principles' drafters of 'reinforc[ing] identity politics' in spite of 'the whole school of thought [i.e. queer theory] wanting to debunk such identities'.[198] They have been deemed insensitive to those who either live 'in a society that lacks any notion of sexual orientation or gender identity' or who want to be free of such categories altogether.[199] An author has warned that the Yogyakarta Principles are generally 'bereft of gender analysis and in danger of subsuming "gender" under "gender identity"',[200] which might effectively 'erase the female subject and her gender-specific experience of human rights abuses'.[201] In addition, the Principles' Special Rapporteur, Michael O'Flaherty, has himself warned that some of them are rather vaguely expressed, thereby creating dangerous interpretative lacunae.[202] He has described, for example, Principle 21 as being unclear as to whether a religious community is permitted in international law to ostracise or even excommunicate people because of their actual or perceived gender identity or sexual orientation.[203]

Given the clear intention of the Yogyakarta expert group to avoid the ubiquitous categorisations and taxonomies related to gender and sexual rights, including the LGBT matrix, the critique of the alleged attempt to re-establish identity politics seems somewhat misguided. The insistence on 'hard' even if open-ended (unnamed) notions of sexual orientation and gender identity seems, however, to be a mediatory step between the apparent necessity to legally foreground the operative concepts upon which sexual and gender diversity could be protected and the need for social and cultural sensitivity in matters relating to human gender/sexual subjectivity formation, often expressed in queer theory. The balancing act, espoused in reification of the two notions albeit in a maximally open manner, appears necessary to intervene in the supranational legal space with an authoritative jurisprudential move. Could this have been done whilst still allowing for persons who wish to be free from these ideas altogether?[204] Perhaps not without taking the risk of providing the opposition forces – who maintain, anyway, that the two notions are not to be found in their respective societies' histories and worldviews – with powerful ammunition. Or maybe the drafters have failed to notice another striking similarity between human belief and gender/sexual systems, in that one can both claim the freedom *of* and *from* the categories and taxonomies pertinent to them.

The lack of the expressly recognised female subject, *sui generis*, in the Yogyakarta Principles confirms the drafters' calculated reluctance to emphasise any specific sexual/gender entity, in hope of the universal application of the two notions they have set to ascertain. Broadening this goal to include gender and, potentially, sex as associable yet different categories must have seemed to them unnecessary or even risking further confusion in this generally convoluted area of international law. With a plethora of strong(er) international legal mechanisms relating specifically to sex and gender, it appears that the elucidation of gender-specific (as opposed to or even in addition to gender identity-specific) human rights in the Yogyakarta document would, indeed, erode the clarity of method and categorical approach that the Principles generally espouse. But, is there a room, nonetheless, for improving some of their supposedly vague language?

The ambition of the Yogyakarta Principles to become the defining instrument in international human rights law related to human sexual and gender diversity is undoubtedly too high. Even though they have managed, in a relatively short time, to become one of the most cited and relied upon 'soft law' documents in transnational gender/sexual legal affairs, the Principles cannot be a substitute for international human rights jurisprudence, which necessarily follows a somewhat slower pace in deliberating matters of gender/sexual rights. They remain, instead, an important auxiliary source. The somewhat imprecise language of some of the Principles will hardly prevent supra-national courts and other legal mechanisms to adjudicate upon the matters they seek to address and thereby achieve greater clarity regarding the applicability of international law in those specific situations. Whilst sexual orientation and gender identity have, indeed, won their place in international human rights law, owing to a wide array of important legal developments, the lack of an international treaty specifically containing these notions still represents a challenge for effective supra-national legal prohibition of discrimination and violence against gender-variant and sexually diverse individuals and collectives, especially in the countries outside the reach of the regional European and Inter-American human rights judicial systems.

This is by and large due to the virulent opposition movements, spearheaded by the OIC and other inter-state political establishments. The situation is, however, also aggravated by the sinister political goals of the 'allies' of/in the social movements for sexual/gender diversity. We now briefly turn to both of these disconcerting phenomena.

The (Muslim) Opposition and (Some) Discontents: The Sexuality and Gender of a Body Politic

Since the beginning of the new millennium, opposition to the concepts of sexual orientation and gender identity and, less overtly, any sexual or gender diversity outside a strictly heteronormative ethos at the UN level in particular and in transnational diplomacy in general, has been most vehemently led by the OIC. In its insistence on combatting an increasingly resolute protection of sexual/gender diversity in international human rights law, the OIC has arguably superseded even the Holy See and other Christian-conservative state, inter-state and non-governmental groups. Citing 'Islamic tradition' and, more specifically, the mainstream *shari'a*-related jurisprudence (*fiqh*), as the basis of its non-pluralist gender/sexual politics, the OIC effectively seeks to monopolise (and politicise) a majoritarian 'Islamic view'. Of course, similar convergences have first occurred on the national level, whereby in a great number of the key OIC member states the *theopolitical*[205] elites have sought and gained power by reimagining the tenets of Muslim faith in accordance with their own visions and interests.[206] More often than not, such power claims have relied heavily on the post-colonial condition of their respective societies, with sexual/gender politics at the forefront of their ideological regiments. In fact,

> [t]he differences between colonial and postcolonial regimes in the area of sexual politics are more of degree than of substance: the tropes are similar. If 'tradition' was seen (and constructed as) the site of 'moral decay' in colonial days, now 'tradition' is invested with nostalgia and reconfigured as a site of heteronormative 'normalcy', while the West is seen as the site of perverse desires.

In the process of inventing itself as a viable nation-state, patriarchal heterosexual reproductive relations are (re)inscribed as normative, while [any] autonomous sexual practices (whether heterosexual or same-sex) and same-sex practices in general are (re)constructed as marginal. Political and religious leaders join in mobilizing emotions to naturalize this fiction of the 'always-already' patriarchal, heterosexual nation.[207]

The OIC has but extended this travesty to the supra-national level. In a recent letter to the president of the UN Human Rights Council, provoked, *inter alia*, by the Resolution 17/19 on Human Rights, Sexual Orientation and Gender Identity, adopted in 2011 CE by that UN organ,[208] which explicitly invokes the Universal Declaration of Human Rights as a basis for protecting sexual and gender diversity, the Pakistani Ambassador to the UN in Geneva sought to explicate the standpoint of the OIC as follows:

The OIC States are deeply concerned by the introduction in the Human Rights Council of controversial notions like 'sexual orientation and gender identity'. The OIC countries have been consistent in their opposition to the consideration of these controversial notions in the context of human rights at international fora.

We are seriously concerned at the attempt to introduce in the United Nations concepts that have no legal foundation in any international human rights instrument. The international community only recognizes those rights enumerated in the Universal Declaration of Human Rights which were codified in subsequent international legal instruments.

We note with concern the attempts to create controversial 'new notions' or 'new standards' by misinterpreting the Universal Declaration of Human Rights and international treaties to include such notions that were never articulated or agreed to by the UN membership. These attempts undermine not only the intent of the drafters and signatories to these human rights instruments, but also seriously jeopardize the entire international human rights framework.

We are even more disturbed at the attempt to focus on certain persons on the grounds of their abnormal sexual behaviour, while not focusing on the glaring instances of intolerance and discrimination in various parts of the world, be it on the basis of colour, race, gender or religion, to mention only a few.

It must also be recognized that the international community agreed during the World Conference on Human Rights, held in Vienna in 1993, that while considering the issue of human rights, national and regional particularities and various historical, cultural and religious backgrounds must be borne in mind. From this perspective, the issue of sexual orientation is unacceptable to the OIC.[209]

The letter is typical of a relatively simplistic OIC approach to the recent developments in human rights law relating to sexual orientation and gender identity. The OIC bloc is to be recognised as a 'persistent objector' to these 'controversial new notions' because it considers that their very deliberation in the UN fora may lead to disintegration of the international human rights system. This is based on 'various historical, cultural and religious' differences of the Muslim-majority states that ought to be borne in mind – the differences which, apparently, bar them from acknowledging sexual and gender plurality. As demonstrated in the subsequent chapters of this book, this assertion is fictitious by all those accounts: historical, cultural and religious. Yet it appeals to the neo-conservative masses, spellbound by forcefully heterosexualised post-colonial moral discourse. It gives a 'sense of order', no matter how unreal and historically, culturally and theologically falsified, to populations bereft of voice and political power, which, teleologically, bestows upon their undeserving leaders political legitimacy.

Unable to assert control over international developments relating to gender/sexual rights, the OIC has moved to introduce a separate 'regional' 'Islamic' human rights system, epitomised in the newly founded Independent Permanent Human Rights Commission (IPHRC) of the OIC. The IPHRC is made up of 18 representatives: six from each of the three OIC 'sub-regions' (the Middle East, Asia and Africa). It has pledged to 'seek to advance human rights and serve the interests of the Islamic Ummah in this domain, consolidate respect for the Islamic cultures and noble values and promote inter-civilizational dialogue'.[210] According to an early analysis, however, the three key areas of its future involvement shall be (1) promoting 'an alternative discourse on women's rights, centred on the family' and 'in opposition to [the established] women's sexual and reproductive rights'; (2) opposition to 'a narrow "Western" conception of sexuality'; and (3) advocacy for the concept of 'defamation of religion'.[211] That this might indeed be the case demonstrates, for example, the election of the Egyptian diplomat, Wael Attiya, to the IPHRC, who has already championed all of these goals before the UN by 'staunchly supporting the traditional family and opposing same-sex marriage, abortion and legislation of prostitution'.[212] For his tireless efforts in 'protecting the institution of the family', Attiya was given the *Stand for the Family Award* of the ultra-conservative American organisation Family Watch International.[213] 'Women's rights' have also been *officially* announced as one of the IPHRC's priority concerns.[214]

The formation of the IPHRC has been marketed as the OIC's benevolent attempt to 'fall within [the] trend of regional and sub-regional [inter-governmental organisations] having their own instruments and mechanisms'.[215] Epitomised in the ECtHR and the Inter-American Court and Commission of Human Rights, these regional groupings are 'arguably more effective than the UN given their closer proximity to situations, familiarity with issues and the confidences amongst member-States'.[216] Hence, the OIC now 'has a similar opportunity to tailor the work of the IPHRC to the *cultural and religious contexts* of its member-States to render it as effective as possible'.[217] These are, however, dangerous analogies. Unlike the Council of Europe and the OAS, the OIC has not endeavoured to create an independent *judicial* human rights body; instead, it was contended that 'the adversarial or juridical nature of existing international mechanisms has hindered effective implementation of human rights'.[218] The IPHRC's work is, thus, more likely to reflect the OIC's attempt to introduce a novel 'Muslim law of nations' (*siyar*), a parallel supra-national legal system spearheaded by these nations' ruling elites instead of independent judicial organs.[219] One of the arms of the new *siyar* would focus specifically on human rights 'in Islam', thereby comprising a 'human rights *siyar*'.

The idea of a human rights *siyar* seems to have been anticipated by the Universal Islamic Declaration of Human Rights (UIDHR), adopted by a group of prominent Islamic scholars in 1981 CE.[220] This document mimics the Universal Declaration of Human Rights (UDHR) in almost everything but the source of authority. Whereas the UDHR seeks to locate the origins of the universal human rights in 'the inherent dignity [...] of all members of the human family', the UDIHR proclaims that 'Allah (God) has given mankind through His revelations in the Holy Qur'an and the Sunnah of His Blessed Prophet Muhammad an abiding legal and moral framework within which to establish and regulate human institutions and relations'.[221] It may well be that the difference in philosophical foundations of the two declarations is not problematic *per se* and that the two views may be, in a pluralist society, concomitantly accommodated. The problem lies, however, in the adjudicatory organs established by the authority of the two declarations, or, more specifically, in the subsequent interpretation of both 'universal' and 'Islamic' human rights. Whose jurisprudence? For whom and against whom? Whose idea of justice and whose politics?

The power of legal abstraction – being precisely in the space and the need it creates for the subsequent judicial or quasi-judicial interpretative processes – was to be seized by the Muslim-majority state elites on a supra-national level soon after the scholarly exercise in Paris with the UIDHR has shown them the ropes. In contrast with the subsequent scholarly interventions in this field, which sought to provide a theoretical ground for understanding human rights from a Muslim perspective,[222] the political establishments moved to adopt a series of multilateral documents which seek to create an *alternative* to universal human rights, namely the human rights *siyar*, epitomised in reemploying the *language* and the *selected* contents of international human rights treaties in order to declaratively enlist 'Islamic' or 'Arab' human rights.[223] These developments, however, occurring mostly in the 1990s CE, produced a relatively modest impact. In Muslim-majority societies, human rights were still seen as either universal – a view propounded by those who have begun to actively use them to address numerous social injustices – or as entirely alien to Muslim traditions. In international relations, apart from creating novel opportunities for the members of Muslim inter-governmental organisations to meet and formally address carefully selected human rights issues *inter se*, the overall impact of these declarations was similarly small. They were not seen as part of evolving international human rights law, but rather as a separate legal/political system. The idea was, however, never completely abandoned and, in its latest reappearance, has taken the form of the IPHRC. The Commission, a permanent body designed to intervene on a regular basis in burning global discussions concerning the interests of the OIC, is arguably better placed to finally make the human rights *siyar* a viable concept, yet its political character will necessarily arise serious questions as to its impartiality and credibility outside the circles of Muslim inter-governmental co-operation.

Opposition to the elaboration and protection of sexual and gender plurality in international law thus seems to be in significant decline. Far from the power exhibited in the events surrounding the 2003 CE Brazilian Resolution on sexual orientation and human rights,[224] ultimately withdrawn due to enormous diplomatic pressure,[225] the OIC bloc and its allies can no longer prevent the recurrence of the notions of gender identity and sexual orientation in an ever increasing number of international legal documents. It is, therefore, likely that they will eventually adopt a more defensive policy similar to that of the Holy See, which now maintains that 'violence against homosexual persons is not acceptable and it should be rejected, even though this does not imply an endorsement of their behavior'.[226] But the danger to integrity and relevance of the colossal achievements of the social justice movements for sexual and gender diversity before the UN and other international legal fora seems to be more and more coming from other directions, i.e. from their self-proclaimed 'allies' as well as, arguably, from within 'their own ranks'.

There is today a substantial body of critique reproaching the global northern *body politic* for 'prid[ing] itself on its adherence to freedom, human rights, and tolerance, [whilst] its own misogynous, homophobic and racist past is conveniently ignored'.[227] It seems that the very nature of liberal regimes, such as that of the United States of America (USA) or the United Kingdom (UK), which seeks to monopolise the concepts of 'freedom' and 'progress' for its own political ends, requires a perpetual search for opportune moments in which thriving social movements can be co-opted to showcase these regimes' 'tremendous commitment' to their cause, even if that cause was utterly repugnant to them only a little while ago.

In the USA, owing to its federal legal system and the utterly contrasting general attitudes towards sexual and gender diversity from state to state, civil rights claims based on sexual orientation (and, to a considerably lesser degree, gender identity) have yielded a complex patchwork of legislation ranging from a broad protection to state-sponsored discrimination of LGBT Americans.[228] Despite the years of its own meek policies on this matter and strong opposition from Republican and other right-wing circles, the Obama administration has recently decided to step up its 'pro-LGBT' stand, with a focus on *international diplomacy* as well as domestic legal reforms.[229] In her Human Rights Day speech, delivered at the Palais des Nations in Geneva on 6 December 2011 CE, the then Secretary of State Hillary Clinton made what many pundits have applauded as a historic speech, in which she exclaimed – probably more than a half century after the coining of this rallying cry – that 'gay rights are human rights, and human rights are gay rights'.[230] She went on to admonish cultural relativist claims against sexual diversity, which she conspicuously located 'outside the West':

> Some seem to believe [that homosexuality] is a Western phenomenon, and therefore people outside the West have grounds to reject it. Well, in reality, gay people are born into and belong to every society in the world [...]. Being gay is not a Western invention; it is a human reality.[231]

The speech was attended by a group of representatives of the global LGBT movement, carefully selected and brought by an American non-governmental organisation, the Council for Global Equality, to represent diverse regions of the world.[232] The same organisation later published a group photograph of these activists with Hillary Clinton and a summary of their praises for her 'pitch-perfect', 'passionate', 'courageous' and 'powerful' address.[233] A photo op for the Secretary of State's new 'global triumph' could not have been better staged and everyone seemed to be ready to once again recognise the supremacy of US 'human rights leadership' in the world, despite all of its previous shortcomings.[234] This imperialist encroachment on decades of social struggle, including struggle at the UN level and 'outside the West' (which the speech seemed to be primarily addressing), elicited, however, no critical response. Even if it were potentially justifiable, perhaps purely pragmatically, to turn a blind eye to the overall unimpressive record of US governments in 'defending' gender/sexual rights, in their own country or elsewhere, were the global social justice movements for sexual/gender diversity still unscrupulously ready to embrace a 'drone-happy' regime as their new transnational ally?[235]

In a similar opportunistic attempt, the UK prime minister, David Cameron, threatened to withhold British aid to some Commonwealth countries in Africa that retain or have considered expanding criminalisation of homosexuality. In October 2011 CE, Cameron warned that the British nation, as 'one of the premier aid givers in the world', wants 'to see countries that receive our aid adhering to proper human rights'.[236] Prior to this address, the Prime Minister was, in fact, urged to 'apologise for Britain's imposition of anti-gay laws on Commonwealth counties in the nineteenth century, during the period of colonial rule'.[237] His message, instead, was more reminiscent of bygone colonialist ultimatums and, hence, was deplored both by the African civil society movements struggling for sexual/gender diversity and by their adversaries – the African political elites adamant to recast their societies as 'traditionally' heteronormative. In the words of one prominent activist,

[e]ven when well intentioned, the shrillest voices advocating for Global South nations (whether in the Commonwealth or not) to expand justice and equality for their LGBTI citizens have too often been tone deaf. The chorus coming from the powers who gave us the sodomy laws in the first place has shifted to singing morality in a different key, often appealing more to righteousness than to shared values. And they have outshouted those of us working within our own nations to build ownership for a vision of postcolonial justice, national pride and liberty that includes sexual autonomy.[238]

It is, indeed, peculiar how often the language of political economy and humanitarianism, employed not only by political leaders but also by civil society 'interventionists' coming from the former colonial powers, retains same-old imperial overtones. A head of a London-based charity that claims to be 'help[ing] local groups and individuals challenge the legality of laws which criminalise private consensual sexual activity between adults of the same sex, wherever those laws exist in the world',[239] observed cheerfully in a recent interview:

We will fundraise, and there is something rather charming that
you can say to somebody: 'If you give us £50,000, I can more or
less guarantee that you will have decriminalised homosexuality in
Tonga'. And actually, you know, that's great.[240]

By the time such self-indulgent prophecies are proven wrong, however,
the 'exotic' locales and former colonial playgrounds are bombarded with
unwanted and insensitive media attention and foreign 'assistance'
projects, often with disastrous consequences. The more recent in a
serious of such systemic failures concern the situations in Iran[241] and
Pakistan,[242] as well as an inadequate campaign before the UN Human
Rights Council.[243]

One of the most outspoken critics of such malevolent political
'correspondence between nonnormative sexualities, race, and patholo-
gized nationality', Jasbir K. Puar, calls it *homonationalism*, and, exploring
particularly the American political landscape, she describes it as
a phenomenon closely related to the state war machine.[244] For her,
'sexual exceptionalism, regulatory queerness, and the ascendancy of
whiteness'[245] are the defining characteristics of the homonationalist
American politics, threatening to spill over to other regions of the world.
On the one hand, Clinton's photo op exercise as a champion of global
LGBT human rights, whilst her state's military interventions continue
to violate international humanitarian and international human rights
law, seems to be a pertinent example of this political trend. The narrative
of exoticised and racialised non-heterosexual and gender-variant global
southern communities, 'saved' for 'a fistful of dollars' (or pounds) by
their global northern benefactors displays, on the other hand, illustrates
what Rahul Rao, another important voice of discontent, explicates as

> a condescension that comes out of being embedded in cultural
> contexts that are seen to be developmentally superior, by virtue of
> having already [...] won the liberties that distant sexual
> minorities now struggle for (the assumption being that they
> struggle for the *same* liberties).[246]

Indeed, the neo-Orientalist[247] and neo-colonial traits amongst and
around the movements for sexual and gender diversity seem to signal the
ascendance of neo-liberal *homonormativity*[248] as a governance strategy

closely related to global northern imperialistic political and economic projects. In such form, it also represents an attempt to salvage the precarious liberal site of international law from further 'disordering' and 'de-normativisiation' caused by the renaissance of sexual and gender (legal) politics. Being a clandestine tactic, seeking to co-opt and infiltrate rather than openly disrupt the diverse movements for sexual and gender plurality, it is arguably more dangerous than the OIC and other neo-conservative opposition blocs. The good news is that it has been recognised as such and that it attracts an ever-growing number of fierce critics, many of whom come from *within* the groups that it had set off to re-colonise.[249]

The difficult task of the contemporary gender/sexual diversity movements is, therefore, to resist a variety of hegemonic streams, both at the national and transnational levels, whilst fostering, interrogating and implementing the developments in human rights law *to the extent* that they suit their own specific social justice claims. In other words, if human rights law is to resist both neo-liberal and cultural relativist encroachments, it needs to be a pluralist site *par excellence*, open for contestation and *transculturation,*[250] where the idea of a human right, including that based on one's sexual orientation or gender identity, carries *transformative* rather than (re-)normative social power.

Empire of Law and Subjectivity

In this chapter, the categories of sexual orientation and gender identity have been analysed in relation to international law and its principal historical environment: the European legal and social ethos, with its complex ideological baggage. The idea has been to introduce a system historiographically, legally, politically, theologically and anthropologically *comparable* with that of a Muslim ethos on sexual and gender difference, which is interrogated in the next chapter of this book.

I have described, first, the imperialistic European traits that have demarcated the ascendance of international law and that, arguably, have never really left the field, despite the period of decolonisation and subsequent attempts at pluralisation of global legal power. Human rights have been used and misused by each side in this post-colonial statist struggle, thereby often being reduced to a commodity traded between inter-state interest-blocs. It is against this troublesome backdrop that I have developed a historicised account of criminalisation and decriminalisation of sexual and gender difference.

I have argued that Greco-Judaic and Romano-Christian prescriptive and prohibitive models of gender and sexuality were gradually introduced across early Christendom, culminating in a series of colossal social and legal reforms in the period between the eleventh and thirteenth century CE. These changes had occurred concomitantly with the development of the Western Church's imperialistic tendencies and are, indeed, aetiologically inseparable from the Crusades, Reformation, Counter-Reformation and subsequent European colonialism. Their crucial intent had been to mobilise and control an increasingly powerful middle-class in the interest of the ruling Church and state elites, by creating the model 'male' and 'female' legal subjects and outlawing and silencing all diverging gender/sexual expressions. The offence of 'sodomy' had been introduced as a particularly salient form of religious and cultural transgression, applicable to both sexual and gender 'sins', especially if allegedly committed by a political opponent. In sixteenth-century CE England, 'buggery' laws were introduced and subsequently replenished across the British Empire. In late eighteenth-century CE revolutionary France, however, 'the pyres of Sodom' and all related persecutory laws were abolished and replaced with police control and oppression. These developments have provided a historical basis for three general trends in the post-1960 CE world of independent nation states.

The first trend was that of 'domestication' of colonial 'sodomy laws' and forceful heteronormativisation of a newly independent society, as a politically motivated act of 'cultural' or 'religious' sovereignty. The second trend, pursued by some former French dominions, was to introduce 'sodomy laws' for the first time, again as an act of 'cultural' autonomy. The third trend, however, was that of some African states, which elected to remain free from 'sodomy laws' and other politico-legal expressions of post-colonial anxiety. Meanwhile, the global north has begun an irreversible process of decriminalisation of same-sex sexuality and recognition of some forms of gender-variance, which gradually reoriented the political imaginary of the 'East'-'West' divide: the Occident has seemingly become ready to embrace the 'libertine' gender/sexual ethos, once relegated to 'licentious' Orient, whilst the southern societies have refashioned themselves into 'neo-Victorian' bastions of compulsory heteronormativity. I have argued, however, that this post-colonial trade-off must be primarily regarded as political opportunism, rather than as a 'culturally' or 'religiously' motivated development.

In international law, human rights related to sexual and gender diversity, via the increasingly common legal categories of sexual orientation and gender identity as intrinsic characteristics of human subjectivity and behaviour, were first claimed as a protected domain of one's *private* life. With the *public* sphere still tightly safeguarded by a heteronormative social and legal ethos, the landmark judgements of the ECHR and the UN Human Rights Committee might have been intended to leave only a shallow imprint on the international legal affairs, limited in scope and potential for further jurisprudential developments. That could not have been further from the truth. The last three decades witnessed an explosion of gender- and sexuality-related activism, inter-state diplomatic wars and, ultimately, supra-national human rights case law and 'soft law' (especially the UN declarations, resolutions, statements and unreserved support from the key UN human rights experts), which have firmly established the notions of sexual orientation and gender identity within the domain of international human rights law. These long-awaited victories have bolstered social movements for sexual and gender diversity, but they have also made them prone to abuse by some ominous political 'allies' and an emerging neo-liberal 'interventionist' off-shoot in the global north. I have argued, however, that there is a developing critical consciousness of these problematics *within* the diverse movements for sexual and gender plurality. Interestingly enough, this consciousness is increasingly emanating *particularly* from Muslim sexually diverse and gender-variant analysts, with their intersectional experience of social discrimination.[251] They are potentially uniquely placed to rebuke the hegemonic agendas of both the re-normative 'Western' neo-liberal gender/sexual politics and the elitist Muslim heteronormativised cultural relativist governance strategies, epitomised by the OIC's attempts to introduce its own human rights *siyar*.

It is precisely this *transformative* critical potential of Muslim sexually diverse and gender-variant subjectivities that this book is set to explore – an ability to navigate through the conflicting and tumultuous legal, political and social landscapes, seemingly for centuries, whilst retaining a mediating and meditative selfhood and sense of community.

CHAPTER 3

SEXUAL AND GENDER DIVERSITY IN ISLAMIC LAW AND THE MUSLIM WORLD

Researching Islamic law today remains an elusive and highly complex endeavour, despite the dramatic surge in studies across the world purporting to provide for a more nuanced or novel understanding of its historical and current emanations. As this chapter inevitably shows, there exist conflicting historiographies and hermeneutical expropriations of this phenomenon, not least because neither its adherents (Muslims) nor its scholars (from within and without the *umma* – the 'community of believers') can agree on what Islamic law really *is*. As Norman Calder, one of its foremost researchers, cautioned shortly before his untimely death, 'the connotations of the phrase "Islamic law" are in part a product of western perception and have been introduced now to Muslim societies through linguistic calques like Arabic *al-qanun al-islami*. There is no corresponding phrase in pre-modern Muslim discourse'.[1] 'There', Calder claimed, 'the two terms which expressed the commitment of the Muslim community to divine law were *fiqh* and *shari'a*'.[2] But equating either (or both) of these terms-of-art with the clumsy construct of 'divine law' obfuscates even further their original elaborations.

Shari'a is inferred from a single verse of the Qur'an (45:13), whereby it denotes a 'pathway to be followed'. Historically, this verse was revealed to Muhammad many years before the 'Medinan period' of the Qur'anic revelation, when most of the legal provisions were set out. Hence, it is highly unlikely that it had meant *only* 'holy law', at least for the early *umma*.[3] Some scholars therefore prefer to describe it as a 'total discourse', in which 'all kinds of institutions find simultaneous expression: religious, legal, moral and economic'.[4] As such, it supposedly 'displays what [Max] Weber calls "substantive rationality", one in which law, morality, religion and politics are not distinguished'.[5] But even this view – although significant in resisting the nowadays-ubiquitous temptation to simply 'translate' *shari'a* as 'Islamic' or 'divine law' – fails to acknowledge that the defining aspect, the very 'totality' of the *shari'a*, is that it is *God's way* – one that is never fully comprehensible nor attainable for the human being. *Shari'a*, in short, always already needs interpretation, and *fiqh* – literally meaning 'understanding' – has developed as a specifically *legal* attempt to do so systematically. Out of the 'totality' of *shari'a*, and also from other sources,[6] classical *fiqh* had sought to infer jurisprudential connotations for an ever-expanding and diverse *umma*. In doing so, it had, indeed, become the leading legal discourse, albeit – as we shall see – by no means the only one. The human agency in deducing *fiqh* had also been consistently and readily acknowledged: while striving to understand the divine, the scholars of *fiqh* (*fuqaha'*, sing. *faqih*) had carefully reiterated their fallibility. Where can one, then, locate the domain of 'holy law' and similarly evasive yet separate discipline of Islamic law?

To answer this question, it is necessary to interrogate the philosophical, historical and socio-political perspectives of the Islamic legal tradition; a simple 'historiography of *shari'a*' will not suffice.[7] On a philosophical plane, one needs, for instance, to engage with the common perception that 'Muslim legal philosophy has been essentially the elaboration and the analysis of [divine] law *in abstracto* rather than a science of the positive law emanating from judicial tribunals'.[8] The legal Realist renditions are, however, notably different, focusing on the law 'as applied' rather than on the law 'as conceived'.[9] To be sure, these considerations have a long and complex history, which is, perhaps, best preserved in classical Muslim works of legal theory (*usul al-fiqh*) and positive law (*furu' al-fiqh*), and best exemplified by the recurrent theoretical question of the role of the judge (*qadi*) in Islamic law-making.[10] The abundance of at times fierce debates amongst the *fuqaha'* on these matters suggests that the tension between practice and theory of law could never be fully resolved; but it also reveals an exceptional diversity in the understandings of what the law *is* (or ought to be) in a Muslim community, ranging from 'hard' Islamic Natural law theories to proto-Realist views.[11] The plurality within the body of *fiqh* signals, of course, an even greater multiplicity of perspectives on the function and meaning of law in Muslim thought and society at large. In this light, a blind over-reliance on classical *fuqaha'* in search of Islamic law (past and present) seems unjustifiable. 'All law is always law interpreted,'[12] but the interpreters are many and their techniques are various.

The pre-eminence of *fiqh* in the existing historiographies of Islamic law poses not only hermeneutical but also a methodological problem. As soon as one realises that the Islamic legal tradition comprises actors and literary genres *outside* the domain of classical jurisprudence, it becomes apparent that their accounts in the mainstream historical narratives have been exceptionally rare. Muhammad Khalid Masud is, therefore, adamant that

> [a] history of Islamic law of the pre-modern Muslim world is still to be written. What we have is a history of Muslim jurists (*fuqaha'*), and of the development of their doctrines as schools. Some, often scanty, information about the laws introduced by Muslim rulers, judgments of qadis (judges), and judicial procedure is available, but existing histories of Islamic law do not take them into account. Consequently our knowledge about the relationship between law and state is influenced greatly by Muslim jurists' vision of law and state.[13]

Arguably, our understanding of the relationship between law and society, or of law *in* society, is equally marred. As a recently published study has shown, even *medical* treatises of Muslim scholars may sometimes be exceptionally beneficial for one's understanding of Islamic law in a certain historical context.[14] The problem of limiting explorations of the Islamic legal tradition to studies of *fiqh* was, however, first recognised in the context that Masud evokes above – that of the role of *siyasa*, or administrative justice/policy,[15] in Islamic law. Amr Shalakany has argued, apropos, for the distinction between *scripturalism* as 'a decidedly pre-Realist historiography' of Islamic law, which is 'a legal history of and about jurists'[16] and in which there is no place for *siyasa*,[17] and a *new historian* approach, which holds that certain domains of Islamic law 'had historically transformed under an alternative conception [...] where *shari'a* and *siyasa* were considered one and the same, and *not* under the mantle of *fiqh*'.[18] This distinction builds upon an earlier rift between the contemporary Islamicists, whereby Shalakany's principal scripturalists – Joseph Schacht and Noel J. Coulson – were opposed by an increasingly influential stream of scholars for portraying Islamic law as 'rigid and unchanging after its formative period, and therefore divorced from the exigencies of developing Muslim society'.[19] The opposition – most vocal in the works of Wael B. Hallaq[20] – set out to prove that 'change did occur in [classical] Islamic law and it was certainly not rigid and unchanging in the later centuries'.[21] But these were not exactly the *new historian* accounts, because their research was still largely focused on (classical) *fiqh*. Furthermore, there was little consensus as to *where* and *how* to locate the enunciated change in law.[22] Still rather scarce, the *new historian* works, then, stand in contrast both with those of the scripturalists and those of their *fiqh*-centred scholarly opposition. The contrast is primarily methodological: society and legal practice are analysed *first*, via a plethora of sources, and *then* compared and contrasted with the prevailing legal doctrines.[23] Jurists' law – whether capable or not of change *causa sui* – is contextualised and historicised in a broader societal paradigm.

Socio-political studies of Islamic law follow a similar route. Understood as a part of a larger edifice,[24] classical Islamic law is not only found in *usul* and *furu'* works,[25] but also inferred from statecraft which, according to the philosopher Al-Farabi (*c*.872/258–950/339 CE/AH), was to be achieved through *ri'asa* ('rulership') by means of *siyasa*.[26] In various periods of Muslim history, state (political ruler's) law – while never failing to pay lip service to God's 'pathway' (*shari'a*) – had served as an effective replacement of the *fiqh* norms, even when they were dealing with the so-called 'rights of God' (*haqq Allah*) against what had been deemed as the most serious of human transgressions (*hudud*, sing. *hadd*).[27] These developments have not occurred (just) as a consequence of an absolutist *raison d'état*; rather, their historical, political, philosophical and, indeed, legal foundations merit a more nuanced approach – one in which questions of class, political economy and social ethos play an important role. In a similar vein, the more recent attempts to 'return to *shari'a*' in the post-Westphalian Muslim polities cannot be analysed simply as a 'religious' and 'legal' phenomenon, bereft of its historical and socio-political context.[28] The Islamic legal tradition is, on the whole, replete with turbulent political events: from an initial Arab (but 'non-nationalist', 'universalist') *umma*, Muslims have undergone the processes of imperialisation, internationalisation, sectarian separatism, colonisation, decolonisation, nationalism and bloc-politics (to name but a few) – all of which have had a distinct legal outlook. Islamic law, even in its most idealistic mode (the one that sees itself infinitely close to God's 'pathway'), could hardly assume a place separate from these changing tides.

If the elaborations and applications of Islamic law are to be found in Muslim philosophical, communal and political experience as well as in the works of classical *fuqaha'* and other legal sources, then an integrative analysis *across* these fields needs to be devised so as to provide for an appraisal of sexual and gender diversity in the Islamic legal tradition – which is the purpose of the present chapter. This approach is, however, a compromise between the scripturalist and *new historian* approaches in as much as it does not shy away from recounting a *fiqh*-based narrative of (classical) Islamic law, whilst complementing or challenging it with other legal and non-legal sources, events and themes from the Muslim past. Reflecting the structure of the previous chapter, however, here I make a distinction between a discursive genealogy of sexual/gender laws and social mores, on the one hand, and what can be termed as a (current) post-colonial condition of Islamic law,[29] on the other. Hence, the first part of this chapter revisits the 13 centuries of Muslim history prior to the twentieth/fourteenth century CE/AH struggle for sovereignty, independence and/or decolonisation of nation states with a significant percentage of Muslim population. In this chapter, the problematic yet pervasive periodisation of 'formative', 'classical', 'post-classical' and 'colonial'/'nationalist' Islamic legal tradition is followed more or less, but only as a springboard for a series of discussions on philosophy and socio-political reality of Islamic law, which inevitably complicate and challenge that linear approach. Some topics of interest – such as the criminal offence of *liwat* (anal sex) or the religious and social role of the *khuddam/aghawat*[30] – are discussed within this framework, but only to showcase particular historical interpretations or phenomena.

Throughout the history of Islam, claims of a trans-historical and, arguably, trans-cultural nature have been made on the theological plane, and some of them, indeed, have taken a *legal* form (e.g. the justification for the *hudud* punishments). That, however, does not make these inescapably *human* hermeneutical interventions somehow foreclosed to historical, theological, social and *legal* critique (hence the numerous cases of the past and present-day resistance to the *hudud*). Critical accounts of major theological, philosophical and legal debates relating to sexual and gender diversity in the Muslim society thus accompany this chapter's underlying historical narrative.

The second section of the chapter briefly assesses the relevant laws and their socio-political milieux in Muslim coloniality and post-coloniality. It has been said that, from the mid-nineteenth/thirteenth century CE/AH 'onward, the history of law in the Muslim world is in large part a history of displacement, replacement, and substitution of the body of the law'.[31] The lasting influence of European imperialism, as well as the related rise of nationalism and overall political and economic transformation in what have become the Muslim-majority states, has changed the landscape of Islamic law to an unprecedented degree. In a similarly dramatic way, sexual/gender propriety and its surrounding legal rules have undergone a comprehensive and systematic change, perhaps so much so that 'what passes in present-day Saudi Arabia, for example, as sexual conservatism is due more to the Victorian puritanism than to Islamic mores'.[32] As a result, (what is understood as) contemporary Islamic law is, often, a strange mixture of reformist tendencies – spanning as wide a horizon as the revival of certain jurisprudential techniques from the first centuries AH to practically brand-new terrain of 'Islamic finance' – and the antiquated colonial legislation. Its stances on gender and sexuality, including with reference to the notions of sexual orientation and gender identity, resemble the medieval Christian inhibitions while purporting to be true to an 'Islamic rationale'. That is, however, a mainstream view of Islamic law, which has been challenged by a variety of interpretative alternatives, ranging from feminist to sexual/gender-pluralist hermeneutics.[33] This chapter, in conclusion, attempts to shed fresh light upon such debates, arguing for a decolonised and de-normativised view of human subjectivity (and human subjectivity-formation) in Muslim social and legal ethos.

Dynamics of Desire: Towards an Interruptive History of Islamic Law

Writing about the sixteenth-/ninth-century CE/AH Mediterranean world,[34] the French historian Fernand Braudel posits the 'three movements of historical time'.[35] The first movement, le temps géographique ('geographical time'), deals with relations between humans and the environment; its fluctuations are almost imperceptible and largely irresistible. The second movement, le temps social ('social time') is Braudel's favourite: the longue durée history proper that explores epochal characteristics of human cultures, economies and societies. The third and last movement, le temps individuel ('individual time'), is that of events: the histoire événementielle of notable persons and (their) politics that is inevitably courte durée.[36]

Social historians mostly agree that, 'in discussing discourses of sex [and gender], a long-durèe [sic] historical method is required, [although it] may sometimes be mistaken for an essentialist approach'.[37] Thus, with its focus on 'great events and major figures', Eva Cantarella finds the method of l'histoire événementielle guilty of 'neglecting the underlying social reality and ignoring the existence of millions and millions of anonymous individuals'.[38] It is only due to the rise of longue durée historical analyses, claims Cantarella, that

> new historiographic subjects were born, the different and marginal
> from every epoch: the sick, the old and young, homosexuals,
> women – subjects, all of them, whose history is not determined by
> events, but rather by mental attitudes, ideologies, practicalities of
> everyday life and their position in a socioeconomic context.[39]

It is, however, precisely the birth of the new 'historiographic subjects' that makes the longue durée method problematic in the context of the present study. The ex post eventum construction and categorisation of human sexual and gendered subjectivities has been, after Foucault,[40] criticised as a neo-Orientalist 'incitement to discourse'.[41] According to this view, an epistemological and ontological model of human self-identification, although specific to certain global northern contexts, attempts to universalise and institutionalise itself by (re)defining the historical and present-day Arab and Muslim sexual/gender landscape.

This assumption lacks the necessary nuance in addressing the complex ways in which sexual/gender discourses operate and traverse the geopolitical boundaries, but it is indicative of the 'ontic effect' a *longue durée* historical project may have on the actors and field of its study. It may produce, rather than 'just' describe, historical subjectivities of a certain type and taxonomy (e.g. 'male', 'Turk', 'eunuch') by recounting their *continuous* existence over a long period of time. It may *incite them into being*, practically *ex nihilo*, by looking through the lenses of a different time and world(view), inapt to notice the detail.[42]

While the 'ontic effect' is, to a certain extent, inevitable in any historical analysis, I want to propose that the over-generalising attitude in the *longue durée* method can be diminished by integrating into it certain elements of both *le temps géographique* and *le temps individuel*. This is to suggest that systematic interruptions of the linear time in which historical epochs are conceived can result in a better understanding of complex, locale-specific phenomena as well as of more general discourses and historical conditions in which they inhere. In dealing with the *histoire événementielle*, for example, one may wish to explore how certain events or individual achievements have influenced the more general groups or attitudes in the researched society. Attention to *le temps géographique*, on the other hand, may improve one's understanding of the relationship of the studied phenomenon with its non-human environment. As I embark, on the following pages, on a historical journey into Islamic law and its sexual/gendered subjects, I argue that the interruptions I consciously deploy along the way will help me to come up with a less normative and determinist account.

On Indeterminacy and Form(ul)ation: From Early Umma *to Eponymous* Fuqaha'

This sub-section revisits the first four centuries of Muslim history, which scripturalist studies of Islamic law usually describe as the 'formative period'. Its exact time-span is, however, a matter of some controversy:

> Until recently, it has been thought that this period ended around the middle of the third century [A]H (ca. 860 [CE]), when, following Joseph Schacht's findings, we thought that the all-important legal schools, as personal juristic entities, had come into existence and that, again after Schacht, Islamic law and legal

theory had come of age. More recent research, however, has shown that Schacht's findings were largely incorrect and that the point at which Islamic law [understood as the science of *fiqh*] came to contain all its major components must be dated to around the middle of the fourth/tenth century, an entire century later than had originally been assumed.[43]

The corresponding political developments were swift and turbulent. The Muslim calendar begins with the Hijra in 622 CE – the flight of the Prophet Muhammad from Mecca to Medina. He died only ten years later, leaving his nascent polity in a state of turmoil, known as the Wars of *Ridda* ('Return', 'Apostasy').[44] The unrest ended with the consecutive succession of four of Muhammad's companions (*sahaba*) as his 'deputies' (*khulafa'*, sing. *khalifa* or, in an Anglicised form, caliph): Abu Bakr, 'Umar, 'Uthman and 'Ali, collectively known in the mainstream Sunni accounts as *al-khulafa' al-rashidun* ('the rightly guided caliphs'). The Sunni sources describe this period as the Era of Felicity (*'asr al-sa'ada*), 'when the community of believers was ruled in accordance with prophetic inspiration',[45] despite the rather tumultuous circumstances of their accessions and reigns.[46] The era ended in 661/40 CE/AH with 'Ali's assassination and a rampant civil war, in which the schism between the Sunni and the Shi'a originated[47] and which gave rise to the new dynasty of the Umayyads (661/41–750/132 CE/AH).

By the time the Umayyad caliphs ascended to power, *al-rashidun* had already conquered Syria, Armenia, Egypt, Cyprus and all of Persia. The new rulers styled themselves as 'deputies of God' rather than 'deputies of the Prophet' and subjected the new Muslim polity – now with the capital in Damascus – to a process of rapid imperialisation. Moreover,

> [t]here is plenty of evidence to suggest that the Umayyad caliphs did in fact function as arbiters of 'religious' issues, acting for example as judges (*qadis*) and as articulators of God's law, and also that many Muslims regarded them and their office as central to their understanding of what it meant to be a Muslim.[48]

For this, the Umayyads had stood accused by the later generations of straying from the path of *al-rashidun* and of turning the caliphate into *mulk* or 'secular' kingship. After they suffered the defeat from the

'Abbasid dynasty, they fled across North Africa to al-Andalus (Andalusia), where they founded the Caliphate of Córdoba, which lasted until the mid-eleventh/fifth century CE/AH.

The 'Abbasids (750/132–1258/656 CE/AH) moved the capital to Baghdad, 'adopted Persian styles of government and courtly culture, and promoted the Persian aristocracy to eminent positions of state'.[49] Their ruling style was arguably more akin to that of *al-rashidun* and their at least formal deference to the legalistic worldviews espoused by the emerging class of *fuqaha'* seemed to have earned them a wider social respect. However, their reign was soon reduced to that of nominal sovereigns, under the new military dynasties that arose in the tenth/ fourth and eleventh/fifth centuries CE/AH,[50] and threatened by rival caliphates,[51] only to be formally ended with the Mongol conquest of Baghdad in the thirteenth/seventh century CE/AH. Our focus is, however, on the times of the strong 'Abbasid Caliphate, i.e. prior to the mid-tenth/fourth century CE/AH, when the schools of *fiqh* became a definitive feature of the Muslim legal landscape.

The story of Islamic law begins with the descent of the Qur'an, more precisely its so-called 'Medinan period', during which most of the 500 or so verses of a 'legal nature'[52] were revealed to Muhammad. It has been contended, however, that the 'legal matter of the Qur'an consists mainly of broad and general propositions as to what the aims and aspirations of Muslim society should be,' and that it is 'essentially the bare formulation of the Islamic religious ethic'.[53] Yet God's voice proper, as transmitted by the Qur'an, has been rather consistently interpreted as clear enough in condemning 'indecency' (*fahisha*), of which adultery/fornication (*zina*) later came to be seen as the only 'sexual crime' warranting a *hadd* punishment.[54] A typical Qur'anic verse, 17:32, thus warns: 'And approach not *zina*; surely it is *fahisha*, and it is evil (*sa'a*) as a way'.[55] Another verse, 4:15, alluding to 'indecency' of an unknown type, enjoins Muslim *men*: 'As for those of your women who commit *fahisha*, call four of you to witness against them; and if they witness, then detain them in their houses until death takes them or God appoints for them a way'. The later commentators disagreed as to whether the type of 'indecency' that God reprimands here is, in fact, *zina* or even same-sex sexual activity.[56] Also, the fact that God's Qur'anic voice seems to address *men only* has led some exegetes to conclude that 'the Qur'an itself [. . .] is founded upon male sexual experience'.[57] Whether this is true or not, there are no other Qur'anic references to sexual activity between women.

Conversely, the condemnation of the 'deeds of Lot's people' ('amal qawm Lut), based upon the Qur'anic rendition of the Biblical parable about the Prophet Lot, appears to link fahisha with sexual acts between men. The following is a typical example, out of 14 references to Lot scattered throughout the Qur'an:

> And Lot, when he said to his people: 'What, do you commit such fahisha as never any being in the world committed before you? See, you approach men lustfully (shahwa) instead of women (min dun al-nisa'); no, you are a people that exceed (musrifun)'. And the only answer of his people was that they said: 'Expel them from your city; surely they are folk that keep themselves clean (tahir)'. So We delivered him and his family, except his wife; she was of those who tarried (ghabirun). And We rained down upon them a rain; so behold thou, how was the end of the sinners (mujrimun)![58]

Those men who 'exceed' (musrifun) and 'approach [other] men lustfully' (shahwa), instead of women, are thus counted amongst the 'sinners' (mujrimun) deserving of divine wrath. To be sure, Lot's people were not destroyed only because of that sin, i.e. their fahisha was not solely of a sexual nature.[59] A more likely reason for the Qur'anic condemnation is that 'the people of Lot cried lies to the [prophetic] warnings'[60] and exceeded in all things sinful, so much so that their destruction had become inevitable. Moreover, a recent analysis has concluded that the Qur'anic phrase that repeatedly describes men who approach other men lustfully 'instead of women' (min dun al-nisa') actually means 'besides the women' and casts a new light on Lot's (and God's) disapproval of such behaviour:

> He [Lot] is not talking about men in general who have sex with other men in general rather than with women in general. He is denouncing the men who sexually assault these specific men (those who are vulnerable as strangers and taken under his protective hospitality) while leaving aside the sexual relationships with the women who are their wives. This fact warns us that their crime was not homosexuality in a general way

or even sex acts per se; rather it was their intention that made their actions immoral. Their sexual assault was driven by their infidelity and their rejection of their Prophet. [61]

Indeed, the fact that Lot's wife ('who tarried') and *all* of Lot's people – women and children included – had been the subject of divine wrath seems to indicate that they were *generally* excessive 'evildoers' (*zalimun*),[62] rather than that they engaged in any *specific* sinful act. Nevertheless, some Muslim exegetes linked Lot's name, as well as the 'deeds of his people' ('*amal qawm Lut*), with the non-Qur'anic term *liwat*, which came to mean the act of penetrative anal sex (whether male-male or male-female). It is difficult to establish when exactly *liwat* was first described as a form of *zina*, since there remain but scarce indirect sources relating to at least a century and a half following Muhammad's death.[63] But what is certain, as we shall see, is that this matter[64] remained the subject of incessant juristic disagreement (*ikhtilaf*) throughout the times of classical *fiqh*.

The Qur'anic depiction of gender has been the subject of much (relatively recent) research and debate, not least because *male* scholars had in fact produced the entirety of classical Islamic hermeneutics.[65] Contending that the patriarchal bias of these scholars has left a significant trace on the common understanding of gender amongst Muslims, Islamic feminists and other contemporary exegetes endeavour to 're-listen' to the voice of the Qur'an from a new angle, one that no longer addresses *men only*, nor is heard and explained exclusively by Muslim male elites. The singularity of the (human) self, in which the male and the female (characteristics) inhere, is narrated in the Qur'an on numerous occasions;[66] it offers, perhaps, the best starting point for one seeking to conceive of a less androcentric and hierarchical Muslim gender order:

> O humans, reverence your Sustainer (*Rabb*) who created you from a single self (*nafs*); created, of like nature, its mate (*zawaj*) and from them twain dispersed countless men and women. Reverence God, through whom ye demand your mutuality.[67]

Asma Barlas argues, after Fazlur Rahman,[68] that the term *nafs* ('self', 'person') was misinterpreted as 'soul' by early Muslim scholars who, under Hellenic influences, 'invented a typology of spirit, soul, and body, in which the spirit occupied the highest place and was associated with man, and the soul occupied a lower rank and was associated with woman'.[69] 'This typology', claims Barlas, 'allowed them to read sexual [and gender] hierarchy and inequality even into [the above Qur'anic verse]'.[70] In contrast, the non-patriarchal exegeses emphasise an underlying egalitarian ethos in the way the story of the origin and nature of human creation is narrated in the Qur'an. Out of a sexless and non-gendered self, humans are given a mate (zawaj), so that they may 'dwell in tranquillity' with them.[71] In fact, 'of everything We have created pairs, so that ye may receive instruction'.[72] And although these pairs may be of male and female traits,[73] they needn't be conceived of as mutually exclusive (i.e. 'opposite'); for, even one's zawaj is, ultimately, of one's own (original) nature.[74]

Besides the Qur'an, the sunna, or Muhammad's 'trodden path' preserved in the hadith literature, is often described as the second most important source (usul) of Islamic law and jurisprudence.[75] Yet the authenticity of oral reports ('ahadith, sing. hadith) about Muhammad's life has been a highly controversial issue in every historical Muslim community, even after some ardent and painstaking standardisations, occurring mostly from the ninth/third to the eleventh/fifth century CE/ AH and resulting in written collections deemed 'reliable' (sahih).[76] Writing, as opposed to memorising and orally transmitting the Qur'an, let alone some other reports, was in itself unthinkable for Muhammad and the early umma. The meaning of the Qur'an – God's speech par excellence – comes alive[77] only in recitation:

> God has sent down the very best speech (ahsan al-hadith) as a message, with matching similes, which makes those who reverence their Rabb shudder so that their hearts and bodies become receptive to the remembrance of God – this is guidance of God with which God guides whomsoever God wills.[78]

As ahsan al-hadith, the Qur'an is sufficient and needs no other 'speech' (hadith),[79] especially not a cacophony of conflicting oral reports:

> At first, the Prophet Muhammad forbade the writing down of reports of what he said or did in everyday life. The Prophet distinguished what he said in revealed language (included in the

evolving Qur'an) from what he pronounced of his own opinions, instructions, or decisions. Yet his followers regarded his decisions and opinions as God's guidance for them; in this light, the Prophet forbade them to write down anything that he said or did which was not explicitly the Qur'an.[80]

Even though Muhammad reportedly agreed that some of his praxis be preserved in a written form after his death, it would be very difficult to imagine that he would allow his *sunna* to become an all-important source of law for the future times and their exigencies, second only to the Qur'an itself. And, although the 'first three generations after the death of the Prophet', when *al-khulafa' al-rashidun* reigned from Medina (631/10–661/41 CE/AH), are, indeed, 'the most obscure period in the history of Islamic law',[81] it seems that his early 'deputies' (caliphs) shared a similarly non-textual – one could say proto-Realist – approach to the law and Qur'anic hermeneutics:

> The only principle they observed consistently was the public good {*maslaha*} above all else. Therefore, we often see them acting in accordance with the dictates of that good, irrespective of the text, no matter how decisively clear-cut it is, when special circumstances demand a deferment of the text.[82]

Muhammad himself was 'content to proffer *ad hoc* solutions as [legal] problems arose',[83] in a manner that certainly could not delineate the boundary between the 'law' and *siyasa*. The often-ambiguous Qur'anic voice was, thus, heard to be (humanly) understood and (by necessity, imperfectly) followed in varying circumstances: the result was, if any, the 'law applied' rather than 'black letter' law of any kind. This appears to be the main reason why legal doctrine – by means of the *hadith* literature – had to be 'back-projected'[84] onto the first *umma* by later *fuqaha'*.

The surviving *'ahadith* attributed to Muhammad's contemporaries[85] paint a generally bleak picture of the acceptance of sexual and gender diversity amongst the first Muslims. The 'deeds of Lot's people' are frowned upon in these reports, and usually deemed punishable by death. Women's sexuality, though, is not of particular interest, so for such 'deeds' to be ascertained at least one man had to be involved.[86] Gender variance seems to have also provoked Muhammad's strong disapproval.

A typical *hadith* thus reads: 'The Prophet cursed [female-like] men (*al-mutakhannathin min al-rijal*) and [male-like] women (*al-mutarajjulat min al-nisa'*) and he said, "Turn them out of your houses"'.[87] A recent study of these reports, however, argues against their authenticity and concludes 'that the Prophet Muhammad never condemned an actual person for [same-sex] relationships or meted out punishment for [same-sex] intercourse'.[88] It also describes the reports condemning gender variance *tout court* as a gross exaggeration, for Muhammad, in reality, banished only one *mukhannath* ('male-born effeminate') named Hit, after discovering the signs of their sexual attraction towards the Prophet's wives,[89] to whom they previously had an unrestricted access as one of those ('male-born' persons) described in the Qur'an as 'lacking interest in women' (*min ghayr uli irba*).[90] There are, in fact, 'canonical' *'ahadith* that convey a strikingly different narrative of sociality and intimacy amongst the first Muslims[91] from that of the dominant 'back-projections'. But this oral tradition on the whole – in its *standardised*, written form – speaks more of political conditions and moral dilemmas of the later times,[92] than of Muhammad's polity and laws that it purportedly describes.

Other sources of Islamic law, traditionally considered secondary to the Qur'an and *sunna*, relate predominantly to certain 'jurisprudential' faculties and techniques, such as *ijma'* (consensus), *ijtihad* (independent reasoning), *qiyas* (analogical deduction), *ra'y* (arbitrary opinion) and so on.[93] Some of these methods obviously exceeded the 'realm of law', whatever it may have been amongst the early *umma*,[94] whilst others were antithetical to one another.[95] Still others were thought foreclosed for future generations (of jurists),[96] only to be revived in the wake of anti-colonial struggle[97] and re-claimed as important instruments of change (in contemporary Islamic law).[98] From Muhammad's time, however, at least until the early 'Abbasid period, these sources were used indiscriminately; that is, by rulers, administrators and judges, according to the exigencies of a specific problem and their *individual* preference. Precedents were important, yet also many and often conflicting.[99] In an ever-increasing empire, this posed a considerable political and legal challenge.

The systematisation of 'law' and its sources – the process eventually leading to *usul al-fiqh* (legal theory) of the classical period – began primarily out of a *sunna*-related conflict. As Wael B. Hallaq argues, until 'the 80s/700s [AH/CE], the main representatives of the legal profession were the proto-[judges], who, for all intents and purposes, were not only government employees and administrators of sorts but also laymen who [...] had no particular legal training'.[100] Their legal decisions were mostly based on their *ra'y*, which followed 'either a *sunna madiya* (past exemplary actions, including those of the Prophet and the caliphs) or commonsense. They also increasingly resorted to the Qur'an'.[101] By the end of this period, however, a novel *profession* emerged – that of *hadith* collectors and memorisers (*muhaddithun*) – and Muslim lands saw a rapid surge in what was presented, even sold, as prophetic *sunna*.[102] In the same time, individual Islamic scholars (*ulama*, sing. *'alim*) began to surface, sometimes particularly interested in the studies of law (Islamic, customary or foreign, including ancient Greek and Roman). These developments as well as a profound cultural and political complexity of the post-*rashidun* caliphates, provided a backdrop for an important formative episode in the history of Islamic law: the quarrel between *ahl al-hadith* ('traditionalists') and *ahl al-ra'y* ('rationalists'), which subsided only towards the end of the tenth/fourth century CE/AH.[103]

The juridical programme of *ahl al-hadith* 'was just as their name suggests: [that] of collecting hadith. Not an organized school in the later sense, they had no separate training in jurisprudence'.[104] They condemned both *ra'y* and *qiyas* as the sources of adjudication and accused the opposite camp of using these methods to evade the injunctions of the *hadith*. In particular, they vociferously opposed the doctrine of the created Qur'an, which some of the adherents of *ahl al-ra'y* accepted along with the broader theological movement of *ahl al-kalam*.[105] Amongst the four eponymous scholars of what later became the dominant Sunni schools of jurisprudence (*madhahib*, sing. *madhhab*) – Abu Hanifa (699/80–767/148 CE/AH), Malik ibn Anas (711/93–795/179 CE/AH), Abu 'Abdullah ibn Idris al-Shafi'i (767/150–820/188 CE/AH) and Ahmad ibn Hanbal (780/164–855/241 CE/AH)[106] – only the oldest of them, Abu Hanifa, belonged to *ahl al-ra'y*, while others adopted distinctly traditionalist views. Hence, Malik reportedly said to his disciples of Abu Hanifa: 'If he came to your columns, here, and tried to persuade you with his *qiyas* that they were wood, you would think that they were wood'[107] His reliance on independent reasoning was such that Abu Hanifa related the *hadith* literature only from a few Kufan *ulama*.[108] Per contra, Ibn Hanbal apparently thought that whoever aspired to qualify as a jurist must have first memorised at least 500,000 *hadith*.[109]

The rift between the 'traditionalists' and 'rationalists' set the domain of Islamic law onto a new course. Whilst the judges (*quda'*, sing. *qadi*) were made, under the early 'Abbasids, increasingly bound to the hierarchical apparatus of the State and their judicial functions substantially and procedurally restricted,[110] a *profession* made *prominent* through the debates between *ahl al-hadith* and *ahl al-ra'y* – that of expert jurists: the *fuqaha'* – attained an elevated and semi-autonomous position.[111] Their independence was, in a way, a political trade-off. Weakened by rival claims to power and a dangerous gap between the ruling elite and their subjects, 'the government was in dire need of legitimization, which it found in the circles of the legal profession. The legists served the rulers as an effective tool for reaching the masses, from whose ranks they emerged and whom they represented'.[112]

It is difficult to imagine what the landscape of Islamic legal tradition would look like, had these reforms not taken place.[113] To be sure, both *quda'* and the emerging *fuqaha'* retained or at least fought for some independence from the State. Some studies suggest that the process of formation of the *madhahib*, which was more or less completed by the end of the tenth/fourth century CE/AH,[114] had to do both with the demands of the government *and* the *fuqaha'*'s resistance thereto.[115] That is, the all-important schools of jurisprudence functioned *also* as *guilds*, the medieval syndicates defending their interests from and before the rulers.[116] The question of creativity and transformative effect on (both 'formative' and 'classical') Islamic law of the *quda'*'s legal opinions (*fatawa*, sing. *fatwa*)[117] is debated amongst Islamicists in a similar context.[118] Despite all this, it seems inevitable to conclude that the doctrinal and administrative grip on the legal profession made the later generations of jurists and judges somewhat *priest-like* in terms of their *canonised* approach to public morals, law, politics and religion.[119] This, in turn, resulted in a peculiar form of 'legal schizophrenia',[120] evident, for example, in a wide range of Muslim literature of the time, wherein sexual and gender diversity elicited formal (and formulaic) disapproval, only to be given – a few pages later – a detailed documentary, poetic or esoteric account.[121]

This is to say that a drama began to unfold in the twilight of the 'formative era' of Islamic law. The more the legal discourse became a stylised and formalistic manifesto of what the law and society *ought* to be, the less it was able to attend to their manifold controversies and complexities. Everyday social bargaining thus entered 'the shadow of the law',[122] for the prevalent legal praxis was less and less capable – or, indeed, willing – to grapple with the society's multifaceted exigencies. And while the office of the *qadi* still provided for some legal dynamism, the proto-Realist times were fast approaching *rigor mortis*.[123]

Nowhere is this legists' 'loss of touch' more clearly discernible than with regard to the undoubtedly vibrant world of sexual and gender plurality that existed amongst the early *umma*. It is no wonder that the Qur'an itself adorns its detailed descriptions of the heavenly garden with ambiguous creatures such as gender-unspecific *huriya'*,[124] with 'wide and beautiful eyes',[125] and *wildan al-mukhalladun* (immortalised youths), whom 'when you see [...] you think them scattered pearls'.[126] These were not only properties of the hereafter. Studies of *mukhannathun*, male-born subjectivities of an 'evasive' gender identity (that seemed to change with different generations), or those of *nisa' mudhakkarat* ('male-like women'), demonstrate that gender-variant Muslims lived freely – even thrived – amongst the early *umma*.[127] To complicate the matter even further, gender binaries were not only crossed and defied in daily life, but also in the *performance* of class and (sub-)culture, such as in the case of 'the *ghulamiyyat,* girls dressed as boys in an erotic fashion' at the 'Abbasid court.[128] At the same time, references to same-sex sexuality, intimacy and sociality are so abundant, especially in the early *adab* (belles lettres) and *mujun* (poetry of humorous licentiousness) literature, and are written 'by people of all socioeconomic classes, from rulers to religious clerics to middle-class poets and tavern singers',[129] that it is patently impossible to imagine them being of purely allegorical nature. It seems that same-sex sexuality was not necessarily stratified by age or role, as it was previously thought, 'but rather according to the appetites and desires of the individual beings who sought these relations'.[130] Class, however, was undoubtedly an important factor; hence, the '"beloveds" [*haba'ib*] depicted in *belles lettres* and poetry tend to be from the artisanal and working classes, sons [and daughters] of grocers, ironworkers, and so forth'.[131] Still, early sources often celebrate the power of love to defy all ephemeral boundaries, including those of class and religion.[132]

Not only did the plurality of gender and sexual expressiveness inform the corporeal and social experience of the early Muslims; it also was an intriguing part of their spiritual life. For instance, the predominantly Sufi practice of gazing at the beauty of a beardless boy (*nazar ila al-amrad jamil*) rested upon the idea that such boy 'was considered a "witness" (*shahid*) to the beauty of God and the glory of His creation'.[133] Permissibility of such meditative acts was always a matter of debate, especially amongst the jurists, but it took many centuries before they were eventually abandoned. All the more so as it appears that the early legal treatises on these matters, coupled with a pragmatic sense of (moral) justice of the proto-judges, offered an underlaying (if not always readily apparent) sensibility, even appreciation, for *unruliness* in human attempts to *experience* this life[134] and *therefore* foretaste the garden of the hereafter.[135]

It is in contrast to this sophisticated (il)legality of Muslim ethos that the will to 'state the law' emerged, epitomised in the ascendance of the *madhahib*. The contemporary Islamicists mostly agree that the formation of schools of *fiqh* was particularly influenced by a class-related transition: 'a movement from a jurisprudence which is a predominantly oral and socially diffuse informal process towards a jurisprudence which is a complex literary discipline, the prerogative of a highly trained and socially distinct elite'.[136] It also had distinct regional connotations.[137] For instance, Abu Hanifa was born in Kufa, which he and other jurists made into one of the strongholds of *ahl al-ra'y*. What hence emerged as the school of Kufa later came to be known by the name of the Hanafi *madhhab*.[138] Similarly, the Medinan school of jurisprudence was later associated with its native jurist and distinct representative of *ahl al-hadith*, Malik ibn Anas.[139]

Amongst the later generations of Sunni Muslims, Abu Hanifa, Malik, Shafi'i and Ibn Hanbal were reified as the scholars (*mujtahidun*, sing. *mujtahid*) of 'peerless ability',[140] so much so that their doctrinal contributions (to the studies of *fiqh*) had to be thoroughly imitated (*taqlid*), instead of looking, by means of *ijtihad*, for novel interpretations. This was a distinctly Positivist move,[141] designed to 'limit the omnipresent plurality of legal opinion'[142] that characterised the entire 'formative era' of Islamic law:

> The formation of the legal schools by the middle of the fourth/ tenth century [AC/CE] was achieved through the construction of a juristic doctrine clothed in the authority of the founding imam,

the so-called absolute *mujtahid*. Juristic discourse and hermeneutics were the product of this foundational authority which was made to create a set of positive principles that came to define the school not so much as a personal entity of professional membership, but mainly as an interpretative doctrine to be studied, mastered, and, above all, defended and applied.[143]

The founding scholars' authority was, however, constructed more or less arbitrarily[144] and *ex post eventum*.[145] The later Positivists thus little cared for the eponyms' well-documented hesitation to assert their legal opinions in absolute terms.[146]

In the new environment, the sharp differences between *ahl al-hadith* and *ahl al-ra'y* gradually faded away, primarily to the detriment of the latter group.[147] In this sense, the lasting influence of Abu 'Abdullah ibn Idris al-Shafi'i, often recognised as the 'master architect' of the entire system,[148] is particularly significant. Shafi'i, a skilful traditionalist, dedicated much of his intellectual vigour to the thesis that the *hadith* literature, if properly systematised, *is* in fact the *sunna*,[149] and as such representative of 'the *unmediated* authority of the Prophet'.[150] Even though the larger theoretical construct, within which Shafi'i elaborated this assertion, soon lost its appeal to the *mujtahidun*, the overall effect on the later generations of *fuqaha'* was such that it, indeed, produced the classical source-hierarchy, one in which *sunna-qua-hadith* always takes precedence over the jurisprudential methods such as *qiyas* or *ijtihad*.[151] This is, however, not to say that 'the gate of *ijtihad*' was thus closed, since, in the post-formative period, each school went on to perfect some novel (subsidiary) interpretative techniques[152] and even the *fatawa* of a *qadi* or a *mufti* (jurisconsult) had the potential to be incorporated into the body of authoritative legal doctrine of a particular *madhhab*.[153] Yet the overall turn towards Positivist legal traditionalism in the subsequent 'classical era' of Islamic law cannot be denied.

What was, then, the law on sexual and gender diversity *as stated* in the schools of *fiqh*? What were the modalities of its implementation and the ways society responded to them? Moreover, were there any *other* instances of Islamic law, outside the realm of *fiqh*, that may have dealt with this phenomenon? To answer these queries, I proceed, first, with a brief elaboration of the approach devised by classical *fuqaha'* to the offence of *liwat*. This judicial concept is then historically, socially and legally examined in the context of the relatively brief Seljuk period (*c.*1040/431–1194/590 CE/AH), when – as it is often stated[154] – Islamic law and philosophy reached its 'golden' zenith.

The First Interlude: Hudud and Liwat in Classical Fiqh

The scholars of classical *fiqh* generally divided the criminal offences and their respective punishments into four categories: *hudud*,[155] *qisas*,[156] *diyya*,[157] and *ta'zir*.[158] The *hudud* (sing. *hadd*) were understood as 'limits prescribed by God',[159] whose punishments were therefore fixed, whilst *ta'zir* offences were, by definition, always punished at the discretion of the *qadi*. The jurists more or less agreed that only the following transgressions could be categorised as *hudud*: highway robbery (*hiraba, qat' al-tariq*), theft (*sariqa*), adultery and fornication (*zina*), false accusation of *zina* (*qadhf*), apostasy (*irtidad, ridda*) and intoxication (*sharb al-khamr*). The *hudud* were made subject to the strictest evidential procedures, arguably inferred from the Qur'an. For example, 'in any other area of the law, confession (*iqrar*) was irrevocable, but not so in the *hudud* (except in *qadhf*) where a *hadd* proven by confession was cancelled upon the withdrawal of that confession'.[160] Furthermore, 'the testimony of a secondary witness (*shahada 'ala al-shahada*), otherwise admissible in law in general, was inadmissible in *hudud*, as was any written communication between judges (*kitab al-qadi ila al-qadi*)'.[161]

Zina, as the only 'sexual crime' amongst the *hudud*, was defined 'as sexual intercourse that (a) involves actual penetration, (b) by persons of full legal competence, (c) outside of a man's right to such intercourse [typically via marriage], and (d) without any doubt whatsoever (*shubha*)'.[162] There were only three ways to prove *zina* – by confession,[163] witness testimony or the refusal of the accused to deny committing the offence by taking the oath.[164] In order for witness testimony to be considered valid, four male witnesses[165] of impeccable moral repute (*'adl*) must all appear in the same court session to testify, 'in extreme detail and in unambiguous (*sahir*) language',[166] to 'having personally seen the act of "*ilaj*" or penetration *in flagrante delicto*'.[167]– Failure to abide by these strict requirements renders the witnesses reliable to the *hadd* offence of *qadhf*, for which a fixed corporal punishment (80 lashes) is prescribed. If, in spite of all these measures, *zina* was eventually established, then the perpetrators were sentenced to the capital punishment – usually by stoning to death[168] – if they were married, or 100 lashes if they were unmarried.[169]

Due to the stringent evidential requirements, zina was 'nearly impossible to establish'[170] and thus very rarely, if ever, punished. Some fuqaha' maintained that 'it is a condition that the witnesses are four' for the hadd offence of zina 'because God the Exalted likes [the vices of] his servants to remain concealed [satr], and this is realised by demanding four witnesses, since it is very rare for four people to observe this vice'.[171] Public confession and witnessing in a zina case was thus condemned as 'contrary to what is most appropriate' (khilaf al-awla).[172]

The majority of the madhahib – with the notable exception of the Hanafis – maintained that liwat is a form of zina. Abu Hanifa reasoned, and most of his followers agreed, that 'since the male organ is not inserted into the vulva', anal sex could not be construed as a hadd offence.[173] Rather, this act was liable to a ta'zir (discretionary) punishment. Having established this, the Hanafis scholastically concluded that the perpetrators of liwat should suffer comparatively less than those who are sentenced for hudud offences. Hence, the death penalty was generally not an option[174] and, 'if chastisement took the form of whipping, the number of lashes should not exceed thirty-nine, which is one less than the lowest number of lashes in a case of hadd'.[175] It seems that the adherents of now-extinct Zahiri madhhab followed the same logic, since one of its most prominent representatives, the Andalusian jurist and philosopher Ibn Hazm (994/384–1064/456 CE/AH), prescribed as little as ten lashes for liwat.[176] Even as a lesser-than-zina-offence, liwat was still considered to be of the kind warranting the public principle of concealment (satr), so it would find its way into the Hanafi qadi's courtroom only on a very exceptional and rare occasion.

Other schools of fiqh that classified liwat as a form of zina often distinguished between liwat al-akbar ('grand liwat') and liwat al-asghar ('petty liwat'), denoting male-male and male-female anal sex, respectively. For the Malikis and the majority of Shi'i madhahib, 'petty liwat' was reprehensible but ultimately permissible act, while other schools considered it to be a hadd offence liable to the fixed punishments (and evidential requirements) prescribed for zina in general.[177] The punishments for liwat al-akbar, as a form of zina, also varied to some extent, depending on the offender's role and marital status. The Shi'a and Maliki jurists made all offenders liable to unconditional stoning.[178] The majority of Shafi'is and Hanbalis did the same, while some notable adherents of these two *madhahib* accorded the death penalty only to 'active' and/or married offenders, with 'passive' and/or unmarried perpetrators being liable to 100 lashes.[179] Eventually a minority of Hanafi jurists, contrary to Abu Hanifa and other notable representatives of this school of *fiqh*, also adopted the latter view.[180]

Overall, despite the wide and apparent juristic disagreement (*ikhtilaf*) across the *madhahib* as to the nature and punishment of *liwat*, this offence was primarily viewed as a matter 'between God and the offender(s)', rather than 'between the offender(s) and the society', save in some isolated cases where the perpetrators were seen as either exceptionally ostentatious or *politically* problematic, the former being the situation comparable to 'political sodomy' in the medieval Christendom. The fact that the sexual relations amongst the women were altogether exempt from this paradigm[181] also suggests that patriarchal 'Islamic jurisprudence was concerned exclusively with [very specific male-related] acts rather than preferences, proclivities, tendencies, or personalities'.[182] There was, in other words, no explicit attempt to outlaw certain expressions of gender identity or sexual orientation, although they may have been frowned upon by the patriarchal *fuqaha'*. Instead, a highly formalistic and deliberately unenforceable system was devised to deter (*zajr*) only the most 'excessive' cases of *zina* and *liwat*, whereas the society's sexual/gender pluralism was to be 'quietly' condoned. One could, therefore, regard it as the case of *fiqh*'s premeditated disconnect with the Muslim social fabric, or, perhaps, as the very opposite – a self-subversive mechanism of legal redefinition of what seemed to be the pre-given heteronormative matrix. And, controversially, probably the both of those extremes were true to some extent.

The Second Interlude: Siyasa *and* Liwat *in the Great Seljuk Empire*

The purpose of this sub-section is to provide an example of the historical and social aspects typically surrounding the theoretical discussions of Islamic law in its 'classical period'. The *fuqaha'*'s discourses on *liwat* are, thus, provided with a geopolitical, social and religious *framework* of the century and a half of Seljuk domination over Iraq and Persia (1040/431–1194/590 CE/AH), when 'a fluid set of purely military governments'[183] reduced the office of the 'Abbasid caliphs – the once-mighty 'deputies of the Prophet' – to a mere 'player in the complex pattern of rule in Iraq'.[184] Following the decline of the Seljuk dynasty, in 590 AH, the 'Abbasids rose once again to a short-lived renaissance, which was abruptly terminated in 656 AH, when Mongol armies destroyed Baghdad and massacred its inhabitants. The 'Islamic Golden Age' was, thus, over, and so was the so-called 'classical period' of Islamic law.

Much like the rest of the late 'Abbasid time, the Seljuk period was characterised by social and legal insecurity, not least because the non-Arab militarised ruling class[185] often felt compelled to make a show of force towards a largely hostile local population. Hence, 'public punitive rituals, often unpredictable and excessive in their violence, were a constant spectre in the lives of ordinary [citizens]'.[186] But the military nature of governance also meant a great deal of decentralisation, so much so that the civil leaders (a'yan) and ulama led their affairs with an extraordinary degree of autonomy.[187] The perceived need for a public use of coercive force by the Seljuk government and the contrasting requirement of a theological justification of such behaviour in the interest of social stability led the rulers and Sunni ulama into a novel form of political partnership. In exchange for their scholarly and personal liberty, the ulama redefined the concept of siyasa (Persian: siyasat), which previously meant simply 'statecraft', to thenceforth signify both (virtuous) 'governance' and (just) 'punishment'. According to the new ideology, 'punishment by the repressive state apparatus served to preserve the awe (hayba) that the ruler required to keep his domain pacified'.[188] Or, in the poet's verse:

> The wolf will not attack the ewe in the desert,
> the partridge will not flee the hawk in its flight;
> all creatures retract their claws for fear of punishment (siyasat),
> be it a lion's paw or the claws of a hawk.[189]

Having received a univocal endorsement by the Islamic scholars, the ruler's criminal justice system could now safely venture into the domain of Islamic law. The discretionary offences and punishments (ta'zir) no longer required a qadi; rather, in the Seljuk period, 'it appears that ta'zir was more often inflicted directly by the repressive state apparatus on the authority of the ruler, especially as a punishment for reasons of state expediency (siyasa)'.[190] The contemporary fuqaha' made no objection to this unprecedented merger of *ta'zir* and *siyasa*. '*Ta'zir* is an educative measure (*ta'dib*) taken by the sultan', explained Abu'l-Hasan al-Sughdi (d. 1069/461 CE/AH),[191] while Abu Ishaq al-Shirazi (d. 1083/476 CE/ AH) wryly confirmed that the political ruler may deploy *ta'zir* 'as he sees fit'.[192] Consequently, the police (*shurta*) or even the market inspector (*muhtasib*) resorted to *ta'zir* without any prior consultations with the *qadi*.[193]

It scarcely needs to be said that these developments, unless treated as a temporary aberration (which, as we shall see, they were not), cast serious doubts over the postulates of scripturalist historiographies of Islamic law, which treat the domain of *fiqh* as a fully separate entity from that of the *siyasa*.[194] If 'secular' state apparatus, by the (legal) power vested in the autocratic ruler (who is *not* a caliph), is entrusted to mete out the 'divine law' (even though *ta'zir*, at least theoretically, requires a *legist*'s knowledge of the *shari'a*), then the entire system collapses for the lack of even rudimentary coherence.[195] The only option left, hypothetically, would be to give up on *ta'zir* altogether; that is, to sever it somehow *ad infinitum* from the *corpus juris* of classical *fiqh*. This is, however, far from what transpired. The *fuqaha'* retained their *theoretical* sway over *ta'zir*, while in practice it became a symbol of state power. The 'divine' and 'secular' merged in yet another normative instance, thereby making the *locus* of Islamic law even more difficult to find.

Let us now examine the dominant discourses on *liwat* in the *fiqh* literature on substantive law (*furu' al-fiqh*)[196] from the Seljuk period, *as well as* some exemplary collections of legal opinions (*fatawa*)[197] from the same time. The inclusion of the selected *fatwa* anthologies should help us grasp the 'law as applied' as well as the 'law as conceived' (in the *furu'* works). The Realist approach is employed throughout, including in the subsequent examination of other historical sources. Because their stand on *liwat* was different from the majority of classical *fuqaha'*, and, also, due to their particular prominence in the Seljuk-led society, our discussion focuses on the Hanafi *madhhab*. But, since the minority of the Hanafi jurists shared, in a broad sense, their convictions with most of the other *madhahib vis-à-vis* the necessity to construe *liwat* as a form of *zina*, their arguments – presented here – convey a general sense of the legal debates that took place on this matter in the Seljuk period.

Within the Hanafi *madhhab*, two hermeneutical approaches to the question of *liwat* emerged, which remained mutually exclusive and therefore divided the jurists into two camps. The smaller camp, which claimed to follow some of the earliest Hanafi authorities (notably the third-century AH jurists Abu Yusuf and Muhammad al-Shaybani), considered *liwat* to be a *hadd* offence, for at least three reasons: (1) the *sahaba*, according to the *hadith* literature, agreed that this act is punishable by death, but disagreed as to the best method of execution;[198] (2) *zina* and *liwat* have the same *lexical* root in the Qur'anic word for 'indecency' (*fahisha*), so they deserve to be punished equally;[199] and (3) the implied semantic 'function' (*ma'na*) of the Qur'anic revelation on *liwat* is the same as that on *zina*.[200] Regarding the last of the three propositions, they argued that *zina* could be defined as a premeditated action aimed at (a) penetrating a genital with another genital (*farj*) (b) in an impermissible way, (c) while knowing that it is an offence, (d) in order to waste semen, provoked by (e) a natural carnal desire.[201] They further claimed that *all* of these elements (a–e) are present in the act of *liwat* – including a *natural* carnal desire (e) – hence, it needed to be understood as a *hadd* offence.

The majority of the Hanafis, however, found each of these arguments to be fallacious and claimed, *per contra*, that 'no Qur'anic directive, Prophetic *hadith*, or consensual decision (*ijma'*) was available that could serve as basis for a legal rule (*hukm*) against [*liwat*]'.[202] This meant something extraordinary: that *liwat*, in principle, for these *fuqaha'*, was not a punishable offence (in this world); the only possible but not (re)commendable avenue was that of *ta'zir*.

They arrived at this conclusion after a systematic analysis of each of the presented arguments of the opposite camp. (1) The *hadith* literature discussing the possible methods of execution for the crime of *liwat* on the authority of the *sahaba* was *all* found to be untrustworthy, without exception.[203] (2) The lexicographical argument was rejected on the basis that the two nouns – *zina* and *liwat* – describe two different kinds of behaviour. 'After all, if they were the same, why would there be a need for two different verbs (*zana* and *lata*) to denote the same action?'[204] (3) The semantic argument was more complex, so the majority group of the Hanafi *fuqaha'* took on each of its elements in order to refute them, if need be, in their own right.[205] (a) As far as penetration of a genital (*farj*) with another genital was concerned, Kasani, for example, recalls that the definition of *zina* was, in fact, an unlawful 'penetration of the female genital by the male genital [*ilaj farj al-rajul fi farj al-mar'a*]' and explains that *zina* is committed only if an act of penetration (*ilaj*) involves the *qubl* (vagina), not just 'any' *farj*.[206] (b) The impermissibility of *liwat*, for this group, was not the point. This act was, unquestionably, morally reprehensible *in this world* for all the Hanafis, although some proposed that it could be quite different in the hereafter, where *liwat* might be stripped of its social perils and thus reduced to pure pleasure.[207] The point was, rather, that the act did not deserve legal punishment. Like with many other forbidden things (*haram*), it was up to individual Muslims to resist the temptation of engaging in it. In other words, it was a quintessentially *private* matter.[208] (c) To know that *liwat* is an offence implied, for the oppositional minority camp, that they could prove, under any circumstances, that the perpetrators of *liwat* knew that what they were 'acting upon' was not their rightful 'property'. Sexual acts were, indeed, often legally defined as a part, so to say, of 'property law': the permissibility of an intercourse depended on whether the 'penetrator' lawfully *possessed* the vagina (*qubl*) in question. Since *qubl* was, theoretically, the only 'acquirable' *farj*, the offenders in a *liwat* case always already knew that what they were doing was *legally* wrong. The majority Hanafi camp responded to this imputation by reversing the logic of the entire construct: clearly, in *liwat al-akbar* ('grand', male-male *liwat*), the absence of a husband as the only potential 'proprietor' in such matters thwarted this line of reasoning,[209] while in *liwat al-asghar* ('petty' *liwat* between the spouses) the minority's opinion had some merit. In either case, however, the *mens rea* of the individuals involved was not in itself sufficient to constitute an offence. (d) The majority agreed that the wastage of semen as a by-product of *liwat* was outright deplorable (*mahin*), but it also stressed that this act was, at least, safe from the worse perils, such as unwanted procreation, confusion of the lineage and fatherless life of the children born out-of-wedlock – all of which were potential consequences of the *hadd* offence of *zina*.[210] (e) Finally, the Hanafi majority did not readily disagree with the opposition's proposition that *liwat* was a product of a *natural* carnal desire. Sarakhsi opined, for example, that it was as a matter of Qur'anic principle, rather than natural predispositions, that the people differentiated between same-sex and different-sex intimacy.[211] Overall, in the Seljuk 'period, there seems to have been quite a vigorous debate about this topic, including beyond the confines of the intra-Hanafi controversy'.[212] It is remarkable, then, how rarely it is evoked today in the scholarly works on Islamic law.

Even though, for the considerable majority of the Hanafi *madhhab*, in the heyday of classical *fiqh*, *liwat* principally meant no punishable offence, let alone a *hadd*, other schools still maintained quite the opposite view. One would expect, therefore, that the punitive view of *liwat* had left its imprint in legal practice, discernible through the *fatawa*, court records and other historical materials. Moreover, in the state in which frequent and ruthless public punishments became a defining feature of the ruler's *siyasa* – a legal(ised) 'necessity', as it were – it would come as no surprise if a Seljuk version of the French medieval *les bûchers de Sodome* ('the pyres of Sodom') had emerged, upon which the culprits had been burnt to death. And, yet, not a single trial is recorded, nor an execution for *liwat* mentioned, in meticulously kept Seljuk chronicles.[213] The *fatwa* collections are equally silent.

But, what of the *ta'zir* avenue? In his analysis of the *taz'ir* case law, Christian Lange suggests that the (im)permissibility of same-sex relations seemed to depend chiefly on social class and the degree of public visibility they may have attained. In other words, 'there was acceptance of such relations as long as they remained within the private circles of the courtly élite'.[214]But once, supposedly, 'they entered the public arena, [. . .] punishment was likely to follow'.[215] There is, however, no evidence whatsoever for this conclusion. Reflecting upon the sole case which might lend some support to his argument, Lange writes: 'It appears that the homoerotic nature of the [Seljuk] sultan Sanjar's relationships to his slave-boys Sunqur and Qaymaz, his submission to their whims, which their outré behaviour threatened to reveal to the public, was a significant factor leading to their execution'.[216] But this was *not* a case of a *ta'zir* punishment for *liwat*. Instead, in view of the perpetually politically contested reign of the Great Seljuk Sanjar (*c.*1084/477–1157/552 CE/AH), and his eventual downfall and humiliation due to *hereditary* controversies, the execution of his slave-boys was more likely consequence of a court intrigue.[217] Moreover, it is even theoretically implausible that the sultan himself could have been 'indirectly' punished for a *taz'ir* offence in the Seljuk period, in which both *siyasa* and *ta'zir* were the inextricable property of the ruler's majesty. In the absence of any other low or high profile *ta'zir* case even remotely relating to *liwat*, it seems, indeed, that the punitive view of anal sex did not find its ally in the state-imposed system of criminal justice.

One can conclude, then, along with the Hanafi *fuqaha'*, that *liwat* was *generally* seen in Islamic law of the period as a deplorable but ultimately *unpunishable* vice. It was treated this way not only because of the unquestionable Hanafi influence in the society, but also because the state legal system, partly or fully outside the purview of *fuqaha'*, found no reason to intervene, even for the sake of public political rituals. Finally, it was not punishable also because the other schools of *fiqh*, which equated it with *zina*, maintained the strictest evidentiary requirements suitable for a *hadd* offence. Hence, in this case study, all shades and instances of Islamic law seem to be, effectively at least, in a peculiar harmony with one another.

It may be puzzling how the formalist and highly theoretical classical *fiqh* – still very much on the outside of the vibrant and culturally, gender-wise and sexually pluralist Muslim society – the repressive state and that society itself ended up in a largely symbiotic relationship. From a legal Realist perspective, however, what emerges as the 'law' is always already a product of social bargaining, political trade-offs and incongruous but co-existent moral narratives. Classical *fiqh*, in its ivory tower, theoretically did not need to conform to the more permissive social ethos of the population at large. Nor did the ruling class necessarily have to comply with a lenient Hanafi discourse on what still largely figured as a contemptible vice. The priestly class of jurists and the ruling class of Seljuks remained detached from other social strata, each in their own right. It seems, nevertheless, that a complex network of social, political and legal relationships produced a climate – indeed, a larger social ethos – in which the 'law' could neither construe nor prosecute *liwat* as a punishable offence. And that 'law', in its social totality, 'as stated' *and* 'as applied', *was* – there and then – Islamic law.

Some 'Post-Classical' Dilemmas: Mamluk and Ottoman (Re-)Visions of a Muslim Self

It is by now apparent that the present chapter does not attempt to produce a grand 'total' narrative of Islamic law '*erga omnes*', that is, as conceptualised and practiced in each and every historical Muslim polity or community. Here, instead, a *longue durée* trajectory of theoretical and substantive features of *some* Muslim normative systems is *interrupted* with the shorter, more intensive and politically and culturally mindful studies of legal and social phenomena relating to sexual and gender diversity.

The underlining proposition is, of course, that the paradigm of Islamic law meant something conceptually and practically different for each 'epoch' and, to a large degree, every historical Muslim polity and community. It is, nonetheless, *possible* to conceive of a *longue durée* trajectory of Islamic law of some kind – as have, indeed, numerous historiographies on the subject. What critical *courte durée* interventions, however, attempt to expose, at the very least, is the ultimately *imprecise* and socially and politically conditioned nature of that project.

This chapter proceeds with an examination of Islamic law in its 'post-classical' phase, focusing on two specific historical Muslim polities: the Mamluk regime in Egypt and Syria (1259/648–1517/922 CE/AH)[218] and the Ottoman Empire from the conquest of Constantinople (1453/857 CE/AH) until the beginning of the Tanzimat ('Reorganis-ation') period (1839/1255–1876/1293 CE/AH).[219] Each of these polities is important for this book in its own right: the Mamluks for politico-military changes that ushered in a new social and familial *modus vivendi*, and for further amalgamation of the *fiqh/siyasa* dyad under their patronage and the Ottomans for their comprehensive legal and administrative reforms. Admittedly, all these are occurrences within the so-called 'Sunni Islamic tradition', but their significance undoubtedly transgresses the doctrinal and political Sunni/Shi'a divide. Notwith-standing the excellent studies in Shi'i formation of a Muslim self,[220] it is my opinion that the phenomena this chapter is set to explore can saliently be observed even if one chooses to keep one's focus solely on the Mamluk and Ottoman lifeworlds and legal legacies. The geopolitical and temporal span of my analysis, however, broadens when, in the final interlude in this chapter, I analyse the phenomenon of male-born castrated *khuddam/aghawat* subjectivity.

In thirteenth/seventh and fourteenth/eighth century CE/AH, the great Muslim cultural and political centres in the Eurasian heartland were, quite literally, overrun by the Golden Horde, a federation of Mongol tribes.[221] The cities – their libraries and palaces – were pillaged and destroyed, and their inhabitants massacred 'without regard to sex and age'.[222] But the cultures and spirituality of the conquered lands soon allured the invaders:

The Mongols, many of whom had adopted Buddhism, were especially attracted by the Sufi form of Islam. In 1295 [CE],

Ghazan Khan, chief of the Ilkhan clan and ruler of Iran, became a Sunni Muslim. His conversion ruptured the unity of the Mongol people. The Golden Horde were the next to adopt Islam (1313 [CE]). From now on, the Mongol states entered the power politics of the Islamic world.[223]

The Mongols, however, came with a comprehensive system of (codified) laws of their own, known as the *yasa* (Mongolian: *ux зacaz*), and they never quite grew accustomed (nor felt compelled to adhere) to the pre-existing Muslim laws. The *yasa* allowed them to worship as they pleased, whilst being most determinate in matters of military discipline and mores.[224]

The Mamluks (Ottoman Turkish: *Memlukler*) rose as a military caste of highly trained Muslim slave-soldiers,[225] who were, at least since the 'Abbasid times, regularly purchased from (non-Muslim) tribes around the Caucasus and the Black Sea. Their social status in Muslim polities steadily grew, and when their leader, Sultan Baybars, defeated both the crusading Franks (1249/647 CE/AH) and the previously invincible Mongol army in Syria (1260/658 CE/AH) – Ibn Khaldun praised them as the 'saviours of Islam'.[226] The Mamluks centralised their power in Cairo and ruled over much of Egypt and Syria until they suffered defeat from the Ottomans in 1517/922 CE/AH. In Egypt, they retained a high, semi-autonomous status even thereafter, so their power dwindled only with the arrival of Napoleon Bonaparte's troupes in Cairo, in 1798/1213 CE/AH.[227]

Overall, the 'Mamluk phenomenon' lasted close to 1,000 years and is often regarded as unparalleled to any other 'slave army' in human history.[228] Each generation of Mamluks was always purchased anew from the steppes of Eurasia and married to slave-women of the same origin. 'Neither the wealth nor the status of [Mamluk] was heritable. Upon the death of a warrior, his property, house, goods, [wives, concubines] and slaves were sold for the benefit of the Treasury'.[229] The Mamluk was, thus, 'a "life peer", and Mamluk society was a one-generation nobility'.[230] The Mamluks had no ties whatsoever with their natal families; also, their children (*awlad al-nas*) could not become soldiers: they 'were ejected from the upper class and were assimilated in the civilian population'.[231] During the Mamluk reign in Cairo, '[d]ivorce and remarriage were [...] common in this class and indeed in all classes.

A table of the marriages of twenty-five Mamluk women shows that seven of them married four or more times and that not one married only once'.[232] Members of the Mamluk family, however, spent their lives almost entirely in a mono-gendered surrounding. In fact, the rise and prosperity of the male-born castrated subjectivity (*khuddam/aghawat*)[233] in this period, as a powerful class in its own right,[234] seems to be directly associated with the government's obsession with keeping women and men separate from each other. The *khuddam/aghawat* – themselves a one-generation nobility of sorts[235] – were usually also the upbringers of the young Mamluks and quite often their military commanders.[236] The young Mamluk novice, once taken away from his natal family, was brought into two separate, socially constructed 'households': one with his wives and concubines,[237] which he rarely had a chance to interact with, and another, a military unit, in which he would spend most of his life. The first 'household' was, thus, by and large a female-only familial domain,[238] whereas the Mamluk military unit (*buyut*, 'house') was a social sphere resembling a form of patriarchal male-only family:

> Within [these] units, [...] there existed some identification with and special feeling for one's cohort (*khushdashiyya*) as well as for one's patron (*ustadh*). Kinship idioms were used: the patron was called 'father' (*walid*), the mamluk 'sons' (*awlad*) called each other 'brothers' (*ikhwa*; sg. *akh*), sometimes distinguishing 'older brothers' (*aghawat*; sg. *agha*) [notice the cognate/euphemism shared with the *khuddam*] from 'younger brothers' (*iniyyat*; sg. *ini*) and *ta'ifa* was used in the sense of 'family' (as well as 'faction') for mamluks. Even other mamluks were regarded as outsiders (*gharib*) who could not become part of such families.[239]

It is no wonder, then, that such male and female close-knit 'households' generated the various modalities of same-sex intimacy and sexuality, of which '[c]hroniclers of the day not infrequently' report.[240] Those relationships are also mirrored in the Mamluk-era poetry and (to a lesser extent) prose.[241] What makes them different from the same-sex narratives from other contemporary Muslim polities[242] is precisely the overall environment produced by the 'Mamluk phenomenon', in which *all* kinship ties have been radically redefined. And, perhaps the most intriguing and idiosyncratic feature of the gendered and sexual subjectivities introduced or re-imagined within this social system was their 'one-generationness', an inability to even symbolically extend oneself beyond the confines of one's own biological existence. In this sense, many inhabitants of the Mamluk lifeworlds – the noble *khuddam/aghawat*, men, women and their children (*awlad al-nas*) – differed from the predominantly Arab population over which they ruled. The only category capable of escaping the predicaments of this status were the *awlad al-nas*. But their rite to passage to the 'multi-generational' world necessarily involved a break with their natal families. Another not inconsiderable element of separation of these Mamluk subjectivities from the larger population was their ethnic origin and – what came to be an increasingly socially constructed difference – their race. Most Mamluks spoke but elementary Arabic and were perceived as 'white'; they were also the only social class who had the right to own the 'white' slaves. The *khuddam/aghawat*, on the other hand, were divided into 'white' and 'black'. The 'one-generationness' and 'foreignness' were, thus, the defining categories of a Mamluk self, which undoubtedly framed not only their social but also their gender and sexual experience.

In matters of law and politics, the Mamluk regime introduced significant changes to the systems developed in the earlier caliphates. Initially, the institution of the caliph was retained, primarily, perhaps, because of the then-perceived need to legitimise the Mamluk rule. Hence, Sultan Baybars (r. 1260/658–1277/675 CE/AH) installed a junior member of the 'Abbasid dynasty as the caliph in Cairo. The same caliph, however, relinquished all of his political power in favour of Baybars. Not only that; he went on to transfer his religious and jurisdictional functions to the sultan as well: 'I entrust to you the interests of all Muslims and I invest you with all with which I am invested in the matters of religion', he proclaimed before the victorious Baybars.[243] Henceforth, the Mamluk sultan 'came to be seen as the guarantor in his own territory of contracts, marriages and [the *hudud*-based] [p]enalties – critical legal acts whose religious legitimacy formerly depended on the [caliph]. The Sultan-Caliph had arrived'.[244] The *ulama*, unabashed, confirmed the legitimacy of this transfer.[245]

The sultans, in turn, sought to provide an environment in which the Sunni schools of *fiqh* could thrive, as well as to minimise their internal strife:

In 1265 [CE], Sultan Baybars decided to treat the four Sunni law schools on an equal footing and to create for each of them the post of a chief qadi in the major cities of his empire. Mamluk Sultans and military leaders consequently founded charitable foundations [awkaf] to support Sunni law schools, and appointed scholars to or dismissed them from the posts of judges, market inspectors (muhtasibs), professors in institutions of higher – mostly legal – learning (madaris), administrators of charitable foundations, and treasury functionaries, thus on the one hand controlling access to the major offices of public life and on the other forming alliances and clientele relations with groups of scholars.[246]

The ulama in general and the fuqaha' in particular sought the support of Mamluk dignitaries in dealing with what by then became an elaborate system of the competing approaches to legal theory, legal practice and legal education.[247] Scholars whose approach went beyond the doctrinal consensus, or whose interpersonal conflicts with the mainstream academe members sometimes even threatened their own life, needed the protection of Mamluk authorities even more. Such was the position, for example, of the famed historian Ibn Khaldun, who had spent his last years in Mamluk Cairo, where many a distinguished émigrée sought refuge from an intercontinental epidemic of the plague and the political strife befalling other Muslim polities. The Mamluk regime thus managed to turn Cairo into the new cultural, philosophical and legal centre of the Sunni intelligentsia, but it also ensured that the dominant discourses on Islamic law fully conformed to its rule. The Mamluk hegemony then gradually extended beyond the walls of Cairo, into all territories under their control.

A case in point is that of Takiyy al-Din Ahmad ibn Taymiyya (1263/661–1328/728 CE/AH), a famous Hanbali jurist whose trials and tribulations but, also, doctrinal contributions to the merger of fiqh and siyasa had become a token of the Mamluk legal reform. He spent almost all his life in Damascus, which under Mamluk rule was slowly reclaiming some of its past glory. Ibn Taymiyya, however, fought tirelessly with its authorities and engaged in painstaking refutations of the 'excesses' of many Sufis, Shi'a, Christians and Mongols of any faith. His scholarship was, thus, deeply divisive, so he constantly 'tried to forge alliances with members of the Mamluk elite in order to find political backing for his religious doctrine'.[248] Mamluk dignitaries, on the other hand, sought to exonerate Ibn Taymiyya from the accusations of his many opponents that his teachings were heretical by asking him to interpret them as a (mere) Hanbali view, which was not obligatory for scholars of other schools. He refused and retorted by branding his enemies, *tout court*, as infidels.[249] For such an attitude, he was imprisoned many times and eventually banned from writing. He, also, died in prison.

Before his demise, however, Ibn Taymiyya penned a doctrine[250] that his faithful disciple, Ibn Qayyim al-Jawziyya, further perfected – that of *siyasa shar'iyya*.[251] The doctrine claimed its universal validity amongst the Muslims, yet its more immediate goal was to bestow upon the Mamluk regime full religious authority for its comprehensive legal and administrative reforms. *Siyasa shar'iyya* was not to be understood as a

> system of rulers and norms but the religious purpose underlying these norms in its practical political form. The concept underlines the necessity of a strong political apparatus for the practice of religion and assigns a religious dimension to the exercise of all public functions (*wilayat*), all of which are supposed to fulfil the *hisba* commandment, that is to command the good and forbid the evil.[252]

The doctrine revolutionised both the substance of and jurisdictional authority in Islamic law. According to Ibn Qayyim al-Jawziyya, the word *qadi* was but 'a name that applies to each and everyone who issues decision in a conflict between two parties or who arbitrates between them, no matter whether he is a caliph, a sultan, a deputy, or a governor'.[253] The strict norms of evidence established by classical *fiqh*, were the first to be revisited by the new theopolitical apparatus, entrusted with deliberating upon and meting out the new, reformed *fiqh*:

> A new stream of *fiqh* on evidence thus emerged at the hands of this rising legal elite during the thirteenth and fourteenth centuries [CE], developing new notions of proof and procedure that, from the fifteenth century onwards, became part and parcel of the post-classical legal doctrine. Signs ('*alamat*) and indications (*amarat*) became admissible as evidence under this religious normativity.[254]

Of course, what transpired within the domain of *fiqh* was merely a reflection of broader legal reforms. The Mongol *yasa* 'became a model of sorts' for the powerful dynasties in the region; not necessarily in substance, but as an example of how to effectively conceive of a separate legal system of the ruling elite: the Mamluks, thus, 'came to believe that they too possessed a *yasa* [...] which governed relations amongst themselves'.[255] On another level, the Mamluks also carried on (from the 'Abbasids) and further developed the institution of *mazalim* ('grievances'): a system of courts founded on the sovereigns' prerogative to hear, adjudicate upon and rectify the wrongs suffered by their subjects. 'Its paradigmatic form is that of the sovereign sitting in his court, aided by his functionaries, giving public audience to any of his subjects to plead for justice against, typically, powerful persons who have usurped [their] rights'.[256] Although Mamluk sultans were careful enough to ensure that each *qadi* or a *mufti* present in the *mazalim* court participated, to some extent, in the decisions that were made,[257] it was ultimately the sovereign's will that shaped – and made legitimate – this entire system. The *mazalim* standards of justice were, thus, largely *ad hoc* and commonsensical, based on the prevailing ethos of the ruling class and its customary laws.[258] Yet, with the sultan vested with caliphal powers, further reinforced by the *siyasa shar'iyya* doctrine, the borderline between the *mazalim* and other forms of Islamic justice became more blurred than ever.

It is this state of affairs of Islamic law that the Ottomans inherited, following their victory over the Mamluk regime in 1517/922 CE/AH. But an entire century before, whilst fighting the Byzantine forces for control of Constantinople/Istanbul, the rising Ottoman sultans created their own system of law: that of *kanun* (Arabic: *qanun*),[259] a cognate with Christian *canon* law (Greek: κανών; Hebrew: *kaneh*). We turn, now, to this peculiar example of a Muslim polity and legal culture.

The Ottoman Empire emerged at the turn of the fourteenth/eighth century CE/AH in Turkish Anatolia, from a welter of smaller emirates, united by Osman I. By the mid-fifteenth/ninth century CE/AH, it began with considerable legal reforms, which eventually enabled the central government, epitomised in the near-absolute sovereignty of the sultans and their ruling class (*askeri*),[260] to effectively and efficiently exercise control over vast conquered lands.[261] The reforms were described as meritocratic, practical and innovative.[262] They were, generally, composed of two distinctive and highly systematic interventions: étatisation of the Hanafi *madhhab* and its *fiqh*, and introduction of sultanic public law, known as *kanun*.

The overwhelming presence of the Hanafi school of *fiqh* in the territories controlled by the Ottomans, in the formative stages of the Empire, ensured that this *madhhab* became the official one. The State transformed the Hanafi thought into a nearly 'unambiguous body of legal rules', by enjoining the judges to systematically determine the most authoritative Hanafi views and turn them into enforceable legal principles.[263] The State reserved – and exercised – the right to declare null and void judgements divergent from the majority view. Also, if the sultans disliked the prevailing Hanafi view on some matter, they were free to order the judges to follow a minority opinion, instead.[264] Thus created, the Ottoman-Hanafi body of *fiqh* served as a form of state law in almost everything but the name. To balance this troublesome intrusion, the Ottoman sultans, who also saw themselves as caliphs, solemnly pronounced that they were bound by the overarching principles of God's 'pathway' (*şeriat*; Arabic: *shariʿa*). This meant that for any action perceived to be contrary to *şeriat*, the sultan risked being punished or even deposed by the Hanafi head jurisconsult (*müftü*; Arabic: *mufti*) of Istanbul, known as *şeyhülislam* (Arabic: *shaykh al-islam*). On several occasions, this indeed happened, but only as part of a larger political plot against the incumbent ruler. Instead, the reorganisation of the Hanafi doctrine of jurisprudential precedence and a wide incorporation of the Hanafi scholars into the *askeri* class, led to a full-fledged étatisation of this branch of *fiqh*.[265]

The second pillar of the Ottoman reforms – and, indeed, the crucial feature of the state legal system as a whole – was the introduction of *kanun*, the law(s) enacted by the sovereign. It provided codified legal standards to be followed in all parts of the Empire, and thus made the Ottoman government administratively and politically superior to all other previous or contemporary Muslim states. A typical code (*kanunname*) of *kanun* dealt with the topics that the sultans and their jurisconsults found underdeveloped in or inapplicable to the Ottoman-Hanafi body of *fiqh*, 'such as fiscal law, land law, organisation of the state and criminal law'.[266] It consisted of sultanic edicts (*ferman*), 'given in individual cases, but made to apply in one region or in the entire empire [. . .]. Since [. . .] such orders were bound to the person of the ruler, they had to be reconfirmed whenever a new [s]ultan came to power'.[267] This requirement made the *kanun* 'a cumulative discourse, each sultan propounding his own decrees while largely maintaining the sultanic laws of his predecessors'.[268] It also allowed them to accommodate change and respond dynamically to the exigencies of various regions of the Empire.[269] On the one hand, the *kanun* rested solely on the sultan's authority: as the lawgiver and supreme jurisprudent. Any uncertainty in interpretation 'were to be referred "to the capital" [...]; and, whereas the [*şeyhülislam*'s *fatawa*] were not legally binding on the [judges], the [sovereign's *ferman*] were'.[270] On the other hand, the judge (*kadı*; Arabic: *qadi*) was made the exclusive agent of the enforcement of *kanun*, whose verdict was strictly required prior to any punishment.[271] The government servants were thus barred from taking justice in their own hands, and the *kanunname* were read out in public, so as to inform the citizens of their duties and rights. The citizens were free to obtain a copy of a *kanunname*, for a fee (120 *akçe*), or to ask the local court to issue them a certified copy of a sultanic rescript of justice ('*adaletname*), for a smaller fee, which they could use to familiarise themselves with or prove their rights.[272] Although primarily introduced to balance the sultanic legal prerogatives, these were tremendously significant improvements to the citizens' access to law and justice. However, the overall effect on the legal profession – particularly on the office of *kadı* – was that, by the sixteenth/tenth century CE/AH, almost *all* of its members 'were ranked, graded and pensioned under central state offices'.[273] The *kanun* thus provided for a more just but centralised and, by and large, state-sanctioned Islamic legal system.

Perhaps the most interesting feature of the *kanun* system is that it gradually made the drastic *hudud* punishments *obsolete*.[274] The earliest Ottoman *kanunname* relating to criminal law[275] dates back to the reign of Mehmed II, who conquered Constantinople in 1453/857 CE/AH and brought an end to the Byzantine Empire. But it was around 1534/940 CE/AH, during the reign of Sultan Süleyman I, also known as *Kanuni* ('the Lawgiver'), that the most significant *kanunname* was enacted (usually referred to as the *Kanun-i Osmani*).[276] Its criminal provisions (in chapters 1, 2, 3 and 15), developed under the guidance of Süleyman's *şeyhülislam*, Ebussu'ud Efendi (Arabic: Abu'l-Su'ud), were so far-reaching that the Islamicists and legal historians often dub them as (the first) Ottoman Criminal Code.[277] The *Kanun-i Osmani* remained the most substantial collection of sultanic law in the Empire, and 'subsequent sultans were given new copies as they came to the throne',[278] to which they would, on rare occasions, introduce but minor changes.[279] It is intriguing that the very first chapter of *Kanun-i Osmani* is entirely devoted to sexual offences. It opens with a significant provision:

> If a Muslim commits *zina*, if it is proven by the *şeriat* [i.e. by Sunni *fiqh*] and the perpetrator is a married man, and if the perpetrator has a property of over a thousand *akçe*, he should pay a fine of 300 *akçe*. If he is of medium sized property of up to six hundred *akçe* he should pay 200 *akçe*. Below this, up to 400, a fine of 100 [will be demanded]. If his property is smaller, a fine of 50 *akçe*, and if his situation is strict poverty [*gayet fakir olsa*], 40 *akçe* will be taken.[280]

This regulation, alongside many other provisions of the *Kanun-i Osmani*, thus 'fiscalised' the offence of *zina*: what amounted to a fixed *hadd* death penalty was from now on to be punishable by a fine, in some cases not exceeding 40 *akçe*. The same was true for the other *hudud* and a whole host of new crimes; in some cases, however, discretionary (*ta'zir* or *siyasa*) corporal punishment was also allowed, in addition to a fine.[281] An exemplary provision thus reads:

> If [a person] kisses [another] person's son or approaches him on his way and addresses [indecent words] to him, [the *kadı*] shall chastise [the offender] severely and a fine of one *akçe* shall be collected for each stroke.[282]

But even with the new evidential requirements in place, much lower than in the case of *hudud*, this offence or, indeed, *zina* and *livata* (Arabic: *liwat*), were almost never tried in the Ottoman courts,[283] which indicates that the principle of concealment (*satr*) was still duly observed.[284] An exception was made for the cases in which a serious crime was known to be a 'common habit' (*'adet-i müstemirreleri*) of the offender. Rudolph Peters, for example, reports of a 1713/1125 CE/AH trial, in the town of Çankırı, for the same-sex gang rape of a beardless youth (*şabb-ı emred*), which ended with the recommendation of the presiding *kadı* that the culprits be executed *because* they were already known as rapists.[285]

The legal reforms, however extensive, made, seemingly, no attempt at curtailing one aspect of the Ottoman society that was, by then, rather commonly spoken of – and most certainly exaggerated – by European observers:[286] its thriving sexual and gender diversity. Whereas numerous recent studies – of which those by Khaled El-Rouayheb[287] and Dror Ze'evi[288] are of particular merit – seek to reframe this phenomenon as a consequence of the complex Ottoman medico-ethical discourses on the human (gendered and sexual) self, it is still difficult to ascertain which specific role the then-prevalent discourse on Islamic law – as a state-sanctioned *and* personal moral system – played in the construction of Ottoman Muslim subjectivities. It seems that the general reluctance of the Ottoman legists to treat sexual and gender diversity as *punishable* transgressions – an attitude comparable to that of the Seljuk and Mughal societies – provided for a lacuna in which this phenomenon could be legally tolerated, if still routinely frowned upon, as a 'matter between God and the transgressor'. At the same time, there is no doubt that the social appeal *and* repugnance of sexual and gender 'irregularity' owed much to its *class* and *political* dimension; that is, to its association with the *askeri* exceptionalism.

Paradigmatic to a class-specific intimacy and sociality was the Ottoman institution of *devşirme* ('collection'), which flourished in fifteenth/ninth and sixteenth/tenth century CE/AH: 'By the terms of this system, recruiters would venture into the Ottomans' [South East] European provinces roughly once each year and select a certain percentage of boys from the population of the Christian villages'.[289] The levy was obligatory, and its subjects had to swear their absolute, life-long loyalty to the sultan; but it also offered nearly 'limitless opportunities to the young men who became a part of it'.[290] Hence, a number of recruits came through voluntary accessions, and, at a later stage, Bosnian Muslims were also allowed to join the ranks.[291] The *devşirme* novices perceived as exceptionally promising were sent to the *enderun* ('innermost') college, where they were schooled into the top of the *askeri* class: viziers (even grand viziers), scientists, teachers, provincial administrators and officers of the sultan's elite *yeniçeri* ('new corps') infantry (in English known as the Janissaries).[292] The novices distinct in their 'bodily perfection [...] and intellectual ability', became the sultan's personal pages (*iç oğlanları*).[293] Others enrolled in *kalemiye* colleges, for scribes, or *ilmiye* institutions, for the *ulema*, or joined the military (especially the *yeniçeri* troops).[294] Unlike Mamluks, the *devşirme* boys were not necessarily deprived of all contact with their natal families and were often able to help their relatives succeed in various Ottoman offices.[295] Like Mamluks, however, they were '[s]et apart by dress and privilege'[296] from the tax-paying lower-class (*reaya*).

The lifeworlds of the *devşirme* recruits, especially *iç oğlanları* and the *yeniçeri* troops, were habitually mono-gendered, the borderlines of which were, like in the Mamluk society, guarded by the subjectivity of a male-born castrated *ağa* (Arabic: *agha*).[297] Marriage was uncommon for the members of the *yeniçeri*, while the entire system of the sultan's court rested upon the principle of gender segregation.[298] Same-sex intimacy and sexual relations were, thus, widespread amongst these recruits and other *askeri*.[299] But because they occurred in a class-specific environment, they were chiefly seen as a form of 'otherness' in the larger society, provoking mixed and complex reactions. It was only in a later period that a gender-ambiguous subjectivity emerged, capable of crossing class-barriers of an Ottoman self: that of the *köçekler* (sing. *köçek*), the cross-dressing prepubescent (male-born) dancers who performed *both* in the sultanic palaces and in city taverns.[300] *Per contra*, the *devşirme* recruits – and sociality, sexuality and gender expressions associated with them – remained a Mamluk-like class phenomenon, although, without doubt, more culturally influential on the whole.

Conducted from the *askeri* centre, the Ottoman Islamic law reform was primarily aimed at producing and maintaining a new form of Muslim state, in which gender, sexual, class and even religious difference were rather pragmatically employed at the service of central government: towards its administrative, military and cultural advancement. While 'bypassing' the *hudud*[301] and other 'classical' aspects of Sunni jurisprudence, the new sultanic public law became the salient feature of a revisited idea of Islamic justice, in which *siyasa*, Hanafi *fiqh* as well as much improved and diversified legal practice and legal education played a pivotal role in construing the Ottoman ruler as a sultan *and* as a caliph. This system, epitomised in the *Kanun-i Osmani*, remained in place for a very long time, with the first significant changes introduced only in the nineteenth/thirteenth-century CE/AH Tanzimat ('Reorganisation') era.[302]

The Third Interlude: Khuddam/Aghawat *in the Interstices of Law*

The final 'interruptive' phenomenon this chapter briefly explores relates to the practice of castration of male children, purportedly outside the purview of a Muslim state or family, who were then sold to Muslim polities as the one-generation noble slaves known as *khuddam* (sing. *khadim*) or *aghawat* (sing. *agha, aǧa*).[303] The deployment of such slaves at the rulers' courts and in their military service had been, of course, a common practice of many historical polities, starting with the Assyrians from about tenth century BCE, over the ancient Roman and Chinese empires, to those contemporary to the early Muslims, such as the late Byzantium.[304] In Muslim caliphates, the *khuddam* were present most probably already during the Umayyad era.[305] What is certain is that they became an inextricable component of the court and army elite of the 'Abbasids and, subsequently, of the Seljuk, Fatimid, Mamluk and other caliphates, as well as of each of the three great medieval Muslim 'gunpowder empires': the Ottomans, the Mughals of the Indian subcontinent and the Safavids of Persia.[306]

During the Seljuk period, for example, the *khuddam* 'served variously as harem guardians, tutors to crown princes, and pleasure companions to the rulers'.[307] They were mostly imported from Africa, later specifically from Abyssinia. The Fatimids extended the import policy to populations known as *saqaliba*, coming from various Slavic and other Eastern European tribes, primarily with a view to turning them into elite slave soldiers. The guardianship over the imperial harem, on the other hand, was the primary role reserved for the Mughal and Safavid *khuddam*, coming from a wide variety of the Eurasian peoples.[308] The Ottoman *aghawat*, however, took on all of those roles and became, arguably, the single most influential one-generation nobility. The Abyssinian *aghawat* guarded the Ottoman sultan's harem, ran the financial and military affairs of the palace and – importantly – guarded the tomb of the Prophet Muhammad in Medina, at least since Salah al-Din's time (r. 1174/569–1193/589 CE/AH).[309] The Medinan society of Abyssinian *aghawat*, as the *exclusive* guardians of Muhammad's tomb, as well as their society at the Ka'ba in Mecca, remarkably survived into *our time*.[310] Similar *aghawat* societies are also known to have 'appeared at the tombs of sultans in Cairo, [...] at the Dome of the Rock of Jerusalem, and at the tomb of Abraham in Hebron'.[311] Cairo was the primary 'entry point' for the Abyssinian *aghawat*, so their Cairene societies were particularly significant and influential during the Mamluk and Ottoman eras.[312] In contrast, the Eurasian *aghawat* in the Ottoman court guarded the threshold between the space reserved for the sultan's (male) visitors and the harem (i.e. not the harem itself), and their influence was more or less limited to the Ottoman Anatolian and European provinces.

However important the religious role of the *khuddam/aghawat* who guarded most treasured Muslim sanctuaries, their contribution to the history of Islamic law goes well beyond it. The Medinan *khuddam*, for instance, famously formed a row in the mosque (*saff al-khuddam*) so as to intimidate the Shi'i attendants who used to stone the Sunni preacher Siraj al-Din al-Ansari with gravel, during his Friday sermons. This earned them a considerable repute amongst the Sunni *fuqaha'*, which supposedly helped their society to survive the subsequent political and religious upheavals.[313] A case in point is, also, that of the Ottoman chief harem *agha* (*kızlar ağası*) Beşir, who founded numerous libraries and schools in order to preserve and disseminate the Hanafi doctrine.[314] Although their 'making into' *khuddam/aghawat* was regarded as contrary to Islamic law,[315] the *fuqaha'* never disputed their remarkable contributions to the legal profession. How, then, this subjectivity's existence may have influenced the legists' and societal perceptions of sexual and gender diversity?

The position of the *khuddam* appears to have been similar to the persons born with 'ambiguous' genitalia and chromosomal order – today usually termed *intersex* – whom Muslim jurists called *khuntha*.[316] The *fuqaha'* distinguished between those of 'discernible' (*khuntha ghayr mushkil*) and 'intractable' (*khuntha mushkil*) sex/gender; whereas the former were ordered either into 'menfolk' or 'womenfolk', the latter posed an insurmountable obstruction to their 'ideal' binary patriarchal world: Where should the *khuntha mushkil* stand when praying in the mosque? What is their rightful inheritance share? What should they wear? Should they marry, and if so, whom? Who should inspect them, if they need a doctor? Who, after all, should perform the *ghusul* (a ritual ablution involving full bath) when they die, and how should they be buried?[317] The jurists went to great pains, trying – unconvincingly – to answer these and many other questions relating to non-binary sexual/gender selfhoods. Their crude biological approach caused them anxiety and embarrassment, yet they knew no better way to relate to this 'conundrum'. For all the same reasons, it seems, classical *fiqh* is interested in the *khuddam* in as much as their sexual prowess, or the lack thereof, is concerned.[318] As the act of castration would not necessarily fully remove one's sexual sensation and desire, the *fuqaha'* were considerably concerned with the *khuddam*'s potential 'indecent' behaviour.[319] In other affairs, however, they were seen as 'comparable to men': hence, their male names and masculine pronouns, or the permissibility of their marriage with women.[320] But the lives of the *khuddam* surpassed greatly this formal designation.

Liminality, as it were, was inscribed on a *khadim/agha*'s body, and on its social role. Their bodily 'otherness'[321] – although, invariably, a source of awe and respect in Muslim societies – compelled the *khuddam* to seek and form their own societies, outside of the dominant binary phantasm. Even their names, sometimes, attested difference: Sünbül ('Hyacinth') Ağa, Reyhan ('Sweet Basil') Ağa, Mercan ('Coral') Ağa, Yapraksız ('Leafless') Ağa and many more, idiosyncratic to *khuddam* only.[322] Their common social role – as the guardians of the *threshold* between men and women – seems only to have exacerbated their need to escape the continuous violence of the affairs on either side of that threshold. On the other hand, at least in some cases, the traumatic and by and large involuntary nature[323] of the *khuddam*'s inception into 'khadimness' must have caused a very complex and tumultuous relationship with their self-perceived 'manliness'. These and many other aspects of the *khuddam*'s lifeworlds fully escaped the imagination and normativity of the then-dominant concepts of/in Islamic law.

Whereas Muslim societies accommodated (albeit not unproblematically) the phenomenon of 'khadimness' in many ways, the law – *qua* *fiqh* or even *qua* 'law as applied' – preferred to turn a blind eye to it altogether, rather than to engage with its manifold complexities. In that the law revealed its acute patriarchal condition, which was systematically exposed and challenged only by much later scholarly enterprises. 'Khadimness', thus, in its times, remained a token of a legally induced crisis of masculinity,[324] in which the patriarchal male legist delimited the domain of law to his own narrow comfort zone.

Islamic Law in (Post-)Colonial Macrocosm: Modernity and its Others

Over the past 200 years or so, the domain of Islamic law – its formats and contents, its theory and practice and, most importantly, its *umma* as a whole – has undergone dramatic, unprecedented changes. The world it emerged into and shaped for over a millennium gradually disintegrated and disappeared, leaving the new generations of Muslims with mere *mise-en-scène* elements of the bygone past: architectural masterworks, social narratives, languages and cultures. But the legal and political landscape, which *constituted*, above all, the domain of Islamic law, metamorphosed beyond recognition, thereby posing an enormous challenge to the new Muslim scholars, polities and communities eager to rethink or restore the law *inspired* by God's numinous 'pathway' (*shari'a*).

The revival, whatever it may have been, was never going to be an easy task. For the most part, the *institution* of *fiqh* – its social and legal environment, and, by extension, its very *fuqaha'* – was gone, never to return. Some attempts at resuscitating it to the new world – most notably in Saudi Arabia – remained but a façade for political manipulations. Instead, new *hybrid* laws arose, state-sanctioned and codified, furthered and practiced by a novel legal elite through new legal institutions. Those who conflate *fiqh* with *shari'a* thus lament the loss of the former as indicative of the nearly certain death of the latter.[325] The ideal *shari'a*, however, could not have left the field, much like the relevance of the Qur'an, as God's trans-temporal and trans-historical *speech*, for Muslims of any generation or polity, could not diminish due to different social circumstances. What did, however, change was the human interpretation of God's 'pathway' and God's speech, along with the exegetical enterprises developed to take on this task *systematically*. And, with them, the realm of Islamic law – that humanly affair which always already incorporated dynamism and flexibility – entered a radically different new phase.

Several interconnected phenomena, all of distinctly European origins, arguably caused the fundamental transformation of Islamic law. First came European colonialism, which, by the beginning of the twentieth century CE, swiped through some nine-tenths of the Earth's territories,[326] including, of course, many Muslim polities. The colonisers either outright abolished the institutions of Muslim justice and lawmaking, like in the 'French' North Africa, or gradually transformed them into legal Frankensteins, as with the Anglo-Muhammadan law of 'British' India.[327] Then came European modernity, fuelled by the rising power of European capitalism, from which emerged its paramount institution – the nation state.[328] This tide left no human polity unaffected. Even the once-formidable empires, such as that of the Ottomans, although never directly colonised, transformed and succumbed under its mighty spell. Finally, there emerged an *intra-Muslim* divide, between intellectual modernists and theopolitical revivalists – a distinction that is ideological rather than 'purely' legal, as we shall see – which dominates the field until the present day.

Against this backdrop and only relatively recently, the new hermeneutical currents began to coalesce, of hybrid origins and systems of knowledge; inevitably, it seems, in the globalised world of today. They took the challenge of breaking the waves of patriarchy and both the Muslim modernist and theopolitical revivalist precepts of what the law ought to be in a Muslim community. And, what is particularly significant for this book, sexual and gender diversity within the contemporary (and historical) *umma* became for those hermeneutics a case study – even, for some, the key problematic – though which one can (and *ought* to) rethink the domain of Islamic law today.

The above trajectory is intimated in this chapter in the following order: First, a brief analysis of the making of Anglo-Muhammadan law in India is juxtaposed to the Tanzimat era and its aftermath, in the declining Ottoman Empire, so as to exemplify two distinct, though interrelated, ways in which European imperial interests, and their ideological cursors, entered the field of Islamic law and influenced, directly or indirectly, its subsequent transformation. Second, the European concept of modernity and the nation state, as well as troublesome Muslim reactions to them, are revisited through a series of examples from across the new Muslim-majority polities, including that of Saudi Arabia, whose leaders averred to have resisted the European encroachments and to have recreated, instead, an environment similar to that in which classical *fiqh* had emerged. Third and finally, the contemporary hermeneutics attempting to un-spell the domain of Islamic law from its colonial and theopolitical charms, especially in relation to Muslim sexual and gender diversity, are given due consideration.

Hybrids and Capitulations: Reforms in 'British' India and in Late Ottoman State

Despite its long and uncanny presence in India through the workings of the East India Company, it was not before the second half of the eighteenth century CE that the British Empire began large-scale administrative and legal reforms, epitomised in the so-called Hastings Plan.[329] This project 'conceived a multi-tiered system that required exclusively British administrators at the top, seconded by a tier of British judges who would consult with local *qadi*s and *mufti*s (*mulavi*s) with regard to issues governed by Islamic law'.[330] The imperative of the Plan, and of subsequent, ever more direct administration over India, was to learn, systematise and employ the local legal 'customs' in the service of British colonial interests.[331] To achieve this, the British aimed at compiling the 'digests' of 'Hindu and Mahomedan laws' to be used by 'native interpreters of the respective laws', albeit in courts established by the British Empire and overseen by British judges.[332] The British colonisers were baffled by the leniency of the Islamic system of justice and by what seemed to them as the arbitrary position of the *quda'* (judges) in charge of its administration.[333] For this they largely blamed the absence of codified laws and of any 'effective' judicial institutions.[334] Selected volumes of classical *fiqh* literature were, thus, (inaccurately) translated into English to qualify as the *new law codes*. This unprecedented 'act of translation-cum-codification represented a replacement of the native system's interpretive mechanisms by those of English law'.[335] To turn a treatise of an individual jurist into black-letter law meant, indeed, to break away, procedurally and substantially, with Islamic legal tradition *tout court*. In order to mask the enormity of this sinister operation, the British included the 'native experts'[336] as co-producers of what was thenceforth known as Anglo-Muhammadan law. The resulting enterprise transformed the field of Islamic law 'totally and beyond recognition'.[337] It was, however, but an important *intermediate* phase: 'By the end of the {nineteenth} century {CE}, and with the exception of family law and certain elements of property transactions, all indigenous laws had been supplanted by British law'.[338]

   In the Ottoman Empire, however, the changes occurred without the overt legal interventions of the European imperial powers; some of them, in fact, were introduced precisely as acts of defiance against European encroachments. And yet they were unmistakably of European character and origin. On the one hand, the ever increasing and intensifying Ottoman capitulations (*imtiyazat*, 'concessions') to the European states, following the Empire's continuous military defeats, provided the economic and political background to the Tanzimat era (1839–76 CE). On the other hand, the Ottomans' growing interest in European cultures and institutions beyond their immediate reach constituted an internal catalyst for change. The shrinking Empire, increasingly troubled by the 'national awakenings' of its non-Muslim subjects (hitherto organised into the *millet* system),[339] embarked thus on the substantive, far-reaching reorganisation. It emerged

under the 'Noble Rescript' – a programme of comprehensive legal and societal reconstruction developed by Mustafa Reşit Paşa (1800–58 [CE]), a high-ranking Ottoman politician. The *millet* system was abolished, in favour of the new general principle that everyone is equal before the law, regardless of religion. A parliamentary system was created and the empire passed its first Constitution (1876) in which both the role of religious authorities and the sultan's powers were restricted. Several penal codes were promulgated, most notably the 1858 Ottoman Penal Code, an almost verbatim translation of the 1810 French Penal Code, which – apart from the apostasy offence – officially abolished all *hudud* penalties, including that for *zina* [...]. This code also decriminalised [all forms of male same-sex sexual acts]. A new civil code, the Mecelle (Majalla), was promulgated in 1868 [CE] and fully completed in 1876 [CE]. Despite the attempts to model it on its French counterpart, the Mecelle was eventually drafted with the reference to the classical Hanafi jurisprudence and its subsequent Ottoman (re)interpretations. It covered contracts, torts and some principles of civil procedure, while family law was left outside its domain [...]. The Tanzimat also reformed the army, financial and administrative systems [...]. Most importantly, however, it thoroughly reformed the educational system and established universities and academies, within which the new young intelligentsia would be raised, including the future reformist Mustafa Kemal.[340]

What started as a desperate effort to overhaul the Empire that the Europeans mockingly dubbed the 'sick man of Europe' thus gradually gave way to an aggressive economic, social, political and legal 'Westernisation', which culminated in Mustafa Kemal Atatürk's reforms (*Atatürk Devrimleri*) abolishing the sultanate (1922 CE), proclaiming the Turkish Republic (1923 CE) and bringing to an end the (Ottoman) caliphate (1924 CE). Obviously, as the introduction of the *Mecelle* attests, there were some strong attempts along the way to revamp the failing system of sultanic law and thus resist European legal hegemony. Indeed, the *Mecelle* continued to be used by a number of emerging nation states well after the demise of the Ottoman Empire.[341] But the concomitant and interrelated forces of Turkish nationalism,[342] the phantasm of European scientific and cultural 'progressiveness' (as, perhaps, the key rallying cry of liberal ideology 'marching eastwards') and the capitalist takeover of the Ottoman economy remained unstoppable. And the 'progress' these reforms eventually achieved was, of course, only to be measured by the new, European standards.

The curious story of *crime passionnel* is a case in point. According to both Muslim and European legal traditions, steeped in patriarchy, 'a killer can validly plead that he has killed his wife or close female relative and/or her paramour because he found them engaged in act of unlawful sexual intercourse'.[343] Both Anglo-Muhammadan and the new Ottoman laws thus explicitly retained the defence of 'passion', based on the notion of the husband's 'honour' that extends, as it were, onto his wife as his rightful 'property', with European moral standards clearly upholding such a construct. The Ottoman Penal Code from 1858 CE, which – in reliance on its French counterpart – abrogated the *hudud* and all forms of *privately* committed *male* same-sex sexual acts, thus reads in Article 188:

> He who has seen his wife or any of his female *mahram*s [close relatives] with another in a state of disgraceful adultery and has beaten, injured, or killed one or both of them will be exempted [from liability] (*ma'fu*). He who has seen his wife or one of his female *mahram*s with another in an unlawful bed and has beaten, injured or killed one or both of them will benefit from an excuse (*ma'dhur*).[344]

The same patriarchal logic continued to inform the legislation of the new Republic. Atatürk's Penal Code from 1926 CE, for example, defined *all* sexual crimes as the offences against *ırz* ('honour', 'purity') and provided, in Article 462, for a significant reduction of sentence for any *crime passionnel*.[345] The infamous 'honour killings' – as acts *par excellence* of *crime passionnel* – thus triggered no effective change in the law in Turkey well until the twenty-first century CE.[346]

European and Muslim Modernism: On Futility of Resistance from a Nation State

The ideological make-up of European colonialism owes much of its zeal to European Enlighenment thought, which 'has, from the first, posited itself as the wellspring of universal learning, of Science and Philosophy, uppercase,'[347] while maintaining a highly condescending view of all other systems of knowledge, deemed 'primitive' and parochial. The linear and un-interruptive world history, civilisations and cultures were thus seen as evolving towards the European centre, where Knowledge and Skill obtained, which were to lead it thenceforth towards a united humanity. The Enlightened Europeans construed themselves as the *omphalos* (ὀμφαλός; 'navel') of the world, and thereby its rightful proprietors, with other, less 'civilised' and 'progressive' peoples at their due service. The concept of modernity – as 'an orientation to being-in-the-world', as 'an ideology of improvement through the accumulation of knowledge and technical skill', as 'the pursuit of justice by means of rational governance' – was, therefore, closely related to the colonial project.[348] It served, primarily, as a *shifter*:[349] 'to situate people – recursively, in mutually reinforcing oppositions – on the near or the far side of the great divide between self and other, the present and prehistory, here and there,'[350] with Europe on the near and the rest of the world on the far side of an ideal humanity.

The *inherent* European modernity thus bestowed upon the colonial masters the 'right' of conquest and exploitation, for it was but through such 'civilising' efforts that the world was ever able to move *forward*, to *develop* and, ultimately, to flourish. And crucially, 'to install a long-term and efficient mechanism for the economic exploitation of the colonies, the nation state system, with all its legal arsenal, had to be exported as an essential first act'.[351]

The concept of *modern* nation state, then, not only originated in Europe; it remained, throughout, its chief colonising tool. It may be tempting to assume that nation state was, somehow, a 'logical next step' for Muslim laws and polities, after the demise of their caliphates and empires. But, as we have seen, even the most elementary moves towards one such state presupposed – and constituted – a radical break with the symbiotic and complex relationship between Islamic law and the Muslim polities of the past, leading to gradual annihilation of *both* of these tender microcosms.[352] Even 'mere' codification of *fiqh* works *qua*

'Islamic' laws and their subsequent subjection to the alien *stare decisis* rule,[353] a rudimentary step towards their full étatisation, altered the pluralist nature and the very place this literature had possessed prior to such intervention. It turned them into an antithesis of Islamic law, a rigid and hybrid monstrosity that eventually became their agonising swan song. What is more, and for very much the same reasons, no nation state, despite the turgid claims of the leaders of some new Muslim-majority polities, could ever hope to become an 'Islamic state' either:

> The notion of an Islamic state is in fact a postcolonial innovation based on a European model of the state and a totalitarian view of law and public policy as instruments of social engineering by the ruling elites. Although the states that historically ruled over Muslims did seek Islamic legitimacy in a variety of ways, they were not claimed to be 'Islamic states'. The proponents of a so-called Islamic state in the modern context seek to use the institutions and powers of the state, as constituted by European colonialism and continued after independence, to regulate individual behavior and social relations in ways selected by the ruling elite.[354]

The becoming of *national* Islamic law was thus predestined to be a tumultuous, multifarious and, ultimately, *impossible* process. But, while many individual states have tried and failed, mostly in the second half of the twentieth century CE, an intellectual movement arose, already at the turn of the same century, which purported to salvage Islamic law on the meta- *and* supra-national level, by very means of the omnipresent modernity. It is known, controversially, as Islamic modernism.

The movement's first notable representative[355] was the Egyptian intellectual and jurist, Muhammad 'Abduh (1849–1905 CE), who sought to equip the emerging 'Muslim nations' with a theoretical approach befitting the new 'age of science and reason', and thus to 'set them on the path to progress'.[356] Building on the postulate that sound human reason is, *sui generis*, able to recognise the difference between right and wrong,[357] 'Abduh's approach focused on a commonly accepted doctrine of classical *fiqh*, known as *dar'a ta'arud al-'aql wal-naql* ('repulsion of conflict between reason and revelation'),[358] which stated that if 'there appears to be a contradiction between reason and revelation [in the Qur'an or *sunna*] concerning any particular issue, it is because one or the other has been misunderstood'.[359] 'Abduh, however, claimed that 'reason is not simply a partner to revelation but can in effect *displace it* as a guide to human action'.[360] This was, of course, a huge leap, that brought his theological approach safely in line with the European Enlightenment's ideas of the supremacy of human reason. The rational Muslim, 'Abduh claimed, needs to engage with the present world, *as if* it were the hereafter, and work tirelessly towards an Islamic political, scientific, cultural and, indeed, legal renaissance. For that, *ijtihad* (independent reasoning) was to be revived – even *severed*, if necessary, from 'a law [*fiqh*] frozen in time'[361] – and used wherever and whenever possible, until both spiritual *and material* 'progress' is achieved in all spheres of Muslim life.

'Abduh's student, Muhammad Rashid Rida (1865–1935 CE), tried to perfect his master's scholarship by reclaiming certain other concepts of classical *fiqh*, apart from the *ijtihad*, and giving them a new place and functions in his theory of Islamic law. Central to his theory was the notion of *maslaha* (public good), which classical jurists employed mostly in connection with legal causation (*ta'lil*).[362] For Rida, this was an independent principle, to be used in law and 'everyday life' (*mu'amalat*) wherever the dictate of 'worship' (*'ibadat*) does not preclude it explicitly. Although *maslaha* was still normally to be inferred from 'the general spirit and intention of the law'[363] (*maqasid*) – another import from classical times[364] – it could, if there was a necessity (*darura*), go even further – *beyond* revelation – until a new, *Natural* Islamic law of sorts is created to meet the exigencies of the modern time.[365]

Similar approaches were devised by a number of later scholars. The Egyptian scholar, 'Abd al-Wahhab Khallaf (1888–1956 CE), for example, calls for a legal theory and practice in which modern *ijtihad* and *maslaha* take a central place and in which Islamic *legislation* (*tashri'*) – that is, *codified* and *state-enacted* Islamic law – is not only plausible but necessary, in order to preserve 'the spirit of the Qur'an' in the new time.[366] In principle, however, this new legal reasoning would traverse the borders of nation states and be applicable to all Muslims.

The Islamic modernist legal thinkers accrued a considerable number of followers across the *umma*, since they were perceived as *restorers*, rather than radical reformers, of Muslim legal traditions. This is, however, not to say that *all* of their contemporary or later jurists were ready to accept their methodological approach. A notable opponent has been, for instance, the Syrian jurist, Muhammad Sa'id Ramadan al-Buti (1929–2013 CE), who calls this stream of scholarship *maslahawi* (for its expanded reliance on *maslaha*) and accuses it of being *primarily* postulated upon the European Utilitarian legal thought, rather than Muslim legal tradition of any kind.[367] As such, for Buti, it is a 'religion of its own kind',[368] separate from the domain of Islam (and its laws). This is, of course, a familiar trope of every counter-reformist thought. But, what distinguishes Buti from other fierce opponents of Islamic modernism is that he bases his rebuttal on a comparative critical analysis of both European and Islamic modernist legal thought, making the roots of the latter all the more visible. The later generations of modernist thinkers, such as Abdolkarim Soroush (b. 1945 CE), give Buti's concerns a novel context, since they propose that pre-modern Islamic legal tradition be dismissed *tout court*, as intrinsically archaic and irrelevant, in favour of a new search for the 'essence of *shari'a*'.[369]

Meanwhile, Muslim governmental and inter-governmental experimentations with Islamic law gave the modernist and counter-modernist discourses of Muslim intellectuals and jurists only passing attention. Instead, the rising theopolitical elites of Muslim-majority nation states overwhelmingly chose to introduce their own take on legal modernity, epitomised in the municipal legislation of highly diverse origins that nevertheless claimed an 'Islamic identity'.[370] In Pakistan, for example, the political and military attempts to 'Islamise' an intrinsically hybrid legal landscape – composed of *mixed* British colonial, Anglo-Muhammadan, modern secular and idiosyncratic customary laws – led to the introduction of a new 'digest' of the codified *hudud*, which, then, gave a *carte blanche* to the state elite to wreck havoc amongst the most vulnerable elements of the Pakistani society.[371] One state, however, claimed that the turbulent tides of modernity have never reached its shores, and that Islamic law it abided by has remained free from codification and étatisation of any kind. This state was the Kingdom of Saudi Arabia.

Founded in 1932 CE by 'Abd al-Aziz al-Sa'ud (1876–1953 CE), Saudi Arabia became a regional powerhouse soon after the discovery, in 1938 CE, of its vast oil reserves. The new king gave an exclusive concession for their exploration and export to the United States of America, thereby earning a powerful and faithful ally for many decades to come. The house of Sa'ud traditionally maintained a close alliance with the revivalist religious movement of Muhammad ibn 'Abd al-Wahhab (1703–92 CE), commonly known today as Wahhabism. When the Sa'ud family became the hereditary royal dynasty of Saudi Arabia, they elevated the Wahhabi views into an official doctrine of the State, and Ibn 'Abd al-Wahhab's descendants assumed the leading positions amongst the Saudi *ulama*. In turn, the Wahhabi scholars made concerted efforts to revive the 'post-classical' doctrine of *siyasa shar'iyya* of the Damascene jurist Ibn Taymiyya,[372] which bestows upon an autocratic political ruler full religious legitimacy. The Saudi state is, then, politically controlled by the Sa'ud family, religiously governed by the descendants of Ibn 'Abd al-Wahhab and fully protected from the external powers through their close economic and military ties with the United States of America.

Owing to this peculiar sharing of power, Saudi Arabia is, indeed, a somewhat special case amongst the contemporary Muslim-majority polities. Sunni (overwhelmingly Hanbali) *fiqh*, as interpreted by theoretically independent contemporary *fuqaha'*, is recognised as the law of the land and state regulations (*nizam*) are not allowed to contravene it.[373] In criminal trials, for example, the *quda'* (judges) are obliged to uphold the high evidential requirements for the *hudud* allegations, and are given relative discretionary powers in the *ta'zir* cases. However, 'many *ta'zir* offences are now defined by legislation',[374] and there exists a distinctly modern hierarchy of courts, with higher courts including three judges per trial, instead of the traditional single *qadi*.[375] Also, despite the *quda"s* opposition, the Saudi kings continuously use their *siyasa* prerogative to impose legislation and tribunals dealing with matters of their special interest, such as commercial, labour and traffic regulations.[376] Overall, the 'neo-classical' façade of the Saudi legal system serves by and large to justify the *de facto* sharing of power amongst its ruling elite. Wherever the pretence of classical *fiqh* runs contrary to the rulers' interests, it is instantly replaced in favour of a modernist solution. The very concept of nation state thus proves to be an insurmountable obstacle to resurrecting any 'classical' environment of Islamic law, even in the 'exceptionalist' Kingdom of Saudi Arabia.

From Feminist to Sexual/Gender-Pluralist Hermeneutics: Islamic Law in Post-Modern Futurity

By now, it is evident that the Muslim *modern condition* developed into a Janus-like phenomenon: a two-faced reaction to European modernity with an intellectual, meta-national side and its politically opportune, statist alterity. Even the counter-modernist discourse of some Muslim intelligentsia, or, indeed, Saudi 'exceptionalism' as a revivalist project *par excellence*, remained *within* the modernist totality, for they found neither a methodology nor a geopolitical locus which would allow them to truly pursue an alternative route (hence, they were merely reactionary, not revolutionary projects).

That Muslim modernity owed much to the European colonial legacy is plain from its rigid and historically alien discourse on gender and sexuality, which sought to drastically redirect the Muslim ethos towards a distinctly European normativity:

> In the 20th century [CE], histories of Arabic literature have been radically re-written, and even the most famous works, such as *The Arabian Nights* (*Kitab 'alf layla wa-layla*), or *Diwan* by the 10th century [CE] libertine poet Abu Nuwas, have had their 'obscene' contents heavily expurgated. Identity terms such as *shudhudh jinsi* (sexual perversion) have been introduced to construe *homosexuality* and its binary opposite *heterosexuality*, following the European model. For the first time in the history of Muslim communities, *people*, the fellow Muslims, instead of certain illicit *acts*, have received blanket condemnation. States, jurists and scholars have now joined hands in defence of *naturalised* normative *heterosexuality* and neo-Victorian sexual puritanism.[377]

Muslim governments moved to criminalise sexual and gender diversity,[378] while maintaining a strict patriarchal and androcentric binary gender system. The bulk of modernist intelligentsia, in turn, ensured that such measures were made consistent with their new social construction of a Muslim historical *and* present-day self. We read, thus, in Abdelwahab Bouhdiba's famed study, *Sexuality in Islam*, first published in 1975 CE:

> Islam remains violently hostile to all other ways of realizing sexual desire [than that between a man and a woman joined in

matrimony], which are regarded as unnatural purely and simply because they run counter to the antithetical harmony of the sexes. As a result a divine curse embraces both the boyish woman and the effeminate man, male and female homophilia, auto-eroticism, zoophilia etc. All these deviations involve the same refusal to accept the sexed body and to assume the female or male condition. Sexual deviation is a revolt against God.[379]

The above statement, indeed, neatly summarises the enormity of this discursive enterprise. The anti-modern 'deviants' finally became 'a type of life, [...] a species'[380] in the Muslim lifeworlds *as well*, thereby erasing the 'embarrassing' distinction between the early European sexual and gender modernity – with its rigid and 'medicalised' morality – and its 'licentious', Orientalised Muslim counterpart. Once the 'deviants' were defined and safely rooted out from the historical and contemporary Muslim self-representations, the new, 'progressive' society was finally within reach. And, it was only right to do so determinedly, 'in the name of Islam', *as such*.

Against the prospects of one such modern 'Muslim' society, Islamic feminist movements arose in the past half a century, building upon the parallel streams of post-colonial critique, post-modern gender studies and other forms of feminism(s) a *new Qur'anic hermeneutic*.[381] By defining the modernist sexual and gender bias as a bias *against* God's Qur'anic voice, Islamic feminists sought to expose such patriarchal misconceptions 'to critical scrutiny and public debate'[382] and thus eventually wrestle the *umma* from its all too powerful grip.[383] At the same time, they engaged in historical and exegetical debates over the laws and polities that governed the Muslim communities in the past, pointing out their deep-seated patriarchal ethos which undoubtedly augmented the later, modernist transitions.[384] But, as the focus slowly shifted towards pre-modern Muslim patriarchies, some exponents of the Islamic feminist discourse toned down their initial critique of European modernity, coming close to be seduced, as it were, by some of its defining tenets, such as that of human 'progress'.[385] Overall, the discourse is today composed of miscellaneous feminist approaches to Muslim laws and societies. It purports to re-imagine both the Muslim past and its futurity, towards a pluralist vision of Islamic law 'as it was', 'as it is' and 'as it ought to be'. Although it remains duly critical of Islamic law 'as attempted' by modern nation states *and* by classical *fuqaha'*, Islamic feminism is ultimately concerned with gender justice and 'gender *jihad*'[386] in all spheres of Muslim life: communal, relational, personal. In that, it is by and large a legal Realist discourse, for it takes note of the 'bargaining in the shadow of the law'[387] that nonetheless contributes to social constructs – and contestations – of gender.

A stream of distinct sexual/gender-pluralist hermeneutics has recently joined these debates,[388] calling specifically for 'sexuality-sensitive interpretation of the Qur'an [that] would complement and support gender-sensitive interpretation of the scripture (to which feminist Islamic scholars [...] are dedicated) as well as race-sensitive and class-sensitive interpretations'.[389] Scott Siraj al-Haqq Kugle, one of its most notable representatives, devised seven guiding principles of such hermeneutics:

> (1) the inherent dignity of all human beings as bearing the breath of God; (2) the sacredness of life such that all persons may pursue the highest spiritual aspirations of well-being in this world and salvation in the next; (3) the ethic of pluralism, for God creates diversity as an ethical challenge to meet the other, care for the other, and understand the other as a way of coming to fully know oneself; (4) order with justice, for God's message is eternal yet complex, announcing principles and promoting their flexible application in ever-changing social circumstances; (5) God's speech is meaningful, such that interpretation is the right and obligation of all Muslims to discover what God intends behind, within, and through scripture's words (within the constraint of the linguistic limits and grammatical construction of the words); (6) faith complements reason, such that the Qur'an must be understood in the light of observed experience, scientific exploration, and reasoned argument about human nature; (7) love is the goal, for, though the Qur'an urges us to build societies based on moral order requiring rules and laws, the deeper goal behind this order is the promotion of loving sincerity between each person and God, between individuals of the faith community, between members of every family, and between sexual partners.[390]

Kugle's ethical approach, although 'inspired' throughout by Muslim modernist thought, remains careful enough not to dispense with Islamic

legal and social traditions. Instead, he uses them comparatively, in order
to substantiate his thesis that gay, lesbian and transgender Muslims – as
he calls them – need to be reintegrated into and fully accepted by the
larger *umma*. For this, he avers, the Qur'an has to be 'liberated', *hadith*
critiqued, *fiqh* reassessed, Islamic law reformed, *nafs* ('self', 'person' or, in
his rendition, 'spirit') revived and Islamic humanism – epitomised in
one's pious admission that 'only God knows best' – fully embraced.[391]
While interrogating the Muslim legal and social past, Kugle is always
already oriented towards the future, aiming at producing a substantial
guidebook to Muslim communities on how to confront their inherent
sexual and gender diversity. In that, his analysis is antithetical to the
Muslim modernist project, although it strives to integrate some of its
postulates as well. As a quintessentially proleptic, 'forward-looking'
hermeneutic, this approach analyses the past primarily in search of the
principles that can be employed in the future; not for the sake of
'unstoppable' human 'progress', but so that the *umma* can rekindle its
long-lost touch with the trans-temporal *peace* of the Muslim faith.
However, some other exponents of this globally emerging stream engage
in a decidedly more *materialist* – though, at the same time, less
essentialising (in terms of sexually diverse and gender-variant
subjectivities discussed) – critique of Islamic law and Muslim societies,
seeking to expose their pre-modern *and* modern biases.[392]

Neither Islamic feminism nor Muslim sexual/gender-pluralist
hermeneutics are, then, willing to concede that the *shari'a* could ever
have 'died', along with 'its' classical *fiqh*.[393] Quite the contrary, their
dynamic and historically grounded analyses of Islamic law – as an
intrinsically pluralist and multidimensional phenomenon – and of an
equally vibrant and variegated *umma*, give rise to the hope that the
continuity and future of Islamic legal tradition are, indeed, imaginable
beyond its bleak colonial and modernist renditions.

Interruptive Pasts of Discursive Legalities

This chapter has sought to retrace a genealogy of Islamic law and its
complex relationship with human sexual and gender diversity, by
offering an *interruptive* historical sketch. The 'formative', 'classical',
'post-classical' and 'colonial'/'modern' periods of Islamic legal tradition
were, thus, analysed each in their own right, albeit only as a *longue durée*

background to more specific – and often cross-periodical – legal, social, political and philosophical phenomena that have shaped Muslim sexual and gendered selfhoods.

Three key interludes from the pre-modern past have explored, respectively: the construction of and relations between the concepts of *hudud* and *liwat* in so-called classical jurisprudence (tenth/fourth to thirteenth/seventh century CE/AH); the rise of *siyasa* and the juridical, political and social treatment of *liwat* in the Seljuk period (eleventh/fifth and twelfth/sixth century CE/AH); and, finally, the role of the *khuddam/aghawat* in Islamic law and Muslim societies. The first two interludes are, then, decidedly *courte durée*, one being more abstract and the other fully anchored in the Seljuk lifeworlds[394] and experience. In contrast, the third interlude is *almost* trans-temporal, for it stretches back to, at least, the early 'Abbasid dynasty and continues until the present day. Other pre-modern sections are more 'conventional' in their treatment of the historical threads of Islamic law: First, the four 'formative' centuries of Islamic legal tradition are revisited, focusing on *al-khulafa' al-rashidun* ('the rightly guided caliphs'), the Umayyad and the 'Abbasid caliphates, and on the 'traditional' sources of the law – the Qur'an and the *sunna* in particular – and on their treatment of sexual and gender diversity. Second and lastly, the 'post-classical' period is reviewed though the legal and social lenses of Mamluk and Ottoman societies.

The tumultuous modern past and present of Islamic law have been assessed in relation to the colonial invention of Anglo-Muhammadan law in 'British' India and the late Ottoman Empire's legal and social reorganisation; the radical reforms introduced by European and Islamic modernism; and, finally, the ascendance of Islamic feminism and Muslim sexual/gender-pluralist hermeneutics. In that section, the problematic emergence of the modern nation state and its meddling with Islamic law, as well as the ideas of the Islamic modernist intelligentsia seeking to reinvent this field of inquiry, have been given special attention.

I have argued that the developments marking the 'formative' period of Islamic law attest to a highly dynamic social and legal landscape, in which *no* uniform approach to sexual and gender diversity simply could emerge. In this era of individual scholars and judges having rather *practical* conceptions of what (Islamic) law is, or ought to be, and a widely sexually- and gender-pluralist yet, for the most part, politically unstable society, the legal and philosophical battle between *ahl al-hadith* ('traditionalists') and *ahl al-ra'y* ('rationalists') epitomised the diversity of opinions, legal analytics and hermeneutics. With the ambiguous Qur'anic narrative on sexuality and gender, the 'rationalist' interpretations may have led to an Islamic law radically different from its much later heteronormative imaginations. But the 'traditionalist' current prevailed, and with it, the *hadith* literature of varying veracity and political motivations, which generally gave rise to a negative legal discourse on sexual and gender diversity. This discourse, however, did not permeate and shape *all* societal and legal sectors. On the contrary, it was but one of the general ways in which the early Muslim *umma* and its legists were able and willing to see the Muslim lifeworlds and their intrinsic laws.

In the 'classical' period of Islamic law, the continuous plurality of juridical opinions (*ikhtilaf*) on sexual and gender diversity corresponded, in some ways, to the general social attitude that such matters were mostly *private*, that is, within the purview of one's personal relationship with God, and therefore protected from the intrusion of the law and the State. Consequently, as my analysis of the Seljuk society has shown, same-sex sexual acts were not tried and punished *at all*, neither judicially nor extra-judicially. A dominant Hanafi stream of the *fuqaha'* concluded, in fact, that *liwat*, whilst reprehensible, was *de jure* unpunishable in this world, and potentially permissible in the hereafter. Other schools of jurisprudence disagreed, but still made this offence *de facto* unpunishable, due to the high evidential requirements.

In the 'post-classical' era, there emerged imperial Muslim societies in which new forms of 'one-generation nobility', kinship, sociality, sexuality and gender relations occurred, epitomised in the 'Mamluk phenomenon', in *devşirme* and in the elevated social and political roles of the *khuddam/aghawat*. Islamic law, in its theoretical and practical as well as 'formal' and 'informal' emanations, became closer to the State than ever before, so much so that sexual and gender 'transgressions' were thenceforth, at least in the Ottoman example, to be defined and punished by sultanic law, although still adjudicated upon by the *quda'*. But even the pervasive Ottoman *kanun*, with their detailed catalogues of sexual offences and significantly lowered evidential requirements, did not make the trials for such crimes any more frequent at now improved and ubiquitous Ottoman courts. If anything, they 'fiscalised' sexual and gender 'transgressions' along with other offences, which effectively meant that *zina*, for example, was liable to a fine, rather than to more drastic *hadd* punishment. Meanwhile, the class-divided society negotiated and developed its sexual and gender relations accordingly, with the upper-class' gender and sexual diversity pragmatically employed at the service of central government. The *fuqaha'* made no effort to oppose such policies; what is more, they made them legally and theologically justifiable, as in the case of Ibn Taymiyya's doctrine of *siyasa shar'iyya*. If something was still 'unclear' or 'contestable' from their point of view, such as the phenomenon of 'khadimness', the jurists preferred to disregard it or couch it in its *artful* vocabulary,[395] rather than to openly produce an opposing account.

When the European nation state system replaced the old Muslim polities, Islamic law was rather forcefully 'entexted'[396] and turned into *modern* political manifestos *par excellence*. I have argued that this move, alongside the Islamic modernist ideology of 'progress' that 'relegated the scientific study of Islamic legal history to second-class status in legal scholarship',[397] represents a departure so radical that it ultimately renders the entire domain of Islamic law a nonentity. Neither 'modern' nor 'national' Islamic law can be imagined *ex nihilo*, and even less so from the European Enlightenment's standpoint or colonial legal hybridis-ations. Islamic law of today and, even more crucially, of tomorrow, needs to critically reconnect with its pluralist past, and through that, with its variegated sexual and gender subjectivities. Islamic feminism and Muslim sexual/gender-pluralist hermeneutics offer one such possibility, thereby promising a fruitful continuation of Islamic legal tradition.

Throughout the centuries, a vivid sexual and gender diversity has been an intrinsic element of Muslim social and legal ethos. While some specific acts – rather than orientations, proclivities and subjectivities – may have been frowned upon and discouraged by (patriarchal) Muslim jurists, there can be no doubt that Islamic law – as a *discursive practice* constitutive, at least, of the triad of the law 'as it ought to be', the 'law as applied' and the 'bargaining in the shadow of the law' – has never sought to infringe upon one's (Muslim) *self*, including its sexual and gender dimensions. It is upon this vital historical fact that sexually diverse and gender-variant Muslims can firmly (re-)build their relationship with Islamic law.

CHAPTER 4

MUSLIM SEXUAL AND GENDER DIVERSITY IN CONTEMPORARY PAKISTAN

No visit to Lahore, an ancient Punjabi city often dubbed the cultural capital of Pakistan, can ever be complete without the stroll through its magnificent citadel, a gem of Mughal architecture in its 'classical age'. Inside, the controversial emperor, Akbar the Great (r. 1556–1605 CE), who gave it its existing base structure, would make a daily public appearance at the balcony (*jharoka*) of the public hall (*Diwan-i 'Amm*) and discuss law, statecraft and philosophy with his Muslim, Hindu and Christian protégés. Akbar was eager to learn and to thoroughly improve the state of his dominions. From these learned conversations, substantive reforms sprang forth, giving the Islamic legal tradition of the Indian subcontinent its idiosyncratic contours. When Akbar would get weary of worldly affairs, he would retreat to the citadel's more private quarters, which included a zenana (women's harem), guarded by *khwajasara*.[1] The Mughals are long gone, but cultural memory never doth run smooth: zenana and *khwajasara* are today gender-variant subjectivities. Many of them live, ironically, just *outside* the citadel, in the inner city's infamous Heera Mandi ('Diamond Market') neighbourhood. But those few hundred metres, which separate *Diwan-i 'Amm*, in its marble glory, and Heera Mandi, a red-light district, are as difficult a journey as in olden times. The roadblocks abound: of caste and its afterlives, of law and its empires, of modernity and its discontents, of an Indic and Muslim selfhood unintelligible to the burgeoning capitalist markets of desire. What follows is but an attempt to walk that perilous walk.

Through a critical ethnographic account of law and society in Pakistan, this chapter seeks to understand how sexually diverse and gender-variant Muslims navigate the high seas of human rights law and Islamic law in a Muslim-majority postcolony, which prides itself on being an 'Islamic republic'. My focal point is the Pakistani province of Punjab, especially its capital, Lahore, in which the bulk of my conversations and observations took place, mostly in 2011 CE. Although many of my interlocutors were from and lived in other parts of the country, the specific *ethnoscape*[2] of this brief case study is predominantly a Punjabi one. But the story of Punjab, as we shall see, is in many ways the story of Pakistan *tout court*, as well as it is, paradoxically perhaps, a paradigm strikingly similar to that of Bosnia and Herzegovina, the country – and ethnoscape – in which I grew up. The field, in other words, seemed to me strangely *familiar* in many respects, and no doubt the *feeling* was mutual for a number of my respondents. However, it also *felt* a world apart from the Lahore I first encountered, some ten years before. Punjab, by and large, continues to be the litmus paper of Pakistani social and political affairs: a phenomenon both beneficial and deeply detrimental for its populace.

My interlocutors on this journey were primarily individuals and families – of *various* types – whose selfhoods transgress the heteronormative codes of human subjectivity; I interviewed, however, also a number of 'others' – lawyers, judges, civil society activists and academic researchers – who were directly involved in (re)shaping and (re)framing their lifeworlds. In these conversations, the law of the everyday – its manifold discourses and social conditionality – came to be just as important as abstract legal reforms. A legal Realist landscape, thus, almost gratuitously, *presented itself*, thereby providing this research project – inclusive of historical explorations pursued in the two preceding chapters – a much-needed *local* contemporary context. But, as such, it necessarily relies on the specific social and legal history of the subcontinent *as well*, preserved through the mnemonic conduits of various kinds and forms. My interlocutors' self-perceptions and narratives are, thus, interspersed with observations from the literature, so as to produce a critical account of the phenomena hereby explored. The researcher is not a 'mere' spectator, although observation is the key.

The conversations featured in this chapter have originally been led in Punjabi, Urdu, Khwajasara Farsi[3] and English, either directly or via an interpreter. These languages *as such* – their class/caste (subliminal and overt) effects, interrelatedness and mutual intelligibility – form an important subtheme of this inquiry. The names of my interlocutors, where mentioned, are either real or pseudonyms, as per their personal request. The 'real' in present context, though, can be a somewhat elusive concept. By way of example, one of the respondents' *khwajasara* name is Chandhi, while her street name is Shazia. Neither of those is the name which she goes by in her natal family, nor the name given to her at birth. She has not renounced any of them (i.e. they are all 'real' to her): they are, quite simply, *situational*. Furthermore, what could be termed the politics of anonymity seems to be a patently class-specific endeavour, which is why the great majority of the non-governmental organisations I have been in touch with are *not* mentioned by their names. My interlocutors' self-perceptions are rigorously respected throughout: they are described *only* by terms and by personal pronouns they attribute to themselves; neither gender nor an identity marker is ever arbitrarily deployed. Their identity politics, or the lack thereof, remain a fluid but increasingly turbulent terrain, conductive of the recent tectonic social, economic and political perturbations on a larger scale.

More than anything else, the following pages represent an attempt to reassess and re-establish the primacy of vernacular knowledge, as a prerogative of any critical project.[4] For it is but in the circuits of a specific *locale* – in its historical, social and political *placedness* – that a legal narrative, of whichever geographical or temporal scale and proportion, can ever hope to attain its *material* form; its realisation. Neither Islamic nor international human rights law can *exist* today, in Pakistan or elsewhere, *unless* they make sense – or are translatable and intelligible – in vernacular knowledge systems. And it is in such systems that they will encounter, and benefit from, their most apposite critique.

What are, then, the seas of international human rights law and Islamic law like, when viewed from a Pakistani vessel? Is there a barrier (*barzakh*) between them, like in the famous Qur'anic tale,[5] so that they do not mix when they meet? Moreover, who are their gender-variant and sexually diverse navigators? In order to address these queries, the present chapter is divided into five thematic sections. First comes an introduction to Pakistani – and Punjabi – law and society. It is followed by a note on contemporary Muslim organising around sexuality and gender, and on subjectivities that may or may not have something to do with it. Then, what I call the *khwajasara* tropes – a register of social, political, religious and gender/sexual discursive practices – are given a closer look, only to reveal an intricate web of human selfhood, which defies any simplistic identitary script and engages creatively with the Pakistani/Punjabi social, religious and legal landscape. Fourth, various – mostly class-stratified – circuits of knowledge and subjectivity formation are engaged, as pertaining to the particular forms of Muslim sexual and gender diversity that I encountered during my fieldwork. Finally, a series of specific questions relating to municipal and international law – including the domains of Islamic law and human rights – are addressed, providing a rationale for the concluding remarks.

Law and Society in Pakistan and Punjab

Relentlessly reiterated, the foremost image of Pakistan in the foreign media and political analyses is that of a society in perpetual crisis, dangerous and unpredictable, evermore approaching its seemingly inescapable demise. An American policy maker thus warns his concerned readership: 'Pakistan was born in great violence, and it is becoming a more violent place. Partition in 1947 [CE] led to hundreds of thousands of deaths and millions of refugees. Now Pakistan is wracked by terrorist bombings, assassinations, and even firefights in its major cities'.[6] A compatriot of his, and author of numerous books on the subject, could not agree more:

> It [Pakistan] has become a violent state, with attacks on its core institutions, notably the police, the army, and the Inter-Services Intelligence Directorate, and assassinations of Benazir Bhutto [in December 2007 CE], its most important politician; Salmaan Taseer [in January 2011 CE], a serving governor; and Shahbaz Bhatti [in March 2011 CE], the only Christian minister in the Cabinet. Moreover, Pakistan has the dubious distinction of being the most unsafe country in the world for journalists and diplomats.[7]

The same mantra is repeated in academic accounts, in which we are reminded, for example, that '[s]ince September 11, 2001 [CE], Pakistan has emerged as a pivotal front in the U.S. war on terrorism' and that, therefore, the country's 'very political destiny is distorted by the unfolding global struggle against al-Qaeda and other militants, such as the Taliban, who have found a home in Pakistan'.[8] The US drone raids and, most significantly, the killing of Osama bin Laden on 2 May 2011 CE in Abbottabad, a city not far from Islamabad, are thus seen as 'necessary' interventions into the affairs of a volatile, violent state, on the brink of failure.[9] Even Louise Brown, a long time researcher of Heera Mandi, tells us of her post-September 11 visit to Lahore: 'This is not the Pakistan I know [...]. I [...] feel apprehensive. I'm frightened of big men in Pathani-style turbans, and even more scared of small men in Pathani-style turbans. I have an unfounded but hard-to-shake feeling that small, thin ones are the angriest'.[10]

To be sure, an eerie atmosphere has, indeed, descended on Lahore. The foreigners were nowhere to be seen; instead, the army checkpoints have mushroomed along the busy city streets in what some of my interlocutors described as 'the parade of (false) military efficiency'. My documents were regularly checked by security officers of various types, but since they did not happen to read Bosnian (I did not carry my passport with me), they would simply gloss over my ID card and return it to me hastily. Everyone seemed to have some kind of weapon on them and bombings, violent demonstrations and shootings were commonplace. But that was just one piece of the intricate Pakistani/Punjabi mosaic of daily life. Far from the Armageddon imminent in the prognoses of non-Pakistani analysts, Lahore and its inhabitants seemed to have absorbed the anxieties over 'weak state', home-grown terrorism and the US interventionism into a plethora of everyday relations and discourses. A young Muslim woman who headed an underground middle-class collective of 'queer people in Lahore' – as she called them – explained this to me: 'Our understanding of violence and our tolerance for violence is very, very different from that in other places'. But how do the law and politics fit into this precarious frame?

Pakistan[11] emerged on the world map of nation states in 1947 CE, following the long political battle of its founder, Muhammad Ali Jinnah (1876–1948 CE), 'to bring about Islamic renaissance',[12] which for him meant that the Indian Muslims and Hindus should part ways in search of their respective post-colonial destinies:

The dramatic events surrounding India's independence from British colonial rule in 1947 [CE], followed by its partition along imagined religious lines, forming separate Muslim and Hindu entities, resulted in the formation of a Muslim-majority state named Pakistan [...]. The new state was curiously composed of two territorial units – East Pakistan (now Bangladesh) and West Pakistan (now Pakistan) – physically separated by over 1,000 miles [...]. Pakistan was envisaged by its founders as a Muslim democracy, wherein religion was the key 'cohesive factor' among culturally and politically variant Muslim groups. A liberal bourgeois ideology, with largely symbolic Muslim elements, was thus developed to galvanise the support of various elements within Muslim communities, as well as to appeal, to some extent, to both Indian and British political establishments. Facing continuous and grave challenges – first, an open-ended and seemingly insolvable armed conflict with India over the Kashmir border; and then, a civil war that led to the partition of its east wing, which became, in 1971 [CE], a new independent state called Bangladesh – Pakistani ruling elites, both civilian and military, relied on the power of a strong centralised state.[13]

Except that the State was never quite 'strong'. Jinnah, Pakistan's foremost leader, whose authority kept together various political factions, died little more than a year after independence. His sudden death spurred fierce 'battles over succession that [...] roiled the country. As the fractious divisions grew more visible and seemingly intractable, a senior military officer, General Mohammed Ayub Khan, seized power in a coup a decade after independence'.[14]

Repeating the same scenario, the military, in fact, have ruled for 33 years since the country came into existence (1958–71, 1977–88 and 1999–2008 CE). And, as with every polity governed by martial law, the periods of army rule have been fraught with drastic displays of firepower, absolutism and less-than-fortunate theopolitical alliances. General Muhammad Zia-ul-Haq (r. 1977–88 CE), for example, who sought to restyle himself as a (right wing) Muslim reformer, imposed, through presidential ordinances, his own version of *hudud* (*hudood*) criminal laws[15] and founded the Federal Shariat Court.[16] But, when this court demanded, in its famous *Bakhsh* case,[17] that stoning to death (*rajm*) be

removed from his ordinance on *zina*, General Zia replaced all but one –
the only dissenting vote in the *Bakhsh* case – of the court's judges.
Unsurprisingly, the new court reversed the previous decision and found
that *rajm* did not run contrary to the 'Injunctions of Islam'.[18] In
another example, General Pervez Musharraf (r. 1999–2008 CE)
suspended, in 2007 CE, the chief justice of the Supreme Court of
Pakistan,[19] Iftikhar Muhammad Chaudhry. This sheer display of
dictatorial might gave rise to the 'Lawyers' Movement', which
eventually led to Musharraf's downfall and the reinstitution of
Chaudhry and all other previously deposed judges, on 21 March
2009 CE, by the new civilian president, Asif Ali Zardari (r. 2008–
13 CE). These dramatic events have led to an unprecedentedly
independent position of the Supreme Court, especially from the then
executive authorities in Pakistan.

Formal Judicial System of Pakistan
The judicial system of Pakistan is derived from English common law –
its quintessential colonial bequest – and is formally based on the much-
amended Constitution of 1973 CE.[20] Speaking to me in 2011 CE, a judge
of the Supreme Court of Pakistan underlined the discrepancy between
this system and its constituencies:

> We have sixty-four years of the so-called post-independence
> history. And yet, the first ever constitutional judgment *in Urdu*
> was decided only six months ago. The terminology, the jargon, the
> concepts [. . .] – it's all in English. The [British] Empire never left.
> So, where is the process to reach out to the community? This is,
> really, a fundamental issue for our judiciary. Nobody reads our
> judgments in English. Even those 1% of the population who are
> familiar with the language don't understand this *legal* English.
> And, what about those 99% who don't understand it at all?

Be that as it may, the judicial elites seem little concerned with the
exclusionary aspects of their work. Rather, the legal vernacular *tout court*
is heavily Anglicised, and its users are expected to appreciate it *as such*.[21]
To conceal this blatant colonial legacy, discursive 'ornamentations' from
classical Sunni *fiqh* are also sometimes deployed, as well as hybrid phrases
such as 'Injunctions of Islam'. But those are by no means in balance with

the ubiquitous presence of a common law legal structure and, even more importantly, the antiquated colonial legislation.[22] As a chief token of General Zia's 'Islamisation' of the law, the Federal Shariat Court operates as a special court outside the formal judicial hierarchy,[23] with 'a mandate to review the validity of Pakistani laws in accordance with the "Injunctions of Islam"', either *suo motu* (on its own motion) or in response to a citizens "petition".[24] But, importantly, the Constitution, Muslim personal law and procedural laws are *not* under its jurisdiction[25] and it is bound by the Supreme Court's interpretation of any question of law.[26]

Constitutional Law: Fundamental Rights and Case 63/09

The incumbent Constitution of 1973 CE establishes Pakistan as an 'Islamic' republic and 'makes the lofty declaration that all the existing laws should be brought into conformity with the "Injunctions of Islam" and no new law should depart from such course either'.[27] However, the entire Chapter 1 of the Constitution is also dedicated to what it terms 'Fundamental Rights', including: security of person (§9); safeguards as to arrest and detention (§10); right to fair trial (§10(A)); prohibition of slavery and forced labour (§11); right to privacy (§14(1)); freedom from torture (§14(2)); freedom of assembly (§16); freedom of association (§17); freedom of speech and expression (§19); freedom of religion (§§20–22); property rights (§24); equality of citizens (§25; §25(2) reads: 'There shall be no discrimination on the basis of sex'); right to education (§25(A)); various safeguards against discrimination in services (§27) and in respect of access to public places (§26); as well as right to preservation of language, script and culture (§28). Section 8(1) boldly states: 'Any law, or any custom or usage having the force of law, in so far as it is inconsistent with the rights conferred by this Chapter, shall, to the extent of such inconsistency, be void'. How, then, are the unspecified 'Injunctions of Islam' interpreted in relation to the constitutional obligation to respect a wide range of 'fundamental rights'?

The Supreme Court judge I interviewed in Lahore was of the opinion that 'human rights sell' in his court, the proof of which he found in 'hundreds of letters of complaints [petitions] that are received in the human rights division' of the court. 'People approach the Supreme Court because they don't get their redress anywhere else', he said; 'although, I do realise that it will take some time for the things to get on the executive side, because, there is a degree of – perhaps I should term it – the absence of sensitivity'. Nevertheless, he averred, 'there have been instances where the common societal merits have very meaningfully been altered by the combination of the law and gender'. Indeed, Pakistani feminist organisations and lawyers have constantly used Section 25(2) of the Constitution in human rights litigation at the Supreme Court.[28] But, although it explicitly outlaws 'discrimination on the basis of sex', this section has not yet provided for any domestic sexual orientation litigation. The prevalent view amongst the potential beneficiaries of such litigation is that it would not succeed; not so much because of the antiquated[29] colonial Section 377 of the Penal Code 1860 – which is the only existing piece of legislation in Pakistan that criminalises (certain) same-sex sexual acts – but because it would be deemed 'repugnant to the Injunctions of Islam'. This is despite the fact that no Pakistani law specifically addressing its Muslim population – including the infamous Offence of Zina (Enforcement of Hudood) Ordinance 1979 – mentions or is implicitly related to *liwat* or any similar transgression.[30] In contrast, the Supreme Court litigation on behalf of *khwajasara* – a Pakistani gender-variant subjectivity – has recently yielded some rather surprising results.

In 2009 CE, shortly after his reinstatement as the chief justice of the Supreme Court of Pakistan, Iftikhar Muhammad Chaudhry decided, *suo motu*, the Human Rights Constitutional Petition 63/2009 (hereinafter 'Case 63/09')[31] in favour of the applications, thereby granting the *khwajasara* community a series of fundamental rights. Dr Muhammad Aslam Khaki, a lawyer for *khwajasara*, who were represented by Bobby, also known as Almas Shah, argued the case from what he calls 'an Islamic perspective',[32] invoking the concepts of classical *fuqaha'* such as *khuntha mushkil* (people of 'intractable' sex/gender).[33] Khaki described a variety of discriminatory practices against these *citizens of Pakistan*, which run contrary to both constitutional and Islamic law. He told me that, 'in the beginning, even some judges smiled in what seemed to be a farcical case, because that is how these people are often seen – as comediennes. But when I spoke of gruesome violations of their rights, everyone became very serious'. As a result of the Chief Justice's decision, *khwajasara* were, *inter alia*: (a) given a 'third gender/sex' status, which was to appear on all of their official documents, including the ID cards; (b) given the right to vote as *khwajasara* and to contest elections; (c) guaranteed a series of (previously denied) inheritance and property rights; (d) assured protection against abuse by the police and other organs of the State; and (e) promised substantial help in social and health care, as well as in education and employment, to be provided by various provincial governmental agencies. The implementation process of these provisions included a series of orders, issued by the Chief Justice, mainly as a critique of various provincial authorities who failed to adopt a proactive approach to the fundamental rights and welfare of *khwajasara*. In addition, some of the leading *khwajasara* activists, such as Bindiya Rana, whom I interviewed in September 2011 CE, ensured through subsequent petitions to the Supreme Court that one need not be medically examined in order to be recognised as *khwajasara*, for the purposes of the benefits guaranteed by the Case 63/06 decision. Overall, the case, on its outset, looks like a prime example of a successful marriage of Islamic law and human rights law at the highest domestic judicial level. But, is it entirely so?

To begin with, in Case 63/09 as well as in the subsequent judicial orders, *khwajasara* are called a variety of names – such as 'unix', 'eunuchs' and 'she-males' – that must have been thought to be either appealing to the court's audience or an expression of the still-incomplete search for political identity of this subjectivity.[34] They are, also, described as having 'gender disorder in their bodies',[35] which makes them 'suffer throughout their life'.[36] Because of societal oppression, 'the she-males are compelled to live an immoral life including offering themselves for dancing etc';[37] 'there are such miserable stories about she-males, which cannot be explained in open Court'.[38] Hence, the State has to 'provide maintenance to them on account of disability'.[39] After all, '[t]hey are creatures of Allah Almighty, therefore, their social life is to be respected'.[40] 'Needless to observe that eunuchs in their own rights are citizens of this country and subject to the Constitution of the Islamic Republic of Pakistan';[41] therefore, 'their rights, obligations including right to life and dignity are equally protected. Thus no discrimination, for any reason, is possible against them as far as their rights and obligations are concerned'.[42] The rights of *khwajasara* are in these documents closely related to their perceived gender/sexual deficiency and the misery associated with it.[43] As God's creatures and the citizens of Pakistan, they are to be saved from immorality, although their social life is deserving of respect. These contradictory overtones suggest that the citizens' 'fundamental rights' go hand in hand with their 'fundamental obligations' (indeed, they are referred to as 'rights, obligations'); state protection is guaranteed only to moral citizens, those whose gender difference is, quite simply, a form of 'disability'. Human rights sell in the Supreme Court of Pakistan, but for a hefty price.

The Punjabi Paradigm: Social as Legal Ethos

Fortunately for *khwajasara* and other subjectivities outside the societal mainstream, Pakistan's legal landscape extends well beyond the realm of formal law. If one is to understand how sexual and gender diversity is negotiated in everyday contexts – that is, by and large, 'in the shadow of the law'[44] – the province of Five Rivers (Persian: *panj* – 'five'; *ab* – 'water'; i.e. Punjab), all five of which remained on the Pakistani side of the border with India, offers an intriguing example.

Following a troublesome century of British colonial rule (1849– 1947 CE), Punjab was partitioned between India and Pakistan: 'An estimated twelve million refugees were on the move in Punjab in the summer of 1947 [CE], Muslims moving westward to Pakistan and Sikhs and Hindus moving eastward to India'.[45] Most of the hundreds of thousands of people who died in partition violence 'were killed in the Punjab, and most of the killing took place over the course of only a few weeks'.[46] These massacres were only the final step of the *communalisation* – under colonial rule – of formal political arenas for the Sikhs, Hindus, Muslims and, increasingly, Christians of the Punjab, which resulted in the late-nineteenth-century CE rise of 'religious-reform organizations that produced new, modern, and increasingly communal religious identities'.[47] These modernist reforms – coterminous with *nationalist* developments elsewhere, *especially* in Bosnia[48] – pitted the different religious communities against each other and thus created a highly volatile social and political environment. Such a society was, arguably, more easily controlled by a relatively minuscule colonial elite, but it was bound to explode in the wake of a large-scale political transformation. The partition of Punjab was, thus, a paradigm for the partition of 'British' India into independent Pakistan and India, as well as for the subsequent fate of its displaced populations.

Prior to these dramatic events, however, the landscapes of cultural memory associated with the Mughal Empire[49] were probably most vividly preserved precisely in Punjab, which was one of its important centres. But the Mughal customs and lifeworlds, still detectable in the customs and lifeworlds of the Punjabis (of various creeds), did not preclude development of the rich Punjabi vernacular culture and system of knowledge. For instance, the Punjabi *qisse* (epic-romances; sing. *qissa*) 'served as both high literature and popular entertainment, and were widely accessible due to their being composed in a vernacular language and disseminated through oral performance and printed media'.[50] Some of the greatest *qissa* authors, such as Waris Shah (1722–98 CE) and Bulleh Shah (1692–1758 CE), have firmly remained the source of vernacular wisdom in Punjab, even though, in the case of the latter poet, 'the most prominent in his universal approach is his love for men'.[51] In fact, gender and sexual diversity, evoked as both mystical and sensual experience in such literary works, has survived as an integral part of the Punjabi cultural memory and, therefore, as a vernacular *sense of being*. During my research in Punjab, I was told, repeatedly, by people of various social and educational backgrounds, that I 'cannot study those things *here* without going back *at least* to Bulleh Shah'. On my insistence that I was *primarily* interested in legal narratives on sexual and gender plurality, they would convincingly argue that classical Punjabi literature has much to do with how law is *understood* and applied in their society. For instance, the Supreme Court judge I interviewed, himself an expert in the Punjabi verse, locates the vernacular wisdom, including wisdom about law, in the fast-disappearing Punjabi *oral tradition*, as a form of 'illiterate' education:

> If you meet with any senior citizen here, aged 65 or above, they will be able to discuss with you any topic, including law, with references to the leading lights of our tradition. I often converse with one such person. And, when I ask him, how much had he studied, he answers, 'I'm illiterate'. What he means is that he hasn't had any formal schooling, and yet he has been educated in *these* things and he has a *much* more intelligent look into the issues than our very erudite legal scholars and judges. He is still alive and we still meet. Just out of sheer interest, I provoke a subject and he gives me some very sound opinions. Just to illustrate, one day I mentioned to him this loud *azan* [Arabic: *adhan*; the Muslim call for prayer], which is very disturbing. It was meant to be serene and in tune, you know; not like this. He immediately *explained* to me that this is something which is forbidden in Islamic law, because it

causes so much distress, and then he quoted Bulleh Shah. Very apt. Very, very apt. And then he cited, of all things, the *Muqaddima* of Ibn Khaldun. And, he says, 'I'm illiterate'. He knows Waris Shah – pages and pages of Waris Shah – by heart. That used to be our traditional education, our wisdom, which has now almost disappeared.

Whilst the circuits of vernacular knowledge slowly make their way into formal law,[52] the still-existent alternative dispute resolution mechanisms – such as that of *panchayat* – remain important communal sites where law and justice are discussed, and meted out, *in defiance* of the hybrid colonial-theopolitical legal culture. 'There is a saying in the Punjab', the Supreme Court judge told me quite proudly, 'that the person, the witness, who speaks the truth in court and lies in a *panchayat* is not the son of his father. So, that's the level of resistance. You don't speak the truth in court and you don't tell lies in the *panchayat*'. I asked him about his somewhat paradoxical position as a judge from the *vernacular* perspective. 'Of course', he replied, 'I'm in the position where I have to abide by all these laws: they are the laws of the land. That *is* what I'm doing. But whenever there is an opportunity, within the Supreme Court or elsewhere, I do come up with alternatives'. In a similar manner, Adeel, a married working-class member of the conservative Sufi movement *Minhaj-ul-Qur'an*,[53] who was *also* in a same-sex relationship, told me how the stories of the Punjabi Sufi male lovers from pre-colonial times, who were *also* accomplished literati and Muslim scholars, have helped him and his many friends to negotiate the difficult questions of law, spirituality and sexuality from a non-mainstream perspective. What is more, these vernacular insurrectionary circuits of knowledge seem to persistently challenge *both* sides of the formal law coin in Pakistan: the British colonial and the modern nation state 'Islamic' law. As such, they are deeply embedded in the Pakistani/Punjabi experience of sexual and gender diversity, and they help it thrive, against all the odds.

Sexually Diverse and Gender-Variant Muslims: Toward *un Pèlerinage Inclusif*

This seems to be an exciting time for sexually diverse and gender-variant Muslims around the world. The number of their community-based organisations is steadily increasing,[54] whilst their underground networks persist despite societal – and, often, governmental – oppression. A group of 'musulmans inclusifs, progressistes, réformistes, partisans d'une représentation de l'islam apaisée, égalitaire et non sexiste',[55] has recently completed 'un pèlerinage inclusif avec l'imam Amina Wadud, à la Mecque et Médinah'.[56] They regarded this trip as an extraordinarily important new chapter in their lives as Muslims. The group, led by a famous female imam, tried to pray together in gender-mixed rows, especially while in Mecca, eliciting often a violent response by the police and other pilgrims.[57] Being on a *pèlerinage inclusif*, these Muslims – of various cultural, gender/sexual and political backgrounds – tried to reach out to a broader *umma*; they were *there* primarily *as Muslims*. But they were frowned upon (by *some* other Muslims) nonetheless, for being *different* Muslims than those in the majority.

The dynamics of inclusion and exclusion in relation to the larger *umma* remain the central preoccupation of the collectives of sexually diverse and gender-variant Muslims *everywhere*. I was told by Ayesha, an *ad hoc* prayer-leader of one such collective in Lahore, that the point was 'not to make the spectacle out of it'. Rather, 'the purpose is that you feel that, spiritually, you are fine. In the community of God, it's okay'. And that community, or rather the lack thereof, starts with one's natal family.[58] Conversely, as we shall see, if one's sociality includes proclivities and practices that the society at large finds unacceptable, new forms of kinship and community will be sought, and formed, in spite of one's social or economic status. And, within them, various circuits of knowledge and subjectivity will have been negotiated and developed, which may or may not have to do with similar groupings *elsewhere*. So, although their faith and hieropraxis, or even their ethnoscape, may be of a very similar kind, such Muslim collectives will not necessarily be composed of subjectivities that are comparable or in conversation with each other. That is because of a variety of economic, social, political, linguistic and historical connotations, which may play a decisive role in one's self-definition *sui generis*, including one's self-understanding and experience of gender and sexuality.

In Lahore – as well as throughout Punjab and Pakistan – Muslim sexually diverse and/or gender-variant subjectivities *do not* form a single, larger community (or a cluster of communities), nor do they rely on any singular identitary taxonomy. Instead, there are *historically-* and *class-specific* subjectivities, each in a flux of social renegotiation to be sure, which may here and there have formed loose political alliances, but which are *still* reliant on *separate* systems of knowledge and sociality. Their self-understanding, accordingly, cannot be subsumed under any globalised form of episteme – including *queer* and *LGBT* – even though they are explored, and used, in *certain* class-based Pakistani/ Punjabi circuits.

Their relationship with the larger *umma* is similarly complex. *Khwajasara* and *zenana* subjectivities, for example, consider certain spiritual practices to be a vital part of their selfhood. But those practices do not necessarily belong to a *single* religious community. In the pluralist context of the Indian subcontinent, they can be simultaneously performed by nominally Muslim, Hindu, Sikh, Christian and various other communities. In Indic cultures, this plurality is often perceived as a source of one's creative and vibrant spirituality, but it can also become an exclusionary mechanism, especially when – as in Punjab – nominal religious identities carry profound historical and class/caste connotations.

During my fieldwork in Punjab, I began to explore these conundrums by turning, first, to those subjectivities that – in name and in praxis – exist, or claim to have existed, for centuries, having shaped and negotiated their ethnoscape through numerous productive social and legal relations. This was *not* to designate them as the exclusive 'indigenous' informants of this study, but in order to interrogate a broader cultural and historical context. I then approached more recent phenomena in the Pakistani/Punjabi subjectivity formation by interacting with groups and individuals with a vested interest in sexual/gender diversity, trying, wherever and whenever possible, to navigate across the deep societal divide along the – *primarily* – class/ caste fault lines. It is, hence, in this order that my ethnographic research is presented on the following pages. It does not attempt to provide a totalistic view of Muslim sexually diverse and gender-variant subjectivities in Pakistan or even in Punjab, nor do their collective and individual narratives offer a singular vision of how burning questions about law, human rights and religion should be addressed *in the vernacular*. Rather, what follows is a look through the kaleidoscope of human subjective formations, in search for the ways in which Islamic law and international human rights law intersect in a contemporary locality.

The *Khwajasara* Tropes*

'Here in Pakistan, we say *khwajasara*. It's a more respectful term than the others', says Kajol, an office assistant in her mid-twenties. 'We become *khwajasara* when a spirit – called *murid* – enters us'. She touches her chest and smiles placidly. 'Once *murid* is within oneself, one feels very special about oneself and then one can consider oneself *khwajasara*'. The term *khwajasara* has recently been reclaimed by the Pakistani gender-variant subjectivity that is in the rest of the subcontinent still designated as *hijra* (pl. *hijre*).[59] In Punjab, specifically, *khwajasara* are also known as *khusre* (sing. *khusra*). None of these terms is, however, considered to invoke much respect (*izzat*) from the larger society, which *khwajasara* – as a subjectivity and as a political and social movement – now publicly beseech.

Although sexual and gender-variance had been a salient feature of Indic cosmology and sociality for a great many centuries,[60] in Pakistan/ Punjab it is most commonly associated with 'Mughal times' (*Mughalan da wela*). The (chief) guardians of the zenana (women's harem) at the Mughal imperial court were known by their Persian title – *khwajasara*.[61] Most of them were male-born castrated subjectivities. It is, however, evident from the historical sources that *khwajasara* were also a subjectivity engaged in a plethora of other professions,[62] and that they were often of Abyssinian origin (*habshi* or *habashi*). Across the Muslim sultanates in the Indian subcontinent, the *habshi* wielded a great deal of power, and some *khwajasara* from this ethno-political grouping even managed to seize the throne.[63] However, the steady decline of the Mughal Empire, which began around 1757/1170 CE/AH with an ever-increasing influence of the British colonisers, came to be the swan song for the zenana culture and *khwajasara* dignitaries. Some 100 years later, for reasons still not entirely clear to historians, the zenana was no longer just a harem, or a secluded place for female inhabitants in general, but also a subject position aetiologically linked to *hijre* and *khwajasara*, the latter of which were now mostly known as *khojay* (sing. *khoja*).[64] Under British rule, all of these gender-variant subjectivities were primarily classified, and controlled, in accordance with their presupposed 'morality' and social status.

In 1870 CE, Syud Ahmed Khan Bahadur, an Indian politician and a 'native informant' to the British colonial authorities, explained the distinction between *khojay* (*khwajasara*), *hijre* and *zenana* in the following terms. *Khojay* or '*khaja sarais*', as he also calls them, 'act as custodians of the zenanas of the Indian princes and noblemen; and as they are exclusively confined to their master's domicile, no opportunity is afforded them of outraging public decency by any immoralities'.[65] *Per contra*, those who are known as *hijre* (Bahadur calls them '*hijrahs*') 'earn a livelihood by dancing and singing in the public streets, an occupation which might be deemed excusable, did they not eke it out by giving themselves up to other abhorrent practices'.[66] Finally, *zenana* (he terms them '*zanana*') 'are eunuchs [*sic*] not by castrations, but whose impotence is caused by some defect of birth, by accident, or other natural causes. They mix and associate with those of the second class [i.e. with *hijre*], and imitate and view with them in their obscene and disgusting depravity'.[67] Consequently, the British authorities in India passed in 1871 CE the Criminal Tribes Act, which included, in Part 2, the category of 'eunuch' that was 'deemed to include all persons of the male sex who admit themselves, or on medical inspection clearly appear, to be impotent'.[68] The Act deprived the class of 'eunuch' of inheritance and property rights and subjected it to forced registration. This marked the beginning of the ultimately unsuccessful British campaign to do away with this class of 'abominable natives' altogether:

> the various [colonial] legislators, judges, and police officials did not want to end the *practice* in which the eunuchs [*sic*] were involved. Instead, they wanted to end the class itself. They used words such as 'eradicate', 'extinguish', 'extirpation', or, in words somewhat less active, 'die out'. This language points to a desire to eliminate the group, indicating a dislike of the group, rather than just the practices in which the class were depicted as engaging.[69]

The existing class and caste system was, however, not to be disturbed by this vicious campaign. While *hijre* and *zenana* were earmarked for elimination, *khojay* were to be exempt from criminalisation by virtue of their membership of upper-class households.[70]

By the beginning of the twentieth century CE, the terms *khojay*, *hijre* and *zenana* were used interchangeably for what came to be the lower-class gender-variant wanderers, of various faiths,[71] dressed in 'women's clothes'. The Censuses of 1891 and 1901 CE still described them as 'castrated men, [and] counted women in their ranks',[72] presumably as household members.[73] But, in society, these subjectivities were increasingly associated with 'habitual sodomy'.[74] In Punjab, for example, they also came to be known as *mukhannasat* ('the effeminate ones'; singular: *mukhannas*): 'the begging and sodomitical caste of Muslims'.[75] Some *hijre* would, thus, insist upon their asexuality and impotence, possibly in order to avoid being criminally charged for sodomy (under §377, Indian Penal Code 1870): 'We are broken vessels and fit for nothings; formerly we guarded the harems of kings – how could they admit us into the zanana if there was the least danger?'[76] Meanwhile, the academic interest and research in these subjectivities surged, unleashing onto them all the hefty sexological and cultural stereotypes of the day. Thus, in the various post-1950s CE studies, *hijre* were described as 'hermaphrodites',[77] 'transvestites',[78] 'passive homosexuals',[79] 'male prostitutes',[80] 'hermaphrodite prostitutes',[81] 'male-homosexual transvestites',[82] 'sex-perverted male[s], castrated or uncastrated',[83] 'sexo-aesthetic inverts coupled with homosexual habits',[84] 'inverts of the object choice',[85] 'abominable aberrations',[86] 'labelled deviants'[87] and, finally, as belonging 'neither to the category of men nor to that of women'.[88] This last imputation became, as of late, particularly popular, with academic studies discussing *hijre*'s 'third sex'[89] and/or 'third gender'.[90] It was, however, recently rebuffed as being insensitive of an 'Indian logic', which stipulates that,

> where X is hijra and A is male, we can postulate that
> X is A;
> X is not A;
> X is not non-A;
> X is both A and non-A; and
> X is neither A nor non-A;
> and likewise a similar set of possibilities is conjured by rendering A as female rather than male.[91]

If one applies the same formula to the contemporary distinctions between *hijra* and *zenana* subjectivities, whereby *zenana* can – and do – assume both the X and A positions, the equation becomes even more complex, thereby ultimately resisting being 'rationalised' into a 'computable' (sex/gender) category. Claire Pamment dubs this specific trope *hijraism* and describes it as 'the gift of heroically upsetting the tyranny of boundaries and the secure world of logos, offering a cultural frontier that disturbs the hegemonic designs of the established orders'.[92] 'This means', she told me, 'that they [*hijre*] subversively move their ways through the society'.[93] And, I am tempted to add, through academic studies, too.

Origins, Kinship and Sociality

Most of the Pakistani *hijra* and *zenana* collectives nowadays self-identify as *khwajasara*, and they often stress the high position their gender-variant ancestors used to have in the Mughal courts. Bindiya Rana, a foremost Sindh-based *khwajasara* social and political leader, summarised this historical narrative as follows:

> During the Mughal period, *khwajasara* were really valued in the society, because they used to teach manners to the young children, especially young girls. They also taught them about spirituality and about music and dance. They were very, very well respected during that time. They were especially sought after as teachers because they could teach both men and women, whereas a male teacher could only teach boys. They were also considered to be closer to God because they were a mixture of both genders. But with the subsequent social changes, *khwajasara* were less and less sought after and they eventually had to go and live amongst themselves. Before they used to live in the palaces; now, they were living in their own dwellings.[94]

Good manners, apparently, play an important role in *khwajasara* cultural memory.[95] But so do the social transformations instigated by British colonial rule:

> The changes started occurring once the Mughals were no longer in real power. Once the white men came to India, the powers of the Mughals were slowly finishing off. The Mughals were then forced to take customs of the white men, and to receive all sorts of orders from them. It also got worse and worse, as more and more technology came in and more and more people went abroad to receive education. By the time of India and Pakistan's partition,

khwajasara were only there to dance and sing at weddings. And that was it. They were no longer perceived as valuable for the society in any other way.[96]

In this account, the interconnected perils of colonialism, modernity and their reproduction as a form of non-vernacular *knowledge* are strikingly obvious. At the same time, despite the nationalist propaganda, a number of my interlocutors who perceived themselves as *khwajasara*[97] did not consider India as being *foreign* in any way.[98] On the contrary, they are productively connected to the Indian collectives similar to their own through shared spiritual, cultural, familial and political practices. And, as I was repeatedly told, that is also where *they are from*. The Punjabi *khwajasara*, unlike their Indian counterparts,[99] trace their origins in the story of Madayantī[100] or Mainandi,[101] an ancient Indian princess:

> It all started in India. It started with Mainandi. Mainandi was born *khwajasara*. A man came up to her and said, 'Mainandi, you are so graceful. Can I be like you?' She said, 'No! Please ask forgiveness from God! You cannot be *khwajasara*. You are *zenana*.' But he went to the field of sugarcanes and he sliced off one sugarcane. He sharpened it and, with it, he emasculated himself. Then he went back to Mainandi and said, 'Look, I'm like you now! Am I not *khwajasara*?' But Mainandi was so depressed that she asked God for forgiveness and to open the earth beneath her. So, a crack appeared beneath her feet and swallowed her.[102]

This narrative, supposedly originating in India,[103] is common amongst *khwajasara* in Lahore.[104] Two of its aspects are of particular importance: it serves to distinguish between *zenana* – described as *men* who hopelessly endeavour to 'imitate' *khwajasara* – and 'real' *khwajasara*, and it is connected with the ritual of emasculation (*nirban*; in India: *nirvan*). Neeli explained:

> The very first *khwajasara* in the whole world was Mainandi. We trace our origins through her [...]. When a *khwajasara* becomes *nirban*, she sometimes takes Mainandi's name. Because, once you become *nirban*, you also become very beautiful. So, whenever a *khwajasara* becomes *nirban*, she assimilates Mainandi

and becomes as beautiful as she was [. . .]. And, on the first night when a person becomes *nirban*, Mainandi appears before her and curses her. So, those *khwajasara* who become *nirban* in the name of Mainandi – and not all of us do – they burn a *diya* [an oil lamp; plural: *diyay*]; and they keep on burning *diyay* every day of their life, in the name of Mainandi.

A number of *khwajasara*, however, do not opt for *nirban*, whilst at least some *zenana* are known to undergo this ritual operation as well.[105] Hence, the boundaries between these subjectivities, where still existent, are those of *zat* ('caste', 'class', 'kinship group') rather than those of gender, sexual and spiritual experience.

The intimate social relations of those who self-identify as *khwajasara* or *zenana* are usually forged through four distinct forms of *familial life*: (1) the relations with their natal family; (2) the *guru/chela* ('master'/ 'apprentice') relationship; (3) the *ma'an/dhi* ('mother'/'daughter') relationship and (4) the relations with their *giriya* ('boyfriend', 'customer', 'male partner'). Let us briefly examine each of them.

Whether male-born or intersex, my gender-variant interlocutors[106] all strongly claim that they have been drawn to the *khwajasara* lifeworlds ever since their early childhood. This *call* is typically explained as a combination of biological,[107] behavioural[108] and circumstantial[109] traits, but it can also be a deeply spiritual experience. Kajol told me:

> It all started at a very young age. I've met someone who also had a *murid* inside them in a very spiritual way. We've respected each other because we've understood each other. It is like a herd of buffalos [*mujhan*]. A buffalo [*majh*] will not end up with the sheep or something. Somehow, a buffalo will always find and connect with another buffalo. [. . .] You know, God has made us this way. Even though people say it's wrong, and that we are doing something that we shouldn't, and sometimes even throw stones at us. Whatever they say, at the end of the day, God has made us. We are God's creatures. That is all.

In order to answer this call, one has to sever the bonds with one's natal family to some extent. In certain cases, this happens very early on,[110] in others, it is around the time one reaches puberty. My interlocutors all had to leave their parental homes, but they continued, apparently, to maintain a good relationship with their natal families, especially with their mothers and sisters. Upon entering a *khwajasara* household (*dera*; pl. *deray*), the young *chela* ('novice', 'apprentice'; pl. *chele*) chooses her *guru* (pl. *guru*), who is also *khwajasara*. '*Guru* provide for us', said Kajol. 'As long as we are good *chele*, they take care of us. This relationship is forged through the ritual, an initiation party [...]. Later in her life, the *chela* becomes a *guru* herself'. The *guru* are also the *chele* to other, higher (*bare* and *bare-bare*) *guru*. On top of the pyramid, some 15 very old *gurus*[111] exert control over the entire population of *khwajasara* in Pakistan.

The *khwajasara* lineage is carefully traced through the *guru/chela* form of kinship, and it is the responsibility of the *bare-bare guru* to keep such familial records in the safe place. As Bindiya Rana explained:

> I know, for instance, that my *guru*'s *guru*'s *guru*'s *guru*'s *guru* was so-and-so in India. We don't know it only verbally; we also have a register [*khata*] that we make a family tree with. Whenever I get a new *chela*, during the initiation ceremony, I will make that *guru* – the first *guru* on the list – her *guru* as well. When we put on a scarf [*dupatta*], during that ceremony, we recite all the names of the *guru* of the past. So, we keep their names alive that way. We even have certain documents of our *khwajasara* ancestors, when they had received some tip or a reward from the Mughal emperor. Those are kept with the *guru* around Pakistan and India [...]. They will not give them no matter what. The documents will be passed down to the next big *guru* who comes down the lineage. Because, these are the proofs of our existence and of our value, as it used to be hundreds of years ago.

The existence of such records (*khata*) clearly attests to the complexity of *khwajasara* subjectivity, as a *familial* and a *cultural* trope. But it is also evidence of this collective's mnemonic battle against the tides of the 'official' histories – those that had systematically dislocated the *khuddam*, *aghawat*, *khwajasara* and other gender-variant subjectivities into a liminal, trans-historical space. The preservation of *khwajasara* lineage is, thus, not just an appeal for *izzat* in the society at large; it is a vernacular history *par excellence*.

What keeps a *dera* together is not only the hierarchical *guru/chela* system. It is also a less structured and congenial *ma'an/dhi* relationship that *khwajasara* establish amongst themselves. The *ma'an* takes care of her *dhi* even though the *dhi* might be a *chela* of another *guru*. 'But it is also like a mother-in-law and daughter-in-law relationship', explained Jala and Gangha facetiously, in front of their *ma'an* Saima. 'We always fight with each other. There's always some fuss'. Just like one can change a *guru*, a *dhi* can change her *ma'an*, too. 'These relationships are like your characters in a soap opera', Saima concluded wryly.

Even more dramatic is one's relationship with the *giriya*. Those *khwajasara* who are sex workers[112] usually find their *giriya* amongst the male customers, others through various social activities.[113] 'I have a boyfriend for two years now', said Kajol. 'My life has changed since we are together, and I'm quite happy now. My previous *giriya* was very different; he used to beat me and always just ask for sex. At the end, I had to leave him'. The new *giriya*, however, 'takes care of me. He is a very pious Muslim. I would like us to get married'. Such marriages, indeed, take place, and are usually officiated by a senior *guru*. The married *chele* either leave their *dera*, or they are regularly visited there by their husbands. Furthermore, in certain rare cases, the *giriya* does not have to be a man 'all the time'. In Saima's *dera*, her *chele* showed me the wedding photograph of a husband with carefully combed beard and his *dupatta*-clad wife. *Both* of them were, in fact, *khwajasara*. And *both* of them sometimes wore 'men's' and 'women's' clothes.

Saima's *dera*, like many others, was a simple half-open-air flat, amidst a busy lower-class neighbourhood in Lahore. There were children running around the rooms (chasing a large and very loud rooster), whom several of her *chele* babysitted for the neighbouring families. Some of the rooms were used for prayer, others for cooking and social events, still others for sex work. 'If you live in one place for a long time', Saima explained, 'people eventually learn how to respect you. Despite some problems that we may have had, here we all help each other'. I wondered if sex work somewhat disturbed this neighbourly solidarity. 'When people say stuff to us', Saima replied, 'I tell them: Give us a better job, and we won't do what we do. We have no other way to feed ourselves'. As a form of 'invisible labour',[114] sex work has been an intrinsic part of

Lahore's vernacular economies since time immemorial. As of recently, some *khwajasara* political groupings have moved to demand it be treated as a profession, and its 'invisible labourers' as workers, entitled to the common set of labour rights. Yet in neighbourhoods like Saima's, *all* labourers have but very limited access to their rights. And this, along with other factors, seems to be an important aspect of the lower- and working-class neighbourly solidarity.

Spirituality

The Muslim–Sufi hieropraxis, in its South Asian vernacular, is kept alive and amidst the Punjabi *khwajasara* lifeworlds. Although quite a few *khwajasara* in Lahore are not nominally Muslim, but Christian,[115] they all share in this spiritual tradition. Hence, many *khwajasara* of Lahore visit and dance at the shrines of the Sufi saints (*pir*), follow the contemporary sages (*pir*),[116] engage in *zikr* (Arabic: *dhikr*)[117] and consider that there is a *murid*[118] within each of them. There seems to be no compulsion in *khwajasara* hieropraxis. Said Kajol, 'You know, I am a Christian, but we, as *khwajasara*, we all come and live and pray together. When the Muslim *khwajasara* fast, I fast with them [...]. But, I do not *have to* become like them. I do it because of friendship'. Saima, a Muslim, followed the *pir* named Hussain. 'When one becomes a disciple of a *pir*', she said, 'one is taught how to become a better person, how to immerse oneself in *salat*,[119] how to perform *dhikr*. But this all comes from a personal effort. There is no obligation among *khwajasara* to follow a *pir*'.

Jala, a Christian, followed the *pir* called Shahbaz. 'I often go to his *dergah* [shrine]', she said. 'We go there and pray for ourselves and for our families. We dance there and join our hands in prayer'. She also used to visit specifically Christian festivals, dedicated to Mary, the mother of Jesus. 'On Thursdays', she told me, 'I burn some incense, in the name of my *pir* Shahbaz. I also make *kiri* [a sweet dish made of rice] and give *zakat* [alms] in the name of another saint from Baghdad'. It seems that all *khwajasara* regularly give alms (*zakat*), even though some of them earn their living by begging for 'money gifts' (*wadhaian*). Sharing one's earnings, however minimal, animates the concept of *izzat*, so central in *khwajasara* morality and sociality.[120] For all the same reasons, it seems, one also needs to share in the spiritual experience of others. Bindiya Rana averred:

We are mostly Muslims, but we do not hate people of any other religion. There is nobody that we hate. If we have friend who is a Hindu, we will celebrate with her in a Hindu temple; if friend is a Sikh, we will go to *ghilja* [also *gurdwara*, a Sikh temple]. We respect everybody and we love everybody.

She added, somewhat apologetically, that this was not mere rhetoric. 'This is a part of our *culture*. This is something *we do*'.

Those *khwajasara* who regularly visit and pray in the mosques and churches did so either in their 'men's clothes' or in their regular 'women's' dresses'. Jala used to go to church every Sunday, dressed in her 'women's' attire. 'They laugh at me, but they also seem happy [to see me] and they meet with me after the service', she said. Neeli, a Muslim, used to go dressed 'as a man' every Friday to a large mosque, for the *jumu'a*.[121] This did not mean, however, that she was not recognised there as *khwajasara*:

> Some people ask me: 'Your people also go to mosque?' And my response is always: '*Alhamdulillah!* [Praise to God!] We are Muslims, too, and this is God's house, so we can come whenever we want'. They have no response to that. I tell them: 'This is God's house; if you have anything to tell to me, you can do so outside, but this is God's house and I can come whenever I want to'. Then, they really have nothing to say.

Neeli had a considerable network of non-*khwajasara* friends in her mosque. 'I know many people there', she said. 'We shake hands and make small talk. [For instance,] I have a friend there who likes other men. His name is Feisal. Another friend, Dershem, is *hafiz Qur'an*.[122] We sometimes go for the *jumu'a* together'. The societal barriers were thus fought and transgressed in the company of friends, who may or may not share one's gender or sexual diversity. They were challenged *from within*, through the membership in a particular congregation, and also *from without*, through solidarity with the nominal religious 'others'. Sexuality and gender were neither irrelevant nor *exclusively* relevant for these productive alliances; they were, quite simply, part of a *larger* spectrum of social relationships in which the Punjabi *khwajasara* – and others – negotiated their communal spiritual experience.

Law, Politics and Society: Limitless Solidarity, Limited Co-operation

In 1936 CE, *hijre* were given the right to vote – albeit as 'men' – in colonial India.[123] It signalled the rise of their political movements, which have since developed throughout the partitioned subcontinent. In the early 1960s CE, a temporary ban on *'hijra* activities' in Pakistan, imposed by General Mohammed Ayub Khan (r. 1958–69 CE), was successfully challenged by a Karachi-based *hijra* political collective. In 1990 CE, in Abbottabad, a *hijra* and *zenana* representative, Mohammad Aslam, contested local elections, arguing that both men and women had failed as politicians.[124] But in order to run for office, Aslam had to prove before a judge 'that he [*sic*] was a "real man"'.[125] Eventually, Aslam's name appeared on the ballots, and some 7,000 residents of Abbottabad circled it, which was 'insufficient to win a seat but enough to expose the crude phallicism of governance'.[126]

At the turn of the twenty-first century CE, *khwajasara* arose as a reclaimed and unified Pakistani political identity of several 'traditional' gender-variant subjectivities (*khojay*, *hijre* and *zenana*). Bindiya Rana, along with some other senior representatives of *khwajasara* collectives across the country, undertook to reform the political profile of *khwajasara* public actions. Others, like the Rawalpindi-based *khwajasara* community leader Bobby, also known as Almas Shah, prioritised the engagements with Pakistan's formal legal system, most notably though the Human Rights Constitutional Petition 63/2009 ('Case 63/09') before the Supreme Court. The key facets of the *khwajasara* political movement in the twenty-first century CE seem to be a broad, civic solidarity platform and a strategic, decidedly limited co-operation with governmental and non-governmental sectors.

The success of the Case 63/09 was undoubtedly an enormous boost for the legal, political and social organising of *khwajasara*. Although the decision of the Chief Justice of the Supreme Court of Pakistan still awaits full implementation, at the national and provincial levels, Bindiya Rana and her *khwajasara* comrades have managed to secure a wide range of benefits by referring to their Case 63/09 victory. She elaborated:

> Through the assistance of the Supreme Court and various high courts, we were able to get the provincial health ministries to recognise our needs and to provide us with free medical care, at the

expense of the government. We were able to get the *zakat* funds, whenever we required them. We were also able to get involved in the Income Support Programme, which is a kind of governmental unemployment support scheme. You get 2,000 to 3,000 rupees a month if you can show that you are unemployed. We have got that, but we are still unable to benefit from it, because one needs to have an ID card in order to receive the funds. We were also able to give notice to the high courts of all things that the police do to us, including rape, torture and everything. We even took NADRA [National Database and Registration Authority] to court [for failing to issue new 'third gender' identity cards], but there it was found out that they themselves do not have the authority to order the third gender box to appear on the ID cards. It's only the Supreme Court. So, now we are waiting for the Supreme Court to order implementation of its own decision. Only then we will be able to receive other benefits that, as citizens of Pakistan, we are entitled to. We will then stage new protests for those other benefits. But, for the time being, we are waiting for our ID cards.

The recognition of the 'third gender' citizenship seems to be, also, a strategy for political participation. 'Once we get the ID cards', said Bindiya Rana, 'we are going to demand that there be specific allocated seats for us in the National Assembly as well as in the provincial parliaments. That will be the next step'. The need for a new quota system was, thus, interpreted as the quest for a *separate* political space. Bindiya was adamant:

> The governments in Pakistan change constantly – today it's one person, tomorrow it's someone else – and we wouldn't want to be part of that environment more than we have to, really. We want to be independent. We don't want to be part of a big political party with all of its in-fighting and backstabbing business. We want to be free. We will run independently.

This exceptionalism, based not only on the decades of disappointing engagement with the State, but also with the non-governmental sector, is further reflected in the refusal of several *khwajasara* organisations to receive financial assistance from either state or non-state donors. 'We do not want and do not expect *such* help', said Bindiya. 'Our organisation doesn't even take money from the government. If we start taking money from them, then we'll have to do what they say'.

The opposite approach was, however, adopted with regard to civic solidarity and syndicated action. 'A few years ago', remembered Bindiya, 'the price of sugar went up. I got together 400 *khwajasara* and we went out to the Karachi press club and staged a peaceful demonstration. We are capable of creating a lot of attention, which can be good for everyone'. She also told me that, when her political collective was formed, 'one of the first things that we have done was to put up some medical camps; *not* for *khwajasara*, but for women and children, throughout Sindh and Baluchistan'. Such actions are consistent with the overarching principle of *izzat* and they have greatly influenced the recent positive change in public opinion about *khwajasara* in Pakistan, which seemed to be evident to *all* of my interlocutors.

Finally, the media attention given to the Supreme Court's decision in Case 63/09 in particular has been creatively utilised by a number of *khwajasara* to voice their grievances and demands. Neeli opined that, at the very least, the public reaction was one of 'confusion':

> There hasn't been a huge change but there has been some since the [Case 63/09] ruling by the Chief Justice. And, as a result of that decision by the Chief Justice Chaudhry, our voice had come to the media. And now, people in the society who used to look down on *khwajasara* are confused. They don't know what to think. That's not too bad for a start.

When formal law is used in conjunction with sustained efforts 'in its shadow', the prospect of substantial societal changes no longer escapes one's political horizons. Despite the fact that the historic decision in Case 63/09 remains largely unimplemented, the *khwajasara* collectives have used it ever since to initiate a series of important social and political reforms. For them, then, this decision has become the 'law as it ought to be' rather than the 'law as applied': it entered the sites of everyday bargaining as a moral, rather than coercive device.

It certainly takes an *exceptional* set of skills and sensitivities to *transform* an unenforced black-letter verdict into the tool for social change. Given the relevant historical and cultural contexts, those who self-identify as *khwajasara* may be uniquely placed to challenge the normativity and social inadequacy of both Islamic law and human rights law, as they are played out in contemporary Pakistan in relation to sexual and gender diversity. But, can the 'confusion' created by the post-Case 63/09 developments be conducive of any *broader* effects? To wit, what about the *other* sexually diverse and gender-variant Punjabis/Pakistanis? It is to their lifeworlds and their legal narratives that this chapter now turns.

The Circuits of Class and Knowledge: 'Why Don't We Go Across the Canal?'

As in the rest of the country, there are numerous underground collectives of sexually diverse and – to some extent – (non-*khwajasara*) gender-variant subjectivities in Lahore, most of which are either Muslim-majority or exclusively Muslim. But they rely on and reproduce *markedly* different circuits of knowledge, primarily divided along class/caste fault lines. Some rare attempts have been made, either through individual initiatives or incentives provided by non-governmental funding bodies, to traverse, even if only temporarily, some class/caste divisions. My interlocutors,[127] however, agreed that they have been deeply traumatic and ultimately unsuccessful. That, said Waheed, a middle-class Punjabi activist, is particularly true of the funds provided by the HIV/AIDS prevention networks towards establishing community-based organisations (CBOs), which are sometimes opportunistically created by '*men* who have been in the business for a long time'.[128] It is, therefore, necessary to examine how these separate circuits of knowledge, and subjectivities constructed thereupon, engage the law and society, each in their own right. This is not to say that there are no commonalities amongst these groups, or that *some* class/caste barriers cannot be productively overcome. Rather, this is to acknowledge – and problematise – what Jamila, a middle-class community leader, succinctly put:

> Somebody will always ask that class-related question, for which we don't have an answer: 'Why don't we work with *those* [working- and lower-class] kinds of people? Why don't we go across the canal [that separates Defence, an affluent upper- and middle-class

neighbourhood, from the inner city slums]?' And, the answer to this is always: 'How do we *do* that?' Because, the thing is, you can walk into the old city and say: 'We are here to liberate you'. But that's neither an ethical nor a viable option. You have to be aware that *we* do not *represent* the queers of Pakistan. We just represent the people *who we are*.

The move towards collective *representation* and the identity politics exclusively based on one's sexual or gender difference is, in fact, a relatively recent challenge in Pakistan, mostly faced by the middle-class collectives. It is they who are approached by international organisations and asked to come up with 'broader identity platforms'. But it is also they, as we shall see, who are increasingly aware of the perils of such representational exercises. Perhaps because of Punjab's historical and cultural specificities, even those circuits of knowledge that seem susceptive to global sexual/gender discourses attempt to critically engage, rather than straightforwardly adopt such discourses. However, the situation is getting increasingly complex, not least because of the surge in neo-liberal international projects in need of 'local communities' *capable* of carrying them out.

What follows is an attempt to *comparatively* examine two *broadly* conceived lifeworlds – of working-class and of middle-class Muslims in Lahore – and the place for (non-*khwajasara*) gender-variance and sexual diversity in them. The idea is to expose both divergent and convergent traits, politics and discursive practices related to these class-stratified subjectivities, exemplified in my interlocutors' personal accounts of personhood and collective action. A caveat is, however, in order. This is a remarkably fluid terrain. As some of the protagonists of the ensuing narratives passionately underline, even *khwajasara* tropes should not be understood as an essentialised identity, despite the recent political decisions to do so. Everyday sexual and gender diversity defies crude categorisations. 'It's like a bubble', explained Waheed. 'Sooner or later, it will burst and you will find yourself in an uncharted territory'.

Selfhood, Communality and Communicability

'When I changed my life, a few years ago, my parents were annoyed with me', said Adeel somewhat anxiously. Precluding any unwarranted conclusion, he proceeded to elaborate the cause of the parental distress:

'I started keeping my beard and praying five times a day'. Adeel was a member of a religious movement that pledges to 'revive, once again, the *exterminated* moral and spiritual values of Islam'.[129] The suspicion of what lies behind the benevolent public face of many a revivalist organisation is common amongst Lahori working-class families, like Adeel's. His sexual life seemed to be of less interest to them. Some (female) members of his natal family knew that, besides being married to a woman, Adeel was also in a same-sex relationship with another member of his Muslim revivalist movement. 'We should be able to love whoever we want', he averred, 'but we need to start thinking away from lust. It seems that the lustful behaviour among men is becoming more and more widespread in the society. We need to come up with an effective solution for it'.

Adeel vividly partakes in a large and diverse circuit of knowledge that combines the vernacular Sufi tradition of his class with the contemporary, mainstream 'international' discourses on Islamic law and morality. For Muslims like him, there is no need to call one's divergent gender/sexual proclivities and practices *any particular name*. They are Muslims; that is all that *really* matters. All answers to their queries are, therefore, to be sought and found in Islamic spiritual, legal and social tradition. But it is a long and difficult journey:

> I have re-read, for example, some collections of the *hadis* {*hadith* } and studied the question of *lavat* {*liwat* }. I am still not sure what to believe. Sometimes I think these feelings are wrong and sometimes I don't. The human being has some feelings that are natural, that are instilled in them. No matter how hard you try to divert from those feelings, they always come back, because they sooth you and comfort you.[130]

On the one hand, then, the communities that Adeel used to interact with face a modernist morality disguised as Muslim 'international' knowledge, which has revived selected versions of classical *fiqh* and retained a relatively uncritical approach to the *hadith* literature. On the other hand, however, the vernacular, still mostly *oral* tradition of same-sex love and intimacy has also survived, and it continues to creatively inform contemporary Punjabi Muslim circuits. 'I was utterly shocked to hear the stories of {male} Punjabi Sufis being in love with other men', said Adeel, 'especially because those men were *also* great spiritual masters'.

The dilemmas that Adeel and his spiritual and social circles faced are, in a sense, nothing new. Long before the colonial and modernist interventions into the Punjabi lifeworlds, the religious and social reforms instigated by the Mughal emperor Akbar the Great (r. 1556/963–1605/1013 CE/AH) and, then, opposed and reversed by one of his successors, Aurangzeb (r. 1658/1068–1707/1118 CE/AH), were nothing short of a Muslim version of the Reformation and the Counter-Reformation of the Western Church,[131] and they are, as such, still alive in the Punjabi cultural memory. The pluralism of thought and knowledge, including about Islamic law, is therefore an intrinsic part of Adeel's lifeworld, despite attempts to suppress it:

> Our *ulama* [religious scholars, sing. *'alim*], in their *khutbay* [sermons, sing. *khutba*], always warn: 'Don't interpret! Don't interpret! Come and consult with *us* if you have any problem in your mind'. But it is already happening. We have all those different schools of thought [*fiqh*]. Also, only in Punjab, there are more than forty different Muslim denominations, because every *jamaat* [community, organisation], every movement, every congregation, every circle – either in the mosque, in the town or somewhere else – they all have their own way of seeing certain things.[132]

And while such circles remain centres of intra-religious debate, they are also places of largely mono-gendered sociality and intimacy.[133]

Outside of those circles, the everyday environment of the working-class Muslims is *also* saturated with examples of same-sex familial, social and sexual life. Kajol elaborated:

> Sometimes a woman is not attracted to men, and she feels special about herself. I know, for example, of two women who live together, even though one of them has children. One of the two women dresses more like a man. She also takes care of that other woman. She sells fruit, while the other woman stays behind.

I asked her if there was any term that describes *that* type of relationship. 'No, there is no specific name for it', she replied, 'but it's like *niyana* with a *niyana*'.[134]

Across the canal, however, the middle-class circuits of knowledge, in part in reaction to global taxonomies of sexual and gender difference (e.g. 'LGBT', 'queer'), are increasingly sensitive to 'the name game', as Fauzia, a community leader, ironically dubbed it. The answers are sometimes sought in the vernacular:

This male member [of our group] came up [one day] and said, 'I was with these women who are a couple and they called themselves *hamzan*'. Now, *hamjins* is your standard word for same-sex relations. *Ham* is 'the same', and *jins* means 'sex'. *Zan* is the word that stands for 'woman'. It is our feminine. So *hamzan* is a really sweet, poetic term that I've never heard before. And I quite liked it. So, we kind of try to invent a language.[135]

But, Fauzia *also* added, 'I'm a missionary for the "queer". I like it because it's an umbrella term that, I find it, allows more. And I find "lesbian" as a restrictive term; "bisexual" even more so'. Nawaz, a male member of the same middle-class collective, explained passionately:

I see both 'gay' and its broader version – 'LGBT' – as problematic because it is used just for convenience or for funding purposes. Moving on to 'queer': very post-modern, questioning a lot of traditional forms of knowledge, but also foreign. Well, I recall conversations we had in [this] group. We were all young folks, getting together, having conversations about sexualities. Somehow, we were all interested in exploring post-modern interpretations of this framework. We preferred, *if necessary*, to use the term 'queer', because sexualities are *so complex* that some of us would get confused and say, 'I don't know what these labels really mean and do they in any way relate to me'. 'Queer' can further *confuse* this confusion, but, at least, 'queer' is *queer*. As the word suggests, yes, it's queer because *it doesn't know* what it is. And it does not want to be stuck in some box. So, in that sense, 'queer' for us was a very interesting exposure.

The problematics of global taxonomies, however, become even more pronounced in an *inter-class dialogue*. Jamila remembered one such instance:

One woman considers 'lesbian' to be a little more than a swearword. We have had a conversation with her once. She is not part of our [middle-class] group; she has her own [working-class] group. She said: 'Why are you saying lesbian? Why do you keep calling me a lesbian?' And she got quite upset. That was *the language thing*. Because, even though both my partner and I are fluent in Urdu, and she is fluent in Punjabi also, the language of the high, complex thought *for us* is English. But *for the woman* we were speaking to the language of the complex thought was Urdu. So, we were having a great deal of trouble explaining why 'lesbian', for *us*, although it may sound bad and it has been used badly, is now a reclaimed word. We didn't venture into *where* it doesn't mean something bad anymore. The reclaimed version of the word simply wasn't on her radar.

The language *tout court* – not only its terms for sexual/gender difference – is an enormous challenge to communication both *within* and *between* some class-based circuits of knowledge. Jamila told me that certain members of her collective 'are still a different middle-class subset than I am. I am understood to be elite. Not necessarily monetarily, but class-based, because of my language and education'. She explained that their 'language of the high thought is Punjabi'; hers was not. They were also 'male and gay, which means that they can speak the language of *khwajasara*; there is some commonality of culture'. For her, though, visiting the *khwajasara* households for some interviews had been 'a horrendous experience', since the linguistic, class and cultural gap was 'almost palpable'. Fauzia also recalled that her middle-class queer and Muslim collective was visited once by 'a working-class female couple'. The couple spoke a different language than the majority of the members of Fauzia's group, and 'felt incredibly uncomfortable' at the community meeting. 'They joined us for the party as well', she remembered, 'and their drinking culture was different. So, then, *we* were uncomfortable. We became "we" because of class. In short, *they* will never join us again'. The language is, thus, only an indicator of broadly divergent sociality, which draws sexually diverse and gender-variant Muslims of Lahore into separate social milieux. How, then, did these different forms of sociality affect the spiritual experience and praxis of my Lahori interlocutors?

Spirituality

'It's a huge experience. Really moving. We do it, but we do it *for ourselves*. We are very quiet and cautious about that'. Ayesha was talking about the hieropraxis of her underground group, which was performed in strict privacy: 'We have had Friday prayers. A mixed group, led by a woman, led by a man, men and women standing together without any objection'. They were also thinking of starting a Qur'an study group. 'The purpose is not a statement', she explained. 'The purpose is that we share our spiritual experience with each other'. It could also be an act of solidarity, for those they felt close to. 'When the Pakistani poet Ifti Nasim passed away, a few months ago', Ayesha recalled, 'we did absentia funeral prayers for him'. Their communal spiritual practices were, however, primarily tailored as a personal support mechanism, having understood that each member of the group was in a different place on their religious journey from the others. For one member, Hassan, 'the religion was a major struggle and a major source of liberation'. For Ayesha, 'the religion was also a major struggle and has not been the major source of liberation as such. But, for me, it has definitely been the case of having faith that it will get sorted out'. In such a communal context, she said, 'you have to start with basic things'. That is, with faith, prayer, quiet studies and solidarity.

A similar story unfolded across the canal. 'Even though there are many people like me', explained Adeel, 'we are quite scared of what would happen to us, had our views become known. So, at the moment, we have no choice but to keep silent'. Since their everyday social environment was more mono-gendered and public, Adeel and his friends were less keen to break away with the general Muslim sites of common worship, in order to create their own. 'Currently, we offer prayers five times a day and, when we feel very spiritual, we go to mosque and sit down together', he said. That way their spiritual unity with the rest of the *umma* helped them understand better their own religious journey. That unity, however, was chiefly one of silence; one that attested an oppressive majoritarian view. 'Most of the *ulama* here think of these things in a very negative way', said Adeel. 'Also, almost everything that is available to read here, coming from a Muslim point of view, has been negative in that sense'. How long can a predominantly oral vernacular knowledge hold out against such omnipresent negativity?

It was encouraging to see that both Adeel's and Ayesha's collectives *had faith* that their sustained focus on 'basic things' would, as they both enthusiastically affirmed, 'get us *there* eventually'. Just *where* that next stop is on their parallel journeys and *what* it might consist of remains to be seen. Inevitably, however, it will involve a renewed search for historical, legal and social narratives within the Muslim traditions that might unspell and disrupt the current majoritarian views of sexual and gender difference. 'At the moment', concluded Ayesha, 'it is about making the private and public spaces of our faith *comfortable* to us'.

Law, Politics and Society: Between Our Niyyat *and Their Agenda*

'Our organisation can be very off-putting', said Jamila of her middle-class collective. 'It is because we often have to explain that we don't do media and don't do government. Because [the people in non-governmental sector] assume that having such an organisation *means* doing government and media. And we don't engage either'. There was an overwhelming consensus among sexually diverse Muslim circuits in Lahore that working with the media and government in Pakistan would be a detrimental move. 'I mean, we don't really want to be on the radar that way', explained Fauzia. 'Once we have thousands of people behind us, we can come in with the media. But, when there are just a few of us, we are really easy to shut up'. Several left-wing parties have been identified as potential allies, but the co-operation was for the time being limited to underground political organising. A similar platform was shared with some workers' unions and a popular Lahori movement for civic action. Finally, 'certain individuals from within the women's organisations, feminist organisations, are good', said Ayesha, and then quickly added: 'But that's a dangerous game, because they are very well established, and one would not want to be instrumentalised. We are very wary of that'.

Engaging the formal legal system was, apparently, not an option either. 'People from outside [the country] or even Indians are, like, "But why aren't you working on 377? We've done it"', told me Jamila. 'And, their 377, I don't really know the details, to what extend it was an issue. But for us, it's a non-issue [. . .]. I think it would just catalyse more hatred and homophobia'. Jamila referred to the historic decision by the High Court of Delhi on 2 July 2009 CE to 'read down' §377 of the Indian Penal Code of 1860 CE to the effect that same-sex sexual acts amongst consenting adults were no longer considered to constitute a criminal offence, which, sadly, has since been reversed by a two-member bench of the Indian Supreme Court.[136] Jamila concluded:

> In *our* environment, 377 would be a symbolic gesture. And, maybe that would mean something. But, we don't have law enforcement. What difference does it *really* make? The only laws that are enforced are the politically salient ones. Things like 377? Not really. Law is instrumentalised when needed, but for us there are many other forces that work much better than the law. Law is *just there*.

I wondered what my interlocutors made of the Case 63/09. Notwithstanding its many shortcomings, this Supreme Court decision has undoubtedly revitalised the *khwajasara* political movements. 'I very strongly feel, and I am not the only one', replied Fauzia, 'that it is the 377 decision [in India] that led the Supreme Court of Pakistan taking notice of *khwajasara*. Because these guys [in India] are doing this thing, we will try to project the soft image of Pakistan to the world as well'. She acknowledged, however, that the positive decision in the Case 63/09 was a response to 'the movement from among *khwajasara*' as well. Still, Fauzia was adamant, 'it was an opportunistic thing for the Supreme Court to do'. The law, then, is perhaps not *just there*. It has regional connotations, which can be seized and used in everyday social and legal bargaining. Ayesha seemed to agree: 'When people are building a movement, something happens in the region, and the movement finds traction; whereas, it wouldn't previously find such traction'.

My interlocutors, however, were quick to point out to what some of them described as a *phallocentric* system and logic behind the recent legal victories for *khwajasara*. Fauzia explained:

> Pakistan's traditional system is reflected in [the Case 63/09]. What's generally thought here is that they [*khwajasara*] are *defective* and that's why you have to be benevolent. That's how the Supreme Court has thought about *khwajasara*. So, these poor defective *men* weren't men anymore, but we wanted them to be, so let's help them out. It's incredibly problematic.

Waheed was less sceptical about the Pakistani legal system as a whole, including the motivations behind the Supreme Court's decision in Case 63/09, but he was nevertheless certain that sexual pluralism was not to be defended by means of formal justice. 'Pakistani law is flexible', he said, 'not so monolithic as some might think, but there are some touchy areas relating to religious elites'. Those areas, it seems, include same-sex sexuality.

Some of the underground sexually diverse Muslim groups, therefore, focused on other activities. Jamila and her colleagues collaborated with a large US-based LGBT organisation, 'on research and outreach' within Pakistan. She described it as a continuous struggle, within what sometimes seems to be an unequal partnership ('at times it feels like the employer-employee situation', she said), to maintain a locally sensitive approach. 'That's primarily because our [partner organisation] has an Asian focus. These big LGBT organisations, they are divided by continents', she explained. 'And, therefore, we are now a single entity, or even if still understood as conglomeration, we are the single conglomeration'.[137] She went on to exemplify these anxieties through various situations, which cannot be described here for the reasons of anonymity and security. But her conclusion was one of uncertainty as to the potential consequences of this precarious partnership:

> I don't want to say it's a humongous imperialist agenda, but mostly I don't want to say that because I can't see what an end game of that kind of agenda would be. I don't know if I feel colonised. And I don't know if I'm replicating that on the people [in the country we, as an organisation, interact with]. That's a huge responsibility to figure out. And, we are not doing a very good job in figuring it out. Part of me is, like, you don't have the resources, not even the material resources, but you also don't have emotional momentum resources for all huge ethical implications of the things that we are doing. And you are doing it for one *niyyat* – one intention – so, the intention there is good, and as the proper Muslim people we believe that if your intention is good then everything will come up good. So, that's part of these efforts. On the other hand, your intention only goes so far. Sometimes I think people are incredibly co-optive.[138]

Similar anxieties were experienced by my interlocutors who worked with HIV/AIDS prevention networks. Waheed described what he called the *commodification* of human rights and the *commodification* of HIV/AIDS-affected communities:

> In the HIV industry, there is an increased focus on human rights, as its extension of some kind. By claiming that rhetoric, it justifies its expansion and the involvement of money. The new rhetoric is that HIV cannot be prevented, unless you ensure human rights [...]. [Also,] there is a realisation in the *khwajasara* community that they are some sort of commodity, that they have been given certain value in the not-for-profit world.

These are no simple matters. My middle-class interlocutors considered navigating the troublesome waters of the civil society sector a difficult but indispensible task. My working class respondents, however, felt less ready to engage with what seemed to them an inherently exploitative system. In that, they were ideologically closer to those *khwajasara* collectives that limit their co-operation with both governmental and non-governmental agencies to the instances deemed strictly necessary. But nobody described those positions as permanent. 'It has only just started', muttered Fauzia gloomily, as if sensing a coming thunderstorm.

Lessons in the Vernacular: How to Dismantle an Epistemic Bomb

Having ventured into the lifeworlds of Lahori sexually diverse and gender-variant Muslims, and having listened to their narratives of the past and the present, this chapter now turns to the five themes that sum up its primary intention: to locate a contemporary vernacular voice and agency in the larger (than life) genealogies and politics of international human rights law and Islamic law. The first story is, primarily, a cautionary tale of how *not* to intervene in the vernacular space in the present context. The other four stories briefly examine the limits and future potentials of (1) formal municipal law, (2) international law, (3) human rights and (4) Islamic law in Pakistan, as they relate to sexual and gender diversity.

The Spectacle of Intervention

Writing in the precarious environment of 1967 CE Paris, Guy Debord begins his widely influential book, *The Society of the Spectacle*, with the following thesis: 'The whole life of those societies in which modern conditions of [capitalist] production prevail presents itself as an immense accumulation of spectacles. All that once was directly lived has become mere representation'.[139] In a similar fashion, neo-liberal *interventionism* into 'client' societies – whether military, economic, political or 'humanitarian' – reveals itself in countless acts of *spectacular representation*. The (real) lives of the *subjects* of such representational acts are always already *irrelevant*; what matters is the spectacle itself.

On 26 June 2011 CE, the then Deputy Chief (and later *Chargé d'Affaires*) of the US Mission to Pakistan, Richard E. Hoagland, hosted 'Islamabad's First Ever Gay, Lesbian, Bisexual, and Transgender (GLBT) Pride Celebration'. The event was publicised at the US Embassy's official website, as a gesture of 'support for human rights, including LGBT rights in Pakistan, at a time when those rights are increasingly under attack from extremist elements throughout Pakistani society'.[140] Fauzia described the chaotic aftermath of this seemingly benevolent 'celebration':

> We had the protests [against the 'pride celebration'] all week and then for a month. Editorial upon editorial upon editorial, in newspapers in English and in Urdu. 'American agenda in harbouring support to these deviants'. 'We really need to bring back the proper Islam'. 'America is making everybody gay'. 'It's another way for them to take over our nation and corrupt us'. You know, that language, that discourse. I mean, it was an Eid for everybody, for the homophobes.

The event shocked and outraged *all* the collectives of sexually diverse and gender-variant Muslims in Pakistan that I have been in touch with. Jamila summed up the general sentiment:

> Oh my God! That was horrible! It's become like a landmark for us. It outed us in ways that are absolutely unacceptable. I've had conversations with the people from the [US] Embassy. I got

invited to that event. I didn't go and the woman called right after this became the news. She called me generally and I happened to be in Islamabad so I went and had a chat with them. I have no problem with the US Foreign Service doing its own gay pride in an embassy. I even have no problem with them inviting some gay people from Pakistan just to go and hang out with the Embassy staff. Whatever. For certain people, those are inroads into another universe and they go for them. But, they put it on their website as a press release. I mean, you are either stupid or you are callous. To see the current situation in Pakistan with the US and then do that, and make a statement like 'We stand with the gay population of Pakistan'. Please don't stand with us! Please stand very, very far away from us! Please! People are trying to shoot you. They will kill us first. Please, go away. Please don't fuck with us this way. It has *huge* consequences.

Jamila explained that she and her colleagues 'conveyed this message the best we could'. But whether that will stop future acts of brazenly apathetic spectacular representation is yet to be seen.

Meanwhile, the *khwajasara* activists engage in the battle against another kind of the societal spectacle of representation, one in which their political agency is being systematically denied on a *domestic* level. Neeli elaborated:

The government of Pakistan is not really willing to help us. If they were, the police wouldn't be harassing us. The politicians have authority to order the police to change their behaviour. But we are the *tamasha* [spectacle]! They look at us, make fun of us, and call us all kinds of nasty names.

The dilemma, then, for sexually diverse and gender-variant Muslims in Pakistan is *how* and *where* to claim their legal, political and social space, between the foreign spectacle and the domestic *tamasha*. For lower classes in general, privacy is often but an unattainable luxury: one, then, is forced to engage the society in the best way one can. For others the retreat from the public is possible to some extent, but that is not necessarily a comfortable position. While tactics and interpretations may vary, the concept of *izzat* seems to permeate – and trouble – all

Muslim subject positions in their relationship with the *umma* at large. Hence, *un pèlerinage inclusif* is every now and then undertaken to the sites of common worship, and of symbolic Muslim unity, albeit in a quiet – spectacle-free – mode. The dialogue has commenced, even if *one* side is still not entirely aware of it. And it is, by and large, led in the vernacular.

If the locality of one's culture and its bargaining rules provide the best environment for social and spiritual reforms, how can the surrounding legal landscapes be utilised to offer the necessary support? Which laws to use/change/demand, if any, and why? Moreover, which legal histories and narratives can help derail the domestic and international political projects commonly attached to legal discourses, in order for them to make sense and work in the vernacular?

Domestic Law

Let us, once more, return to the formal legal system of Pakistan. There can be no doubt that its current hybridity – oscillating between an antiquated colonial(ist) *corpus juris* and the conflicting theopolitical visions of 'Islamic' law – poses an enormous challenge for any meaningful reform. The selective implementation mechanisms of formal domestic law are, then, only the most obvious symptom of its long and potentially terminal malady. Remarkably, the most damning verdict on this system comes right from its core. The Supreme Court judge with whom I spoke described it in the following terms:

> The formal court mechanism has become very oppressive, exploitative system, used mainly by those who are affluent and influential as a tool to oppress their opponents, who are less privileged, less affluent, less moneyed. It's a very, very pernicious system [...]. The system needs very, very drastic changes. I would say, *it needs to be abolished*. It is that pernicious; it is that bad. Barring certain areas of expertise, say, corporate law, issues of securities of the market. But, by and large, in the realm of the main disputes, of people on the streets, it is not working, it will not work, it cannot work.

The main issue for this judge and for the majority of my interlocutors is, clearly, that the domestic legal system is *not vernacular enough*. Laden with an alien and insidious *ratio juris* – be it of colonial or of Muslim theopolitical provenance – it presents itself as an antithesis of the local systems of knowledge.

Still, reforms have been attempted at the formal legal level, and, arguably, the most successful ones have been those accompanied by a parallel, thorough societal *translation* through bargaining in the shadow of formal law. One such example was when, in 2006 CE, 'after decades of advocacy by women's and other civil society organisations',[141] the Criminal Law Amendment (Protection of Women) Act substantially revised the infamous Offence of Zina (Enforcement of Hudood) Ordinance 1979, making it much less harmful for women.[142] The other example is, plainly, the success of the Case 63/09, *despite* the lack of its formal enforceability. Importantly, both of these legal battles have been won by combining vernacular interpretations of Islamic law and constitutional (fundamental rights) law. One, therefore, could envision that, for example, §377 of the Penal Code 1860 be dismantled as 'repugnant to the Injunctions of Islam' *and* unconstitutional. Obviously, the vernacular knowledge of Islamic law and fundamental rights – as well as of their respective *histories* – would be indispensible in this process. And even if the process would not immediately result in an increased *formal* legal protection of the sexually diverse citizens of Pakistan, its *translated vernacular value* might be significant. At any rate, only an *internally* induced and owned[143] reform process could potentially have a positive outcome.

Since the dissatisfaction with the formal domestic legal system is shared by a fairly large and diverse group of critics – from judges to grass-roots activists – the prospect for broader (overt or covert) co-operation amongst them towards a comprehensive vernacular reform does not seem to be too far-fetched. The boundaries of class and incommunicability, however, will have to be overcome or at least temporarily suspended; and that might well be the most difficult of all tasks. Some of my interlocutors have begun to explore the possibilities for inter-class/caste dialogue and, at the very least, they are remarkably class-conscious, which seems to be an elementary ingredient of any insurrectionary knowledge.[144] The formal law, then, is not *just there*; it offers a *paradigm* as well as a *material raison d'être* for a *broader* – even revolutionary – social, political and legal action.

International Law

Amongst my interlocutors, there was a shared and strongly expressed discontent with just about *everything* relating to international law: with what it is and what it used to be; with its foreign[145] and domestic missionaries; with the Pakistani official politicisations of it and with its capacity for change. One of my respondents, otherwise directly involved in the domestic interpretations of the international legal standards, summed up this outrage in the following statement:

> It is sheer hypocrisy. That is how I look at it. It is so deeply problematic for me. It is a farce, this whole international law shebang. It's a good farce. You can see it being worked on, on a daily basis in the United Nations. You can look at what the most common issues are. Just look at Palestine. I really cannot take these things seriously. I can't because, really, it is so patently farcical. For whatever goes on in the Middle East, you always have to blame the Palestinians. So, I don't get upset about this because I can really see through the whole thing. It's a power game; it's a colonial enterprise again. I don't get worked up on this and, in all fairness, I know that I'm just wasting my time on international law. It is that farcical.

It would be wrong to assume that my interlocutors bought into the propaganda of Pakistan's government, exemplified in its role in the Organisation of Islamic Co-operation's (OIC) equally deplorable 'shebang' about 'Islamic human rights' and the accompanying mainstream Muslim theopolitical vocabulary.[146] The government's political use of international law and the international human rights system was, in fact, scorned and 'seen through' in very much the same way. But the persistent 'colonial enterprise' of international law – one that is explored in some detail in Chapter 3 of this book – was remarkably obvious to my respondents.

Speaking of both the involvement of international organisations in the *khwajasara* socio-political plight and of the international mechanisms potentially available as a domestic legal remedy, Bindiya Rana concluded bitterly: 'Nothing good has ever come out of it'. Waheed intimated that mainstream domestic human rights institutions and events were 'little more than the conventions of the [then ruling] Pakistan People's Party', while Fauzia was adamant that the people from these institutions 'have absolutely no interest in our issues', despite their scarce formal expressions of solidarity. *Therefore*, my interlocutors also saw only a limited applicability of the 'soft law' international instruments such as the *Yogyakarta Principles on the Application of International Human Rights Law in relation to Sexual Orientation and Gender Identity* (the Yogyakarta Principles).[147] Waheed explained that 'even CEDAW[148] could only rarely be used here, let alone the Yogyakarta Principles', while Jamila saw them as useful primarily in the context of community awareness:

> International human rights documents cannot be used here to lobby the government or the domestic human rights institutions. I think the Yogyakarta Principles can be used as an empowerment tool, for people to realise that these are also the rights that they might want to claim [...]. But as far as the other structures in Pakistan are concerned, well, they don't care anyway.

I pointed out that at least one of the signatories of the Yogyakarta Principles has had an active role in building Pakistan's domestic human rights system. Jamila answered resolutely: 'They have no interest. They *really* have no interest'.

It is noteworthy that the Yogyakarta Principles, and potentially all other recent developments relating to sexual orientation and gender identity in international law, were *not at all* seen in a negative light by my respondents. But the system *itself* – that is, international law *sui generis* – is what they described as a 'colonial enterprise', potentially beyond repair. Indeed, in the history of the present, the need for *meaningful* decolonisation of international law is just as pertinent as in the decades of the post-World War II anti-colonial struggle, although with new terms of reference (such as that of international 'development' agendas).[149] Yet, in the absence of any workable alternative, it is doubtful that moves to 'dispense with' international law altogether would have a sound political and, indeed, legal purchase. At the same time, the decolonisation strategies would need to work, with an equal force, on debunking the OIC-like misappropriation of supranational legal and political space, which sometimes skilfully employs the 'decolonisation discourse' towards its own political ends. To wit, a greater attention paid to and participation in the well-developed post-colonial critique of international law, including from a 'third space',[150] might reveal some productive avenues for grappling with international law from the Pakistani context. It could even be framed, controversially, as a rescue operation, intending to salvage precisely those elements of the international legal system that are invariably seen by my interlocutors in a positive light.

Human Rights: A Quest for Greater Happiness

Regardless of their disappointment with the domestic and international justice systems, my interlocutors seem to share an unfaltering faith in human rights. Those are not rights preached by neo-liberal missionaries, nor are they rights/obligations deductable from Pakistani constitutional law. They are, instead, rights stemming from a vernacular experience of the self and the society, the rights of everyday, yet anchored in the hope of a classless and non-violent future. Said Bindiya Rana, a *khwajasara* political and social leader:

> God has given us eyes and ears. We know *naturally* what our rights
> are, what they should be and what we should have. We want
> *inclusive* rights that every other citizen enjoys. We don't want any
> special rights. We want the right to choose our profession.
> We want rights where we *can* have jobs. Jobs are very important,
> but nobody hires us. We want housing. Nobody gives us a house
> to rent or even to buy. We want to be able to live in the good parts
> of the city, like Defence. Why should we only have to live in the
> inner city slums? So, we just want to be like everybody else.
> Nothing more, but nothing less either.

For Waheed, the rights were worth fighting for, and they all could be subsumed under four major principles: 'Dignity, freedom, respect and choice'. But these principles, he said, needed to be wrestled from 'neo-liberal commodification; from its ideological market of rights'. Fauzia was sceptical of any transformative potential of 'the fundamental rights enshrined in our Constitution', yet she saw such potential in a discourse that would advocate the freedom from any harm:

> In terms of the idea that you are entitled to *greater happiness* than you
> think, in that sense the rights discourse can be instrumentalised.

And, that's something that I would like to see happen. I would like
to see people feel that they are *entitled* to something more than just
quietly living their lives without anybody bothering them. I would
like them to think that they have a right to freedom from any kind
of harm. And that they should expect to live without harm. Because,
as I said, our threshold for violence is very high. And it's gotten
worse in a last few years.

The entitlement to greater happiness, then, is what gives Fauzia's idea a
universal claim. For Adeel, it was all about love (*'ishq*): a human being's
love for their Creator, and the Creator's endless and unconditional love
for the (human) creature. 'Because of that', he said, 'we should be able to
love whoever we want'. The right to love, then, stems from the God-
given right to life.

In this colourful mosaic, human rights are seen as indivisible
from one's social and spiritual experience, of one's self that is inextricable
from one's nature as a God's *and* human being. One's capacity for
love, happiness and social relationships, including those based on one's
sexual and gender experience, is envisioned as God's precious gift to
humankind. It is both individual and collective. Its *law* is that of the
community with God and with other fellow human beings. As such, it
offers a novel script for understanding human rights law *and* Islamic law
in the vernacular. And, since the vernacular narrative of Islamic law –
according to my interlocutors – is categorically *not* to be found in the
hybrid state law of Pakistan, it calls for a renewed search for the
whereabouts of Islamic law 'of every heart'.[151]

Whither Islamic Law (in Punjab/Pakistan)?
The fallacy of nation states' modernist attempts to reduce the subject
matter of Islamic law to 'no more than positive law, emanating from the
state's will to power'[152] is apparent to my Punjabi interlocutors. This
idea, represented in the state's legal institutions of 'Islamic justice' and
in the corresponding state legislation, is historically and culturally alien
to the Punjabi experience with Islamic law. This experience, which is
rooted in *oral* tradition/transmission and in a heterogeneous cultural
memory that includes both the Mughal 'reformation' and 'counter-
reformation' of an already-pluralist Islamic law, operates today chiefly on
an inter-personal level. It is there, in the *imponderability*[153] of everyday

'subjective' spiritual and cultural practice, that a 'pre-modern' Islamic law can be found: the law that governs Muslim relationships with the self and the other. As the critical historical review in Chapter 4 of this book has shown, *this* Islamic law has never sought to infringe upon one's *self*, including its sexual and gender dimensions. The same is true for the 'inter-personal' Islamic law of my interlocutors' lifeworlds in Punjab. And it is from that source and locus that the Punjabi/Pakistani gender-variant and sexually diverse Muslims *can* – and *do* – engage the non-vernacular apparitions of 'Islamic' law that dominate their legal landscape.

Crucial to this, as well as to all other engagements with non-vernacular laws, is the process of *translation*, which allows for an epistemic shift and 'shadow bargaining' towards the desired social outcomes. The harbingers of this process are dedicated and skilful groups and individuals, fully conversant in the larger insurrectionary vernacular.

Towards Epistemological Primacy of Vernacular Knowledge

This chapter has offered a brief ethnographic insight into the lifeworlds of sexually diverse and gender-variant Muslims in Pakistan, focusing on their *personal* narratives of engagement with law and society. It primarily draws upon my 2011 CE fieldwork in Lahore, the capital of the Pakistani province of Punjab. Owing to the multitude of historical and cultural contexts, the discourses of Islamic law and international human rights law *meet* in the Punjabi ethnoscape, albeit through a complex socio-political exchange. This chapter has sought to unravel the particular aspects of this meeting that relate to sexual and gender diversity.

I have argued, first, that there is a deep-seated tension between the formal laws of the land and the Punjabi/Pakistani social and legal ethos. Even though the state law is used, as in the famous Case 63/09 before the Supreme Court of Pakistan, to allow for social benefits and greater political participation of *khwajasara*, it is not based on vernacular knowledge and, as such, it is always already in need of *translation*. Hence, in search of the relevant translation practices, I have sought to provide a closer, firsthand account of the lifeworlds of sexually diverse and gender-variant Lahori Muslims: their histories, kinship, sociality, spirituality and politics, as well as their intimate legal narratives. I have argued that the discursive practices of my interlocutors do not manage to escape the predicaments of the profound class/caste divide of the Punjabi/Pakistani society, but that they nonetheless create a wellspring of opportunities for countering epistemic, social and political violence through the law of the everyday. And it is from the same vernacular angle that Muslim sexually diverse and gender-variant individuals and collectives can contribute to decolonising international law and the discourses on human rights.

Without any intention to *essentialise* vernacular knowledge or the sexually diverse and gender-variant subjectivities that participate in its production and preservation, I have posited that its epistemological *primacy* is of crucial importance for the success of any future social and legal reforms in Pakistan. The insurrectionary discursive practices of my Lahori interlocutors offer, then, an invaluable script for *understanding* and *doing* the law in a contemporary society.

CONCLUSION

At the close of our historical, legal and anthropological journey – spanning two millennia, three continents and two often-incongruous epistemologies of law and society – it is pertinent to offer some comparative concluding observations. This brief chapter examines the salience of a comparative approach to historical and present-day phenomena related to human sexual and gender diversity, legality, intimacy and sociality in what is today known as international human rights law and Islamic law. It also revisits the potential implications of this study for the contemporary plight of sexually diverse and gender-variant Muslims. In this respect, my concept of insurrectionary vernacular knowledge is given some additional defining contours and examined, in particular, in relation to the *praxis* of both human rights and Islamic law.

Co-Histories in the Making

One way to approach the long social, epistemic and legal processes at the heart of this book is to foreground some peculiar temporal and spatial convergences occurring amongst them. What follows, then, is a series of remarks that loosely form a *co-historical* narrative[1] of sorts: one in which the past and the present intrinsically *coexist* through reiterations of sexual/gender subjectivities, cultural memory and politics, and in which the law is seen as a principal repository of such discursive practices.

Perhaps the first striking fact about the parallel histories of European and Muslim laws is that a major pre-modern reform of both systems occurred at roughly the same time. While western Christendom underwent colossal social and legal changes between the eleventh and the thirteenth century CE, Muslim polities lived through the so-called 'classical period' of Islamic jurisprudence (tenth/fourth to thirteenth/ seventh century CE/AH). In each system, the rise of middle-class powers threatened to challenge the ruling elites and therefore resulted in novel mechanisms of subjugation and control. But, whereas in Europe this led to the invention of the model Christian 'man' and 'woman', which ultimately begot a series of social and legal aberrations, from 'buggery laws' to the Pyres of Sodom, Muslim polities retained a heterogeneous approach to sexual and gender difference. Thus, for example, in some classical *fiqh*, it was perfectly possible to argue that *liwat*, whilst reprehensible, was *de jure* unpunishable in this world, and most probably permissible in the hereafter.

Both Christian and Muslim pre-modern polities endeavoured to distinguish between the public and the private space, with the latter seen as an exclusive country club for the middle and upper social classes. European 'sodomy laws', thus, arose primarily as a 'public' and, often, 'political' offence, which was selectively enforced against 'enemies of the state'. The punitive gaze of Victorian laws and morality into the hitherto 'protected' privacy of its subjects was thus an exceptional and far-reaching legal development, not least because it was diligently exported to all of Britain's overseas dominions. The idea that the law can encroach upon the *private* gender/sexual *space* of its subjects is, thus, quintessentially European and by and large inapplicable to pre-modern Muslim societies. Correspondingly, pre-colonial Islamic law, in theory and in practice, made no resolute attempt to govern the private sphere of Muslims in as much as their sense of sexual and gender self is concerned; the evidentiary requirements for the *hadd* offence of *zina* are an apt example. In addition, Muslim polities accommodated a variety of class-based forms of sociality, intimacy and familial life that stand in sharp contrast with the (later, capitalist) European concept of the 'nuclear family' and its intrinsic normative structure. Of course, this is not to say that Muslim societies were not patriarchal and gender-biased. Importantly, however, the laws of these societies allowed for a greater diversity of same-sex and gender-variant practices and relations *even* in the public space.

Whilst the idea of a 'less-than-human' enemy – who can, therefore, be conquered, killed or assimilated without a serious moral dilemma – was certainly shared by many imperial projects across the world, it was overwhelmingly a European innovation, from the Crusades onwards, to 'otherise' Muslims with a specific and sustained focus on their imputed *sexual* and *gender* 'savageness'. This Orientalist trend first made the Muslim a 'licentious other', warranting tight legal control, and then a 'puritan other', in need of gender/sexual 'liberation', again by means of the law. In either scenario, an 'East-West moral divide' was conjured up with an almost exclusive reference to the sexual and gender difference of the Muslim. And, invariably, a 'colonisation by law' was proposed as a possible solution. As international law is historically complicit in these imperialistic attempts, the cultural memory of Muslim communities carries an understandable discomfort with laws of European (or even *quasi*-European) provenance, of *any* kind. My fieldwork in Pakistan suggests what may be broadly true for any contemporary Muslim-majority community. Yet recourse to contemporary state 'Islamic' laws is an equally problematic endeavour.

Although Muslim 'post-classical' societies had developed an intriguing form of 'legal sociality', one in which a polity and a polymorphous Islamic law coexisted in a variety of mutually dependant relations, it would be a mistake to consider modern Muslim-majority nation states as the rightful heirs to this peculiar symbiosis. This is because the very idea of the nation state, with its intrinsic legal, economic and political mechanisms, *requires* and *produces* a different kind of (human rights) law, which – at least in theory – is there primarily to ensure the citizens' protection both *by* and *from* the State. The powers of the nation state are considerably different from those of pre-modern Muslim polities. They are, historically and operationally, incongruous with those of pre-modern *fuqaha'*, judges, caliphs and other heterogeneous agents of the Islamic law of the past. Codifying, rigidifying and de-pluralising the selective collections of classical *fiqh*, in order for them to serve as the modern 'statutes' of state 'Islamic' law, are processes that are, therefore, antithetical to the very nature of Islamic law in all its variegated historical forms. The attempts of the modern Muslim-majority nation states to develop their specific 'official' versions of Islamic law are thus incongruous with the very tradition of the pluralist *umma* on which they claim to rely. In sum, Islamic law of today *cannot* be subsumed within the concept of state law, just as a contemporary Muslim-majority state *cannot* claim to be an 'Islamic' state.

Both human rights law and Islamic law seem, then, to make sense primarily *in the vernacular*. As the Pakistani case study shows, these two legal systems, in fact, need each other today to effectively challenge the systemic state and societal oppression experienced by sexually diverse and gender-variant Muslims (and many others). To wit, in the vernacular – culturally and historically conscious – contemporary Islamic law and human rights law, it certainly *might* constitute an offence to discriminate on the basis of one's sexual orientation and gender identity. It is so not only because of the recent developments in international law, but also because it goes against an exhilarating social and legal history of sexual and gender diversity in Muslim communities: a history that is still in the making, largely against the odds of European and Muslim modernity, and their aftermaths; yet, a co-history, too – necessarily complicated by those and other social and legal ethea.

Insurrectionary Vernacular Knowledge

The vernacular, however, is a somewhat elusive concept.[2] The idea of insurrectionary vernacular knowledge, as elucidated in this book, corresponds perhaps most closely with what the legal anthropologist Sally Engle Merry has described as *vernacularisation* of human rights language – the process in which this discourse is 'extracted from the universal and adapted to national and local communities'.[3] For Merry, this process can range from *replication*, 'a process in which the imported institution remains largely unchanged from its transnational prototype', to *hybridisation*, 'a process that merges imported institutions and symbols with local ones, sometimes uneasily'.[4] The focus of Merry's analysis of vernacularisation is on *translators*, whom Richard Wilson dubs 'knowledge brokers' because they 'translate human rights talk both downwards into local argot as well as upwards, for instance, when they turn local grievances into funding proposals for international donors'.[5] However, partly due to an exceptionally multidimensional nature of Islamic legal discourses as well as those – as we have seen – of human rights, the terrain of vernacular knowledge examined in this book seems infinitely more complex. Translators are, of course, important, but in some ways *all* of my Pakistani interlocutors could be described as having that role in the various worlds they often concomitantly inhabit. Translations, then, of necessity, go *more* than two ways and are an integral part of daily life in the vernacular. The fact that this daily life, by and large, is both confined to and contested by certain localities – spatial, temporal, linguistic, legal, religio-spiritual, class-based, etc. – accounts for the intrinsic *situatedness* of vernacular translation as social practice. It has also led me to document and reflect upon a particular dimension of the vernacular – that of *resistance*.

In her problematisation of the term 'local', Sally Engle Merry mentions, *inter alia*, its 'recalcitrant particularity'.[6] Related to this, presumably, is her concern that when certain radical ideas are presented by translators as 'compatible with existing ways of thinking, these ideas will not induce change'.[7] I would like to propose an opposite possibility – that radical ideas are often an integral part of vernacular knowledge, which allow it to challenge and survive other, often more powerful and 'mainstream', discursive social practices, such as those of the State and official legalities. Recalcitrant, insurrectionary particularity of the vernacular does not make it a site *free* from power, social oppression and control, of course. Local knowledge sometimes can be as patriarchal and normative as other forms of discursive collectivity. Such knowledge nevertheless has an agency indispensable in uphill battles against colonisations, epistemic and otherwise. This agency both produces and resists certain subjectivities,[8] including those relating to sexuality, gender and religion. The way protest is mobilised in the vernacular may not always be readily apparent, especially to outsiders, as certain radical ideas may require camouflage in the various stages of their elaboration or can be legible only by the specific rationalities of the vernacular. These survival practices make them exceptionally difficult for outsiders to study, as the researcher's unlearning process, in which one is gradually accustomed to lifeworlds and epistemologies other than one's own, is a precondition for any substantial analysis. Furthermore, as Merry helpfully suggests, researchers are also translators of sorts, as they 'typically translate the cultural worlds of the people they study into the cultural worlds of their readers and students'.[9] Therefore, the 'end product' of an analysis is always mediated, partial and contingent. There cannot be an absolute or perfect translation.

Towards the Praxis of Human Rights?

Amongst the myriad philosophical uses of the Ancient Greek word *praxis* (πρᾶξις), one describes it as the process *leading towards* practicing ideas – i.e. the correlative act or space between theory and practice. This may be of some salience for the few final words on the paradox of human rights. A similar approach has been suggested before: 'Instead of asking if human rights are a good idea, [one should] explore[] what difference they make'.[10] This is far from a mechanical pragmatism; rather, it suggests that claims produced *in abstracto* by the historical and present-day repositories of human rights – including international law and state law and the various institutions they rely on – may have material consequences radically incongruent with the professed goals and purposes of such claims and, *mutatis mutandis*, the goals and purposes of institutions and organisations that harbour them.

We have seen that the discursive histories and, indeed, practices of human rights have been largely reflective of the history and practice of imperialism. If neoliberal co-optation and re-colonisation are primarily material loci of human rights, can human rights really be understood as a quest for greater happiness, as my Pakistani interlocutors have emphatically proposed? After all, my empirical findings suggest that such a vernacular concept of rights relies on an altogether different set of values to those professed by the Pakistani state or those that seemingly underpin the international human rights system.

Mark Goodale has described this conundrum as a type of vernacularisation of rights in which local social actors 'have picked apart and appropriated only some aspects of human rights discourse'.[11] He calls it, also, 'the Pandora's box of neoliberalism: when the power of one part of neoliberalism (human rights discourse) is used to resist other parts', such as the 'privatization of utility concerns, the rationalization of land tenure, democratization, the capitalization of property, and so on'.[12] But, can an imperial tool *par excellence* be wrested from empire without causing epistemic and political damage to one's cause? What is more, is that tool truly worth the wrestle?

I want to return for a moment to the concept of human rights as a quest for greater happiness. In *The Promise of Happiness*, Sara Ahmed warns of the dangers of happiness taken as the ultimate goal of human life.[13] 'Ideas of happiness involve social as well as moral distinctions', she submits, 'insofar as they rest on ideas of who is worthy as well as capable of being happy "in the right way"'.[14] In order to escape this normativity, Ahmed proposes to *suspend* belief that happiness is a good thing: 'In this mode of suspension, we can consider not only what makes happiness good but how happiness *participates* in making things good'.[15] In other words, '[i]f we do not assume that happiness is what we must defend, if we start questioning the happiness we are defending, then we can ask other questions about life, about what we want from life, or what we want life to become'.[16] The same rationale could be followed in the case of human rights. If their purported ethical pre-eminence is suspended, if one no longer feels obliged to defend them at all costs, perhaps one makes room for seeing and living other forms of insurrectionary social practice.

This is where a turn to praxis might reveal some additional dimensions of the problem. For the majority of my Pakistani interlocutors, human rights were at once an exigency of spiritual life and a tool used in day-to-day social and political bargaining. Their ethics, at best, were *contingent* upon a larger system of belief and everyday practice that is, remarkably, *at odds* with the world(s) of state and international law. This was, in fact, the core of their insurrectionary consciousness; as Sara Ahmed suggests: 'It is no accident that revolutionary consciousness means feeling at odds with the world, or feeling that the world is odd'.[17] Yet this necessary estrangement, this *otherworldliness*, was not primarily organised around or by the (vernacularised) concept of human rights. The priorities were, clearly, elsewhere.

Towards the Praxis of Islamic Law?

I have already referred, in Chapter 4, to the various instances of praxis relevant for the Islamic legal tradition, from the Prophet Muhammad's 'trodden path', or *sunna*, to the legal praxis of pre-modern scholars and judges that had shaped the defining features of Islamic law. Having postulated the way some of those features had been challenged and reshaped in times of modernity (or, indeed, multiple modernities), it is possible to account for the modern praxis of Islamic law (or, perhaps, 'Islamic' law), too, whose preoccupation and ability to translate 'back and forth' between pre-modern *fiqh* and the exigencies of nation state has been questioned and deemed ultimately unsuccessful, at least by the present author. I have also suggested the concept of the vernacular as central to *locating* the afterlives of Islamic law, posterior or parallel to its modernist overkill. What praxis, then, can reveal and pertain to such sites in contemporary Muslim lifeworlds?

First, it is plain that any praxis constitutive of 'things Islamic', as such, needs to relate, or at least profess to relate, to Muslim hieropraxis, however heterogeneously the latter be conceived. In other words, the harmony of creed ('*aqida*) and life constructed thereupon is an organising concept that, in its collective and individual emanations, presupposes Muslim praxis that may or may not include diverse forms of legality. We have seen, apropos, that the very concept of *shari'a* can and had been construed beyond its nowadays-ubiquitous association with *fiqh*. It is therefore pertinent to ask whether law, of *any* kind, is a helpful ingredient of Muslim life today, *tout court*.

Related to this fundamental question is the state of what in this book has been loosely described as 'the Muslim world'. It is important to reiterate the intimate and relational, as opposed to geographical, nature of this construct, which relies on Muslim lifeworlds and the knowledge they inherit, challenge and/or reproduce. This world is in constant flux, yet it also relies on traditions, on histories and meta-histories, which may not be common to *all* Muslims but are considered important by some. It is this pluralist quality of the Muslim past, as much as the Muslim present, that has informed and sustained my focus on the vernacular and that necessitated an *interruptive* approach to the making of what can, again, only loosely be termed the Islamic legal tradition.

In a related context, Lila Abu-Lughod has argued that 'it might be fruitful to examine how "Muslim women's rights" makes and remakes the world'.[18] It would certainly be salient, *mutatis mutandis*, to ask how 'Islamic law' today makes and remakes the Muslim world, and in particular: 'How, when, and where is the concept deployed? What transformations of social life and individual lives are produced in its name? Who enables that work and is in turn enabled by it? What new paths of power and channels of capital, financial and cultural, does it open up?'[19] These queries could be of particular significance for sexually diverse and gender-variant Muslims. And, if there is a meaningful contemporary praxis of Islamic law in any given locale or context – as there was, for example, on an inter-personal level amongst my Pakistani interlocutors – these questions might draw it out.

A turn to praxis is, ultimately, always a *return* to knowledge that is about experiencing, negotiating, translating, re-appropriating and, indeed, *living* the self and/in the world.

NOTES

Introduction

1. My interview with Neeli, Lahore, Pakistan, 27 September 2011 CE. Neeli self-identifies as *khwajasara*, a Pakistani gender-variant subject position, and she is also an observant Muslim. The interview took place in a *khwajasara* household, amidst the busy lower-class Lahori neighbourhood. *Zenana* is, today, also a gender-variant subjectivity.

2. Pakistan's Permanent Mission to the United Nations in Geneva, 'Aide Memoire on behalf of the OIC' distributed to the delegates of the 59th session of the United Nations Commission on Human Rights, 17 March – 24 April 2003 CE, in response to the draft resolution E/CN.4/2003/L.92 entitled 'Human Rights and Sexual Orientation'. 'OIC' currently stands for the Organisation of Islamic Co-operation. The United Nations Commission on Human Rights was replaced, in 2006 CE, by the United Nations Human Rights Council.

3. See, for example, Abdullahi Ahmed An-Na'im, *Toward an Islamic Reformation: Civil Liberties, Human Rights, and International Law* (Syracuse University Press, Syracuse 1996); Ann Elizabeth Mayer, *Islam and Human Rights: Tradition and Politics* (3rd edn; Westview Press, Boulder 1999); Ruud Peters, 'Islamic Law and Human Rights: A Contribution to an Ongoing Debate' (1999) 10(1) *Islam and Christian-Muslim Relations* 5; Mahmood Monshipouri, *Islamism, Secularism, and Human Rights in the Middle East* (Lynne Rienner Publishers, Boulder 1998).

4. One of the latest publications of this type is Mark S. Ellis, Anver M. Emon & Benjamin Glahn (eds), *Islamic Law and International Human Rights Law: Searching for Common Ground?* (Oxford University Press, New York 2012).

5. Mashood A. Baderin, *International Human Rights Law and Islamic Law* (Oxford University Press, Oxford 2003), p. 117.

6. The margin of appreciation doctrine was developed by the European Court of Human Rights in order to take into effect the fact that the European Convention on Human Rights 1950 may be interpreted differently in various

member states of the Council of Europe. In the cases in which the margin of appreciation doctrine applies, the judges of this court are obliged to take into account the cultural, historic and philosophical differences that underpin the legal systems of the member states. See *Handyside* v *United Kingdom* A 24 (1976); 1 EHRR 737. The other 'moral questions' that, according to Baderin, should be understood as within the Muslim-majority states' margin of appreciation are 'family', 'blasphemy' and 'abortion'; see Baderin, *supra* n. 5, p. 234.

7. See Vanja Hamzić, 'The Case of "Queer Muslims": Sexual Orientation and Gender Identity in International Human Rights Law and Muslim Legal and Social Ethos' (2011) 11(2) *Human Rights Law Review* 237, pp. 261–262.

8. See, for example, Khaled El-Rouayheb, *Before Homosexuality in the Arab-Islamic World, 1500–1800* (University of Chicago Press, Chicago 2005); Dror Ze'evi, *Producing Desire: Changing Sexual Discourse in the Ottoman Middle East, 1500–1900* (University of California Press, Berkeley 2006); Everett K. Rowson, 'The Effeminates of Early Medina' (1991) 111(4) *Journal of the American Oriental Society* 671; Sahar Amer, 'Medieval Arab Lesbians and Lesbian-Like Women' (2009) 18(2) *Journal of the History of Sexuality* 215.

9. See Samar Habib, *Female Homosexuality in the Middle East: Histories and Representations* (Routledge, New York 2007); Jerry W. Wright Jr. & Everett K. Rowson (eds), *Homoeroticism in Classical Arabic Literature* (Columbia University Press, New York 1997).

10. See Scott Siraj al-Haqq Kugle, *Homosexuality in Islam: Critical Reflection on Gay, Lesbian, and Transgender Muslims* (Oneworld, Oxford 2010); Scott Siraj al-Haqq Kugle, 'Sexuality, Diversity, and Ethics in the Agenda of Progressive Muslims' in Omid Safi (ed.), *Progressive Muslims: On Justice, Gender, and Pluralism* (Oneworld, Oxford 2003), pp. 190–234.

11. For a series of anthropological and sociological chapters on the subject, see Stephen O. Murray & Will Roscoe, *Islamic Homosexualities: Culture, History, and Literature* (New York University Press, New York 1997).

12. See especially Samar Habib (ed.), *Islam and Homosexuality* (Praeger, Santa Barbara 2010), Vols 1–2.

13. Samar Habib, 'Introduction' in Samar Habib (ed.), *Islam and Homosexuality* (Praeger, Santa Barbara 2010), Vol. 1, p. xli.

14. *Ibid*, p. xlviii. See also Rusmir Musić, 'Queer Visions of Islam' in Samar Habib (ed.), *Islam and Homosexuality* (Praeger, Santa Barbara 2010), Vol. 2, pp. 327–346.

15. Cf. my interview with Jamila, Lahore, Pakistan, 6 October 2011. Jamila is the leader of an underground middle-class collective of sexually diverse Muslims in Punjab, a Pakistani province of which Lahore is the capital. For a detailed exploration of my fieldwork in Pakistan, please refer to Chapter 5 of this book.

16. Oliver Wendell Holmes Jr, *The Common Law* (Little, Brown, Boston 1963 [1881]), p. 5.

17. 'Jurisprudence, as I look at it, is simply law in its most generalized part. Every effort to reduce a case to a rule is an effort of jurisprudence, although the name as used in English is confined to the broadest rules and most fundamental

conceptions'; Oliver Wendell Holmes Jr, 'The Path of Law' in David Kennedy & William W. Fisher III (eds), *The Canon of American Legal Thought* (Princeton University Press, Princeton 2006 [reproduced from (1897) 10 *Harvard Law Review* 457]), p. 40.

18. 'It is revolting to have no better reason for a rule of law than that so it was laid down in the time of Henry IV. It is still more revolting if the grounds upon which it was laid down have vanished long since, and the rule simply persists from blind imitation of the past'; *ibid*, p. 37.

19. Cf. Roscoe Pound, 'Law in Books and Law in Action' (1910) 44 *American Law Review* 12.

20. Robert H. Mnookin & Lewis Kornhauser, 'Bargaining in the Shadow of the Law: The Case of Divorce' (1979) 88(5) *Yale Law Journal* 950.

21. Karl Llewellyn, 'Some Realism about Realism: Responding to Dean Pound' in David Kennedy & William W. Fisher III (eds), *The Canon of American Legal Thought* (Princeton University Press, Princeton 2006 [reproduced from (1931) 44 *Harvard Law Review* 1222]), p. 150.

22. Hijaz is a region in the west of the present-day Kingdom of Saudi Arabia, which hosts the cities of Mecca and Medina.

23. According to a seminal anthropological account, the term *imponderabilia* denotes 'a series of phenomena of great importance which cannot possibly be recorded by questioning or computing documents, but have to be observed in their full actuality'; Bronisław Malinowski, *Agronauts of the Western Pacific* (Routledge, London 2002 [1922]), p. 18.

24. 'Critique offers possibilities of analyzing [. . .] discourses of power to understand how subjects are fabricated or positioned by them, what powers they secure (and disguise or veil), what assumptions they naturalize, what privileges they fix, what norms they mobilize, and what or whom these norms exclude'; Wendy Brown & Janet Halley, 'Introduction' in Wendy Brown & Janet Halley (eds), *Left Legalism / Left Critique* (Duke University Press, Durham 2002), p. 26.

25. I have attempted to follow the general four-step anthropological approach to enter the field and get 'acclimated to the setting', which involves (1) 'taking in the physical setting'; (2) 'developing relationships with inhabitants (locating potential guides and informants)'; (3) 'tracking, observing [. . .] and asking questions'; and (4) 'locating subgroups and starts (central characters in various subgroups)'; Bruce Lawrence-Berg, *Qualitative Research Methods for the Social Sciences* (Allyn and Bacon, London 2001), p. 155. Since my first visit to Pakistan, in the late 1990s CE, I have developed close relationships with several key informants for this study. Their guidance and a snowballing technique have helped me establish further contacts.

26. John Brewer, *Ethnography* (Open University Press, Buckingham 2000), p. 11.

27. For the purposes of the present research, I conducted 50 unstructured or semi-structured interviews in Pakistan (47 in Lahore, three in Islamabad), in 2011 CE (mainly during the months of September and October). All of them were recorded, after obtaining an expressed permission from the interviewees.

In Chapter 5, some of these interviews are also referred to as *conversations*, in order to set them apart from more formal approaches, which are typically used in sociological rather than in anthropological studies. 40 interviewees were self-identified sexually diverse and/or gender-variant Muslims, mostly from the Pakistani province of Punjab, but also (five of them) from other parts of the country. 15 of those belonged to various middle-class groups, 14 were working-class people, while 11 of them had a lower-class background. Further 10 interviewees were lawyers, judges, civil society activists and academic researchers in Pakistan who were directly involved in the lifeworlds of sexually diverse and gender-variant Pakistani Muslims. Of these interviewees, five were of middle-class and other five of upper-middle-class background. For further details, please see Chapter 5.1 of this book.

28. John Comaroff, 'Notes on Anthropological Method, Mainly in the Key of E', presented at *Workshop on Interdisciplinary Standards for Systematic Qualitative Research*, National Science Foundation, 19–20 May 2005, Washington, DC, USA, available at http://www.wjh.harvard.edu/nsfqual/Comaroff%20Paper.pdf (accessed 1 August 2014), p. 2.

29. Catherine Dawson, *Practical Research Methods: A User-friendly Guide to Mastering Research Techniques and Projects* (How To Do Books Ltd, Oxford 2002), p. 28.

30. Tim Ingold, 'The Temporality of the Landscape' (1993) 25(2) *World Archaeology* 152, p. 156.

31. Clifford Geertz, *Local Knowledge: Further Essays in Interpretative Anthropology* (Basic Books Inc, New York 1983).

32. Cf. Boaventura de Sousa Santos, *Toward a New Legal Common Sense: Law, Globalization, and Emancipation* (2nd edn; Butterworths, London 2002); Boaventura de Sousa Santos, *Another Production is Possible: Beyond the Capitalist Canon* (Verso, London 2006), Vol. 2; Boaventura de Sousa Santos, *Another Production is Possible: Beyond Northern Epistemologies* (Verso, London 2006), Vol. 3; Boaventura de Sousa Santos, 'The World Social Forum and the Global Left' (2008) 36(2) *Politics and Society* 247.

33. Comaroff, *supra* n. 28, p. 5.

34. Cf. Charlotte Aull Davies, *Reflexive Ethnographies: A Guide to Researching Selves and Others* (Routledge, London 2002 [1999]), p. 35.

35. Stephen Valocchi, 'Not Yet Queer Enough: The Lessons of Queer Theory for the Sociology of Gender and Sexuality' (2005) 19(6) *Gender and Society* 750, p. 751. See also Sharyn Graham Davies, *Gender Diversity in Indonesia: Sexuality, Islam and Queer Selves* (Routledge, London 2010), p. 6.

36. Susan Stryker, 'Transgender Studies: Queer Theory's Evil Twin' (2004) 10(2) *Journal of Lesbian and Gay Studies* 212, p. 214. See also Graham Davies, *supra* n. 35, p. 7.

37. See, for example, Alain Pottage, 'Persons and Things: An Ethnographic Analogy' (2010) 30(1) *Economy and Society* 112. In Chapter 5 of this book, I explore the analogical connections between the historical and present-day ethnographic accounts of gender-variant and/or sexually diverse Muslim subjectivities.

Chapter 1   A Critique of Terminological Conundrums

1. The debate, in short, relates to whether (some or all) human rights are culturally relative, i.e. differently applicable in varying cultural and social environments, or they are universal *sui generis,* that is, of the same meaning and importance for all cultures and societies.

2. While essentialists believe that human sexuality and gender identities are 'predestined' forms of an 'essential nature of things', constructionists see them as socially constructed and therefore mutable. See, for example, Kathryn Woodward (ed.), *Identity and Difference* (Sage, London 1997). See also John D. DeLamater & Janet Shibley Hyde, 'Essentialism vs. Social Constructionism in the Study of Human Sexuality: The Use of Theory in Research and Scholarship on Sexuality' (1998) 35 *Journal of Sex Research* 10.

3. Janet Halley, 'Gay Rights and Identity Imitation: Issues in the Ethics of Representation' in David Kairys (ed.), *The Politics of Law* (3rd edn; Basic Books, New York 1998 [1982]), p. 120.

4. These principles outline a comprehensive set of international legal duties relating to sexual orientation and gender identity. See the *Yogyakarta Principles on the Application of International Human Rights Law in relation to Sexual Orientation and Gender Identity,* available at http://www.yogyakartaprinciples. org (accessed 17 August 2014). The Yogyakarta Principles are critically examined in Chapter 3 of this book.

5. For the seminal work on Orientalism, which is understood here as a European ideological creation devised by global northern writers, philosophers and colonial administrators to deal with the perceived 'otherness' of so-called 'Eastern' cultures, beliefs and customs, see Edward W. Said, *Orientalism* (Penguin Books, London 2003 [1978, 1995, 2003]).

6. Amin Maalouf, *In the Name of Identity: Violence and the Need to Belong* (trans. Barbara Bray; Penguin Books, New York 2003 [1996]), p. 9.

7. *Ibid*, p. 143.

8. K. Anthony Appiah, 'Identity, Authenticity, Survival: Multicultural Societies and Social Reproduction' in Amy Guttmann (ed.), *Multiculturalism: Examining the Politics of Recognition* (Princeton University Press, Princeton 1994), pp. 159–160.

9. José A. Lindgren Alves, 'The Declaration of Human Rights in Postmodernity' (2000) 22 *Human Rights Quarterly* 478, p. 490.

10. Wayne Morgan, 'Queering International Human Rights Law' in Carl Stychin & Didi Herman (eds), *Law and Sexuality: the Global Arena* (University of Minnesota Press, Minneapolis 2001 [2000]), p. 212.

11. Sara Ahmed, *Queer Phenomenology: Orientations, Objects, Others* (Duke University Press, Durham 2006), p. 84 (emphasis added).

12. *The Universal Declaration of Human Rights*, Preamble, adopted by the United Nations General Assembly resolution 217 A (III) on 10 December 1948.

13. Michael J. Perry, *The Idea of Human Rights: Four Inquiries* (Oxford University Press, Oxford 1998), p. 5. Similar explanatory systems are built, for example, in James Griffin, *On Human Rights* (Oxford University Press, Oxford 2008); Ari Kohen, *In Defense of Human Rights: A Non-Religious Grounding in a Pluralist World* (Routledge, London 2007).

14. Balakrishnan Rajagopal, 'Introduction: Encountering Ambivalence' in Mark Goodale & Sally Engle Merry (eds), *The Practice of Human Rights: Tracking Law between the Global and the Local* (Cambridge University Press, Cambridge 2007), p. 275.

15. This phrase is borrowed from Martti Koskenniemi's critical history of international law. See Martti Koskenniemi, *The Gentle Civilizer of Nations: The Rise and Fall of International Law, 1870–1960* (Cambridge University Press, Cambridge 2004 [2001]).

16. Cf. Robert McCorquodale, 'The Individual and the International Legal System' in Malcolm D. Evans (ed.), *International Law* (2nd edn; Oxford University Press, Oxford 2006), pp. 307–337.

17. See, for example, Vanja Hamzić, 'Unlearning Human Rights and False Grand Dichotomies: Indonesian Archipelagic Selves Beyond Sexual/Gender Universality' (2012) 4(1) *Jindal Global Law Review* 157. The perils of neo-liberal human rights are discussed in some detail in Chapter 3 of this book.

18. Hilary Charlesworth & Christine Chinkin, *The Boundaries of International Law: A Feminist Analysis* (Manchester University Press, Manchester 2000), p. 201.

19. See, for example, Claus Wilcke, 'Der Kodex Urnamma (CU): Versuch einer Rekonstruktion' in Zvi Abusch (ed.), *Riches Hidden in Secret Places: Ancient Near Eastern Studies in Memory of Thorkild Jacobson* (Eisenbrauns, Winona Lake 2002), pp. 291–333.

20. For a classic account on Aśoka's legacy, see Romila Thapar, *Aśoka and the Decline of the Mauryas* (rev. edn; Oxford University Press, New York 1998 [1961]).

21. See, for example, Ἀριστοτέλης, Ἠθικῶν Νικομαχείων (c.350 BCE); and also Sarah Broadie & Christopher Rowe (eds), *Aristotle, Nicomachean Ethics: Translation, Introduction and Commentary* (Oxford University Press, Oxford 2002).

22. One of the best examples of the ethico-legal reforms pursued by the Prophet Muhammad is his *Constitution of Medina* (c.622 CE), which stipulates numerous civil rights and duties of the citizens of Medina. While the original document has not been preserved, scholars generally accept the authenticity of the copy of the *Constitution* included in Muhammad ibn Ishaq ibn Yasar's *sirat* (biography) of the Prophet. However, even Ibn Ishaq's *sirat* has only survived in the abridged copies of his two students' edited copies of his work. These documents have been reassembled and translated in Alfred Guillaume, *The Life of Muhammad* (Oxford University Press, Oxford 2003 [1955]).

23. Sunni tradition generally regards the rule of the four *khulafa' al-rashidun* (the rightly guided caliphs) as an 'elective authority based on consent', in which many human rights have been duly respected. Bustami Mohamed Khir, 'The

Islamic Quest for Sociopolitical Justice' in Peter Scott & William T. Cavanaugh (eds), *The Blackwell Companion to Political Theology* (Blackwell Publishing, Malden 2004), p. 505. However, the first caliphate lasted only some thirty years, after which it was transformed into *mulk*, a monarchy founded on force. See Ibn Khaldun, *al Muqaddimah (The Introduction)* (trans. F. Rosenthal; Routledge & Kegan Paul, London 1958 [1377]), pp. 598–608.

24. Gayatri Chakravorty Spivak, 'Righting Wrongs' (2004) 103 *South Atlantic Quarterly* 523, p. 524.

25. Spivak explains this subtle twist: 'Only a "kind of" social Darwinism, of course. Just as "the white man's burden," undertaking to civilize and develop, was only "a kind of" oppression'; *ibid*.

26. *Ibid*, p. 527. Joseph A. Massad rightfully asserts that this conclusion is applicable to urban poor as well. See Joseph A. Massad, *Desiring Arabs* (University of Chicago Press, Chicago 2007), pp. 38–39.

27. *Subaltern* are considered those persons and groups who remain outside the hegemonic power structure and whose self-identification is largely inconceivable because of oppression they are bound to endure. For a classic essay on this phenomenon, see Gayatri Chakravorty Spivak, 'Can the Subaltern Speak?' in Cary Nelson & Lawrence Grossberg (eds), *Marxism and the Interpretation of Culture* (University of Illinois Press, Urbana 1988), pp. 271–313.

28. See, for example, Geeta Chowdhry & Sheila Nair (eds), *Power, Postcolonialism and International Relations: Reading Race, Gender and Class* (Routledge, London 2002); Anthony Pagden, 'Human Rights, Natural Rights, and Europe's Imperial Legacy' (2003) 31 *Political Theory* 2; Henry F. Carey, 'The Postcolonial State and the Protection of Human Rights' (2002) 22 *Comparative Studies of South Asia, Africa and the Middle East* 59.

29. See generally Marie-Bénédicte Dembour, 'Following the Movement of a Pendulum: Between Universalism and Relativism' in Jane K. Cowan, Marie-Bénédicte Dembour & Richard A. Wilson (eds), *Culture and Rights: Anthropological Perspectives* (Cambridge University Press, Cambridge 2001), pp. 56–80.

30. See Stephen A. James, 'Reconciling International Human Rights and Cultural Relativism: The Case of Female Circumcision' (1994) 8 *Bioethics* 1, p. 2.

31. *The Universal Declaration of Human Rights*, Article 1, *supra* n. 12 (emphasis added).

32. On moral universality of rights, see Jack Donnelly, *Universal Human Rights in Theory and Practice* (Cornell University Press, Ithaca 1989), pp. 1–2. For an opposite view, see Victor Segesvary, 'Group Rights: The Definition of Group Rights in the Contemporary Legal Debate based on Socio-Cultural Analysis' (1995) 3 *International Journal on Group Rights* 89, pp. 91–93.

33. Guyora Binder, 'Cultural Relativism and Cultural Imperialism in Human Rights Law' (1999) 5 *Buffalo Human Rights Law Review* 211, p. 214.

34. See Jack Donnelly, 'Third Generation Rights' in Catherine Brölmann, René Lefeber & Marjoleine Zieck (eds), *Peoples and Minorities in International Law* (Martinus Nijhoff Publishers, Dordrecht 1993), p. 135.

35. See Binder, *supra* n. 33, p. 221.

36. One of the reconciliatory attempts is Abdullahi Ahmed An-Na'im's proposal to instate a '*process of retroactive legitimation* of the existing international human rights standards', so that they might achieve a greater cross-cultural appreciation. Abdullahi Ahmed An-Na'im, 'Introduction' in Abdullahi Ahmed An-Na'im (ed.), *Human Rights in Cross-Cultural Perspectives: A Quest for Consensus* (University of Pennsylvania Press, Philadelphia 1992), pp. 5–6 (emphasis in original).

37. Jane K. Cowan, Marie-Bénédicte Dembour & Richard A. Wilson, 'Introduction' in Jane K. Cowan, Marie-Bénédicte Dembour & Richard A. Wilson (eds), *Culture and Rights: Anthropological Perspectives* (Cambridge University Press, Cambridge 2001), pp. 4–5.

38. See Fred Halliday, 'Relativism and Universalism in Human Rights: The Case of the Islamic Middle East' in David Beetham (ed.), *Politics and Human Rights* (Blackwell, Oxford 1995), pp. 154–155; Edward Mortimer, 'Islam and Human Rights' (1983) 12 *Index on Censorship* 5, p. 5. Paraphrased in Mashood Baderin, *International Human Rights and Islamic Law* (Oxford University Press, Oxford 2003), p. 13.

39. For instance, the Muslim nationalist agendas instrumentalised by ruling political elites in many Muslim-majority countries, which see human rights, *tout court*, as a threat to their authoritarian regimes. See, for example, Patrick Seale, *The Struggle for Arab Independence: Riad el-Solh and the Makers of the Modern Middle East* (Cambridge University Press, Cambridge 2009).

40. Talal Asad, *The Idea of an Anthropology of Islam* (Georgetown University Center for Contemporary Arab Studies, Washington 1996 [1986]), p. 11.

41. Anastasia Vakulenko, 'Islamic Dress in Human Rights Jurisprudence and the Surrounding Debate: A Critical Feminist Analysis', a PhD in Laws thesis submitted to the University of Nottingham (University of Nottingham School of Law, Nottingham 2008), on file with author, p. 12.

42. *Ibid.* See generally Friedrich Nietzsche, *Zur Genealogie der Moral: Eine Streitschrift* (Reclam, Ditzingen 1988 [1887]).

43. Wendy Brown, *States of Injury: Power and Freedom in Late Modernity* (Princeton University Press, Princeton 1995), pp. 66–67, 71.

44. Judith Butler, *Undoing Gender* (Routledge, New York 2004), pp. 29–30. The purported emancipatory potential of human rights is discussed in some detail in Chapter 5 of this book.

45. Cf. Global Rights, *Demanding Credibility and Sustaining Activism: A Guide to Sexuality-based Advocacy* (Global Rights, Washington 2008), p. 25.

46. Cf. International Council on Human Rights Policy, *Sexuality and Human Rights: Discussion Paper* (International Council on Human Rights Policy, Versoix 2009), p. 44.

47. I.e. if involving two or more persons, a right cannot be exercised without their clearly stated consent.

48. I.e. the minimum age at which a person is considered to be legally competent of consenting to sexual activities.

49. I.e. the exercise of a right must not cause an excessive mental or physical harm. However, sexual acts which involve minor bodily harm are often deemed permissible, provided that they are exercised between the consenting adults.

50. Rosalind Petchesky, 'Sexual Rights Policies across Countries and Cultures: Conceptual Frameworks and Minefields' in Richard Parker, Rosalind Petchesky & Robert Sember (eds), *Sex Politics: Reports from the Front-lines* (Sexuality Policy Watch, Rio de Janeiro 2007), available at www.sxpolitics.org (accessed 6 January 2014).

51. In Foucault's view, these social forces 'obtiendrait qu'on n'en parle pas, par le seul jeu de prohibitions qui renvoient les unes aux autres: des mutismes qui, à force de se taire, imposent le silence ['ensure that one does not speak [of sex], without even having to pronounce the word, merely through the interplay of prohibitions that refer back to one another: mutisms which, by dint of saying nothing, impose silence']'. Michel Foucault, *Histoire de la sexualité: La volonté de savoir* (Gallimard, Paris 1976), Vol. 1, p. 25.

52. Eric Heinze, *Sexual Orientation: A Human Right* (Martinus Nijhoff Publishers, Dordrecht 1995), p. 159.

53. Cf. Global Rights, *supra* n. 45, p. 53.

54. Paul Hunt, *Report of the Special Rapporteur on the Right to Health* (United Nations Office of the High Commissioner for Human Rights, Geneva 2004), UN Doc E/CN.4/2004/49.

55. Although debated in scholarly and activist circles for decades, the notion of 'sexual rights' first appeared on the UN agenda during preparations for the 1994 CE Cairo-based United Nations Conference on Population and Development. See Pınar İlkkaracan, 'Introduction: Sexuality as a Contested Political Domain in the Middle East' in Pınar İlkkaracan (ed.), *Deconstructing Sexuality in the Middle East* (Ashgate Publishing, Burlington 2008), p. 5. See also Sonia Corrêa, 'From Reproductive Health to Sexual Rights: Achievements and Future Challenges' (1997) 5 *Reproductive Health Matters* 107.

56. For the seminal work on social control exerted through an imposed discourse on sexuality, see Foucault, *supra* n. 51.

57. International Council on Human Rights Policy, *supra* n. 46, p. 7.

58. Petchesky, *supra* n. 50, p. 12.

59. *Ibid.*

60. For an example of such view, see generally the website of *Focus on the Family*, available at http://www.focusonthefamily.com (accessed 6 January 2014).

61. See, for example, Judith Butler, *Bodies that Matter: On the Discursive Limits of 'Sex'* (Routledge, New York 1993); Anne Fausto-Sterling, *Sexing the Body: Gender Politics and the Construction of Sexuality* (Basic Books, New York 2000).

62. Cf. Petchesky, *supra* n. 50, p. 13.

63. Cf. Jacques Derrida, 'Choreographies' (1982) 12 *Diacritics* 66, p. 76.

64. The Charter enumerates sexuality- and reproduction-related aspects of the following twelve human rights: (1) the right to life, (2) the right to liberty and security of the person, (3) the right to equality and to be free from all forms of

discrimination, (4) the right to privacy, (5) the right to freedom of thought, (6) the right to information and education, (7) the right to choose whether or not to marry and to found and plan a family, (8) the right to decide whether or when to have children, (9) the right to health care and health protection, (10) the right to the benefits of scientific progress, (11) the right to freedom of assembly and political participation, (12) the right to be free from torture and ill treatment. It is predominantly focused on health and family planning, with little or no attention paid to other aspects of human expression of sexuality, such as sexual and gender diversity or sex workers rights. This Charter is available at http://www.ippf.org (accessed 7 January 2014).

65. Cf. International Council on Human Rights Policy, *supra* n. 46, p. 16.
66. See Alice M. Miller & Carole S. Vance, 'Sexuality, Human Rights, and Health' (2004) 7 *Health and Human Rights* 5, p. 9.
67. Rosalind Petchesky, 'Sexual Rights: Inventing a Concept, Mapping an International Practice' in Richard Parker, Regina Maria Barbosa & Peter Aggleton (eds), *Framing the Sexual Subject: the Politics of Gender, Sexuality and Power* (University of California Press, Berkeley 2000), p. 81.
68. See International Council on Human Rights Policy, *supra* n. 46, p. 16.
69. *Response to Statement on Human Rights and the So-Called Notions of 'Sexual Orientation' and 'Gender Identity'*, read by Syria, UN General Assembly, 63rd Session, New York, 18 December 2008, available in audio-visual form at www.un.org/webcast/ga2008.html (accessed 7 January 2014), transcript on file with author.
70. International Council on Human Rights Policy, *supra* n. 46, p. 46.
71. David Bell & Jon Binnie, *The Sexual Citizen: Queer Politics and Beyond* (Polity Press, Oxford 2000), p. 2 (emphasis added).
72. See, for example, Diane Richardson, *Rethinking Sexuality* (Sage, London 2000); Diane Richardson, 'Constructing Sexual Citizenship: Theorizing Sexual Rights' (2000) 20 *Critical Social Policy* 105; Andrew Kam-Tuck Yip, 'The Quest for Intimate/Sexual Citizenship: Lived Experiences of Lesbian and Bisexual Muslim Women' (2008) 2 *Contemporary Islam* 99, p. 103.
73. Ken Plummer, *Intimate Citizenship: Private Decisions and Public and Public Dialogues* (University of Washington Press, Seattle 2003), p. 14. Paraphrased in Yip, *supra* n. 72.
74. See, for example, Angelia R. Wilson, 'The "Neat Concept" of Sexual Citizenship: A Cautionary Tale for Human Rights Discourse' (2009) 15 *Contemporary Politics* 73.
75. See, for example, Joan Scott, 'Deconstructing Equality-Versus-Difference: Or, the Uses of Poststructuralist Theory for Feminism' in Diana Tietjens Meyers (ed.), *Feminist Social Thought: A Reader* (Routledge, New York 1997), pp. 757–771; Carol Smart, 'The Woman of Legal Discourse' (1992) 1 *Social and Legal Studies* 29; Michele Barrett & Anne Phillips (eds), *Destabilizing Theory: Contemporary Feminist Debates* (Polity Press, Cambridge 1992); Kathy Ferguson, *The Man Question: Visions of Subjectivity in Feminist Theory* (University

of California Press. Berkeley 1993); Elizabeth Grosz, 'Identity and Difference: A Response' in Paul James (ed.), *Critical Politics: From the Personal to the Global* (Arena Publications, Melbourne 1994), pp. 29–33; Judith Squires, *The New Politics of Gender Equality* (Palgrave Macmillan, Basingstoke 2007).

76. See Johanna Kantola & Hanne Marlene Dahl, 'Gender and the State: from Differences between to Differences within' (2005) 7 *International Feminist Journal of Politics* 49, p. 57. See also Hilary Charlesworth & Christine Chinkin, *The Boundaries of International Law: A Feminist Analysis* (Manchester University Press, Manchester 2000), p. 211.

77. Ryan Goodman, 'Beyond the Enforcement Principle: Sodomy Laws, Social Norms, and Social Panoptics' (2001) 89 *California Law Review* 643, p. 722. This assertion draws on John D'Emilio's argument that the 'making of a homosexual minority' in the United States of America had been intrinsically related to an 'ideological configuration of sin, sickness, and crime'. See John D'Emilio, *Sexual Politics, Sexual Communities: The Making of a Homosexual Minority in the United States, 1940–1970* (University of Chicago Press, Chicago 1983), p. 129.

78. Cf. Kate Sheill, 'Losing Out in the Intersections: Lesbians, Human Rights, Law and Activism' (2009) 15 *Contemporary Politics* 55.

79. See, for example, Jeffrey A. Redding, 'Human Rights and Homo-sectuals: The International Politics of Sexuality, Religion, and Law' (2005–2006) 4 *Northwestern Journal of International Human Rights* 436.

80. International Covenant on Civil and Political Rights (ICCPR), UN General Assembly Res 2200A (XXI), 21 UN GAOR Supp (No. 16), p. 52, UN Doc A/6316 (1966), 993 UNTS 3, entered into force on 23 March 1976. Article 18 safeguards the right to freedom of thought, conscience and religion.

81. Declaration on the Elimination of All Forms of Intolerance and of Discrimination Based on Religion or Belief, UN General Assembly Res 36/55 of 25 November 1981, 36 UN GAOR Supp (No. 51), p. 171, UN Doc A/36/684 (1981).

82. Alice M. Miller, 'Human Rights and Sexuality: First Steps Toward Articulating a Rights Framework for Claims to Sexual Rights and Freedoms' (1999) 93 *American Society of International Law Proceedings* 288, p. 301.

83. Katerina Dalacoura, *Islam, Liberalism and Human Rights: Implications for International Relations* (rev. edn; I.B.Tauris, London 2003), p. 13.

84. *Ibid*, p. 17.

85. Cf. *ibid.*

86. Stanley Ingber, 'Religion or Ideology: A Needed Clarification of the Religion Clauses' (1989) 41 *Stanford Law Review* 233, p. 282; quoted in David B. Cruz, 'Disestablishing Sex and Gender' (2002) 90 *California Law Review* 997, p. 1011.

87. For the notion of sexual orientation, see, for example, Robert Wintemute, *Sexual Orientation and Human Rights: The United States Constitution, the European Convention, and the Canadian Charter* (Clarendon Press, Oxford 1995), pp. 6–10; Heinze, *supra* n. 52, pp. 44–49; Ahmed, *supra* n. 11, pp. 65–107; Janis

S. Bohan, *Psychology and Sexual Orientation: Coming to Terms* (Routledge, New York 1996), pp. 13–30. For the notion of gender identity, see, for example, Sally Hines, *Transforming Gender* (Policy Press, Bristol 2007); Stuart Hall, 'Introduction: Who Needs "Identity"?' in Stuart Hall & Paul Du Gay (eds), *Questions of Cultural Identity* (Sage, London 1996), pp. 1–17; Susan Stryker & Stephen Whittle (eds), *The Transgender Studies Reader* (Routledge, London 2006); Paisley Currah, Richard M. Juang & Shannon Price Minter (eds), *Transgender Rights* (University of Minnesota Press, Minneapolis 2006).

88. See, for example, Gregory M. Herek, *Stigma and Sexual Orientation: Understanding Prejudice against Lesbians, Gay Men and Bisexuals* (Sage, London 1998).

89. Matthew Waites, 'Critique of "Sexual Orientation" and "Gender Identity" in Human Rights Discourse: Global Queer Politics beyond the Yogyakarta Principles' (2009) 15 *Contemporary Politics* 137, p. 145. See also Wintemute, *supra* n. 87, Appendix II, p. 267. Robert Wintemute reports that sexual orientation has been recognised as a prohibited ground of discrimination in the United States of America's District of Columbia as early as in 1973 CE. See *District of Columbia Code Annotated*, §§1–2501 to 1–2533.

90. See, for example, Ken Plummer (ed.), *The Making of Modern Homosexual* (Hutchinson, London 1981).

91. For the seminal psychiatric research on the subject that is today rightfully contested by the scholars of transgender studies, see Robert Stoller, *Sex and Gender: On the Development of Masculinity and Femininity* (Science House, New York 1968).

92. See, for example, Stryker & Whittle, *supra* n. 87. See also Currah, Juang & Minter, *supra* n. 87.

93. This assertion is, however, contested by a number of authors. See, for example, Massad, *supra* n. 26, p. 41.

94. There is a bulk of academic literature confirmative of this phenomenon. See, for example, Evelyn Blackwood & Saskia E. Wieringa (eds), *Female Desires: Same Sex Relations and Transgender Practices across Cultures* (Columbia University Press, New York 1999).

95. The Yogyakarta Principles, *supra* n. 4.

96. See generally Chapter 3 of this book.

97. The Yogyakarta Principles, *supra* n. 4, Preamble.

98. Baden Offord & Leon Cantrell, 'Unfixed in a Fixated World: Identity, Sexuality, Race and Culture' in Peter A. Jackson & Gerard Sullivan (eds), *Multicultural Queer: Australian Narratives* (Harrington Park Press, Binghamton 1999), p. 218.

99. This argument is proposed primarily in relation to sexual orientation, yet it clearly implies its applicability to gender identity as well. It is *deliberative* because it encompasses 'potential dissonance between subjectivity and external representation', *conduct-oriented* for being inclusive of those who engage in certain type of sexual conduct (e.g. sex with members of the same sex) without subscribing to certain social labels attached to it (e.g. 'gay' or 'lesbian') and

expressive because it is implicit of the protections accorded to an individual freedom 'to express [. . .] public gender or sexual identities, and publicly voice the need for such protections'; Sonia Katyal, 'Exploring Identity' (2002) 14 *Yale Journal of Law and Feminism* 97, pp. 168–169. Those who oppose the notion of 'sexual autonomy', which is sometimes, rightly or not, equated with the syntagm 'sexual liberty' (*liberté sexuelle*), argue that it problematically covers all aspects of human sexuality, while the concepts of 'sexual orientation' and 'gender identity' are much narrower. See, for example, Robert Wintemute, 'De l'égalité des orientations sexuelles à la liberté sexuelle: Jurisprudence européenne et comparée' in Daniel Borrillo & Danièle Lochak (eds), *La liberté sexuelle* (Presses Universitaires de France, Paris 2005), pp. 161–186.

100. For the seminal study on performativity of gender, see Judith Butler, *Gender Trouble: Feminism and the Subversion of Identity* (4th edn; Routledge, London 1999 [1990]).

101. See, for example, Wintemute, *supra* n. 87, pp. 8–9 and n. 25.

102. See *supra* n. 2.

103. Heinze, *supra* n. 52. Eric Heinze summarises the view of the theologian Hans-Georg Wiedemann, who characterises homosexuality as 'ein Teil unserer ganzheitlichen, vielgestaltigen Sexualität, die zu unserem Personsein gehört ['a part of our holistic, multifaceted sexuality that is part of our personhood']'. Hans-Georg Wiedemann, *Homosexuelle Liebe: Für eine Neuorientirung in der christlichen Ethik* (Kreuz, Stuttgart 1982).

104. Momin Rahman, *Sexuality and Democracy: Identities and Strategies in Lesbian and Gay Politics* (Edinburgh University Press, Edinburgh 2000), p. 42.

105. Momin Rahman, 'In Search of My Mother's Garden: Reflections on Migration, Sexuality and Muslim Identity' (2008) 5(4) *Nebula* 1, p. 22, n. 4 (emphasis in original).

106. In particular, Foucault, *supra* n. 51.

107. See, for example, Christine Delphy, 'Rethinking Sex and Gender' (1993) 16 *Women's Studies International Forum* 1; Anne Fausto-Sterling, *Myths of Gender: Biological Theories about Women and Men* (Basic Books, New York 1992); Stevi Jackson & Sue Scott, (1996) 'Sexual Skirmishes and Feminist Factions' in Stevi Jackson & Sue Scott (eds), *Feminism and Sexuality: A Reader* (Edinburgh University Press, Edinburgh 1996); Diane Richardson, 'Heterosexuality and Social Theory' in Diane Richardson (ed.), *Theorising Heterosexuality* (Open University Press, Milton Keynes 1996); G Vines, *Raging Hormones* (Virago, London 1993).

108. See, for example, Fausto-Sterling, *supra* n. 61. See also Butler, *supra* n. 61.

109. See, for example, Steven Seidman (ed.), *Queer Theory/Sociology* (Blackwell, Oxford 1996), pp. 11–12.

110. See, for example, Morgan, *supra* n. 10, p. 216.

111. Sami Zeidan, 'The Limits of Queer Theory in LGBT Litigation and the International Human Rights Discourse' (2006) 14 *Willamette Journal of International Law and Dispute Resolution* 73, pp. 74 and 96.

112. Cf. Samar Habib, 'Reading the Familiarity of the Past: An Introduction to Medieval Arabic Literature on Female Homosexuality' (2007) 7 (2) *EnterText* 162, p. 167, available at http://arts.brunel.ac.uk/gate/entertext/home.htm (accessed 13 January 2014).
113. For this argument labelled the 'concept of atemporality', see Eve Kosofsky Sedgwick, *The Epistemology of the Closet* (University of California Press, Berkeley 1990), pp. 45–47. Drawing on this concept, Samar Habib explains that '[t] here is no inherent quality to time that makes past cultures automatically different to contemporary ones, on the contrary, the continuity of time itself makes an essentialist, panoramic survey of sexualities all the more important'; Samar Habib, *Female Homosexuality in the Middle East: Histories and Representations* (Routledge, New York 2007), p. 21.
114. *Ibid*, p. 22.
115. Petchesky, *supra* n. 50, p. 13, drawing upon Fausto-Sterling, *supra* n. 61.
116. Wintemute, *supra* n. 87, p. 8 (emphasis added).
117. For instance, for an informed discussion on 'homonationalist imperial sexual exceptionism', see Jasbir K. Puar, *Terrorist Assemblages: Homonationalism in Queer Times* (Duke University Press, Durham 2007).
118. Rictor Norton, 'A Critique of Social Constructionism and Queer Theory', published on-line (2002, 2008) at http://rictornorton.co.uk/extracts.htm (accessed 13 January 2014), Ch. 10.
119. Bohan, *supra* n. 87, p. xvi (emphasis added).
120. See, for example, Butler, *supra* n. 61. See also Butler, *supra* n. 44.
121. Ahmed, *supra* n. 11, p. 96.
122. Noreen O'Connor & Joanna Ryan, *Wild Desires and Mistaken Identities: Lesbianism and Psychoanalysis* (Virago, London 1993), p. 190; quoted in Ahmed, *supra* n. 11, p. 96.
123. The Yogyakarta Principles, *supra* n. 4, Preamble, the definition of gender identity.
124. See generally Hall, *supra* n. 87.
125. Surya Monro, 'Transgender: Destabilising Feminisms?' in Vanessa E. Munro & Carl F. Stychin (eds), *Sexuality and the Law: Feminist Engagements* (Routledge-Cavendish, New York 2007), p. 136. See also Leslie Feinberg, *Transgender Warriors: Making History from Joan of Arc to Dennis Rodman* (Beacon Press, Boston 1996), p. 143.
126. See Waites, *supra* n. 89, pp. 147–148.
127. See, for example, Currah, Juang & Minter, *supra* n. 87.
128. See, for example, Waites, *supra* n. 89, p. 147.
129. For an analysis of the oppressive and ultimately unsuccessful methods to change sexual orientation, used by so-called 'ex-gay' ministries in the United States of America, see Wayne R. Besen, *Anything but Straight: Unmasking the Scandals and Lies behind the Ex-Gay Myth* (Harrington Park Press, Binghamton 2003).
130. For an overview of legal issues pertinent to human rights of gender-variant persons, including the resistance of judicial systems to recognise their right to

gender transition, see Stephen Whittle, *Respect and Equality: Transsexual and Transgender Rights* (Cavendish, London 2002).

131. See, for example, Lori B. Girshick, *Transgender Voices: Beyond Women and Men* (University Press of New England, Lebanon 2008), p. 11 *et passim*.

132. See, for example, American Psychological Association, *Resolution on Appropriate Affirmative Responses to Sexual Orientation Distress and Change Efforts* (2008), available at www.apa.org/about/governance/council/policy/sexual-orientation. aspx (accessed 14 January 2014).

133. For a learned constructionist critique of the voluntaristic mutability of these notions, see Butler, *supra* n. 61.

134. 'It is important to point out that some authors conceptualise gender as being determined by processes concerning sexual orientation, other see sexuality as resulting from gender, whilst still others see gender and sexuality as being interwoven, so that gender identities are shaped by our sexual orientation and vice versa [. . .]. I adopt the latter stance'; Monro, *supra* n. 125, p. 126.

135. Judith Butler asserts that, in order to open up the 'new possibilities for gender' that contest the rigid codes of hierarchical binarisms', it is possible to institute 'a subversion of identity', though 'only *within* the practices of repetitive signifying' by which it has been constructed in the first place. Butler, *supra* n. 100, p. 185 *et passim*.

136. Kenji Yoshino elaborates in detail the process of 'covering', when one's sexual orientation 'is neither altered nor hidden, but is downplayed'; Kenji Yoshino, 'Covering' (2002) 111 *The Yale Law Journal* 769, p. 772 *et passim*.

137. Doris E. Buss, 'Queering International Legal Authority' (2007) 101 *American Society of International Law Proceedings* 122, p. 123.

138. Cf. Morgan, *supra* n. 10, p. 215.

139. On the concept of *compulsory heterosexuality*, referring to the forced institutionalisation of the heterosexual relations as the only permissive form of sociality, see Adrienne Rich, 'Compulsory Heterosexuality and Lesbian Existence' in Henry Abelove, Michele Aina Barale & David M. Halperin (eds), *The Lesbian and Gay Studies Reader* (Routledge, New York 1993), p. 234 *et passim*; quoted in Ahmed, *supra* n. 11, p. 84.

140. In Latin America, for example, the forms of violent heteronormativity have been called *heterrorsexualidad*. See, for example, ILGA-LAC, *A 40 Años de Stonewall Inn: Transfobia, Lesbofobia, Homofobia, Bifobia en Latinoamérica y El Caribe* (ILGA-LAC, 2009), available at http://www.clam.org.br (accessed 15 January 2014).

141. Heinze, *supra* n. 52, p. 40.

142. Rahman, *supra* n. 104, p. 6.

143. Rusmir Musić, 'Queer Visions of Islam' in Samar Habib (ed.), *Islam and Homosexuality* (Praeger, Santa Barbara 2010), Vol. 2, p. 343.

144. See, for example, Tarik Bereket & Barry D. Adam, 'Navigating Islam and Same-Sex Liaisons among Men in Turkey' (2008) 55 *Journal of Homosexuality* 204.

145. For instance, Tom Boellstorff argues that the local categories of *gay* and *lesbi* in Indonesia are only partially translatable and culturally irreducible to 'the English concepts' of gay and lesbian. See Tom Boellstorff, 'Between Religion and Desire: Being Muslim and *Gay* in Indonesia' (2005) 107 *American Anthropologist* 575, p. 575.

146. It is, however, argued that *waria* must be seen neither as a simple 'traditional third gender' role for male-bodied 'feminine' people nor as a precursor to contemporary forms of same-sex desire. See David Valentine, *Imagining Transgender: An Ethnography of a Category* (Duke University Press, Durham 2007), p. 161. See also Boellstorff, *supra* n. 145, p. 9.

147. See, for example, Yik Koon Teh, '*Mak Nyahs* (Male Transsexuals) in Malaysia: The Influence of Culture and Religion on Their Identity' (2001) 5 *International Journal of Transgenderism*, on-line edition, available at http://www.symposion. com/ijt (accessed 16 January 2014).

148. See, for example, Gayatri Reddy, *With Respect to Sex: Negotiating Hijra Identity in South India* (University of Chicago Press, Chicago 2005). As discussed in Chapter 5 of this book, the Pakistani *hijra* subjectivity is increasingly known as *khwajasara*, the latter term being identified as more respectful and historically salient.

149. See, for example, Stephen O. Murray, 'The Sohari *Khanith*' in Stephen O. Murray & Will Roscoe, *Islamic Homosexualities: Culture, History, and Literature* (New York University Press, New York 1997), pp. 244–255.

150. For example, one such individual asserts: 'In the West things are labeled. Here you have to pick a box that you're in. [. . .] They [in the East] don't really do this box. You're you'. Omar Minwalla, B.R. Simon Rosser, Jamie Feldman & Christine Varga, 'Identity Experience among Progressive Gay Muslims in North America: A Qualitative Study within Al-Fatiha' (2005) 7 *Culture, Health & Sexuality* 113, p. 120. Although persistent in calling its protagonists 'gay Muslims', the above study concludes: 'Notably, in our study, Muslim men from Eastern cultures appeared to have a heightened awareness that the process of constructing of a gay identity – that is, constructing homo-social expression into an internal and social identity – is more of a Western process. This may be why some respondents seemed to struggle with and resist the construct of gay, perceiving it as a confining label or a box – a resistance to cultural assimilation'; *ibid*, p. 124.

151. Tom Boellstorff, *The Gay Archipelago: Sexuality and Nation in Indonesia* (Princeton University Press, Princeton 2005), p. 9.

152. See especially Chapters 4 and 5 of this book.

153. In his critical historical account of international law, Martti Koskenniemi documents a deeply rooted prejudice against Muslims that informed the European imperialist project and, by extension, the early international law as well. For instance, Koskenniemi reflects upon an assertion of Henry Wheaton (1785–1848 CE) that 'the international law of the civilized, Christian nations of Europe and America, is one thing; and that which governs the intercourse of

the Mohammedan nations of the East with each other, and with Christian, is another and a very different thing'; Koskenniemi, *supra* n. 15, p. 115; see also pp. 4–5, 104–105.

154. Linguistically, the verbal noun *'islam* is derived from the verb *'aslama*, which in the Arabic language means 'to surrender', 'to submit', 'to accept'. Theologically, this semantic direction is paramount in determination of human relationship with God. See, for example, Toshihiko Izutsu, *God and Man in the Koran: Semantics of the Koranic Weltanschauung* (Keiō Institute of Cultural and Linguistic Studies, Tokyo 1964).

155. This testimony of faith is called *shahada* and it reads in Arabic: *la ilaha illallah, Muhammadun rasulullah.*

156. Daniel Martin Varisco, *Islam Obscured: The Rhetoric of Anthropological Representation* (Palgrave Macmillan, New York 2005), p. 110.

157. Qur'an 30:22 (my translation); see also Qur'an 42:8 and 49:13.

Chapter 2   Sexual and Gender Diversity in International Human Rights Law and Its Originatory Milieux

1. Hersch Lauterpacht, *International Law and Human Rights* (Stevens, London 1950), p. 72.

2. For a historical overview of this process, see Robert McCorquodale, 'The Individual and the International Legal System' in Malcolm D. Evans, *International Law* (2nd edn, Oxford University Press, Oxford 2006), pp. 307–332.

3. A human right can arguably be construed both as 'an ethical justification for setting up, maintaining, and respecting protections of individuals' – in which case it is a *moral* claim – and as 'a type of institutional arrangement in which interests are guaranteed legal protection, choices are guaranteed legal effect, or goods and opportunities are provided to individuals on a guaranteed basis' – which operates, essentially, as a *legal* claim. See Michael Haas, *International Human Rights: A Comprehensive Introduction* (Routledge, London 2008), pp. 3–4.

4. Haas, *supra* n. 3, p. 1.

5. For an excellent study of this issue, see Sundhya Pahuja, *Decolonising International Law: Development, Economic Growth and the Politics of Universality* (Cambridge Studies in International and Comparative Law Series, Cambridge University Press, Cambridge 2011).

6. Cf. Martti Koskenniemi, *The Gentle Civilizer of Nations: The Rise and Fall of International Law 1870–1960* (Cambridge University Press, Cambridge 2001).

7. Martti Koskenniemi, 'What Should International Lawyers Learn from Karl Marx?' in Susan Marks (ed.), *International Law on the Left: Re-examining Marxist Legacies* (Cambridge University Press, Cambridge 2008), p. 31.

8. For instance, China Miéville maintains that international law is *always already* 'made actual in the power-political wranglings of states, ultimately at the logic of capital, in the context of an imperialist system'. Consequently, '[a]ttempts to reform [international] law can only ever tinker with the surface level of

institutions'. See China Miéville, 'The Commodity-Form Theory of International Law' in Susan Marks (ed.), *International Law on the Left: Re-examining Marxist Legacies* (Cambridge University Press, Cambridge 2008), p. 130 *et passim*.

9. For the famous description of international law as a 'wasteland' of theory, see B. S. Chimni, *International Law and World Order: A Critique of Contemporary Approaches* (Sage, New Delhi 1993), p. 15.

10. Antony Anghie, *Imperialism, Sovereignty and the Making of International Law* (Cambridge University Press, Cambridge 2004), p. 254 *et passim*.

11. See Ulrich Beck, *Der kosmopolitische Blick oder: Krieg ist Frieden* (Suhrkamp Verlag K.G, Frankfurt am Mein 2004), pp. 197–244.

12. Adulterous *women* (and, often, their paramours) had faced exceptionally harsh punishments, including death by drowning. See Hammurabi, *Code* (trans. G. R. Driver & John C. Miles, Clarendon Press, Oxford 1960 [1952]), Vol. 2, pp. 51–57 (Articles 129, 133a-135, 142–143); Walter Kornfeld, 'L'adultère dans l'Orient antique' (1970) 57 *Revue biblique* 96–104 *et passim*; Winfred E. Ohlson, 'Adultery: A Review' (1937) 17 *Boston University Law Review* 330; Reuven Yaron, *The Laws of Eshnunna* (2nd rev. edn, Magnes Press, Jerusalem 1988 [1969]); Matitiahu Tsevat, 'The Husband Veils a Wife (Hittite Laws, §§197–98)' (1975) 27 *Journal of Cuneiform Studies* 235.

13. See, for example, Louis Crompton, *Homosexuality & Civilization* (Harvard University Press, Cambridge 2003).

14. Indeed, one must separate the popular (and contestable) picture of libertine ancient Greek and Roman societies, wherein same-sex sexual acts, concubinage, extramarital affairs and gender variance abound, from there and then developed philosophical and legal discourses stipulating, with varying public success, quite a different ethos. Rather than social mores and 'vices' of the Greco-Roman antiquity, those divergent discourses had been studied and re-appropriated by the patristic and late medieval Christian scholars. See, for example, James A. Brundage, *Law, Sex, and Christian Society in Medieval Europe* (University of Chicago Press, Chicago 1987), pp. 10–50.

15. Crompton, *supra* n. 13, p. 539.

16. Relevant Pakistani laws are discussed in Chapter 5 of this book.

17. See generally Anghie, *supra* n. 10.

18. To be sure, in that point in time, this concept was also *geopolitically* Western European, which bore a significant weight in its subsequent dissemination.

19. See, for example, Brundage, *supra* n. 14; Crompton, *supra* n. 13; Eric Fuchs, *Sexual Desire and Love: Origins and History of the Christian Ethic of Sexuality and Marriage* (trans. Marsha Daigle, Seabury Press, New York 1983); Willy van Hoecke & Andries Welkenhuysen (eds), *Love and Marriage in the Twelfth Century* (Leuven University Press, Leuven 1981); Jacques Marie Pohier, *Le Chrétien, le plaisir et la sexualité* (Editions du Cerf, Paris 1974); Robert Briffault, *Sin and Sex* (Allen & Unwin, London 1931); Barbara A. Hanawalt, 'Of Good and Ill Repute': *Gender and Social Control in Medieval England* (Oxford University Press, New York 1998).

20. For a detailed study of this paradigm shift see especially Brundage, *supra* n. 14.

21. Leviticus 20:13. If not stated otherwise, all Old and New Testament quotes are taken from the King James translation of the Holy Bible [1611].

22. Leviticus 18:22.

23. Deuteronomy 22:5.

24. Thomas Browne, 'Religio medici' in William Swann Sonnenschein (ed.): *Thomas Browne: Works* (George Routledge & Sons, London 1884), pt. 2, p. 80.

25. Brundage, *supra* n. 14, p. 62. See also John Bugge, *Virginitas: An Essay in the History of a Medieval Ideal* (Martinus Nijhoff, The Hague 1975), pp. 11–18; Michael Müller, *Die Lehre des hl. Augustinus von der Paradiesesehe und ihre Auswirkung in der Sexualethik des 12. und 13. Jahrhunderts bis Thomas von Aquin* (Friedrich Pustet, Regensburg 1954), pp. 10–11.

26. Origen, 'In Genesim homiliae' in Jacques-Paul Migne (ed.), *Patrologiæ cursus completus... Series Græca* (Imprimerie Catholique, Paris 1857), Vol. 12, p. 192.

27. See, for example, Brundage, *supra* n. 14; Crompton, *supra* n. 13; Fuchs, *supra* n. 19. Patristic times (and studies) generally refer to the period between the Apostolic Age (*c.* 100 CE) to either 451 CE or to the eighth century CE in the history of Christian Church. Most relevant for this period are the writings of the so-called Church Fathers, including St Irenaeus of Lyons, Saint Clement of Alexandria, Origen, St Athanasius of Alexandria, St Cyril of Alexandria, St John Chrysostom, St Maximus the Confessor, St John of Damascus, Tertullian, St Cyprian of Carthage, St Ambrose of Milan, St Jerome of Stridonium, St Augustine of Hippo and St Gregory the Great. Their major works are collected, *inter alia*, in Jacques-Paul Migne's enormous *Patrologiæ cursus completus... Series Latina* (221 Vols) and *Series Græca* (165 Vols), published between 1844 and 1858 by his own Imprimerie Catholique in Paris.

28. Fourteen epistles in the New Testament are attributed to St Paul, with varying certainty: (1) very high likelihood (that St Paul actually had authored them): Romans, 1st Corinthians, 2nd Corinthians, Galatians, Philippians, Philemon and 1st Thessalonians; (2) high likelihood: Ephesians, Colossians and 2nd Thessalonians; (3) very low likelihood: 1st Timothy, 2nd Timothy, Titus, and Hebrews. See, for example, AQ Morton & James McLeman, *Paul, the Man and the Myth: A Study in the Authorship of Greek Prose* (Hodder & Stoughton, London 1966); Karl Kertelge (ed.), *Paulus in den neutestamentlichen Spätschriften* (Herderg, Freiburg 1981); Donald Guthrie, *New Testament: Introduction* (InterVarsity Press, Downers Grove 1990).

29. Crompton, *supra* n. 13, pp. 112–115 *et passim*.

30. Crompton, *supra* n. 13, p. 114.

31. Romans 1:24.

32. All quotes are from Romans 1:26–32.

33. Consider, for example: 'But I would have you know, that the head of every man is Christ; and the head of the woman [is] the man [. . .]. Man [. . .] is the image and glory of God: but the woman is the glory of the man. For the man is not of

the woman; but the woman of the man. Neither was the man created for the woman; but the woman for the man'. I Corinthians 11:3–9. The apostle also orders to the Christian men: 'Let your women keep silence in the churches: for it is not permitted unto them to speak; but [they are commanded] to be under obedience, as also saith the law. And if they will learn any thing, let them ask their husbands at home: for it is a shame for women to speak in the church'. I Corinthians 14:34–35.

34. 'Doth not even nature itself teach you, that, if a man have long hair, it is a shame unto him?' I Corinthians 11:14.

35. 'Let the woman learn in silence with all subjection. But I suffer not a woman to teach, nor to usurp the authority over the man, but to be in silence. For Adam was first formed, then Eve. And Adam was not deceived, but the woman being deceived was in transgression.' I Timothy 2:11–14.

36. Brundage, *supra* n. 14, p. 60.

37. See, for example, Lucius Annæus Seneca, *De vita beata* (trans. Russell Halderman Wagner; Cornell University Press, Ithaca 1923); Lucius Annæus Seneca, *L Annæi Senecæ ad Lucilium epistolæ selectæ* (University of Michigan Library, Ann Arbor 2009); Lucius Annæus Seneca, *De beneficiis* (ed. William Hardy Alexander, University of California Press, Berkeley 1950), Vol. 7; John M. Rist, *Stoic Philosophy* (Cambridge University Press, Cambridge 1977).

38. He was, however, born in Tarsus, from which two eminent Stoic teachers also hailed and which was a town widely known for its schools. See Brundage, *supra* n. 14, p. 60, n. 51.

39. 'In Paul's hierarchy of virtues and vices, complete sexual abstinence was a preferred state, one that Christians ought to strive for; those who could not control their sexual passions, however, had the option of marriage, which would provide them with a legitimate sexual outlet, at the cost forfeiting the higher value of virginity'. Brundage, *supra* n. 14, p. 60.

40. Seneca, *De vita beata, supra* n. 37.

41. Seneca, *L Annæi Senecæ ad Lucilium epistolæ selectæ, supra* n. 37. Ironically, Seneca wrote of these matters while in exile in Corsica, due to his conviction for adultery. See Brundage, *supra* n. 14, p. 21.

42. In his own words, 'rerum naturæ adsentior; ab illa non deerrare et ad illius legem exemplumque formari sapientia est' ('I assent to nature; it is common sense not to stray from it but to be moulded according to its law and example'); Seneca, *De vita beata, supra* n. 37. Ever since, understanding 'sexual crimes' as 'crimes against nature' has become a commonplace of various moral and legal discourses.

43. Brundage, *supra* n. 14, pp. 104–105.

44. St Cæsarius of Arles, *Serm. 142.2* (Corpus Christianorum: continuatio mediævalis, Vol. 103; Brépols, Turnhout 1958), p. 186.

45. There were observant Christian women who disguised themselves in men's clothes so that they could join male-only monastic and ascetic communities. See Jo-Ann McNamara, 'Muffled Voices: The Lives of Consecrated Women in

the Fourth Century' in John A. Nichols & Lillian Thomas Shank (eds), *Medieval Religious Women: Distant Echoes* (Cistercian Publications, Kalamazoo 1984), pp. 23–24.

46. In Justinian's own words, '[i]tem lex Iulia de adulteriis coercendis, quæ non solum temeratores aliarum nuptiarum gladio punit, sed etiam eos, qui cum masculis infandem libidinem exercere audet [...]' ('[t]he lex Iulia, passed for the repression of adultery, punishes with death not only defilers of the marriage-bed, but also those [men] who indulge in criminal intercourse with those of their own sex [...]'); Justinian, *Institutes* (translated by J.B. Moyle; Oxford University Press, Oxford 1911), Book IV, Title XVIII: 4. Moyle's 1911 English translation of *Institutes*, cited above, curiously presents what Justinian clearly worded as male-only offence as gender-neutral. One cannot but wonder what has 'inspired' the translator to 'extend' a Justinian law beyond its original scope.

47. 'Item lex Iulia de adulteriis coercendis [...]'; Justinian, *Institutes, supra* n. 46.

48. See, for example, J.A.C. Thomas, 'Accusatio adulterii' (1961) 12 *Iura* 65. Also, see generally Thomas A.J. McGinn, *Prostitution, Sexuality, and the Law in Ancient Rome* (Oxford University Press, New York 1998). It is a matter of scholarly debate whether Justinian had indeed based his prohibition of male-male sexual acts on the *lex Iulia*, as accepted by James A. Brundage, or simply invented it himself, for the first time in Roman imperial history, as claimed by John Boswell. See Brundage, *supra* n. 14, p. 121, n. 211; John Boswell, *Christianity, Social Tolerance and Homosexuality: Gay People in Western Europe from the Beginning of the Christian Era to the Fourteenth Century* (University of Chicago Press, Chicago 1980), p. 171.

49. Justinian, 'Novellæ constitutiones' in Justinian, *Corpus iuris civilis: Novellæ* (4th edn; ed. Wilhelm Kroll & Rudolf Schoell; Apud Weidmannos, Berlin 1912), Vol. 3, 77:1 & 141:1.

50. Augustine contended that Sodom was a town 'where sexual intercourse between males had become so commonplace that it received the license usually extended by the law to other practices'; Augustine of Hippo, *De civitate Dei* (translated by R.W. Dyson; Cambridge University Press, Cambridge 1998), 16:30, p. 743. The emphasis placed on curtailing the *commonness* (i.e. a widespread nature) of such practice, rather than finding it wrong *per se*, seems to signal a fear of disruption of a well-established social order, rather than an 'essentially sinful' behaviour.

51. A notable exception to this trend can be found in the writings of the German chronicler Abbot Regino of Prüm (d. 915 CE), which discuss in great detail the subjects of marital chastity and sexual continence. See Regino Prumiensis, *Libri duo de synodalibus causis et disciplinis ecclesiasticis* (ed. F.G.A. Wasserschleben; G. Engelmann, Lipsiæ 1840).

52. See, for example, Oscar D. Watkins, *A History of Penance* (2 Vols; Longmans, Green & Co, London 1920); John T. McNeill, *A History of the Cure of Souls* (Harper Brothers, New York 1951).

53. For the seminal work on this period, see Charles Homer Haskins, *The Renaissance of the Twelfth Century* (Harvard University Press, Cambridge 1927).
54. Brundage, *supra* n. 14, p. 177.
55. For a study of legal paradigm shift in the times of Church Reform, see Stephen Kuttner, 'The Revival of Jurisprudence' in Robert L. Benson & Giles Constable (eds), *Renaissance and Renewal in the Twelfth Century* (Harvard University Press, Cambridge 1982), pp. 299–323. See also Knut Wolfgang Nörr, 'The Institutional Foundations of the New Jurisprudence' in Robert L. Benson & Giles Constable (eds), *Renaissance and Renewal in the Twelfth Century* (Harvard University Press, Cambridge 1982), pp. 324–338.
56. Brundage, *supra* n. 14, p. 178.
57. For example, a chapter in the *Decretum* of Bishop Burchard of Worms (*c.*950–1025 CE), which was the earliest major canonical collection clearly advocating for the goals of the reform movement, warns against the perils of lust: it leads to spiritual blindness, insensitivity, shiftiness of the eyes, hatred of the divine commandments, attachment to things of this world, and misery and despair in this life as well as in the eternity. See Burchard of Worms, 'Decretum' in Jacques-Paul Migne (ed.), *Patrologiæ cursus completus... Series Latina* (Imprimerie Catholique, Paris *c.*1850), Vol. 140, p. 977 [ch. 19, para. 6 of the *Decretum*].
58. Thenceforth tolerated albeit with an increasingly negative sentiment, clerical marriage was given a nearly lethal blow by the First Lateran Council (1123 CE), which ruled that ordination to the higher ecclesiastical grades (priesthood, diaconate and subdiaconate) automatically caused a diriment impediment to marriage. The business was completed in 1139 CE by the Second Lateran Council, which decreed that all the remaining clerical marriages, regardless of their ecclesiastical rank or social status, must be broken up and any resistance severely punished. See, for example, Jean Gaudemet, 'Le célibat ecclésiastique: le droit et la pratique du XIe au XIIe siècle' (1982) 68 *Zeitschrift der Savigny-Stiftung für Rechtsgeschichte: Kanonistische Abteilung* 10.
59. In addition to these punishments, the culprits were liable to any municipal or a specific religious community-based penalty for 'unnatural vice'. See Brundage, *supra* n. 14, p. 399. For an exemplary system of non-canonical punishments relating, *inter alia*, to 'unnatural vice', see Indrikis Sterns, 'Crime and Punishment among the Teutonic Knights' (1982) 57 *Speculum* 91. See also Michael Goodich, 'Sodomy in Medieval Secular Law' (1976) 1 *Journal of Homosexuality* 295.
60. Raymond of Penyafort (*c.*1175–1275 CE), for instance, cautioned confessors to refrain from naming or describing this sin to penitents, in order to avoid giving them ideas that had not previously occurred to them. See Brundage, *supra* n. 14, p. 399, n. 392.
61. William Burgwinkle, *Sodomy, Masculinity, and Law in Medieval Literature: France and England, 1050–1230* (Cambridge University Press, Cambridge 2004), p. 32. See also Monique Boutry (ed.), *Petri Cantoris Parisiensis, Verbum*

abbreviatum: Textus conflatus (Corpus Christianorum: Continuatio Mediæualis, Vol. 196; Brepols, Turnhout 2004); Eva Matthews Sanford, 'The *Verbum Abbreviatum* of Petrus Cantor' (1943) 74 *Transactions and Proceedings of the American Philological Association* 33.

62.   *Hugonis Sancto Charo... in epistolis Pauli* (u, fol. 209rb, Venice 1703) quoted in John Baldwin, *The Language of Sex* (University of Chicago Press, Chicago 1994), p. 44, n. 5 (p. 282). Baldwin, however, could not locate the story in question neither in Cantor's nor in St Jerome's writings.

63.   'Hæc pestilentissima sodomorum regina suæ tyrannidis legibus obsequentem hominibus turpem Deo reddit odibilem. Adversus Deum nefanda bella conserere, nequissimi spiritus imperat militiam baiulare, ab angelorum consortio separat et infelicem animam sub propriæ dominationis iugo a sua nobilitate captivat. Virtutum armis suos milites exuit omniumque vitiorum iaculis, ut confodiantur, exponit. In ecclesia humiliat, *in foro condempnat*, foedat in secreto, dehonestat in publico, conscientiam rodit ut vernis, carnem exurit ut ignis, anhelat, ut voluptatem expleat, et contra timet, ne ad medium veniat, ne in publicum exeat, ne hominibus innotescat'; Petrus Damiani, *Liber Gomorrhianus*, 310, 9–17 (emphasis added); quoted in Burgwinkle, *supra* n. 61, pp. 57–58.

64.   See, for example, Jo Ann McNamara & Suzanne Wemple, 'The Power of Women through the Family in Medieval Europe, 500–1100' (1973) 1 *Feminist Studies* 126.

65.   Jacobus de Vitriacus, *Historia Hierosolymitana* (ed. Bongars [Free Library of Philadelphia, Rare Book Department]; Paris 1459 [*c.*1224]), 1:1055–56.

66.   See Robert E. Lerner, *The Heresy of the Free Spirit in the Later Middle Ages* (University of California Press, Berkeley 1972), pp. 10–34.

67.   The Crusades were a series of bloody expeditional wars fought from the eleventh to thirteenth century CE, mainly over the access to the holy places, especially in and near Jerusalem. They were initiated and sanctioned by the Western Church as the 'holy war' against Muslims in Levant and elsewhere, as well as against heretics across Europe (most notably in its northernmost and south-eastern parts). The Crusaders committed innumerable atrocities on their quests and stained the relations of the Western Church and the political realms under its influence with their neighbours in Eurasia and Northern Africa for many centuries to come. For an introductory critical account of the Crusades, see Jonathan Riley-Smith, *The Oxford History of the Crusades* (Oxford University Press, New York 1999).

68.   William of Malmesbury quoted in William Stubbs & Helen J. Nicholson, *Chronicle of the Third Crusade: A Translation of the Itinerarium peregrinorum et gesta Regis Ricardi* (Ashgate, Aldershot 201), pp. 369–370.

69.   'Inter hæc impune procedebat petulans illecebra molles flammisque cremandos turpiter fedebat uenus sodomestica maritalem thorum publice polluebant adulteria. [...] Tunc effeminati passim in orbe dominabantur indisciplinate debachabandur sodomiticisque spurciis foedi catamitæ flammis urendi

turpiter abutebantur [...] hortamenta sacerdotum deridebant; barbaricumque morem in habitu et uita tenebant'; quoted in Marjorie Chibnall (ed./trans.), *The Ecclesiastical History of Ordericus Vitalis* (6 Vols; Clarendon Press, Oxford 1969–80), Vol. IV, pp. 186, 188.

70. Burgwinkle, *supra* n. 61, p. 50.

71. Even William of Malmesbury, in his depictions of 'soft living' under William II, has presumed that all that finery and 'effeminacy' must have been learnt by the young men primarily in order to woo women, rather than other men. See Frank Barlow, *William Rufus* (University of California Press, Berkeley 1983), p. 104 *et passim*.

72. Brundage, *supra* n. 14, p. 473 (references omitted).

73. *Ibid* (references omitted).

74. Ascending, as it were, from the apocalyptic nightmares of St Peter Damian; see *supra* n. 63.

75. James A. Brundage convincingly argues that numerous sexual/gender transgressions continued to be exercised despite the greatly increased penalties attached to them. Some examples include 'Cypriot knights [who] were described as fighting tournaments while dressed as women', apparently without incurring any criminal consequences, and the writings of some contemporary scholars, who found it necessary to explain in detail why the Church allowed only the marriage between a man and a woman, 'which may indicate that [they were] aware, or at least fearful, of attempts to extend social recognition to same-sex relationships through some type of wedding ritual'; Brundage, *supra* n. 14, pp. 473–474.

76. In fact, out of 21,000 trials documented in the London church records from 1470 to 1516 CE, only *one* took place for the charges of sodomy; on this single occasion, the accused was excommunicated as he failed to show up at the trial. See Derrick Sherwin Bailey, *Homosexuality and the Western Christian Tradition* (Longmans/Green, London 1955), p. 147.

77. Formally, *An Acte for the Punysshement of the Vice of Buggerie*; 25 Henry VIII c. 6 (1533); made permanent by 32 Henry VIII c. 3 (1540).

78. *Ibid* (emphasis added).

79. Crompton, *supra* n. 13, p. 362.

80. Formally, *An Acte Restoring to the Crown the Ancient Jurisdiction over the State Ecclesiastical and Spiritual and Abolishing All Foreign Power Repugnant to the Same*; 26 Henry VIII c. 1 (1534).

81. Other similar statutes prepared by Thomas Cromwell include three *Succession to the Crown Acts* (25 Henry VIII c. 22 (1533); 26 Henry VIII c. 2 (1534); and 28 Henry VIII c. 7 (1536)); the *Ecclesiastical Appeals Act* (or the *Statute in Restraint of Appeals*; 24 Henry VIII c. 12 (1532)); the *Act of Conditional Restraints of Annates* (23 Henry VIII c. 20 (1532)); the *Act Concerning Ecclesiastical Appointments and Absolute Restraint of Annates* (25 Henry VIII c. 20 (1533)); the *Act Concerning Peter's Pence and Dispensations* (25 Henry VIII c. 21 (1533)); the *Treasons Act* (26 Henry VIII c. 13 (1534)); *An Act for the Suppression*

of the Lesser Monasteries (27 Henry VIII c. 28 (1536)); and *An Act Extinguishing the Authority of the Bishop of Rome* (28 Henry VIII c. 10 (1536)).

82. A letter from Henry VIII to the Earl of Arran of 1543 CE, quoted in David Dom Knowles, *The Religious Orders in England: The Tudor Age* (Cambridge University Press, Cambridge 1959), Vol. 3, p. 204.

83. Crompton, *supra* n. 13, p. 363.

84. *Comperta*, Entry No. 2 ('Thomas Rede, sub-prior, and three others'), quoted in Crompton, *supra* n. 13, p. 364.

85. Formally, *An Act for the Dissolution of the Greater Monasteries*; 31 Henry VIII c. 13 (1539). The act disbanded 552 major monasteries and houses which remained operational after the enactment of *An Act for the Suppression of the Lesser Monasteries* of 1536 (27 Henry VIII c. 28). By the powers of these two statutes, the total of 825 monastic houses across England were eliminated.

86. Crompton, *supra* n. 13, pp. 365–366.

87. 5 Elizabeth I c. 17 (1563).

88. Cf. Crompton, *supra* n. 13, p. 366.

89. *An Act for Consolidating and Amending the Statutes in England relative to Offences against the Person*; 9 George IV c. 31 (1828), §1 (repeal), §15 (new offence).

90. See the *Offences against the Person Act*; 24 & 25 Victoria c. 100 (1861), §61. Also, see generally Hartford Montgomery Hyde, *The Love that Dared Not Speak Its Name: A Candid History of Homosexuality in Britain* (Little/Brown, Boston 1970).

91. See Criminal Law Amendment Act, 1885 (*An Act to Make Further Provision for the Protection of Women and Girls, the Suppression of Brothels and Other Purposes*); 48–49 Victoria c. 69 (1885), §11.

92. See Sexual Offences Act, 1956, c. 69, §§12, 13.

93. Sexual Offences Act, 1967, c. 60. The age of consent for male-male sexual activity was 21. It was reduced first to 18, in 1994, and then to 16, in 2000. For the relevant legislation, see Criminal Justice and Public Order Act, 1994, c. 33, §§143, 145; Sexual Offences (Amendment) Act, 2000, c. 44. See also *The Wolfenden Report: Report of the Committee on Homosexual Offences and Prostitution* (Stein & Day; New York 1963 [1957]).

94. See generally the Sexual Offences Act, 2003, c. 42. For a brief review of the English laws criminalising male same-sex sexual activities, from the Buggery Act, 1553 onwards, especially in the context of Indian Penal Code, 1860, §377, see Robert Wintemute, 'Same-Sex Love and Indian Penal Code §377: An Important Human Rights Issue for India' (2011) 4 *National University of Juridical Sciences Law Review* 31.

95. For instance, 'Denmark had no sodomy law till 1683 or known prosecutions before 1744. In Sweden there were none before 1600 and very few after. Russia, where male relations seem to have been surprisingly open in the 1600s and 1700s, did not have a sodomy statute until 1832'; Crompton, *supra* n. 13, p. 321 (references omitted). See also Jens Rydström & Kati Mustola (eds), *Criminally Queer: Homosexuality and Criminal Law in Scandinavia, 1842–1999* (Aksant, Amsterdam 2007).

96. See Code pénal du 25 septembre 1791. For a study of 'the pyres of Sodom', see Maurice Lever, *Les Bûchers de Sodome: Histoire des «infâmes»* (Fayard, Paris 1985).

97. Condorcet wrote this in a note to an early edition of Voltaire's *Prix de la justice et de l'humanité*; see François Marie Arouet de Voltaire, *Oeuvres completes de Voltaire* (ed. L.E.D. Moland, 52 Vols; Garnier Frères, Paris 1877–85), Vol. 30, p. 570, n. 4. Also quoted in Crompton, *supra* n. 13, p. 527.

98. For an analysis of the condemnatory views of sodomy expressed in the works of Voltaire, Montesquieu, Marat and Diderot, see Crompton, *supra* n. 13, pp. 500–528. The phrase *le vice ultramountain* (the vice 'across the Alps'), synonymous with what was also known as *le vice italien*, which gained popularity especially in the sixteenth century CE France, suggests that sodomy was an originally Italian import.

99. Napoleon Bonaparte quoted in Michael David Sibalis, 'The Regulation of Homosexuality in Revolutionary and Napoleonic France' in Jeffrey Merrick & Bryant T. Ragan (eds), Homosexuality in Modern France (Oxford University Press, Oxford 1996), p. 92 (emphasis added).

100. *Ibid.*

101. Crompton, *supra* n. 13, p. 528. See also Olivier Fillieule & Jan Willem Duyvendak, 'Gay and Lesbian Activism in France: Between Integration and Community-Oriented Movements' in Barry D. Adam, Jan Willem Duyvendak & André Krouwel (eds), *The Global Emergence of Gay and Lesbian Politics: National Imprints of a Worldwide Movement* (Temple University Press, Philadelphia 1999), p. 183.

102. I allude, of course, to the landmark case of *Dudgeon v United Kingdom*, A 45 (1981); 4 EHRR 149. The European Court of Human Rights ruled in *Dudgeon* that criminalisation of same-sex sexual conduct between consenting adults constituted a breach of the right to private life, protected by Article 8 of the 1950 European Convention on Human Rights. This decision provided a convenient niche for the stream of consequent cases on sexual and gender rights that transformed the European jurisprudence on sexual/gender diversity to a revolutionary extent.

103. To take but an example, the imperialistic legacies in China and Russia and Eastern Europe have yielded comparable yet distinct socio-political clusters, in which the regional forms and colours of communism have taken on the task of preserving the former empires. Thus the ideological contours have largely followed the former imperial fault lines.

  *. Some parts of the following sub-section in this chapter are based on Vanja Hamzić, 'The Case of "Queer Muslims": Sexual Orientation and Gender Identity in International Human Rights Law and Muslim Legal and Social Ethos' (2011) 11(2) *Human Rights Law Review* 237.

104. See, for example, §377 ('Unnatural Offences'), Act No. 45 of 1860 of the Legislative Council for India, which established the offence of 'carnal intercourse against the order of nature'. Prior to this provision, British colonial criminal law in India included, as of 1828, 'crime of buggery', later (in 1837)

replaced with the related concept of 'unnatural lust'. It is, in fact, precisely the infamous 'section 377' that, in name and content, survived in numerous criminal codes of the former British colonies, such as India, Pakistan and Singapore. See generally Alok Gupta, *This Alien Legacy: The Origins of 'Sodomy' Laws in British Colonialism* (Human Rights Watch, New York 2008). See also Wintemute, *supra* n. 94, pp. 42–44.

105. One such gender-variant subjectivity is *khwajasara*, known for their elevated social position in the Mughal imperial courts. See, for example, Claire Pamment, 'Hijraism: Jostling for a Third Space in Pakistani Politics' (2010) 54(2) *Drama Review* 29.

106. Shane Gannon, 'Exclusion as Language and the Language of Exclusion: Tracing Regimes of Gender through Linguistic Representations of the "Eunuch"' (2011) 20(1) *Journal of the History of Sexuality* 1, p. 3.

107. See, for example, §377 of the 1860 Penal Code of the Islamic Republic of Pakistan and §377 of the 1860 Penal Code of the Republic of India. Both of these are, of course, the 'domesticated'/post-independence versions of the Act No. 45 of the [all-British, colonial] Legislative Council for India of 6 October 1860. Note that §377 was read down to decriminalise same-sex behaviour amongst consenting adults in a historic judgement by the High Court of Delhi on 2 July 2009; *Naz Foundation* v *Government of NCT of Delhi & Others*, 2009 (160) DLT 277. See generally Wintemute, *supra* n. 94. However, on 11 December 2013 CE, the Supreme Court's two-member bench (Justices G.S. Singhvi and S.J. Mukhopadhaya) overturned the decision of the High Court of Delhi as 'constitutionally unsustainable', purportedly due to Parliament's sole prerogative to change a law, which cannot be assumed by courts. In Pakistan, §377 remains to date legally unchallenged.

108. An astonishing number of states currently apply *verbatim* 'buggery laws' of their former English colonial administrators. See Botswana: Penal Code, §§164–165, 167 ('unnatural offences'); Eritrea: 1957 Penal Code ('unnatural carnal offences') [inherited from a brief British rule via Ethiopia], §§600, 105; the Gambia: 1965 Criminal Code ('unnatural offences'), §144; Ghana: 1960 Criminal Code (Act No 29) ('unnatural carnal knowledge'), §104; Kenya: Penal Code (Ch. 63) ('carnal knowledge of any person against the order of nature'; 'gross indecency'), §§162–163, 165; Lesotho: common law offence of 'unlawful and intentional sexual relationship per anus between two human males'; Malawi: Penal Code (Cap. 7:01) ('unnatural offences'; 'gross indecency'); Mauritius: 1838 Criminal Code ('sodomy'), §250; Nigeria: Criminal Code Act (Ch. 77) ('carnal knowledge of any person against the order of nature'; 'gross indecency'), §§214–215, 217; Seychelles: 1955 Criminal Code ('carnal knowledge of any person against the order of nature'), §151; Sierra Leone: 1861 Offences against the Person Act ('buggery'), §61; Somalia: 1962 Penal Code ('homosexuality'; 'carnal intercourse'), §§409–410; Swaziland: common law offence of 'sodomy'; Tanzania: 1945 Penal Code ('unnatural offences'), §154; Uganda: 1950 Penal Code Act (Ch. 120)

('unnatural offences'), §§145–146, 148; Zambia: 1995 Penal Code Act ('carnal knowledge of any person against the order of nature'; 'gross indecency'), §§155–156, 158; Zimbabwe: 2006 Criminal Law (codification and Reform) Act ('sodomy'), §73; Bangladesh: 1860 Penal Code ('unnatural offences'), §377; Brunei: Penal Code (Ch. 22) ('unnatural offences'), §377; Gaza Strip (part of Palestinian Authority): 1936 Criminal Code Ordinance ('unnatural offences'), §152; Malaysia: Penal Code ('unnatural offences'), §377; Myanmar: 1860 Penal Code ('carnal intercourse against the order of nature'), §377; Pakistan: 1860 Penal Code ('unnatural offences'), §377; Singapore: Penal Code ('outrages on decency'), §377; Sri Lanka: 1882 Penal Code ('carnal intercourse'; 'gross indecency'), §365; Northern Cyprus: Criminal Code (Ch. 154) ('sexual intercourse against the order of nature with any person'), §171; Antigua and Barbuda: 1995 Sexual Offences Act ('buggery'; 'serious indecency'), §§12, 15; Barbados: 1992 Sexual Offences Act (Ch. 154) ('buggery'; 'serious indecency'), §§9, 12; Belize: Criminal Code (Cap. 101) ('unnatural crime'), §53; Dominica: 1998 Sexual Offences Act ('gross indecency'; 'buggery'), §§14, 16; Grenada: Criminal Code ('unnatural connexion [sic]'), §435; Guyana: Criminal Law (Offences) Act ('gross indecency'; 'unnatural offences'; 'buggery'), §§352–354; Jamaica: Offences Against the Person Act ('unnatural crime'; 'carnal knowledge'; 'outrages on decency'), §§76–79; Saint Kitts and Nevis: Offences against the Person Act ('abominable crime of buggery'), §§56–57; Saint Lucia: 2004 Criminal Code ('gross indecency'; 'buggery'), §§132–133; Saint Vincent and the Grenadines: Criminal Code ('buggery'; 'gross indecency'), §§146, 148; Trinidad and Tobago: 1986 Sexual Offences Act ('buggery'; 'serious indecency'), §§13, 16; Cook Islands: 1969 Crimes Act ('indecency between males'; 'sodomy'), §§154–155; Kiribati: Penal Code (Cap. 67) ('unnatural offences'; 'buggery'; 'indecent practices between males'); §§153–155; Nauru: 1921 Criminal Code ('unnatural offences'; 'gross indecency'), §§208–209, 211; Papua New Guinea: 1974 Criminal Code ('unnatural offences'; 'gross indecency') [inherited via Australia], §§210, 212; 1961 Crimes Ordinance ('indecency between males'; 'sodomy') [inherited via New Zealand], §58; Solomon Islands: Penal Code ('unnatural offences'; 'indecent practices between persons of the same sex'), §§160–162; Tonga: Criminal Offences (Cap. 18) ('sodomy or carnal knowledge'), §§136, 139–140, 142; Tuvalu: Penal Code (Cap. 8) ('unnatural offences'; 'gross indecency'), §§153–155.

109. The inglorious legacy of the United Kingdom in exporting sodomy laws across the world is wholly incomparable with any other European imperial power. There are, in fact *only three countries* in the world today that retain sodomy laws from a former European empire other than that of the United Kingdom. Those are the former Portuguese dominions Angola, Mozambique and São Tomé and Principe that apply the colonial 1886 Penal Code ('vícios contra a natureza'), §§70, 71.

110. See Algeria: 1966 Penal Code ('homosexual act'), §338; Guinea: 1998 Penal Code ('indecent act or act against nature'), §325; Mauritania: 1984 Penal Code

('impudent act against nature'; 'outrage on public decency and Islamic morals'; death penalty for adult Muslim men), §§306, 308; Morocco: 1962 Penal Code ('lewd or unnatural acts'), §489; Togo: 1980 Penal Code ('impudent acts or crimes against the nature'), §88; Tunisia: 1913 Penal Code ('sodomy'), §230. All of these are Muslim-majority states.

111. Rwanda achieved its independence in 1962 CE from Belgium, which seized control over the country (then part of German East Africa) from Germany in World War I.

112. It is a striking fact that Mali (90 per cent of the population Muslim), Niger (90 per cent Muslim) and Chad (53 per cent Muslim) are amongst the *founding members* of the Organisation of the Islamic Co-operation (OIC). Burkina Faso (61 per cent of the population Muslim), Côte d'Ivoire (38 per cent Muslim), Benin (25 per cent Muslim), Central African Republic (11 per cent Muslim) and Gabon (1 per cent Muslim) are *also* OIC member states.

113. The 1969 CE Stonewall riots in New York are often credited as the benchmark of a new social movement in North America and Europe arduously advocating for social acceptance of sexual/gender diversity. In 1972 CE, Sweden became first country in the world to allow transsexual persons to *legally* change their sex, and to provide free hormone therapy, whilst, in 1973, the American Psychiatric Association removed 'homosexuality' from its *Diagnostic and Statistical Manual of Mental Disorders* (DSM-II). In 1977 CE, the Francophone Canadian province of Quebec became the first such jurisdiction in the world to prohibit discrimination on the basis of one's sexual orientation (*orientation sexuelle*); see *Chartre des droits et libertés de la personne* [adoptée le 27 juin 1975 par l'Assemblée nationale du Québec], RSQ *c.* C-12, §10 (originally added via SQ 1977, *c.* 6, §1).

114. Amongst these, the system created by Council of Europe and its member states, governed by the 1950 European Convention on Human Rights (ECHR), was of paramount importance. By that time, it already had a respectable Court and a Commission in place to deal with the implementation of the Convention, whose decisions were binding on all (Council of Europe / ECHR) member states. In 1980 CE, those states were Belgium, Denmark, France, Ireland, Italy, Luxembourg, Netherlands, Norway, Sweden, United Kingdom, Greece, Turkey, Iceland, Germany, Austria, Cyprus, Switzerland, Malta, Portugal, Spain and Liechtenstein. Today, Council of Europe (and ECHR) has 47 member states.

115. For an analysis of this formative stage of global sexual rights movement, see, for example, Alice M. Miller, 'Human Rights and Sexuality: First Steps Toward Articulating a Rights Based Framework for Claims to Sexual Rights and Freedoms' (1999) 93 *American Society of International Law Proceedings* 288.

116. Koskenniemi, *supra* n. 6, p. 102.

117. The Non-Aligned Movement was founded in Belgrade in 1961 CE as a community of states considering themselves outside both the Western and Eastern power blocs. In 1979 CE, Fidel Castro proclaimed that the

Movement's solemn mission was to sustain 'struggle against imperialism, colonialism, neo-colonialism, racism, and other forms of foreign aggression, occupation, domination, interference or hegemony as well as against great power and bloc politics'; quoted in Abayomi Azikiwe, 'Non-Aligned Movement Calls for "New Economic Order"', *Workers World*, 27 July 2009, available at http://www.workers.org/2009/world/nonaligned_0730/ (accessed 8 April 2014).

118. Karl Llewellyn, 'Some Realism about Realism: Responding to Dean Pound' (1931) 44 *Harvard Law Review* 1222, p. 1234. It was contended that the conception of law as a means to social ends, which Llewellyn ascribed to 'real Realists', was but 'a straightforward alloy of [Oliver Wendell] Holmes's instrumentalism and [Wesley] Hohfeld's insistence upon the need for the disaggregation of legal categories'; William Fisher, 'Karl Llewellyn' in David Kennedy & William W. Fisher III (eds), *The Canon of American Legal Thought* (Princeton University Press, Princeton 2006), p. 136. Whatever the case, the 'law in action' paradigm – suggesting an active, *social* component of lawmaking and legal-cum-social reform – has found a substantial ground in the subsequent theoretical and activist approaches to law.

119. Rosalind Petchesky, 'Sexual Rights Policies across Countries and Cultures: Conceptual Frameworks and Minefields' in Richard Parker, Rosalind Petchesky & Robert Sember, *Sex Politics: Reports from the Front Lines* (Sexuality Policy Watch, Rio de Janeiro 2007), p. 12.

120. Sonia Corrêa, Richard Parker & Rosalind Petchesky (eds), *Sexuality, Health and Human Rights* (Routledge, London 2008), p. 28.

121. The governmental delegation that issued the 1985 CE statement supporting lesbian rights was that of the Netherlands. See generally ARC International, *UN General Assembly Joint Statement on Sexual Orientation & Gender Identity: Building on the Past, Looking to the Future* (ARC International, Geneva 2009).

122. It enjoins that the 'human rights of women include their right to have control over and decide freely and responsibly on matters related to their sexuality, including sexual and reproductive health, free of coercion, discrimination and violence'. Four references in the draft text to women's sexual orientation were erased from the final document, due to a last minute compromise. See generally Kate Sheill, 'Loosing Out in the Intersections: Lesbians, Human Rights, Law and Activism' (2009) 15 *Contemporary Politics* 55.

123. For instance, the 1994 CE International Conference on Population and Development in Cairo affirmed women's right to a satisfying and safe sex life; see ARC International, *supra* n. 121, p. 2.

124. See, for example, *Prosecutor v Kunarac* et al, Judgment, Case No IT-96-23 (International Criminal Tribunal for the former Yugoslavia (ICTY), Trial Chamber, 22 February 2001), Judgment (Appeals Chamber, 12 June 2002), paras 393, 409; and *Rome Statute of the International Criminal Court*, adopted on 17 July 1998, entered into force on 1 July 2002; affirming women's rights to sexual autonomy and bodily integrity.

125. Global Rights, *Demanding Credibility and Sustaining Activism: A Guide to Sexuality-based Advocacy* (Global Rights, Washington 2008), p. 55.
126. *Convention for the Protection of Human Rights and Fundamental Freedoms*, ETS 5, 4 November 1950, entered into force on 3 September 1953.
127. *Dudgeon v UK*, A 45 (1981); (1982) 4 EHRR 149.
128. *Norris v Ireland*, A 142 (1988); (1988) 13 EHRR 186.
129. *Modinos v Cyprus*, A 259 (1993); (1993) 16 EHRR 485.
130. *B v France*, A 232-C (1992).
131. See, for example, Article 17 of the International Covenant on Civil and Political Rights, UN General Assembly Res 2200A (XXI), 21 UN GAOR Supp (No. 16), p. 52, UN Doc A/6316 (1966), 993 UNTS 3, entered into force on 23 March 1976.
132. *Dudgeon v UK, supra* n. 127, para. 61.
133. For ICCPR and the right to privacy it enshrines, see *supra* n. 131.
134. *Toonen v Australia*, (488/1992), CCPR/C/50/D/488/1992 (1994); 1–3 IHHR 97 (1994).
135. Michael O'Flaherty & John Fisher, 'Sexual Orientation, Gender Identity and International Human Rights Law: Contextualising the Yogyakarta Principles' (2008) 8 *Human Rights Law Review* 207, p. 221.
136. *Toonen v Australia, supra* n. 134, para. 8.7.
137. In conformity with the UN Human Rights Committee's decision in *Toonen v Australia*, the Australian federal government passed the Human Rights (Sexual Conduct) Act 1994, Section 4, which legalised sexual acts between consenting adults of either sex in private. This act repealed the offending laws in Mr Toonen's native (Australian federal) state of Tasmania, despite an earlier refusal of the Tasmanian Parliament to comply with the *Toonen v Australia* judgment and do away with those laws itself.
138. An often expressed opinion which seeks to challenge the recent international jurisprudence concerning sexual and gender diversity (including that in *Toonen*) argues that 'the categories "sexual orientation" and "gender identity" [...] find no recognition or clear and agreed definition in international law'. Their increasing usage by the treaty bodies and other UN human rights organs thereby 'create[s] serious uncertainty in the law [and] undermine[s] the ability of States to enter into and enforce new and existing human rights conventions and standards'; Statement by the Permanent Observer Mission of the Holy See to the United Nations, 63rd session of the United Nations General Assembly, Item 64(b); available at http://www.holyseemission.org/statements/statement. aspx?id=112 (accessed 21 April 2014). For an opposing view, see Sophie M. Clavier, 'Objection Overruled: The Binding Nature of the International Norm Prohibiting Discrimination against Homosexual and Transgendered Individuals' (2012) 35 *Fordham International Law Journal* 385.
139. *Young v Australia* (941/2000), CCPR/C/78/D/941/2000 (2003); 11 IHHR 146 (2004); *X v Colombia* (1361/2005), CCPR/C/89/D/1361/2005 (2007); 14 IHHR 933 (2007). In addition to these decisions, numerous Concluding

Observations of the UN Human Rights Committee univocally corroborate this stance.

140. For a good survey of the General Comments and Concluding Observations of the UN treaty bodies that mention sexual orientation, see O'Flaherty & Fisher, *supra* n. 135, p. 216.

141. UN Committee on Economic, Social and Cultural Rights (CESCR), General Comment No 20: Non-Discrimination in Economic, Social and Cultural Rights (Para 32), 2 July 2009, E/C12/GC/20 (2009); 16 IHRR 925 (2009), para. 32.

142. 'Ending Violence and Criminal Sanctions on the Basis of Sexual Orientation and Gender Identity', United Nations, Office of the High Commissioner for Human Rights (OHCHR), 23 September 2010, available at http://www. ohchr.org/EN/NewsEvents/Pages/GenderIdentity.aspx (accessed 21 April 2014) (emphasis added).

143. Formed in 2003, ARC International 'plays a unique role in facilitating strategic planning around LGBT issues internationally, strengthening global networks, and enhancing access to UN mechanisms'. It describes itself as 'the only organization with a full-time presence in Geneva committed to advancing LGBT issues within the UN human rights system', which has been 'successful in engaging the support of the UN High Commissioner for Human Rights, ensuring that the records of all UN States on LGBT issues are subjected to international scrutiny, and bringing international support to the work of NGOs in countries around the world'; ARC International, 'About Us', available at http://arc-international.net/about (accessed 22 April 2014). Amongst many strategic tools, ARC International maintains a closed (invitation-only) e-mail list known as SOGI (for 'sexual orientation' and 'gender identity'), which is central to co-ordinating global advocacy on sexual and gender diversity.

144. Rahul Rao, *Third World Protest: Between Home and the World* (Oxford University Press, Oxford 2010), p. 189.

145. *Smith and Grady* v *United Kingdom*, 1999-VI; (1999) 29 EHRR 493.

146. *Lustig-Prean and Beckett* v *United Kingdom*, (1999) 29 EHRR 548.

147. *Salgueiro da Silva Mouta* v *Portugal*, 1999-IX; (1999) 31 EHRR 1055.

148. *SL* v Austria, 2003-I 71; (2003) 37 EHRR 39, para 44. See also *L and V* v *Austria*, 2003-I 29; (2003) 36 EHRR 55.

149. *Karner* v *Austria*, 2003-IX 199; (2003) 38 EHRR 24.

150. *EB* v *France*, Application No. 43546/02, Judgment, 22 January 2008.

151. See *Schalk and Kopf* v *Austria*, Application No 30141/04, Judgment, 24 June 2010, para. 90. See also Loveday Hodson, 'A Marriage by Any Other Name? *Schalk and Kopf* v *Austria*' (2011) 11 *Human Rights Law Review* 170.

152. See, for example, *Van Oosterwijck* v *Belgium*, Application No. 7654/76, Judgment, 6 November 1980; *Rees* v *United Kingdom*, Application No 9532/81, Judgment, 17 October 1986; *Cossey* v *United Kingdom*, Application No. 10843/84, Judgment, 27 September 1990; *B* v *France*, Application No 13343/87, Judgment, 25 March 1992.

153. *I* v *United Kingdom*, Application No 25680/94, Judgment, 11 July 2002, para. 54.
154. *Christine Goodwin* v *United Kingdom*, Application No 28957/95, Judgment, 11 July 2002.
155. *Van Kück* v *Germany*, 2003-VII; (2003) 37 EHRR 51, para. 69.
156. *L* v *Lithuania*, Application No 27527/03, Judgment, 11 September 2007, para. 59.
157. *Christine Goodwin* v *United Kingdom*, supra n. 154, para. 91.
158. See, for example, *I* v *United Kingdom*, supra n. 153, para. 61.
159. This pun was first used in Stephen Whittle, *Respect and Equality: Transsexual and Transgender Rights* (Cavendish Publishing, London 2002), p. 153.
160. See Ralph Sandland, 'Crossing and Not Crossing: Gender, Sexuality and Melancholy in the European Court of Human Rights' (*Christine Goodwin* v. *United Kingdom* [. . .], *I* v. *United Kingdom* [. . .]) (2003) 11(2) *Feminist Legal Studies* 191; Ralph Sandland, 'Feminism and the Gender Recognition Act 2004' (2005) 13(1) *Feminist Legal Studies* 43.
161. *Bączkowski and Others* v *Poland*, Application No. 1543/06, Judgment, 3 May 2007.
162. *Alexeyev* v *Russia*, Applications No. 4916/07, 25924/08 & 14599/09, Judgment, 21 October 2010.
163. Закон Рязанской области о защите нравственности и здоровья детей в Рязанской области, Управление Внутренних Дел по Рязанской области, No. 41-ОЗ, 3 April 2006. The by-laws against 'propaganda of homosexuality among minors' were enacted in Ryazan on 22 March 2006, in Arkhangelsk on 30 September 2011 and in Kostroma Region on 28 February 2012.
164. Закон Санкт-Петербурга о внесении изменений в Закон Санкт-Петербурга об административных правонарушениях в Санкт-Петербурге, 7 March 2012. See also 'Санкт-Петербург стал четвертым российским регионом, запретившим гей-пропаганду', GayRussia (по материалам РИА *Новости*), 11 March 2012, available at http://www.gayrussia.eu/russia/3883/ (accessed 23 April 2014).
165. See, for example, Resolution on Human Rights, Sexual Orientation and Gender Identity, General Assembly of the Organisation of American States, 4 June 2009, GA Res 2504 (XXXIX-O/09), reiterating an earlier resolution of the same title, GA Res 2435 (XXXVIII-O/08).
166. The full text of the Inter-American Convention against All Forms of Discrimination and Intolerance, adopted by the General Assembly of the Organisation of American States on 5 June 2013, is available at http://www.oas.org/en/sla/dil/docs/inter_american_treaties_A-69_discrimination_intolerance.pdf (accessed 23 April 2014).
167. *Atala Riffo y niñas* v *Chile*, Inter-American Court on Human Rights (IACtHR), Judgment, 24 February 2012, para 91 ['la orientación sexual y la identidad de género de las personas son categorías protegidas por la Convención']. The *American Convention on Human Rights* was adopted by the states of Americas on 22 November 1969 in San José, Costa Rica. It entered into force on 18 July

1978. The judicial bodies responsible for overseeing compliance with this treaty are the Inter-American Court of Human Rights and the Inter-American Commission on Human Rights, both of which are organs of the Organisation of American States (OAS). OAS currently has 35 member states.

168. *Juridical Condition and Rights of the Undocumented Migrants*, Inter-American Commission on Human Rights (IACHR), Advisory Opinion OC-18/03, 17 September 2003, Series A No. 18, para. 63.

169. In one such a case, *Marta Lucía Álvarez Giraldo* v *Columbia*, Case No. 11.656, Report No. 71/99 (1999), the Inter-American Commission on Human Rights declared the application admissible because the prohibition of intimate visits in a women's prison for the inmates' same-sex partners may have constituted a breach of the right to respect for private life. However, in a move typical for these cases, it was not decided on the merits because the respondent state adopted a satisfactory remedy.

170. See, for example, the IACHR's swift response to the news of yet another murder of a trans human rights activist in Mexico: 'IACHR Condemns Murder of Human Rights Defender in Mexico', Press Release, IACHR, 20 March 2012, available at http://www.oas.org/en/iachr/media_center/PReleas es/2012/032.asp (accessed 23 April 2014).

171. *AIDS-Free World (on behalf of two petitioners)* v *Jamaica*; submission of petition to the IACHR announced on 26 October 2011; see 'The First-Ever Legal Challenge to Jamaica's Anti-Gay Law', AIDS-Free World, 26 October 2011, available at http://www.aidsfreeworld.org/Our-Issues/Homophobia/The-First-Ever-Legal-Challenge-to-Jamaicas-Anti-Gay-Laws.aspx (accessed 23 April 2014). The discriminatory statute in question is Offences Against the Person Act, 1864 ('unnatural crime'; 'carnal knowledge'; 'outrages on decency'; 'buggery'), §§76–77, 79 – a relict of British colonial law.

172. For an overview of these UN resolutions, see ARC International, *supra* n. 121, p. 2.

173. Organisation of Islamic Co-operation (OIC), formerly known as the Organisation of the Islamic Conference, is an inter-governmental body of 57 member states which claims to represent 'the collective voice of the Muslim world and [that it is] ensuring to safeguard and protect the interests of the Muslim world in the spirit of promoting international peace and harmony among various people[s] of the world'; 'About OIC', OIC/OCI official website, available at http://www.oic-oci.org/page_detail.asp?p_id=52 (accessed 24 April 2014).

174. Statement made by Ambassador Tim Caughley, New Zealand Representative, on behalf of several countries under Agenda Item 17: Promotion and Protection of Human Rights, 15 April 2005, UN Commission on Human Rights, 61st Session, 14 March–22 April 2005, available at http://www.mfat. govt.nz/Media-and-publications/Media/MFAT-speeches/2005/0-15-April-2005a.php (accessed 24 April 2014).

175. UN Human Rights Council, 3rd Session, Geneva, 1 December 2006, available at http://www.norway-geneva.org/unitednations/humanrights/hrc011206 (accessed 24 April 2014).

176. For a summary of these statements, see ARC International, *supra* n. 121.

177. *Universal Declaration of Human Rights* (UDHR), UN General Assembly Res 217A (III) (1948), UN Doc A/810, p. 71.

178. *Statement on Human Rights, Sexual Orientation and Gender Identity*, on behalf of 66 States, under Agenda Item 64(b), UN General Assembly, 63rd session, New York, 18 December 2008, UN Doc A/63/635. The statement was introduced by a cross-regional Core Group of states from all five UN regions and co-ordinated by numerous human rights organisations. The signatory states included three OIC member states (Albania, Gabon and Guinea-Bissau) as well as three states with the OIC observer status (Bosnia and Herzegovina, Central African Republic and Serbia). In March 2009 CE, the United States of America joined the statement as the 67th state.

179. *Ibid*, paras 10–13.

180. *Response Presented by Syria to Statement on Human Rights and the So-Called Notions of 'Sexual Orientation' and 'Gender Identity'*, UN General assembly, 18 December 2008, available at http://www.un.org/webcast/ga2008.html (video) (accessed 24 April 2014). Of 57 signatory states, only 12 were not OIC members (those were the Democratic People's Republic of Korea, Eritrea, Ethiopia, Fiji, Kenya, Malawi, Rwanda, St Lucia, the Solomon Islands, Swaziland, the United Republic of Tanzania and Zimbabwe).

181. *Ibid*.

182. See, for example, 'Ground-Breaking Statement on Sexual Orientation and Gender Identity by Record Number of 85 States', International Service for Human Rights (ISHR), Press Release, 24 March 2011, available at http://www.ishr.ch/council/1033-ground-breaking-statement-on-sexual-orientation-and-gender-identity-by-record-number-of-85-states (accessed 24 April 2014).

183. *Ibid*.

184. 'UN Human Rights Council: Landmark Report and Panel on Sexual Orientation and Gender Identity', ARC International, Press Release, 7 March 2012, available at http://arc-international.net/global-advocacy/human-rights-council/hrc19/press-release (accessed 24 April 2014).

185. *Ibid*. See also, Navanethem Pillay, *High Commissioner's Report to the Human Rights Council on Violence and Discrimination based on Sexual Orientation and Gender Identity*, 15 December 2011, UN Doc A/HRC/19/41, available at http://www.ohchr.org/EN/Issues/Discrimination/Pages/LGBTUNReports.as px (accessed 24 April 2014).

186. The Yogyakarta Principles are available at http://www.yogyakartaprinciples.org (accessed 24 April 2014). See also O'Flaherty & Fisher, *supra* n. 135; Michael O'Flaherty & Gwyneth Williams, 'Jurisprudential Annotations to the Yogyakarta Principles', Human Rights Law Centre, University of Nottingham, November 2007, available at http://www.yogyakartaprinciples.org/

yogyakarta-principles-jurisprudential-annotations.pdf (accessed 24 April 2014).

187. See http://www.yogyakartaprinciples.org/principles_en.htm (accessed 29 April 2014) for the full list of 29 signatories. It includes Asma Jahangir, Chairperson of the Human Rights Commission of Pakistan; Yakın Ertürk, the then UN Special Rapporteur on Violence against Women and a Professor at the Middle East Technical University in Ankara; and Rudi Mohammed Rizki, the then UN Special Rapporteur in International Solidarity and a Senior Lecturer and Vice Dean of the Faculty of Law at the University of Padjadjaran in Indonesia. Professor Robert Wintemute, of School of Law, King's College London, was also amongst the expert signatories.

188. '"[S]exual orientation" [refers] to each person's capacity for profound emotional, affectional and sexual attraction to, and intimate and sexual relations with, individuals of a different gender or the same gender or more than one gender'; Yogyakarta Principles, Preamble. For a more detailed discussion of this definition, see Chapter 2 of this book.

189. '"[G]ender identity" [refers] to each person's deeply felt internal and individual experience of gender, which may or may not correspond with the sex assigned at birth, including the personal sense of the body (which may involve, if freely chosen, modification of bodily appearance or function by medical, surgical or other means) and other expressions of gender, including dress, speech and mannerisms'; Yogyakarta Principles, Preamble. This definition for the first time 'merged' 'gender identity' and 'gender expression' into a single notion, which since has become a standard in a variety of legal and academic sources. For a more detailed discussion, see Chapter 2 of this book.

190. See Michael O'Flaherty, 'Address of the Rapporteur' at the launch of the Yogyakarta Principles, Geneva, 26 March 2007, as paraphrased in O'Flaherty & Fisher, *supra* n. 135, pp. 232–233.

191. *Ibid.*

192. *Ibid*, p. 235.

193. UN Human rights Council, General Comment No. 22: The Right to Freedom of Thought, Conscience and religion (Art 18), 30 July 1993, CCPR/C/21/Rev1/Add4 (1994); 1(2) IHRR 30 (1994).

194. For the relevant ECtHR case law, see, for example, *Kokkinakis v Greece*, Application No 14307/88, Judgment, 25 May 1993; *Masaev v Moldova*, Application No 6303/05, Judgment, 12 August 2009; *Thlimmenos v Greece*, Application No 34369/97, Judgment, 6 April 2000; *Bayatyan v Armenia*, Application No. 23459/03, Judgment, 7 July 2011; *Ahmet Arslan and Others v Turkey*, Application No. 41135/98, Judgment (in French), 23 February 2010.

195. Reacting to the news of the establishment of the first organisation in the United States of America for sexually diverse and gender-variant Muslims, the vice president of the All-Dulles Ara Muslim Society, Iqbal Unus, was quoted saying: 'I don't see how it is possible to be gay and Muslim [. . .]. They are two contradictory things. I can't imagine what circumstances or situations would

bring about any kind of accommodation'; *Washington Post*, 3 April 2000, p. B4; quoted in Irshad A. Haqq, 'Homosexuality and Islam in America' (2000) 5 *Journal of Islamic Law & Culture* 87, pp. 89–90.

196. O'Flaherty & Williams, *supra* n. 186, p. 52.

197. Some early examples include Committee on Economic, Social and Cultural Rights, General Comment No. 20: Non-Discrimination in Economic, Social and Cultural Rights (Art. 2, para. 2, International Covenant on Economic, Social and Cultural rights), E/C12/GC/20, 2 July 2009, para. 32; *Handbook for the Protection of Women and Girls* (Office of the UN High Commissioner for Refugees (UNHCR), Geneva 2008), p. 72.

198. Joke Swiebel, 'Lesbian, Gay, Bisexual and Transgender Human rights: The Search for an International Strategy' (2009) 15 *Contemporary Politics* 19, pp. 31–32.

199. Aeyal M Gross, 'Sex, Love, and Marriage: Questioning Gender and Sexuality Rights in International Law' (2008) 21 *Leiden Journal of International Law* 235, p. 251.

200. Sheill, *supra* n. 122, p. 59.

201. *Ibid*, p. 60.

202. O'Flaherty & Fisher, *supra* n. 135, p. 236.

203. *Ibid*.

204. Cf. Gross, *supra* n. 199, p. 251.

205. I use this term to denote the employment of religion for purely political ends, otherwise known, in Muslim contexts, as 'Islamism' or 'political Islam'. In the absence of 'Christianism' and other comparable neologisms, imputing that ideological indoctrination 'in the name of Islam' is somehow immanent to the profession and practice of the Muslim belief system(s) is at best imprecise and inappropriate.

206. See, for example, Vanja Hamzić & Ziba Mir-Hosseini, *Control and Sexuality: The Revival of* Zina *Laws in Muslim Contexts* (Women Living under Muslim Laws, London 2010).

207. Saskia Eleonora Wieringa, 'Postcolonial Amnesia: Sexual Moral Panics, Memory, and Imperial Power' in Gilbert H. Herdt (ed.), *Moral Panics, Sex Panics: Fear and the Fight over Sexual Rights* (New York University Press, New York 2009), pp. 206–207.

208. UN Doc A/HRC/RES/17/19, adopted at the 34th Session of the UN Human Rights Council in Geneva, 17 June 2011.

209. Zamir Akram, 'Letter to H.E. Ms Laura Dupuy Lasserre, President of the Human Rights Council, from Zamir Akram, Ambassador and Permanent Representative of the Permanent Mission of Pakistan to the United Nations and Other International Organisations', Geneva, 14 February 2012, available at http://blog.unwatch.org/index.php/2012/02/17/letter-from-uns-islamic-group-to-unhrc-president-opposing-panel-on-violence-against-gays/#more-1760 (accessed 30 April 2014) (paragraph numbers omitted).

210. *Statute of the Independent Permanent Human Rights Commission of the Organisation of Islamic Co-operation (IPHRC)*, Chapter III: Objectives of the Commission,

Art. 8; quoted in Marie Juul Petersen, *Islamic or Universal Human Rights? The OIC's Independent Permanent human Rights Commission*, DIIS Report 2012:03 (Danish Institute for International Studies, Copenhagen 2012), p. 19.

211. Petersen, *supra* n. 210, pp. 29–30.

212. *Ibid*, p. 32.

213. Sharon Slater, 'UN Delegates Honored for Standing for the Family', the Family Watch International, 18 November 2010, available at http://www.familywatchi nternational.org/fwi/newsletter/0485.cfm (accessed 30 April 2014).

214. Maha Akeel, 'First Session of IPHRC: OIC Human Rights Body Identifies Women'S Rights, Education, Development and Research as Priority' (2012) 20 *OIC Journal* 28, pp. 28–29, available at http://www.oic-oci.org/journal.asp (accessed 30 April 2014).

215. John Packer & Murtaza Shaikh, 'OIC Independent Permanent Human Rights Commission: A Key Step towards Implementation' (2012) 20 *OIC Journal* 68, p. 68, available at http://www.oic-oci.org/journal.asp (accessed 30 April 2014).

216. *Ibid*.

217. *Ibid* (emphasis added).

218. *Ibid*. However, it was not at all made clear how this might be the case.

219. In the contemporary contexts, *siyar* can also be loosely translated as 'inter-state Muslim "legal politics"' or even 'Islamic international law'. I have opted for a version more reminiscent of its traditional (pre-Westphalian) function, i.e. 'Muslim law of nations'. See generally Shaheen Sardar Ali, 'The Twain Doth Meet! A Preliminary Exploration of the Theory and Practice of *as-Siyar* and International Law in the Contemporary World' in Javaild Rehman & Susan C. Breau (eds), *Religion, Human Rights and International Law: A Critical Examination of Islamic State Practices* (Martinus Nijhoff Publishers, Leiden 2007), pp. 81–113.

220. *Universal Islamic declaration of Human Rights* (UDIHR), adopted by the Islamic Council in Paris on 19 September 1981.

221. See Preamble, UDHR, *supra* n. 177; and Preamble, UDIHR, *supra* n. 220.

222. From a plethora of available studies, see, for example, Abdullahi A. An-Na'im, *Toward an Islamic Reformation: Civil Liberties, Human Rights, and International Law* (Syracuse University Press, Syracuse 1996); Abdullahi A. An-Na'im, *Islam and the Secular State: Negotiating the Future of Shari'a* (Harvard University Press, Cambridge 2008); Mashood A. Baderin, *International Human Rights and Islamic Law* (Oxford University Press, Oxford 2005 [2003]); Ann Elizabeth Mayer, *Islam and Human Rights: Tradition and Politics* (3rd edn, Westview Press, Boulder 1999).

223. These include the *Cairo Declaration on Human Rights in Islam*, adopted by the 19th Islamic Conference of Foreign Ministers, July/August 1990; the *Arab Charter of Human rights*, adopted by League of Arab States, September 1994; and the *Tehran Declaration on the Role of Women in Islamic Societies*, adopted by the OIC Symposium of Experts on the Role of Women in the Development of

Islamic Society, April 1995. For an analysis of these documents, see Sardar Ali, *supra* n. 219.

224. *Draft Resolution on Promotion and Protection of Human Rights (and Sexual Orientation)*, presented by Brazil on behalf of 20 UN Member States, [the former] UN Commission on Human Rights, 59th Session, Agenda Item 17, 17 April 2003, E/CN.4/2003/L.92, available at http://www.un.org/Docs/journal/asp/ws.asp?m=E/CN.4/2003/L.92 (accessed 1 May 2014).

225. The OIC diplomatic resistance seemingly went as far as to issue a threat to boycott an Arab-Latin American trade summit, upon which the Brazilian delegation decided to give in and withdraw the draft resolution. See Françoise Girard, 'Negotiating Sexual Rights and Sexual Orientation at the UN, in Richard Parker, Rosalind Petchesky & Robert Sember, *Sex Politics: Reports from the Front Lines* (Sexuality Policy Watch, Rio de Janeiro 2007), p. 347.

226. Archbishop Silvano Tomasi, Head of the Holy See's Permanent Mission to the UN in Geneva, quoted in Benjamin Mann, 'Vatican Official: UN Gay "Rights" Agenda Endangers Church's Freedom', Catholic News Agency, 8 July 2011, available at http://www.catholicnewsagency.com/news/vatican-official-says-un-gay-rights-agenda-endangers-churchs-freedom/ (accessed 1 May 2014).

227. Wieringa, *supra* n. 207, p. 206.

228. A good example of this diversity in laws and attitudes can be found in the area of family law and anti-discrimination, which in the USA varies drastically by state. On the federal level, the president of the USA has signed into law the Matthew Shepard and James Byrd, Jr Hate Crimes Prevention Act; an Act of Congress, passed on 22 October 2009 CE and signed into law by President Barack Obama on 28 October 2009 CE as a rider to the National Defence Authorisation Act for 2010, HR 2647. This act extends the federal 'hate crimes law' to include the categories of gender identity and sexual orientation. Most importantly, on 26 June 2015, the US Supreme Court decided in *Obergefell* v *Hodges* that the right to marry must be guaranteed to same-sex couples across the country, by virtue of the Fourteenth Amendment to the US Constitution. Prior to this landmark decision, a total of 36 states, Washington DC and Guam used to issue marriage licences to same-sex couples, while many other US states persistently objected to such practice.

229. Domestic legislative changes have also been pursued; see *Obergefell* v *Hodges*, the Matthew Shepard and James Byrd, Jr Hate Crimes Prevention Act, *supra* n. 228, as well as Don't Ask, Don't Tell Repeal Act of 2010, HR 2965, S 4023, which ended a policy in the US Armed Forces to ban from serving all openly non-heterosexual people.

230. Hillary Rodham Clinton, 'Free and Equal in Dignity and Rights', Human Rights Day speech, Palais des Nations, Geneva, Switzerland, 6 December

2011, transcript available at http://www.humanrights.gov/2011/12/06/rem
arks-in-recognition-of-international-human-rights-day/ (accessed 3 May
2014).
231. *Ibid.*
230. The Council for Global Equality is self-described as an American organisation
working 'to ensure that those who represent our country – including those in
Congress, in the White House, in U.S. embassies and in U.S. corporations –
use the diplomatic, political and economic leverage available to them to
oppose human rights abuses that are too often directed at individuals because
of their sexual orientation, gender identity or gender expression'; 'About the
Council for Global Equality', the Council for Global Equality, available at
http://globalequality.wordpress.com/about/ (accessed 3 May 2014).
233. 'LGBT Activists from Around the World React to Secretary Clinton's Speech',
Global Equality Today, the Council for Global Equality Blog, 9 December
2012, available at http://globalequality.wordpress.com/2011/12/07/lgbt-acti
vists-from-around-the-world-react-to-secretary-clintons-speech/# (accessed 3
May 2014). The article informs us that, '[f]or this historic moment in the
LGBT movement, the Council for Global Equality was privileged to bring 14
prominent LGBT activists from around the world to Geneva to be present for
Secretary Clinton's Human Rights Day speech'. An activist from each of the
following countries has attended the speech: Cameroon, Colombia, Croatia,
India, Jamaica, Kenya, Lithuania, Malawi, Moldova, Philippines, Russian
Federation, South Africa, Uganda and Ukraine. Their smiling faces and
passionate 'reactions' adorn this 'picture-perfect' celebration of the US human
rights diplomacy.
234. *Ibid.* On the same page, amongst other panegyrics, Rev. MacDonald
Sembereka of the Malawi Network or Religious Leaders Living with
HIV/AIDS, is quoted saying: 'First and foremost, thank you Hillary
Clinton and the U.S. government for starting a global discussion like
never was done before. To me this has been a speech that touched all aspects
of a discussion that we need to have globally. She covered all the pros
and cons – and now the global discussion begins. I hope that the rest of
the world takes it up'.
235. Barack Obama was described as 'the drone-happy president' for authorising
some 267 'targeted killings' during the first three years in office (as opposed to
52 such strikes under the Bush administration) in Pakistan alone by the US
Army's drones ('unmanned aerial vehicles'); see Glenn Greenwald, 'Obama
Escalates in Yemen – Again', *Salon*, 26 April 2012, available at http://www.
salon.com/2012/04/26/obama_escalates_in_yemen/ (accessed 3 May 2014).
According to a 2014 report by the Bureau of Investigative Journalism, a total
of 319 drone attacks under the Bush and Obama administrations in Pakistan
killed between 2,433 and 3,093 persons, of which 467 to 815 were civilians
and 178 children. In addition, between 1,163 and 1,268 persons were injured.
See generally 'Covert War on Terror: The Data', the Bureau of Investigative

Journalism, available at http://www.thebureauinvestigates.com/category/ projects/drone-data/ (accessed 3 May 2014). The former Special Rapporteur on Extrajudicial, Summary or Arbitrary Executions, Professor Philip Alston, has repeatedly warned that the US drone attacks 'might violate international humanitarian law and international human rights law'; see 'Press Conference by Special Rapporteur on Summary or Arbitrary Executions', United Nations, Department of Public Information, News and Media Division, New York, 27 October 2009, available at http://www.un.org/News/briefings/docs/2009/ 091027_Alston.doc.htm (accessed 3 May 2014).

236. Quoted in 'Cameron Threat to Dock Some UK Aid to Anti-Gay Nations', BBC News UK, 30 October 2011, available at http://www.bbc.co.uk/news/ uk-15511081 (accessed 3 May 2014).

237. Peter Tatchell, 'David Cameron Urged: Apologise for Anti-Gay Laws Imposed by UK', Peter Tatchell Foundation, 27 October 2011, available at http://www. petertatchellfoundation.org/commonwealth/david-cameron-urged-apologise-anti-gay-laws-imposed-uk (accessed 3 May 2014).

238. Colin Robinson, 'Decolonising Sexual Citizenship: Who Will Effect Change in the South of the Commonwealth?', *Opinions*, April 2012, the Commonwealth Advisory Bureau, p. 6, available at http://www.common wealthadvisorybureau.org/fileadmin/CPSU/documents/Publications/April_ Opinion.pdf (accessed 3 May 2014).

239. 'The Human Dignity Trust: Legally Challenging the Illegality of Homosexuality', Human Dignity Trust, available at http://www.humandignity trust.org/pages/ABOUT%20US (accessed 3 May 2014).

240. Jonathan Cooper OBE, CEO of Human Dignity Trust, quoted in Zoe Williams, 'Gay Rights: A World of Inequality', *Guardian*, 13 September 2011, available at http://www.guardian.co.uk/world/2011/sep/13/gay-rights-world-of-inequality (accessed 3 May 2014); also quoted in Robinson, *supra* n. 238, p. 4.

241. The Iran regime is notorious for treating sexual diversity as amongst the most serious criminal offences, often warranting the death penalty. But the media reports and campaigns around this issue, fuelled by certain human rights groups and activists from the global north (e.g. the Italian EveryOne Group), have proven extremely unhelpful and insensitive. Not only are the dramatic reports on 'gay youth' being publicly executed for 'being who they are' at best imprecise (as those individuals might have been executed for reasons other than their sexual orientation or same-sex sexual acts, let alone the fact that they have never self-identified as 'gay'), but such coverage jeopardises the status of those still on death row even further, given that same-sex sexuality is a capital offence *causa sui* in Iran. To make it even worse, the Israeli right-wing propaganda machine, campaigning for a military intervention against Iran, has also picked up this issue, for its own ideological purposes. For one such case, reported in the *Jerusalem Post* as 'the Islamic Republic's campaign to execute gay Iranians [that has] resulted in the public hanging this month of a man identified only as "CH. M."', see Benjamin Weinthal, 'Iran Reportedly Hangs

Gay Man', the *Jerusalem Post*, 29 April 2012, available at http://www.jpost. com/MiddleEast/Article.aspx?id=267868 (accessed 4 May 2014). See also Scott Long, 'Unbearable Witness: How Western Activists (Mis)Recognize Sexuality in Iran' (2009) 15 *Contemporary Politics* 119.

242. Jubilant, perhaps, over the Obama administration's new policy to campaign for lesbian and gay equality *around the world* (but not yet so much in the USA itself), the US Ambassador in Pakistan, Richard Hoagland, and some Gays and Lesbians in Foreign Affairs Agencies (GLIFAA) activists 'hosted an event declared as "Islamabad's first ever Gay, Lesbian, Bisexual, and Transgender (GLBT) Pride Celebration" on June 26, 2011 in the Federal Capital of Islamic Republic of Pakistan. This high profile event was reportedly attended by 75 people including Mission Officers, U.S. military representatives, foreign diplomats, and leaders of Pakistani LGBT advocacy groups who showed their "support for human rights, including LGBT rights in Pakistan at a time when those rights are increasingly under attack from extremist elements throughout Pakistani society". Unthankfully, all the sensational and flowery claptrap peddled around this event turned out to be a disaster for the budding underground Pakistani {movement for sexual and gender diversity} as the US Embassy conveniently oversaw [*sic*] the repercussions this event would have brought in an already critical country [...]. Within a few days, the streets of major urban cities of Pakistan [...] were hailed with the students and political workers of Jamaat-e-Islami, a religious political party, chanting slogans at their highest pitches against homosexuals and America [...]. Banners were displayed in major cities, especially in the federal capital, within a few days demanding persecution of gays and accusing Americans of propagating and imposing this "westernized" idea'; Hadi Hussain, 'US Embassy's Pride Celebrations in Islamabad: More Damage than Support', *Gaylaxy*, 24 August 2011, available at http://www.gaylaxymag.com/blog/index.php/2011/08/ us-embassys-pride-celebrations-in-islamabad-more-damage-than-support/ (accessed 4 May 2014). In addition, all members of the Pakistani social justice movement(s) for sexual and gender diversity that I have spoken with, especially during my fieldwork related to this study, have unanimously condemned this 'pride event' as a dire form of American imperialism, denying that any of their representatives had either been invited to or had attended it.

243. In April 2012 CE, a British charity organised an out of the blue 'global' campaign for same-sex marriage that was supposed to culminate in submitting 'recommendations for action' to the eleven states scheduled for the human rights screening process under the Universal Period Review (UPR) at the UN Human Rights Council. The states under review were Benin, Gabon, Ghana, Guatemala, Japan, Pakistan, Peru, Sri Lanka, the Republic of Korea, Ukraine and Zambia, and the 'recommendations for action' were, in each case, to include an explicit call for legalising same-sex marriage. In preparations of these submissions, the British charity made no consultations with the existing movements for sexual/gender diversity in any of the eleven states. Upon

hearing of this campaign, the representatives of these movements squarely rejected and deplored it, since they felt that bringing up the issue of same-sex marriage before their governments, whilst many of them still fought for decriminalisation of same-sex sexual activities, could only harm their cause. Moreover, they maintained that the hostile media and other reactionary forces in their respective countries could find this insensitive campaign rather useful for further persecution of sexually diverse and gender-variant communities, because the previous allegations of same-sex marriages illegally taking place, especially in some African contexts, have been instrumental in mounting public support for violence and discrimination against these communities. Eventually, the British charity withdrew its UPR submissions and apologised for its ignorance and lack of sensitivity. Due to confidentiality and security concerns, I am obliged to withhold further information.

244. Jasbir K. Puar, *Terrorist Assemblages: Homonationalism in Queer Times* (Duke University Press, Durham 2007), p. xiv.

245. *Ibid*, p. xxiv.

246. Rao, *supra* n. 144, p. 192. He goes on to explain that '[t]he satisfaction that white queers derive from saving brown queers from brown homophobes stems from the confirmation that this heroic gesture seems to provide for something whites have always "known": that "whiteness" (and everything non-racial that this additionally signifies) is superior to "brownness" and will always be so'.

247. Following a well-known seminal study, Orientalism determines a tendency to exoticise and eroticise the subjugated 'Oriental' subjectivities by their 'Occidental' (European) colonial masters and explorers. This phenomenon, which arguably began as early as the late fifteenth century CE, seems to be continuously resurfacing ever since, in various neo-Orientalist fashions. The seminal study of this malicious imperial gaze is, of course, that of Edward W. Said, *Orientalism* (Penguin Books, London 2003 [1978, 1995, 2003]).

248. Lisa Duggan, 'The New Homonormativity: The Sexual Politics of Neoliberalism' in Russ Castronovo & Dana D. Nelson, (eds), *Materializing Democracy: Toward a Revitalized Cultural Politics* (Duke University Press, Durham 2002).

249. For the distinct *Muslim* voices from within the rising critical movements for sexual and gender diversity, see, for example, Ibrahim Abraham, '"Everywhere You Turn You Have to Jump into Another Closet": Hegemony, Hybridity, and Queer Australian Muslims' in Samar Habib (ed.), *Islam and Homosexuality* (Praeger, Santa Barbara 2010); Ayisha A al-Sayyad, '"You're What?": Engaging Narratives from Diasporic Muslim Women on Identity and Gay Liberation' in Samar Habib (ed.), *Islam and Homosexuality* (Praeger, Santa Barbara 2010); Jin Haritaworn, Tamsila Tauqir & Esra Erdem, 'Gay Imperialism: Gender and Sexuality Discourse in the "War on Terror"' in Adi Kuntsman & Esperanza Miyake, *Out of Place: Interrogating Silences in Queerness/ Raciality* (Raw Nerve Books, York 2008). For some other critical perspectives, see Dennis Altman, *Global Sex* (Allen and Unwin, Crows Nest 2001); Paola Bacchetta, 'Rescaling Transnational "Queerdom": Lesbian and "Lesbian"

Identitary-Positionalities in Delhi in the 1980s' (2002) 34 *Antipode: A Radical Journal of Geography* 947; Kath Browne, Jason Lim & Gavin Brown (eds), *Geographies of Sexualities: Theory, Practices and Politics* (Ashgate, Surrey 2007); Arnaldo Cruz-Malavé & Martin F. Manalansan IV (eds), *Queer Globalizations: Citizenship and the Afterlife of Colonialism* (New York University Press, New York 2002); Peter A. Jackson, 'Capitalism and Global Queering National Markets, Parallels among Sexual Cultures, and Multiple Queer Modernities' (2009) 15(3) *GLQ: A Journal of Lesbian and Gay Studies* 357.

250. *Transculturation* is a term coined in 1940 by Cuban anthropologist Fernando Otiz, which denotes the phenomenon of converging and merging cultures; see Fernando Otiz, *Cuban Counterpoint: Tobacco and Sugar* (Duke University Press, Durham 1995 [1940]).

251. Ranging from Muslim post-colonial heteronormativity to neo-Orientalist and/or Islamophobic homonormativity; see, for example, Abraham; al-Sayyad; and Haritaworn, Tauqir & Erdem, *supra* n. 249.

Chapter 3 Sexual and Gender Diversity in Islamic Law and the Muslim World

1. Norman Calder, 'Law' in Seyyed Hossein Nasr & Oliver Leaman (eds), *History of Islamic Philosophy* (Routledge, London 1996), Vol. 2, p. 988.
2. *Ibid.*
3. The same argument is pursued, for example, in Mohammad H. Kamali, *shari'ah Law: An Introduction* (Oneworld, Oxford 2008), p. 2.
4. Brinkley Messick, *The Calligraphic State: Textual Domination and History in a Muslim Society* (University of California Press, Berkeley 1993), p. 3.
5. Sami Zubaida, *Law and Power in the Islamic World* (I.B.Tauris, London 2005 [2003]), p. 11. See also Max Weber, *Max Weber on Law in Economy and Society* (trans. Edward Shils & Max Rheinstein; ed. Max Rheinstein; Simon and Schuster, New York 1954).
6. The Prophet Muhammad's 'trodden path', or *sunna*, features as the second most important such source, with a variety of additional, hierarchically lesser sources that are discussed later in this chapter. *Sunna*, as Muhammad's *praxis* (i.e. the correlative acts between what was to become the theory and practice of the Muslim life), has been transmitted through oral narratives of varying veracity and historical relevance, which have been turned into voluminous written collections, known as '*ahadith* (sing. *hadith*).
7. Apart from misinterpreting the notion of *shari'a*, the historiographical studies that conflate this term-of-art with 'divine law' and Islamic law suffer from one major omission: in search for the '*shari'a* comprehended and applied', they primarily rely on the plentiful works of *fuqaha'* as their bibliographical source; their accounts, thus, turn to be by and large the histories of classical *fiqh*. It is because of these misconceptions that an early yet very influential study claims

that 'Islamic law represents an extreme case of a jurists' law; it was created and further developed by private specialists, a phenomenon well known to the sociology of law'; Joseph Schacht, *Introduction to Islamic Law* (Oxford University Press, London 1964), p. 209.

8. Noel J. Coulson, *A History of Islamic Law* (Edinburgh University Press, Edinburgh 1964), p. 2.

9. See, for example, Kristen Stilt, 'Price Setting and Hoarding in Mamluk Egypt: The Lessons of Legal Realism for Islamic Legal Studies' in Peri Bearman, Wolfhart Heinrichs & Bernard G. Weiss (eds), *The Law Applied: Contextualizing the Islamic shari 'a* (I.B.Tauris, London 2008), pp. 57–78.

10. Robert Gleave, 'The Qadi and the Mufti in Akhbari Shi'i Jurisprudence' in Peri Bearman, Wolfhart Heinrichs & Bernard G. Weiss (eds), *The Law Applied: Contextualizing the Islamic shari 'a* (I.B.Tauris, London 2008), p. 235 *et passim*.

11. On the Naturalist camp, see the excellent study of Anver M. Emon, *Islamic Natural Law Theories* (Oxford University Press, Oxford 2010); for some Realist renditions of *usul al-fiqh*, see Sherman A. Jackson, 'Fiction and Formalism: Toward a Functional Analysis of *Usul al-Fiqh*' in Bernard G. Weiss (ed.), *Studies in Islamic Legal Theory* (Brill, Leiden 2002), pp. 177–201.

12. Bernard G. Weiss, 'Text and Application: Hermeneutical Reflections on Islamic Legal Interpretation' in Peri Bearman, Wolfhart Heinrichs & Bernard G. Weiss (eds), *The Law Applied: Contextualizing the Islamic Shari 'a* (I.B.Tauris, London 2008), p. 376.

13. Muhammad Khalid Masud, 'A Study of Waki''s (d. 306/917) *Akhbar al-Qudat*' in Peri Bearman, Wolfhart Heinrichs & Bernard G. Weiss (eds), *The Law Applied: Contextualizing the Islamic shari 'a* (I.B.Tauris, London 2008), p. 116.

14. See Dror Ze'evi, *Producing Desire: Changing Sexual Discourse in the Ottoman Middle East, 1500–1900* (University of California Press, Berkeley 2006).

15. Depending upon context, *siyasa* can also mean 'governance' and 'punishment'.

16. Amr Shalakany, 'Islamic Legal Histories' (2008) 1 *Berkeley Journal of Middle Eastern and Islamic Law* 1, p. 6. For Shalakany, the seminal works of the scripturalist stream are those of Schacht, *supra* n. 7, and Coulson, *supra* n. 8.

17. At least to the extent of conflating *siyasa* with *shari 'a* (or *vice versa*), which for the scripturalists *is* Islamic law; ibid, pp. 10–27.

18. *Ibid*, p. 60; see also pp. 60–77. In the context of a *new historian* approach, Shalakany cites, *inter alia*, the works of Baber Johansen and Uriel Heyd; further, in relation to the nineteenth century CE reforms of Egyptian criminal law, he refers to Khaled Fahmy's and Rudolph Peters' scholarship. The most promising work is that of Johansen; see Baber Johansen, *The Islamic Law on Land Tax and rent: The Peasant's Loss of Property Rights as Interpreted in the Hanafite Legal Literature of the Mamluk and Ottoman Periods* (Croom Helm, London 1988); Baber Johansen, 'Legal Literature and the Problem of Change: The Case of the Land Rent' in Chibli Mallat (ed.), *Islam and Public Law: Classical and Contemporary Studies* (Graham and Trotman, London 1993),

pp. 29–47. See also Baber Johansen, 'Eigentum, Familie und Obrigkeit im hanafitischen Strafrecht' (1979) 19 *Die Welt des Islams* 1.

19. Robert Gleave, 'Introduction' in Norman Calder, *Islamic Jurisprudence in the Classical Era* (ed. Colin Imber; Cambridge University Press, Cambridge 2010), p. 3.

20. For an exemplary piece, see the much cited Wael B. Hallaq, 'Was the Gate of Ijtihad Closed?' (1984) 16 *International Journal of Middle East Studies* 3. Numerous other Islamicists have followed the suit; see, for example, Gideon Libson, 'On the Development of Custom as a Source of Law in Islamic Law' (1994) 1(1) *Islamic Law and Society* 131; Muhammad Khalid Masud, Brinkley Messick & David S. Powers (eds), *Islamic Legal Interpretation: Muftis and Their Fatwas* (Harvard University Press, Cambridge 1996).

21. Gleave, *supra* n. 19, p. 3.

22. For instance, referring to Hallaq's assertion that a legal opinion (*fatwa*, pl. *fatawa*) of an individual Islamic scholar (*mufti*) has had the potential to leave a lasting impact on the various authoritative jurisprudential doctrines (recorded in the *furu' al-fiqh* literature) in the post-formative era of Islamic law, Norman Calder concludes: 'It is possible to agree with Hallaq's thesis at its most general – that in some sense or another Islamic law was capable of responding to social change – without feeling that he has characterised well either the basic structures of the Islamic legal system or the modality of its accommodation to change'; Norman Calder, *Islamic Jurisprudence in the Classical Era* (ed. Colin Imber; Cambridge University Press, Cambridge 2010), p. 160. See also Wael B. Hallaq, 'From *Fatwa*s to *Furu*'' (1994) 1(1) *Islamic Law and Society* 29.

23. For a good example of the *new historian* scholarship employing this approach see David S. Powers, *Law, Society, and Culture in the Maghrib, 1300–1500* (Cambridge University Press, Cambridge 2002).

24. '[I]n the Islamic world [...], politics and the state were not conceived as a category separate from other forms of activity, but as an integral part of religion, morality, law or clan values'; Antony Black, *The History of Islamic Political Thought: From the Prophet to the Present* (2nd edn; Edinburgh University Press, Edinburgh 2011 [2001]), p. 5.

25. That is, in literary genres comprising legal theory or positive law treatises, respectively.

26. Black, *supra* n. 24, p. 65. See generally Ralph Lerner & Muhsin Mahdi (eds), *Medieval Political Philosophy: a Sourcebook* Free Press of Glencoe, Toronto 1963), pp. 22–94; Abu Nasr al-Farabi, *Mabadi' ara' ahl al-madinat al-fadilah / On the Perfect State* (trans./ed. Richard Walzer; Kazi Publications, Chicago 1998); Abu Nasr al-Farabi, *as-Siyasa al-madaniya al-mulaqqab bi-mabadi' al-mawjudat* (ed. F. Najjar, Imprimerie Catholique, Beirut 1964).

27. Classical *fiqh* literature more or less agrees that there are only six *hudud* offences: highway robbery (*hiraba, qat' al-tariq*), theft (*sariqa*), adultery and fornication (*zina*), false accusation of *zina* (*qadhf*), apostasy (*irtidad, ridda*) and

intoxication (*sharb al-khamr*). For these transgressions, the penalties are (interpreted as) prescribed in the Qur'an. Many of the *hudud* penalties, however, have been *effectively* suspended in various historical Muslim polities, for instance in the Ottoman Empire (1299/698 – 1922/1341 CE/AH) by the enactment of sultanic laws (*qanun*; Ottoman Turkish: *kanun*) that provided for the alternative penalties for the same or similar offences. While the *hudud* were still theoretically punishable in accordance with the Qur'anic injunctions, in reality they were mostly adjudicated upon and punished by means of state law. There are comparable (but not necessarily causally linked) examples in other historical Muslim polities, too, e.g. in the Mughal Empire (*c.*1526/932 – 1857/1274 CE/AH). Later in the present chapter, this topic is explored in some detail in relation to the Ottoman state. The Mughal reforms, pursued during the reign of Akbar the Great (r. 1556/963 – 1605/1013 CE/AH), are briefly discussed in Chapter 5 of this book.

28. See, for example, Vanja Hamzić & Ziba Mir-Hosseini, *Control and Sexuality: The Revival of* Zina *Laws in Muslim Contexts* (Women Living under Muslim Laws, London 2010).

29. On the post-colonial condition of (contemporary) Islamic law, see, for example, As'ad AbuKhalil, 'A Note on the Study of Homosexuality in the Arab/Islamic Civilization' (1993) 32 *Arab Studies Journal* 48; Shalakany, *supra* n. 16, p. 5; Khaled M. Abou El Fadl, *The Great Theft: Wrestling Islam from the Extremists* (HarperCollins, New York 2007 [2005]), pp. 43–44; Amina Wadud, *Inside the Gender Jihad: Women's Reform in Islam* (Oneworld, Oxford 2007 [2006]), pp. 136–137.

30. These are euphemisms used in Arabic to describe the male-born castrated subjectivities present in various historical Muslim societies; the correspondent term in English is 'eunuch' (from Greek: εὐνοῦχος) but its random historical usage to categorise different, often incommensurable forms of sexual/gender variance has been rightly criticised. For a seminal study of *khuddam/aghawat*, see Shaun Marmon, *Eunuchs and Sacred Boundaries in Islamic Society* (Oxford University Press, New York 1995), p. 41 *et passim*; for a critique of the historical usage of the term 'eunuch', see Shane Gannon, 'Exclusion as Language and the Language of Exclusion: Tracing Regimes of Gender through Linguistic Representations of the "Eunuch"' (2011) 20(1) *Journal of the History of Sexuality* 1.

31. Louise Halper, '"Legal Realism" in Tehran: Gender Law and the Transformative State' in Peri Bearman, Wolfhart Heinrichs & Bernard G. Weiss (eds), *The Law Applied: Contextualizing the Islamic shari'a* (I.B.Tauris, London 2008), p. 42.

32. AbuKhalil, *supra* n. 29, p. 32. This claim, while probably exaggerated, describes well the complex relationship that many Muslim-majority states still have with the European colonial heteronormativity and its (out)laws.

33. The latter interpretative system is sometimes also called queer Muslim hermeneutics; see, for example, Samar Habib, *Female Homosexuality in the*

Middle East: Histories and Representations (Routledge, New York 2007); Samar Habib (ed.), *Islam and Homosexuality* (Praeger, Santa Barbara 2010). Another author argues for 'sexuality-sensitive interpretation'; see Scott Siraj al-Haqq Kugle, *Homosexuality in Islam: Critical Reflection on Gay, Lesbian, and Transgender Muslims* (Oneworld, Oxford 2010), p. 41 *et passim*. For an example of scholarship employing one strand of Islamic feminist hermeneutics, see Fatima Mernissi, *Beyond the Veil: Male-Female Dynamics in a Muslim Society* (Saqi Books, London 2011 [1975, 1985]).

34. Fernand Braudel, *La Méditerranée et le monde méditerranéen à l'époque de Philippe II* (Armand Colin, Paris 1990 [1949]), Vol. 1.

35. Richard C. Hoffmann, Nancy Langston, James C. McCann, Peter C. Perdue & Lise Sedrez, 'AHR Conversation: Environmental Historians and Environmental Crisis' (2008) 113(5) *American Historical Review* 1431, p. 1433.

36. Braudel borrows the term *l'histoire événementielle* from the French economist François Simiand. See Fernand Braudel, *Écrits sur l'histoire* (Flammarion, Paris 1969); Gérard Noiriel, '"L'éthique de la discussion": A propos de deux conférences sur l'histoire (1903–1906)' in Lucien Gillard & Michel Rosier (eds), *François Simiand (1873–1935): sociologie, histoire, économie* (Editions des archives contemporaines, Paris 1996), pp. 79–93.

37. Ze'evi, *supra* n. 14, p. 11.

38. Eva Cantarella, 'Gender, Sexuality, and Law' in Michael Gagarin & David Cohen (eds), *The Cambridge Companion to Ancient Greek Law* (Cambridge University Press, Cambridge 2005), available at http://cco.cambridge.org/extract?id=ccol0521818400_CCOL0521818400A017 (accessed 30 June 2014).

39. *Ibid.*

40. Michel Foucault, *The History of Sexuality* (Penguin, London 1978), Vol. 1, pp. 17–35.

41. Joseph A. Massad, *Desiring Arabs* (University of Chicago Press, Chicago 2007), pp. 171–180.

42. The detail, in this sense, alludes to both cultural difference and any inconsistencies with the 'general view of the epoch' that the *longue durée* methodology ultimately strives to produce, challenge or refine.

43. Wael B. Hallaq, *The Origins and Evolution of Islamic Law* (Cambridge University Press, Cambridge 2004), p. 2.

44. Jonathan Berkey, *The Formation of Islam: Religion and Society in the Near East, 600–1800* (Cambridge University Press, Cambridge 2003), p. 71.

45. Zubaida, *supra* n. 5, p. 6.

46. 'Abu Bakr came to power only through a last-minute sleight-of-hand, while 'Umar and 'Uthman were both assassinated. 'Ali was raised to power by the rebels responsible for 'Uthman's death, fought a long civil war against 'Uthman's cousin Mu'awiya ibn Abi Sufyan, and was himself at last murdered'; Berkey, *supra* n. 44, p. 71.

47. The term Shi'a is an abbreviation of *Shi'atu 'Ali*, meaning the 'Faction of 'Ali'.

48. Berkey, *supra* n. 44, p. 79.

49. Zubaida, *supra* n. 5, p. 7.
50. Those were the Persian Buyids (945/333 – 1055/447 CE/AH) and the Turkic Seljuk (Arabic: *Saljuq*; Turkish: *Selçuk*) dynasties (1055/447 – 1194/590 CE/ AH). Buyids were Zaydi Shi'a and Seljuks Sunni Muslims.
51. Those of al-'Andalus as well as the Fatimid dynasty (949/337 – 1171/566 CE/ AH), which ruled over Egypt and North Africa. The Fatimids were Isma'ili Shi'a while the Spanish caliphs were predominantly Sunni Muslims.
52. Zubaida, *supra* n. 5, p. 12.
53. Coulson, *supra* n. 8, p. 11.
54. See *supra* n. 27.
55. The translations of the Holy Qur'an, if not stated otherwise, are mostly mine, although they do rely on a comparative analysis of the examples from various present-day and historical translators. This is because I find none of the well-established English translations sufficiently sophisticated for the purposes of the present study. For verses dealing with Lot, my primary source of relatively acceptable translations is that of Amreen Jamal, 'The Story of Lot and the Qur'an's Perception of the Morality of Same-Sex Sexuality' (2001) 41(1) *Journal of Homosexuality* 1.
56. See Kecia Ali, *Sexual Ethics & Islam: Feminist Reflections on Qur'an, Hadith, and Jurisprudence* (Oneworld Publications, Oxford 2007), p. 81.
57. Wadud, *supra* n. 29, p. 238.
58. Qur'an 7:80–84. Other references to the Prophet Lot appear in Qur'an 6:86, 11:74, 11:77–83; 15:58–77; 21:70–71, 21:74–75; 22:43; 26:160–175; 27:54–58; 29:26; 29:28–35, 37:133–138; 38:12–14; 50:12–14, 54:33–35 and 66:10 (the last verse refers to Lot's wife only).
59. Qur'an 29:28–29 ('And Lot, when he said to his people: 'Surely you commit such *fahisha* as never any being in the world committed before you. What, do you approach men, and cut the way [as in highway robbery], and commit in your assembly dishonour (*munkar*)?'').
60. Qur'an 54:33 (emphasis added). Indeed, in Qur'an 50:12–14, Lot's people are explicitly mentioned amongst numerous other ancient communities that had been punished for failing to recognise God's messengers.
61. Kugle, *supra* n. 33, p. 55.
62. Qur'an 29:31, referring to Lot's people ('We shall destroy the people of this city, for its people are evildoers (*zalimun*).').
63. And even those sources are all *biographical*, which is in itself problematic: 'If Muslim men of religion invented hadith reports to justify their doctrine, as demonstrated by [a number of Islamicists], they probably also invented much biographical information'; Christopher Melchert, *The Formation of the Sunni Schools of Law, 9th-10th Centuries C.E.* (Brill, Leiden 1997), p. xxviii.
64. I.e. whether *liwat* is a form of *zina*, an illicit sexual intercourse liable to a *hadd* punishment.
65. See, for example, Asma Barlas, *'Believing Women' in Islam: Unreading Patriarchal Interpretations of the Qur'an* (University of Texas Press, Austin 2002).

66. See, for example, Qur'an 4:1, 6:98, 7:189, 16:72, 30:21 and 49:13.
67. Qur'an 4:1.
68. Fazlur Rahman, *Major Themes of the Quran* (Bibliotheca Islamica, Minneapolis 1980).
69. Barlas, *supra* n. 65, p. 134.
70. *Ibid.*
71. Qur'an 30:21.
72. Qur'an 51:49.
73. Qur'an 53:45.
74. Qur'an 16:72.
75. See *supra* n. 6.
76. The '*hadith* collectors' (*muhaddithun*) had categorised the *hadith* literature, *inter alia*, in accordance with its supposed authenticity, whereby *sahih* are most reliable and *mawdu'* reports straightforward fabrications, usually with two more categories – *hasan* and *da'if* – between them. Over centuries, the Sunni Muslims came to accept the collections of six ninth/third century CE/AH scholars (Bukhari, Muslim ibn al-Hajjaj, al-Nasa'I, Abu Dawud, al-Tirmidhi and Ibn Maja) as most trustworthy, while the Shi'a rely on somewhat later collections (late third to fifth centuries AH) of the so-called 'Three Muhammads' (Muhammad ibn Ya'qub al Kulayni, Muhammad ibn Babuya and Abu Jafar Muhammad ibn Hassan Tusi). For a recent critical review of the *hadith* literature, see Jonathan A.C. Brown, *Hadith: Muhammad's Legacy in the Medieval and Modern World* (Oneworld, Oxford 2009).
77. According to the historian (and, one could say, proto-sociologist and proto-anthropologist) Ibn Khaldun (1332/732 – 1406/808 CE/AH), it is *recitation* itself that conveys the meaning, so even a written text should never be read mutely, but 'recited aloud in order to mean'; Timothy Mitchell, *Colonising Egypt* (Cambridge University Press, Cambridge 1988), p. 151. See also Abu Zayd 'Abdurrahman ibn Muhammad ibn Khaldun al-Hadrami [Ibn Khaldun], *Muqaddimah* [1377], available, *inter alia*, as *Muqaddimat Ibn Khaldun* (ed. E.M. Quatremere; Maktabat Lubnan, Beirut 1970 [1858]), Vols 1–3, and *The Muqaddimah: An Introduction to History* (2nd edn; trans. Franz Rosenthal; Princeton University Press, Princeton 1967), Vols 1–3. The title of the treatise means 'Introduction', hence it is also well known as *Prolegomena* (from Greek: Προλεγόμενα).
78. Qur'an 39:23.
79. Qur'an 45:6 ('These are God's signs (*ayat*) which We recite unto thee [Muhammad] in truth; then to what other speech (*hadith*) apart from God and God's signs will they believe?'); see also Kugle, *supra* n. 33, p. 126.
80. *Ibid*, pp. 77, 284. This is, controversially, preserved in the *hadith* literature itself. One such report narrates that Muhammad once approached Abu Hurayra and other companions (*sahaba*) while they were writing something and asked what was going on. They replied that they were writing down sayings that they heard from him. Muhammad then asked: 'A book other than

God's Book?' So the companions gathered what they had written onto a pile and burnt it all. See *ibid*, p. 284; Gautier H.A. Juynboll, *The Authenticity of the Tradition Literature: Discussions in Modern Egypt* (Brill, Leiden 1969), p. 50. See also 'Abd al-Hadi al-Fadli, *Introduction to Hadith* (trans. Nazmina Virjee; ICAS Press, London 2002), p. 69.

81. Obscure, that is, 'because of the scarcity of contemporary evidence'; Schacht, *supra* n. 7, p. 15.

82. Mohammed Abed al-Jabri, *Democracy, Human Rights and Law in Islamic Thought* (I.B.Tauris, London 2009), p. 5.

83. Coulson, *supra* n. 8, p. 22.

84. See Schacht, *supra* n. 7, pp. 31–32, 43, 53; Coulson, *supra* n. 8, pp. 64–65.

85. Of whom, two men stand out as the alleged authors – in a long chain (*isnad*) of transmitters – of the most of the *hadith* literature dealing with sexual and gender 'transgressions': Abu Hurayra, a Yemeni Arab who worked as a cleaner and a servant in Muhammad's household, and 'Ikrima, a Berber manumitted slave. In this type of the *hadith*, Muhammad's closest *sahaba*, including the first three *al-khulafa' al-rashidun*, are very rarely mentioned. Both of these individuals have been accused of being utterly unreliable. For instance, Muhammad's 'favourite wife' (according to Sunni tradition), 'A'isha, to whom numerous (Sunni) '*ahadith* have also been attributed, singled out Abu Hurayra as the least trustworthy of all of the companions, while there were great many others who called 'Ikrima a liar (*kadhdhab*). See, for example, Ibn Hazm al-Andalusi, *Asma' al-sahabat al-ruwat wa ma li-kulli wahid min al-'adad* (ed. Sayyid Kurdi Hasan; Dar al-kutub al-'ilmiyya, Beirut 1992 [*c.*1040]), p. 37; Muhammad al-Jazari, *Ghayat al-nihaya fi tabaqat al-qura'* (G. Bergsträßer, Cairo 1932), Vol. 1, p. 515; Taqi al-Din al-Maqrizi, *Mukhtasar al-kamil fi al-du'afa wa 'ilal al-hadith by Ibn 'Adi* (Dar al-jil, Beirut 2001), pp. 577–578; 'Ali al-Qari al-Harawi, *al-Masnu' fi ma'rifat al-hadith al-mawdu'* (ed. 'Abd al-Fattah Abu Ghudda; 2nd edn; Mu'assasat al-risala, Beirut 1978 [*c.*1598]), p. 103.

86. The majority of such '*ahadith* consider male-male anal sex to be, in fact, the mysterious 'deeds of Lot's people'. For numerous examples and a detailed analysis of these reports, see Kugle, *supra* n. 33, pp. 73–127.

87. Muhammad ibn Isma'il al-Bukhari, *al-Jami' al-sahih* (Thesaurus Islamicus Foundation, Liechtenstein 2000 [*c.*842–869]) ['Kitab al-libas', book 77, ch. 62, *hadith* 5947], Vol 3, p. 1213; quoted in Kugle, *supra* n. 33, p. 95.

88. *Ibid*, p. 76.

89. *Ibid*, p. 94 *et passim*.

90. Cf. Qur'an 24:31.

91. Consider, for example, the following (Sunni) *sahih hadith*: 'A man was with the Prophet (peace be upon him) when another man passed by and the former said, "O Messenger of God! I love this man". The Messenger of God asked, "Have you let him know that?" He said, "No". The Messenger of God then said, "Tell him". So he went up to the man and said, "I love you for the sake of God" and

the other replied, "May God love you who loves me for the sake of God'"; Abu Dawud Sulayman al-Sijistani, *Kitab al-sunan* (Thesaurus Islamicus Foundation, Liechtenstein 2000 [*c*.847–888]) ['Kitab al-adab', book 42, ch. 122, *hadith* 5127], Vol. 2, p. 857; quoted in Kugle, *supra* n. 33, p. 73.

92. The majority of contemporary Islamicists make a similar point, including the scripturalists Schacht, *supra* n. 7, and Coulson, *supra* n. 8. Hallaq, for example, claims that, '[i]n fact, the increasing importance and authority of *hadith* as an embodiment of Prophetic Sunna made it attractive to the Umayyad – as well as the early 'Abbasid – caliphs as a tool for enhancing their legitimacy *vis-à-vis* their many opponents'; Hallaq, *supra* n. 43, p. 73.

93. See, for example, Kamali, *supra* n. 3, p. 19 *et passim*.

94. *Ijma'* is one such example, which covered all aspects of 'communal agreement' amongst Muslims, including, at least theoretically, the elected office of caliph. See, however, Coulson, *supra* n. 8, pp. 59, 78.

95. Such is sometimes though to be the relationship between *ra'y* and *qiyas*. In Coulson's interpretation, when 'reasoning became more systematic, [...] *ra'y* gradually gave place to [...] *qiyas*'; *ibid*, p. 40.

96. This relates to one of the greatest controversies amongst the contemporary Islamicists, which is whether 'the closing of the gate of *ijtihad*' (*insidad bab al-ijtihad*), referenced in some medieval sources, ever actually took place. Scripturalist historiographers, Joseph Schacht in particular, argued that, in the early fourth century AH, 'a consensus gradually established itself to the effect that from that time onwards no one could be deemed to have the necessary qualifications for independent reasoning [*ijtihad*] in religious law, and that all future activity would have to be confined to the explanation, application, and, at the most, interpretation of the doctrine as it had been laid down once and for all'; Schacht, *supra* n. 7, pp. 70–71. This thesis was, however, refuted by the subsequent generation of Islamicists, most notably in Hallaq, *supra* n. 20. See also Gleave, *supra* n. 19, pp. 3–4.

97. For instance, in the writings of Muhammad 'Abduh, the late-nineteenth-century CE Egyptian jurist, reformer and political activist, one of the founders of Islamic modernism; see Zubaida, *supra* n. 5, pp. 142–144.

98. *Ijtihad* is emphasised as a necessary ingredient of (any demand for) Islamic reforms in a great variety of contemporary contexts. Abdullahi An-Na'im, for instance, argues, based on a 'clear and strong precedent from the earliest times of Islam [the rule of the second caliph 'Umar], that policy considerations may justify applying a rule derived through *ijtihad* even if that required overriding clear and definite texts of the Qur'an and Sunna'; Abdullahi Ahmed An-Na'im, *Toward an Islamic Reformation: Civil Liberties, Human Rights, and International Law* Syracuse University Press, Syracuse 1990), p. 28.

99. Amongst the (legal) precedents, both *sunna* of Muhammad and that of his *sahaba* (also known as *sunan*, which is plural of *sunna*) played an important (albeit often confusing) role, at least until the late Umayyad period; see Hallaq, *supra* n. 43, pp. 50–52.

100. Hallaq, *supra* n. 43, p. 178. They concomitantly functioned as 'tax-collectors, provincial secretaries of the treasury, police chiefs or story-tellers'.

101. *Ibid.*

102. Melchert, *supra* n. 63, pp. 1–31.

103. *Ibid.*

104. *Ibid*, p. 13.

105. Simply put, our study of *ahl al-hadith* and *ahl al-ra'y* focuses on the *legal* aspects of their disagreements. Its roots, however, run deeper into the domain of theology, which is, indeed, often inseparable from legal problematics. The doctrine of the created Qur'an is one of the main tenets of the so-called Mu'tazili school of Islamic speculative *theology* (also known as *ahl al-kalam*), which flourished from the second until the end of fourth century AH in the metropolitan (and cosmopolitan) settings of Basra and Baghdad, only to be extinguished by force due to its supposed 'heretical' views. The doctrine posits that, due to the perfect unity and eternal nature of God, the Qur'an must have been created, as it could not be co-eternal with God. From this premise, the Mu'tazilites proceeded to claim that God's injunctions are accessible through *ra'y*: because knowledge is derived from reason, reason is the ultimate arbiter in ascertaining what is right or wrong. However, despite the apparent doctrinal similarities, *ahl al-ra'y* should not be equated with *ahl al-kalam*.

106. After whom the four mainline Sunni *madhahib* are called Hanafi, Maliki, Shafi'i and Hanbali school of jurisprudence, respectively.

107. Ibn 'Abd al-Barr, *al-Intiqa' fi fada'il al-thalathah al-a'imma* (al-Qudsi, Cairo 1931), p. 146; quoted in Melchert, *supra* n. 63, p. 10.

108. Ibn Hajar, *Tahdib 'al-tahdib'* (Majlis Da'irat al-Ma'arif al-Nizamiya, Hyderabad 1909 [c.1425]), Vol. 10, p. 449; quoted in Melchert, *supra* n. 63, p. 3.

109. He was reportedly asked: "'How many *hadith* will suffice a man to give juridical opinions? Will 100,000 suffice?" He said, "No". He was then asked, "200,000?" He said, "No". He was asked, "300,000?" He said, "No". He was asked, "400,000?" He said, "No". He was then asked, "500,000?" He said, "I hope so'"; Ibn Abi Ya'la', *Tabaqat al-hanabilah* (ed. Muhammad Hamid al-Fiqi; Matba'at al-sunna al-Muhammadiya, Cairo 1952 [c.1130]), Vol. 1, p. 131; quoted in Melchert, *supra* n. 63, p. 25.

110. Schacht, *supra* n. 7, p. 50.

111. Wary of the consequential loss of their independence, *fuqaha'* famously dreaded the prospect of being appointed to judgeship by the caliphs: 'Abu Hanifa was imprisoned and flogged for persisting in his refusal to serve [as a chief justice (*qadi al-qudat*)]. Yet others resorted to ingenious arguments to escape the predicament'; Hallaq, *supra* n. 43, p. 181.

112. *Ibid*, p. 182.

113. An account predating the final phase of the 'formative period', although anecdotal, may perhaps help us imagine an alternative route Islamic law could have taken, had the independent juristic reasoning managed to survive the subsequent processes of systematisation of the legal profession. When one of

Abu Hanifa's most prominent disciples and the caliph Harun al-Rashid's chief justice (*qadi al-qudat*), Abu Yusuf, died in 182 AH, the Mu'tazili theologian and poet an-Nazzam reportedly declaimed on his grave: 'had he lived, he would have made virgins and boys licit with his *qiyas*'; Melchert, *supra* n. 63, p. 10. See also Ibn Hajar, *Lisan 'al-mizan'* (Matba'at Majlis Da'irat al-Ma'arif, Hyderabad 1912 [*c.*1420]), Vol. 6, p. 301.

114. See Melchert, *supra* n. 63, p. 1.

115. See, for example, George Makdisi, 'The Guilds of Law in Medieval Legal History: An Inquiry Into the Origins of the Inns of Court' (1984) 1 *Zeitschrift für Geschichte der arabisch-islamischen Wissenschaften* 233; George Makdisi, 'La Corporation à l'époque classique de l'Islam' in Daniel Massignon (ed.), *Présence de Louis Massignon: hommages et témoignages* (Maisonneuve et Larose, Paris 1987), pp. 35–49; George Makdisi, *The Rise of Humanism in Classical Islam and the Christian West: With Special Reference to Scholasticism* (Edinburgh University Press, Edinburgh 1990), pp. 16–23.

116. George Makdisi, '*Tabaqat*– Biography: Law and Orthodoxy in Classical Islam' (1993) 32 *Islamic Studies* 371.

117. Which, in the pre-*madhahib* period, are sometimes also categorised as *responsa* and *dicta*: 'By a *responsum* I mean an answer (*jawab*) [of the *qadi*] to a question (*mas'ala*) [...]. A *dictum,* in contrast, is defined as a statement (*qawl, hadith*) which is not preceded by a question in the text'; Harald Motzki, *The Origins of Islamic Jurisprudence: Meccan Fiqh before the Classical Schools* (Brill, Leiden 2002), p. 79.

118. See, for instance, Masud, Messick & Powers, *supra* n. 20; Gleave, *supra* n. 10.

119. Calder argues, apropos, that '[i]n spite of the common (but misleading) cliché that there are no priests, or no clerics, or, even, no mediators, in Islam, between God and his community, it is clear that the jurists functioned precisely as mediators [...]. [They] acquired their status through knowledge and commitment to the *madhhab*, and had a duty to transmit it to the wider community. Their capacity to mediate, that is to reveal and explain the symbols of divine revelation to the community, was intimately related to their participation in the processes of *fatwa*'; Calder, *supra* n. 22, p. 190. The oscillating (but never really absent) level of state involvement in this mediation process makes the legal profession all the more so comparable with (the European notions of) priesthood.

120. Cf. Louis Crompton, 'Male Love and Islamic Law in Arab Spain' in Stephen O. Murray & Will Roscoe, *Islamic Homosexualities: Culture, History, and Literature* (New York University Press, New York 1997), p. 155.

121. *Ibid.* For two excellent examples of such literature, see Ibn Khaldun, *supra* n. 77, and Adib al-Raghib al-Isfahani, *Muhadarat al-udaba' wa muhawarat al-shu'ara' wa al-bulagha'* (ed. 'Umar Taba'; Dar al-arqam bin abi arqam, Beirut 1999 [*c.*982]). For a pertinent discussion of the latter work, see Habib, *Female Homosexuality in the Middle East, supra* n. 33, pp. 48–50. The commonly applied formula by the Muslim literati of the time was to briefly cite the

condemnatory remarks, found in some reputable *hadith* and/or *fiqh* literature, and then proceed with an elaborate account of sexual and gender diversity as observed in the past and contemporary Muslim societies.

122. Cf. Robert H. Mnookin & Lewis Kornhauser, 'Bargaining in the Shadow of the Law: The Case of Divorce' (1979) 88(5) *Yale Law Journal* 950.

123. To paraphrase Coulson, in his symptomatic but imprecise description of the *shari'a* (*qua* Islamic law); Coulson, *supra* n. 8, p. 5.

124. E.g. Qur'an 56:35. The term *huriya'* (also *hur*; sing. *ahwar* (masc.) and/or *hawra* (fem.)) is impossible to translate without damaging its originally intended ambiguity. They are described in the Qur'an as the pleasurable companions of *all* gendered human subjectivities of this world who made it to the heaven: male, female and (many) others.

125. E.g. Qur'an 56:22.

126. Qur'an 76:19. In contrast to the *huriya'*, the Qur'anic text hints at these youths being male-gendered and working as servants (of the paradise's humanly inhabitants), usually as cupbearers. See generally Suzanne Pinckney Stetkevych, 'Intoxication and Immorality: Wine and Associated Imagery in al-Ma'arri's Garden' in Fedwa Malti-Douglas (ed.), *Critical Pilgrimages: Studies in the Arabic Literary Tradition* (spec. edn. of *Literature East & West*; Department of Oriental and African Languages and Literatures, University of Texas at Austin, Austin 1989), pp. 29–48.

127. See, for example, Everett K. Rowson, 'The Effeminates of Early Medina' (1991) 111(4) *Journal of the American Oriental Society* 671; Sahar Amer, 'Medieval Arab Lesbians and Lesbian-Like Women' (2009) 18(2) *Journal of the History of Sexuality* 215, p. 224; Habib, *Female Homosexuality in the Middle East*, *supra* n. 33, p. 18.

128. Franz Rosenthal, 'Male and Female: Described and Compared' in Jerry W. Wright Jr. & Everett K. Rowson (eds), *Homoeroticism in Classical Arabic Literature* (Columbia University Press, New York 1997), p. 25. See also Amer, *supra* n. 127, pp. 226–229; Habib Zayyat, 'al-Mar'a al-ghulamiyya fi al-Islam' (1956) 50 *al-Machriq* 153.

129. Steven M. Oberhelman, 'Hierarchies of Gender, Ideology, and Power in Ancient and Medieval Greek and Arabic Dream Literature' in Jerry W. Wright Jr. & Everett K. Rowson (eds), *Homoeroticism in Classical Arabic Literature* (Columbia University Press, New York 1997), p. 68.

130. Habib, *Female Homosexuality in the Middle East*, *supra* n. 33, p. 49. Both role- and age-stratified relations were, however, also common. For instance, the 'active' and the 'passive' male sexual partner in the act of *liwat* were sometimes called *luti* (with an obvious etymological connection to the 'deeds of Lot's people') and *ma'bun*, respectively. See, for example, Franz Rosenthal, 'Ar-Razi on the Hidden Illness' (1978) 52 *Bulletin of the History of Medicine* 45.

131. Leslie Peirce, 'Writing Histories of Sexuality in the Middle East' (2009) 114 (5) *American Historical Review* 1325, p. 1333. Note, also, an excellent study on the sixteenth-century CE 'beloveds' in Ottoman and European sources: Walter

NOTES TO PAGES 97–99

253

G. Andrews & Mehmet Kalpaklı, *The Age of Beloveds: Love and the Beloved in Early-Modern Ottoman and European Culture and Society* (Duke University Press, Durham 2005).

132. Consider, for example, the story of 'the enduring love between Hind Bint al-Nu'man, the Christian daughter of the last Lakhmid king of Hira in the seventh century [CE], and [a woman called] Hind Bint al-Khuss al-Iyadiyyah from Yamama in Arabia, known as al-Zarqa"; Amer, *supra* n. 127, p. 218. See generally Sahar Amer, Crossing Borders: *Love Between Women in Medieval French and Arabic Literatures* (University of Pennsylvania Press, Philadelphia 2008).

133. Everett K. Rowson, 'The Categorization of Gender and Sexual Irregularity in Medieval Arabic Vice Lists' in Julia Epstein & Kristina Straub (eds), *Bodyguards: The Cultural Politics of Gender Ambiguity* (Routledge, New York 1991), p. 62. See also Annemarie Schimmel, 'Eros – Heavenly and Not So Heavenly – in Sufi Literature and Life' in Afaf Lutfi as-Sayyid Marsot (ed.), *Society and the Sexes in Medieval Islam* (Undena Publications, Malibu 1979), pp. 119–141.

134. Or, as the Qur'an 2:207 rather beautifully describes, to 'sell [themselves] desiring God's good pleasure'.

135. See Ze'ev Maghen, *Virtues of the Flesh: Passion and Purity in Early Islamic Jurisprudence* (Brill, Leiden 2005).

136. Norman Calder, *Studies in Early Islamic Jurisprudence* (Clarendon Press, Oxford 1993), p. 164.

137. This was already postulated by Ibn Khaldun in 1377/778 CE/AH; see Ibn Khaldun, *supra* n. 77.

138. See, for example, Coulson, *supra* n. 8, p. 51.

139. *Ibid*. See generally Ibn Khaldun, *supra* n. 77, but, also, Melchert, *supra* n. 63, p. xix. Melchert identifies Ibn Khaldun's 'definite Maliki bias' for, in his *Muqaddimah*, Ibn Khaldun equates Malik ibn Anas' *ahl al-Hijaz* with *ahl al-hadith*, as if Malik was to be credited as the founder of the entire traditionalist movement.

140. Coulson, *supra* n. 8, p. 81.

141. 'The narrowing of juristic possibilities was no doubt a function of the tendency to increase the level of determinacy of positive legal doctrine, a fact represented in the highly applauded search, on the part of jurists, for those opinions considered to have achieved an authoritative status in the schools [of *fiqh*]'; Wael B. Hallaq, *Authority, Continuity, and Change in Islamic Law* (Cambridge University Press, Cambridge 2004), p. 238.

142. *Ibid*.

143. *Ibid*, p. 236.

144. 'Abu Hanifa and Shafi'i were admittedly jurists of the first calibre [...]. Malik does not appear to have stood on par with them as a legal reasoner or as a seasoned jurist. But he was jurist of a sort, nonetheless. Ibn Hanbal was none of these things. He was in the first place a traditionalist and theologian, and his involvement with law as a technical discipline was rather minimal'; *ibid*, pp. 39–40.

145. *Ibid*, p. 39.
146. Abu Hanifa, for example, was notorious for frequently changing his position. Thus one of his contemporaries, Abu Hamza al-Sukkari, reports in despair: 'I went to Abu Hanifa and asked him about some questions. I went away for some twenty years, then went to him, and lo, he had gone back on those questions. I had given them to people as my juridical opinions (*aftaytu bi-ha al-nas*). I told him of this. He said, "We see one view (*nara' al-ra'y*), the next day we see another and take it back"'. Abu Hamza replied, 'What a wretched man you are'; 'Abdullah ibn Ahmad, *Kitab al-Sunna* (ed. Muhammad ibn Sa'id ibn Salim al-Qahtani; Dar Ibn al-Qayyim, Dammam 1986 [*c.*893]), p. 220; also quoted in Melchert, *supra* n. 63, p. 11.
147. Hanafi *madhhab*, the only amongst the surviving Sunni schools with the roots in *ahl al-ra'y*, lost much of its jurisprudential potency due to the principle of imitation (*taqlid*): 'If some Hanafis, along with others, held high views of the significance of *ijtihad*, they held a correspondingly low view of the possibility of novel and independent *ijtihad* for all who lived after Islamic law's formative period'; A. Kevin Reinhart, 'Transcendence and Social Practice: Muftis and Qadis as Religious Interpreters' (1993) 27 *Annales islamologiques* 5, p. 20.
148. That is, of the viability of the idea of a *madhhab*; see, for example, Coulson, *supra* n. 8, pp. 53–61.
149. As opposed to other possible sources of Muhammad's (or, generally, early Muslim) legal praxis, such as the *sunan* of his *sahaba*.
150. Hallaq, *supra* n. 43, p. 119.
151. These two specific 'secondary' sources Shafi'i understood as being one and the same.
152. Such as Hanafi *istihsan* (juristic preference), Maliki *istislah* (consideration of the public interest) or even Shafi'i *istishab* (natural principle of legal evidence); see Coulson, *supra* n. 8, pp. 91–92. *Ijtihad*, also, continued to play an all-important role in the Shi'i *madhahib*.
153. Hallaq, *supra* n. 22.
154. Christian Lange, for example, calls the second half of the Seljuk period (1118/511 – 1194/590 CE/AH) 'the late classical age of Islamic theology and law'; Christian Lange, *Justice, Punishment, and the Medieval Muslim Imagination* (Cambridge University Press, Cambridge 2008), p. 2. It is, in fact, the entire era of the 'Abbasids (750/132 – 1258/656 CE/AH) that is typically described as the 'Islamic Golden Age', due to its artistic, cultural, philosophical and scientific achievements. This periodisation is, of course, problematic. It is utilised here only as a cursory mark.
155. *Hudud* (lit. 'limits') are offences arguably defined in the Qur'an itself, and thereby given a special consideration in the *fiqh* literature. See *supra* n. 27.
156. *Qisas* (equal retaliation) are a form of Muslim *lex talionis*, defined as the right of the heirs of a murder victim to demand execution of the perpetrator. This right can also be forfeited, in exchange for a fee supplied by the murderer's family (*diyya*), or as an act of charity. Some Shafi'is included *qisas* into the *hudud*

category, and saw it as encompassing not only homicide (*qatl*) but also bodily harm (*jinayat*); see Wael B. Hallaq, *shari'a: Theory, Practice, Transformations* (Cambridge University Press, Cambridge 2009), pp. 310–311.

157. *Diyya* (lit. 'blood money', 'ransom') is financial compensation paid to the heirs of a victim in offences against life.

158. *Ta'zir* (discretionary punishment) refers to offences punishable at the discretion of the judge.

159. Hallaq, *supra* n. 156, p. 310.

160. *Ibid*, p. 311.

161. *Ibid*.

162. 'A *shubha* exists even if a man merely claims, without any proof, that he had married the woman with whom he was accused to have committed *zina* (provided, of course, that the woman is single). Likewise, if a person claims, under oath, that because darkness he thought the woman with whom he is charged with committing *zina* was his wife, he is vindicated'; *ibid*, p. 312. As per the requirement of being a person of full legal competence, slaves, minors and people with mental health issues were exempt from this category. So were non-Muslims, according to the Hanafi and Maliki *fuqaha'*. Shi'i jurists, however, maintained that whoever commits incest or rape (both of which were considered a form of *zina*) needs to be killed, regardless or their legal capacity.

163. As previously noted, the confession of a *hadd* offence could be withdrawn (*ruju'*). According to Schacht, it was 'even recommended that the [*qadi*] should suggest this possibility to the person who has confessed, except in the case of false accusation of [*zina*]'; Schacht, *supra* n. 7, p. 177. Otherwise, in order to be admissible, the confession had to be uttered four times 'by choice' (*ikhtiyar*), i.e. without compulsion or duress of any kind.

164. See Shalakany, *supra* n. 16, pp. 46–47.

165. The Twelver Shi'i doctrine allows, also, the testimony of three men and two women or two men and four women.

166. Hallaq, *supra* n. 156, p. 313.

167. Shalakany, *supra* n. 16, p. 47. Furthermore, it is not sufficient for the act of penetration to be 'partial'; i.e. the perpetrator's 'male organ' must have 'entirely disappeared from sight' (*wa-yatahaqqaq dhalika bi-ghaybubat al-hashafa*); Muhaqqiq Najm al-Din Ja'far ibn Hasan Hilli, *Shara'i' al-islam fi masa'il al-halal wal-haram* (Dar al-Qari', Beirut 2004), Vol. 4, p. 399; see also Hallaq, *supra* n. 156, p. 313.

168. This form of the capital punishment is not found in the Qur'an, but established by reference to the legal praxis of *al-rashidun*. Joseph Schacht claims that stoning to death was 'obviously taken from Mosaic law' by the first caliphs; Schacht, *supra* n. 7, p. 15.

169. Some jurists also stipulate that the latter category of offenders be punished with one year banishment, in addition to being flogged in public. See Hallaq, *supra* n. 156, p. 312.

170. *Ibid.*
171. 'Ali ibn Sultan al-Qari' al-Harawi, *Fath bab al-'inayah bi-sharh al-niqayah* (eds M.N. Tamim & H.N. Tamim; Beirut 1997 [*c.*1601]), Vol. 3, p. 195; quoted in Vanja Hamzić, 'The Case of "Queer Muslims": Sexual Orientation and Gender Identity in International Human Rights Law and Muslim Legal and Social Ethos' (2011) 11(2) *Human Rights Law Review* 237, p. 257.
172. See Zayn al-'Abidin ibn Nujayam, *al-Bahr al-ra'iq sharh kanz al-daqa'iq* (Cairo 1894 [*c.*1560]), Vol. 5, p. 5; Muhammad Amin ibn 'Abidin, *Radd al-muhtar 'ala al-durr al-mukhtar* (Bulaq 1856 [1830]), Vol. 3, p. 156; 'Abd al-Baqi al-Zurqani, *Sharh mukhtasar Khalil* (Cairo 1890 [*c.*1680]), Vol. 7, pp. 176–177; Shams al-Din Muhammad al-Ramli, *Nihayat al-muhtaj bi-sharh al-minhaj* (Cairo 1969 [*c.*1590]) Vol. 8, p. 307; Muhammad 'Ali bn 'Allan, *Dalil al-falihin li-turuq Riyad al-salihin* (Cairo 1938), Vol. 3, p. 20. See also Khaled El-Rouayheb, *Before Homosexuality in the Arab-Islamic World, 1500–1800* (University of Chicago Press, Chicago 2005), p. 123.
173. Ze'evi, *supra* n. 14, p. 55.
174. Save, in some instances, for the case of repeat offenders.
175. El-Rouayheb, *supra* n. 172, p. 119.
176. Hamzić, *supra* n. 171, p. 257. Zahiris were one of the Sunni *madhahib*.
177. See, for example, James T. Monroe, 'The Striptease that was Blamed on Abu Bakr's Naughty Son: Was Father Being Shamed, or was the Poet Having Fun? (Ibn Quzman's Zajal No. 133)' in Jerry W. Wright Jr. & Everett K. Rowson (eds), *Homoeroticism in Classical Arabic Literature* (Columbia University Press, New York 1997), p. 116.
178. El-Rouayheb, *supra* n. 172, pp. 121–122.
179. And, according to some Shafi'i and Hanbali *fuqaha'*, those offenders were also liable to banishment. See Shalakany, *supra* n. 16, pp. 42–48.
180. *Ibid.*
181. Although the individual jurists did deal with the concepts such as *musahaqat al-nisa'* or *sahq*, which describe sexual relations between the women, and sometimes called for their *ta'zir* punishment; see, for example, Ali, *supra* n. 56, p. 77; Amer, *supra* n. 127.
182. Monroe, *supra* n. 177, p. 117.
183. Marshall G.S. Hodgson, *The Venture of Islam: Conscience and History in a World Civilization* (University of Chicago Press, Chicago 1974), Vol. 2, p. 53.
184. Lange, *supra* n. 154, p. 6.
185. Seljuks were a tribe of the Oghuz (Ghuzz) Turks, who became (Sunni) Muslims while living in the lower Jaxartes valley in (present-day) Uzbekistan in the late fourth century AH. Their westward and southward conquests commenced shortly thereafter, with their second ruler Tughril (Turkish: Tuğrul) taking both Isfahan (443 AH) and Baghdad (447 AH). Their confederate ruling style was gradually replaced with the Persian model of (absolute, hereditary) kingship, only to be transformed, at a later stage, to a federation of rulers, albeit with the strong central office of Great Seljuk. In the final years of the Seljuk dynasty, the

government disintegrated along the 'sub-tribal'/'regional' fault lines, and the Turkic generals of the Seljuk sultan began forming their own dynasties. See generally Clifford E. Bosworth, *The Ghaznavids: Their Empire in Afghanistan and Eastern Iran, 994–1040* (Edinburgh University Press, Edinburgh 1963), pp. 205–266; Clifford E. Bosworth, 'The Political and Dynastic History of the Iranian World (AD 1000–1217)' in John A. Boyle (ed.), *The Cambridge History of Iran* (Cambridge University Press, Cambridge 1968), Vol. 5, pp. 1–202.

186. Lange, *supra* n. 154, p. 7.

187. *Ibid.*

188. *Ibid*, p. 14. See also Ann K.S. Lambton, 'Changing Concepts of Justice and Injustice from the 5th/11th Century to the 8th/14th Century in Persia: The Saljuq Empire and the Ilkhanate' (1988) 68 *Studia Islamica* 27; Bernard Lewis, 'Siyasa' in Arnold H. Green, *In Quest of an Islamic Humanism: Arabic and Islamic Studies in Memory of Mohamed al-Nowaihi* (American University in Cairo Press, Cairo 1984), pp. 3–14;

189. *'Gurg ba mesh ta'addi nakunad dar sahra, / tihu az baz tahashi nakunad dar parwaz; / chang dar sar kashad az bim-i siyasat chu kashaf, / chi ki dar panja-yi shir wa-chi ki dar mikhlab-i baz'*; Awhad al-Din Muhammad ibn Muhammad Anvari, *Diwan* (Bungah-i Tarjama u Nashr-i Kitab, Tehran 1959–1961 [*c.*1180]), 256:7–8; quoted and translated from Persian in Lange, *supra* n. 154, pp. 42–43.

190. *Ibid*, p. 217.

191. Abu'l-Hasan 'Ali al-Sughdi, *al-Fatawa* (2nd edn; Dar al-furqan, Amman 1984 [*c.*1065]), Vol. 2, p. 646.

192. Abu Ishaq Ibrahim ibn 'Ali ibn Yusuf al-Firuzabadi al-Shirazi, *al-Muhadhdhab fi fiqh al-imam al-Shafi'i* (Dar al-fikr, Beirut 1980 [*c.*1080]), Vol 2, p. 288.

193. Lange, *supra* n. 154, p. 217.

194. See generally Shalakany, *supra* n. 16.

195. Cf. Johansen, 'Eigentum, Familie und Obrigkeit im hanafitischen Strafrecht', *supra* n. 18, p. 73.

196. Following the bibliographical approach in Lange, *supra* n. 154, the focus of this exercise is, mainly, on the 'mainstream' jurists of the period, in particular 'Ala' al-Din Abu Bakr ibn Mas'ud al-Kasani, *Bada'i' al-sana'i' fi tartib al-shara'i'* (Matba'a al-jamaliyya, Cairo 1910 [*c.*1180]), 7 Vols; Burhan al-Din 'Ali ibn Abi Bakr ibn 'Abd al-Jalil al-Marghinani, *Bidayat al-mubtadi* (Maktabat wa-matba'at Muhammad 'Ali Subh, Cairo 1969 [*c.*1188]); 'Ala al-Din Muhammad ibn Ahmad al-Samarqandi, *Tuhfat al-fuqaha'* (Dar al-kutub al-'ilmiyya, Beirut 1984 [*c.*1140]); Burhan al-Din 'Ali ibn Abi Bakr ibn 'Abd al-Jalil al-Marghinani, *al-Hidaya sharh al-bidaya* (Mustafa al-Babi al-Halabi, Cairo 1975 [*c.*1138]), 2 Vols; Muhammad ibn Ahmad al-Sarakhsi, *al-Kitab al-mabsut* (Dar al-ma'rifa, Beirut 1993 [*c.*1080]), 9 Vols; Muhammad ibn Ahmad al-Sarakhsi, *Le grand livre de la conduite de l'état [Sharh al-siyar al-kabir]* (trans. Muhammed Hamidullah; Türkiye Diyanet Vakfı, Ankara 1989 [*c.*1070]).

197. More specifically, al-Sughdi, *supra* n. 191; al-Hasan ibn Manzur al-Uzjandi al-Farghani Qadikhan, *al-Fatawa* (Dar al-ma'rifa, Beirut 1973 [*c.*1189]); Siraj al-

Din 'Ali ibn 'Uthman Ushi al-Farghani, *Al-Fatawa al-sirajiyya* (Calcutta 1827 [*c.*1190]). Other works, such as Burhan al-Din Mahmud al-Bukhari ibn Maza, *al-Kitab al-dhakhira al-burhaniyya* [*c.*1170], are referenced in the 'post-classical' *furu'* literature as being influential during the Seljuk period (and beyond), but they are, to my knowledge, no longer available.

198. Cf. Sarakhsi, *al-Kitab al-mabsut*, *supra* n. 196, Vol. 9, p. 79.

199. *Ibid*, p. 78. The phase used is '*al-liwata bi-zina min haythu l-ism*', which is, as Christian Lange notes, repeated *verbatim* in other *furu'* works. See Lange, *supra* n. 154, p. 205.

200. Importantly, though, this argument, supposedly, was not arrived at analogically, which would be forbidden to the Hanafi scholars *tout court*, because, according to Abu Hanifa, *qiyas* can never be used for the *hudud* punishments (*la qiyasa fi l-hudud*). Instead, it is, purportedly, of a purely semantic nature (*ma'na*). See Marghinani, *al-Hidaya sharh al-bidaya*, *supra* n. 641, Vol. 2, p. 102.

201. *Ibid*; Sarakhsi, *al-Kitab al-mabsut*, *supra* n. 196, Vol. 9, p. 77; also summarised in Lange, *supra* n. 154, p. 208.

202. *Ibid*, p. 202. See also Sarakhsi, *al-Kitab al-mabsut*, *supra* n. 196, Vol. 9, p. 79; Kasani, *supra* n. 196, Vol. 7, p. 34.

203. See generally Léon Bercher, *Les délits et les peines du droit commun prévu par le Coran* (Société anonyme de l'imprimerie rapide, Tunis 1926), p. 95. See also Lange, *supra* n. 154, pp 202–205.

204. *Ibid*, p. 205. In support of this thesis, the *faqih* Muhammad ibn Ahmad al-Sarakhsi even quotes no other but the second-century AH libertine poet Abu Nuwas, well-known for his licentious verses on male-male love: 'A maid dressed in men's clothes has / two lowers: the *luti* [the 'active' partner in *liwat*] and the *zani* [the 'active' partner in *zina*]' ('*Min kaffi dhati hirin fi ziyi dhi dhakarin / laha muhibbani lutiyun wa-zanna'u*'); Sarakhsi, *al-Kitab al-mabsut*, *supra* n 196, Vol. 9, p. 78. The point is that if Abu Nuwas could distinguish in this verse between the *luti* and the *zani*, then he must have thought of two completely different persons (and personalities).

205. Cf. Lange, *supra* n. 154, pp. 208–211.

206. Kasani, *supra* n. 196, Vo.l 7, p. 33.

207. This was opinion, for example, of the Hanafi jurist and philosopher Abu 'Ali ibn al-Walid al-Mu'tazili (d. 1119/513 CE/AH); see Lange, *supra* n. 154, pp. 211–212.

208. The privacy of such act being defined *in the negative*; that is, construable only because it fell outside the divinely prescribed *hudud* ambit *and* the rational scope of other offences defined by classical *fiqh*.

209. Sarakhsi, *al-Kitab al-mabsut*, *supra* n. 196, Vol. 9, p. 77.

210. *Ibid*; Kasani, *supra* n. 196, Vol. 7, p. 34.

211. Sarakhsi, *al-Kitab al-mabsut*, *supra* n. 196, Vol. 9, p. 77.

212. Lange, *supra* n. 154, p. 211.

213. *Ibid*, p. 199. There is, however, *one* report from this period relating that, in 538 AH, on the streets of Baghdad, a man was captured and killed – in what seems

to be an act of mob violence – for an unspecified 'indecency' involving a young boy. The term *liwat* is not used in the report. See Abu'l-Faraj 'Abd al-Rahman ibn 'Ali ibn al-Jawzi, *al-Muntazam fi tarikh al-umam wa-l-muluk* (Dar al-kutub al-'ilmiyya, 1992 [*c.*1190]), Vol. 18, p. 33.

214. Lange, *supra* n. 154, p. 219.
215. *Ibid.*
216. *Ibid.*
217. See generally Bosworth, 'The Political and Dynastic History of the Iranian World (AD 1000–1217)', *supra* n. 185; Ann K.S. Lambton, 'The Administration of Sanjar's Empire as Illustrated in the *'Atabat al-kataba'* (1957) 20 *Bulletin of the School of Oriental and African Studies* 367; Deborah G. Tor, 'Sanjar, Ahmad b. Malekšah' in *Encyclopaedia Iranica* (online edn.), available at http://www.iranicaonline.org/articles/sanjar (accessed 17 July 2014).
218. This period is often divided into *dawlat al-Atrak* (the State of Turks, 1259/648 – 1382/784 CE/AH), ruled by *Bahri* Mamluks of Turkic origin, mostly from Kipchak and Cuman tribes, and *dawlat al-Jarakisa* (the State of Circassians, 1382/784 – 1517/922 CE/AH), controlled by *Burji* Mamluks of Circassian and Georgian origin. The names *Bahri* and *Burji* come from the two toponyms of the medieval Cairo associated with Mamluks: the river Nile (*bahr al-Nil*), since their barracks used to stand on Cairo's Rhoda Island, and the tower (*burj*) of Cairo Citadel, where Mamluk troupes were also garrisoned. See, for example, Shai Har-El, *Struggle for Domination in the Middle East: The Ottoman-Mamluk War, 1485–1491* (Brill, Leiden 1995), p. 28. Please note that the scope of the present study does not extend to *other* Mamluk regimes, such as their rule over the Delhi Sultanate, from 1206/602 to 1290/689 CE/AH.
219. The lifespan of the Ottoman Empire was, of course, notably longer (623 years) from the presently researched period (386 years). It emerged with Osman I, who declared independence of his emirate from the Seljuk state in 1299/698 CE/AH and flourished as the longest-lasting Muslim empire until its abolishment, in 1922/1341 CE/AH, by Mustafa Kemal (Atatürk).
220. See especially this fascinating portrayal of Qajar Iran (1785/1199 – 1925/1343 CE/AH): Afsaneh Najmabadi, *Women with Mustaches and Men without Beards: Gender and Sexual Anxieties of Iranian Modernity* (University of California Press, Berkeley 2005).
221. The Mongol state, in this period, expanded into the largest contiguous land empire in human history, stretching from North Eastern Europe to the Sea of Japan, from Siberia to South East Asia, including the Iranian plateau and some parts of the Middle East. However, the Maghreb, the Hijaz and the Andalusian caliphates were never conquered.
222. Hodgson, *supra* n. 183, Vol. 2, p. 288.
223. Black, *supra* n. 24, p. 141.
224. Hence, according to the Mamluk-era Egyptian historian al-Maqrizi, in *yasa*, same-sex relations amongst the (male) soldiers were punishable by death. However, in matters of *yasa*, al-Maqrizi is not always the most reliable source.

See, for example, Frédéric Bauden, 'Maqriziana VII: Al-Maqrizi and the *Yasa*: New Evidence of His Intellectual Dishonesty' in Reuven Amitai & Amalia Levanoni (eds), *The Mamluk Sultanate in Egypt and Syria: Aspects of a Medieval Muslim State* (Ashgate, Surrey [*forthcoming*]); Frédéric Bauden, 'Maqriziana IX: Should al-Maqrizi Be Thrown Out with the Bath Water?: The Question of His Plagiarism of al-Awhadi's *Khitat* and the Documentary Evidence' (2010) 14 *Mamluk Studies Review* 159, p. 159.

225. The word *mamluk* (pl. *mamalik*) literally means 'one who is owed' in Arabic.

226. Berkey, *supra* n. 44, p. 182.

227. See generally Thomas Philipp & Ulrich Haarmann (eds), *The Mamluks in Egyptian Politics and Society* (Cambridge University Press, Cambridge 1998).

228. '[N]owhere outside Muslim civilization was there ever created a military slave institution which had been planned so methodologically; which had been created for such a grand purpose; which succeeded in accumulating such an immense power, and in registering such astounding achievements; and which enjoyed such a long span of life'; David Ayalon, 'Mamlukiyat' (1980 [1950]) 2 *Jerusalem Studies in Arabic and Islam* 321, p. 333.

229. Stephen O. Murray, 'Male Homosexuality, Inheritance Rules, and the Status of Women in Medieval Egypt: The Case of the Mamluks' in Stephen O. Murray & Will Roscoe, *Islamic Homosexualities: Culture, History, and Literature* (New York University Press, New York 1997), p. 162.

230. Ayalon, *supra* n. 228, p. 328.

231. *Ibid.*

232. Leila Ahmed, *Women and Gender in Islam: Historical Roots of a Modern Debate* (Yale University Press, New Haven 1992), p. 105.

233. *Khudam* (sing. *khadim*, 'servant') and *aghawat* (sing. *agha*, Turkish: *ağa*, 'sir', 'lord', 'elder brother' – an honorific for people of high office and social repute) were common euphemisms for this subjectivity, with the neutral honorific *agha*/*ağa* becoming dominant in the later periods of the Mamluk state and in the Ottoman Empire. *Aghawat* were a highly respected class/subjectivity in these Muslim polities and the term *khasi* ('castrated one') was rarely, if ever, used. See Marmon, *supra* n. 30, p. 41.

234. See, for example, Jane Hathaway, *Beshir Aga: Chief Eunuch of the Ottoman Imperial Harem* (Oneworld, Oxford 2005), pp. 1–5.

235. Murray, *supra* n. 229, p. 163.

236. See David Ayalon, *Eunuchs, Caliphs and Sultans: A Study in Power Relationships* (Magnes Press, Tel Aviv 1999).

237. In these 'households', 'keeping large harems of concubines and marrying the maximum [allowed] number of wives probably expressed a man's class and power'; Ahmed, *supra* n. 232, p. 104.

238. 'Mamluk women ran their own households, which were huge establishments; one princess had seven hundred household staff. The staff of their households consisted entirely of women, including the treasurer (*khazin-dara*) and the general supervisor (*ra's nauba*). Like the men, the women in this class

established endowments [*awkaf*, sing. *waqf*, Turkish: *vakıf*] for schools, hospices, and mausoleums and also created endowments in favor of their female slaves'; *ibid*, p. 106.

239. Murray, *supra* n. 229, pp. 163–164. The *khuddam* participated in ordering both male and female 'households', but they retained somewhat liminal position in between those social units; a position of their own, nonetheless, which they turned into a form of 'household' or society as well.

240. Ahmed, *supra* n. 232, p. 104. For example, the young Sultan al-Nasir Abu al-Sa'adat Muhammad (r. 1496/901 – 1498/903 CE/AH) 'scandalized his society [. . .] by the "unnatural" interest he showed in the [. . .] Sudanese slaves (*'abid*) who bore firearms, and for their leader, Farajallah, in particular'; Murray, *supra* n. 229, p. 165.

241. See, for example, Everett K. Rowson, 'The Homoerotic Narratives from Mamluk Literature: al-Safadi's *Law'at al-shaki* and Ibn Daniyal's *al-Mutayyam*' in Jerry W. Wright Jr. & Everett K. Rowson (eds), *Homoeroticism in Classical Arabic Literature* (Columbia University Press, New York 1997), pp. 158–191.

242. For one such narrative on the thirteenth/seventh century CE/AH women's same-sex communities and 'schools of pleasure' in the Maghreb, see Amer, *supra* n. 127, pp. 219–221.

243. Quoted in Black, *supra* n. 24, p. 147.

244. *Ibid.*

245. See, for example, Badr al-Din Ibn Jama'a, *Tahrir al-ahkam fi'l-tadbir ahl al-islam* (ed. Fu'ad 'Abdul-Mun'im Ahmad; Dar al-thaqafa, Qatar 1988 [*c.*1300]).

246. Baber Johansen, 'A Perfect Law in an Imperfect Society: Ibn Taymiyya's Concept of "Governance in the Name of the Sacred Law"' in Peri Bearman, Wolfhart Heinrichs & Bernard G. Weiss (eds), *The Law Applied: Contextualizing the Islamic shari'a* (I.B.Tauris, London 2008), p. 260.

247. *Ibid.*

248. *Ibid*, p. 263.

249. 'Abd al-Rahman ibn Qasim al-Asimi (ed.), *Majmu' fatawa shaykh al-islam Ahmad ibn Taymiyya* (Matabi' al-Riyad, Riyadh 1962 [*c.*1320]), pp. 260–268.

250. See Takiyy al-Din Ahmad ibn Taymiyya, *al-Siyasa al-shar'iyya fi islah al-ra'i wa l-ra'iyya* (translated as *Le Traité de droit public d'Ibn Taymiyya*) (trans./ed. Henri Laoust; Institut français de Damas, Beirut 1948 [*c.*1309–1312]).

251. *Siyasa shar'iyya* has been translated in many ways, of which Johansen's 'the political function of the [*shari'a*]' seems to me most pertinent to its original meaning (and ambiguity therein); see Baber Johansen, 'Signs as Evidence: The Doctrine of Ibn Taymiyya (1263–1328) and Ibn Qayyim Al-Jawziyya (d. 1351) on Proof' (2002) 9 *Islamic Law and Society* 168, p. 181. See also Shalakany, *supra* n. 16, p. 70.

252. Johansen, *supra* n. 696, p. 251. Also quoted in Shalakany, *supra* n. 16, p. 70. For a salient study of the *hisba* commandment, see Michael Cook, *Commanding Right and Forbidding Wrong in Islamic Thought* (Cambridge University Press, Cambridge 2004 [2001]).

253. Quoted in Johansen, *supra* n. 251, p. 185. Also quoted in Shalakany, *supra* n. 16, p. 70.

254. *Ibid.*

255. Berkey, *supra* n. 44, p. 221.

256. Zubaida, *supra* n. 5, p. 52.

257. Calder, *supra* n. 22, p. 157.

258. Zubaida, *supra* n. 5, p. 52.

259. The terms-of-art specific to the Ottoman state are transliterated in this book from Ottoman Turkish, rather than Arabic, although the legal profession in the empire relied, of course, on sources from both of these languages. However, the Arabic transliteration is, where appropriate, also included when a specific term is mentioned for the first time.

260. The class system of the Ottoman Empire was based, by and large, on the three groups: the *askeri*, a class of military and court functionaries, the nobility and some *ulama* (Turkish: *ulema*); the *reaya*, a tax-paying lower-class; and the slaves (*kul*). See Vanja Hamzić, 'Turkey' in Vanja Hamzić & Ziba Mir-Hosseini, *Control and Sexuality: The Revival of* Zina *Laws in Muslim Contexts* (Women Living under Muslim Laws, London 2010), p. 186.

261. By the late seventeenth / early twelfth century CE/AH, the Ottoman Empire became the largest Muslim state in the history, controlling much of South Eastern Europe, North Africa, the Middle East and West and South Asia. It was principally made of provinces (*vilayet*) and vassal states with different degrees of autonomy. The Empire also exercised authority over some distant lands, which sought its protection against the regional (or European) rival states. In 1565 CE, for example, the sultan of Aceh (a present-day autonomous region in Indonesia) declared allegiance to the Ottoman sovereign. See generally *ibid.*

262. See, for example, Black, *supra* n. 24, p. 200.

263. By the time of this state intervention, the Hanafi doctrine had already developed a formulaic approach to the distinguished Hanafi precedents, which was arguably more advanced than that of the other Sunni schools. Thus, 'an opinion of Abu Hanifa would have precedence over those of the others, whereas, if no opinion of Abu Hanifa was known, Abu Yusuf's view had to be followed. Only if neither of them had had declared his view on the issue was the opinion of Muhammad al-Shaybani the authoritative one'; Rudolph Peters, *Crime and Punishment in Islamic Law: Theory and Practice from the Sixteenth to the Twenty-first Century* (Cambridge University Press, Cambridge 2005), p. 71. By the same token, Abu Hanifa's view that *liwat* was not a form of *zina* was generally followed, while the opposite view held by Abu Yusuf gradually became obsolete (in legal practice, not in some theoretical works of the later *fuqaha'*).

264. *Ibid.* A recent study goes so far as to argue that these developments led to the 'second formation' of Islamic law, at least in the lands under Ottoman rule; see Guy Burak, 'The Second Formation of Islamic Law: The Post-Mongol Context

of the Ottoman Adoption of a School of Law' (2013) 55(3) *Comparative Studies of Society and History* 579.

265. See Peters, *supra* n. 263, pp. 69–75; Hallaq, *supra* n. 156, pp. 216–218; Black, *supra* n. 24, p. 206.
266. Peters, *supra* n. 263, p. 72.
267. *Ibid.*
268. Hallaq, *supra* n. 156, p. 214.
269. *Ibid*, p. 215.
270. Black, *supra* n. 24, p. 205.
271. Hallaq, *supra* n. 156, p. 215.
272. See Uriel Heyd, *Studies in Old Ottoman Criminal Law* (ed. V.L. Ménage; Clarendon Press, Oxford 1973), pp. 150, 177.
273. Madeline C. Zilfi, 'The Ottoman *Ulema*' in Suraiya N. Faroqhi (ed.), *The Cambridge History of Turkey: The Latter Ottoman Empire 1603–1893* (Cambridge University Press, Cambridge 2006), Vol. 3, p. 210. See also Hamzić, *supra* n. 260, pp. 186–187.
274. Some Islamicists, in fact, argue that the *kanun* outright *abolished* the *hudud*, by *replacing* them primarily with monetary fines. Others adopt a more nuanced approach, arguing that the *hudud* were not clearly decreed inapplicable; instead, by enacting an alternative legal approach to the offences *also* covered in the *hudud*, the latter were *effectively* made obsolete. See, for example, Peters, *supra* n. 263, pp. 44–75. See also Hamzić, *supra* n. 260, p. 192.
275. This is also the earliest historically recorded *kanunname*; the later Ottoman claim, that the *kanun* system was a salient feature of the Ottoman state since its inception, could not be verified. See Zubaida, *supra* n. 5, p. 108.
276. Peters, *supra* n. 263, p. 73.
277. See, for example, Amira El-Azhary Sonbol, 'Class and Violence in Nineteenth-century Egypt' in Peri Bearman, Wolfhart Heinrichs & Bernard G. Weiss (eds), *The Law Applied: Contextualizing the Islamic shari'a* (I.B.Tauris, London 2008), p. 154. See also Peters, *supra* n. 263, p. 73; and Calder, *supra* n. 22, p. 68. For the text and translation of the Code, see Heyd, *supra* n. 272, pp. 54–131. For a highly relevant study on Ebussu'ud, see Colin Imber, *Ebu's-su'ud: The Islamic Legal Tradition* (Stanford University Press, Stanford 1997).
278. Ze'evi, *supra* n. 14, p. 59.
279. Peters, *supra* n. 263, p. 73.
280. Quoted in Ze'evi, *supra* n. 14, p. 59.
281. See, for example, Peters, *supra* n. 263, p. 74.
282. Quoted in *ibid.*
283. Cf. *ibid*, p. 85; Ze'evi, *supra* n. 14, p. 66.
284. This is confirmed in El-Rouayheb, *supra* n. 172, p. 123.
285. Every sentence involving the capital punishment had to be approved by the governor, since the right to take life was understood as the sultan's exclusive prerogative. Rudolph Peters does not reveal whether the culprits in the present case were eventually executed. See Peters, *supra* n. 263, pp. 85–86.

264 NOTES TO PAGE 119

286. So, for example, 'Michael Baudier, a French traveler to Turkey in the 1620s [CE] is shocked to find that [the vice of sodomy] "serves as an ordinary subject of entertainment" in men's everyday conversations. Three decades later his countryman, Monsieur de Thevenot, matter-of-factly notes that sodomy "is a very ordinary Vice amongst [the Turks], which they care little to conceal"'; Joseph A. Boone, 'Modernist Re-Orientations: Imagining Homoerotic Desire in "Nearly" Middle East' (2010) 17(3) *Modernism/Modernity* 561, p. 567. For a recent study on the European Orientalist imaginations of the Ottoman Empire, see Roderick Cavaliero, *Ottomania: The Romantics and the Myth of the Islamic Orient* (I.B.Tauris, London 2010).

287. El-Rouayheb, *supra* n. 172.

288. Ze'evi, *supra* n. 14.

289. Hathaway, *supra* n. 234, p. 4. Apparently, 'the basis for the calculations was one [boy] from every forty of those still living who had been baptized fourteen to eighteen years before'; Stephen O. Murray, 'Homosexuality among Slave Elites in Ottoman Turkey' in Stephen O. Murray & Will Roscoe, *Islamic Homosexualities: Culture, History, and Literature* (New York University Press, New York 1997), pp. 174–175. It is possible, however, that this formula was not always strictly followed in the practice. See generally V.L. Ménage, 'Some Notes on the Devshirme' (1966) 29 *Bulletin of the School of Oriental and African Studies* 64.

290. William L. Cleveland, *A History of the Modern Middle East* (3rd edn; Westview Press, Boulder 2004), p. 46.

291. Stanford Shaw, *History of the Ottoman Empire and Modern Turkey* (Cambridge University Press, Cambridge 1976), Vol .1, p. 114. See also V.L. Ménage, 'Devshirme' in B. Lewis, Ch. Pellat & J. Schacht (eds), *Encyclopædia of Islam* (2nd edn; Brill, Leiden 1965), Vol. 2, p. 211; Murray, *supra* n. 289, p. 176. Conscription of Bosnian Muslims was, however, an exception, since Muslims and Jews were generally exempt from *devşirme*. The exemption, for economical reasons, also applied to Christian citizens in the cities as well as to children of Christian craftsmen in rural towns. It appears that Bosnian Muslims were eventually allowed to join the *devşirme* elite (and be sent directly to serve in the sultan's palaces) because of the general preference for the Bosnians and the Albanians that gradually developed in this class. Before it lapsed, the *devşirme* was extended to Asian provinces of the Empire, but it remained, throughout, a phenomenon primarily associated with the Ottoman provinces in the Balkans.

292. The *enderun* students enjoyed an excellent academic programme, including classes in Islamic law, mathematics, geography, history, administration, art, music, weaponry and physical training as well as Arabic, Turkish and Persian language. 'The [*enderun*] was the principal creative source in Ottoman culture. The great architect Sinan (1490?-1588 [CE]), for example, came originally as a *devşirme* boy from Kayseri'; Halil İnalcık, *The Ottoman Empire: The Classical Age, 1300–1600* (Wiedenfeld & Nicolson, London 1973), p. 88.

293. Albert H. Lybyer, *The Government of the Ottoman Empire in the time of Suleiman the Magnificent* (Harvard University Press, Cambridge 1913), p. 74; also quoted in Murray, *supra* n. 289, p. 175.

294. See generally Shaw, *supra* n. 291, pp. 112–139.

295. Cavaliero, *supra* n. 286, p. 20.

296. *Ibid.*

297. See *supra* n. 233.

298. The socio-physical worlds of the women's harem and male political arena rarely mixed at the imperial court. This is not to say that the harem's inhabitants did not have any influence on politics and society. Some 130 years in the late sixteenth and the early seventeenth century CE are even known as *Kadınlar Saltanatı* (the 'Sultanate of Women'), when the sultans' mothers *(valide)* exercised nearly all imperial prerogatives on behalf of their (mostly still infant) sons. But gender segregation also led to 'blatant and often bizarre misogyny', like in the case of the eighteenth-century CE Sultan Osman III, who 'is said to have ordered the women of Topkapı Palace – five or six hundred at the time – to stay out of sight when he came their way. To prevent accidental encounters, he reportedly had taps attached to his footwear to signal his approach [. . .]. He extended his fantasy of an all-male world by ordering Istanbul's women off the streets on the three days of the week that he himself would be moving about the city'; Madeline C. Zilfi, *Women and Slavery in the Late Ottoman Empire: The Design of Difference* (Cambridge University Press, Cambridge 2010), pp. 73–74. See also Hamzić, *supra* n. 260, p. 189.

299. See generally Murray, *supra* n. 289, pp. 174–186.

300. See Danielle J. van Dobben, 'Dancing Modernity: Gender, sexuality and the State in the Late Ottoman Empire and Early Turkish Republic', MA thesis, Department of Near Eastern Studies, University of Arizona, 2008, pp. 47–53 *et passim*. From the seventeenth century CE onwards, apart from the *köçekler*, there were dancers known as *çengiler* (sing. *çengi*), who initially consisted of both women and cross-dressed men, but in later times came to be women only. See, for example, Eugenia Popescu-Judetz, 'Köçek and Çengi in Turkish Culture' (1982) 6 *Dance Studies* 53.

301. Zubaida, *supra* n. 5, p. 115.

302. The Tanzimat period, paradigmatic of a Muslim polity's encounter with the European legal tradition, is analysed in the second part of this chapter, which deals with the nineteenth-century CE and later developments in Islamic law.

303. See *supra* n. 233.

304. The relatively recent surge in academic interest in this phenomenon is reflected, *inter alia*, in Mathew Kuefler, *The Manly Eunuch: Masculinity, Gender Ambiguity and Christian Ideology in Late Antiquity* (University of Chicago Press, Chicago 2001); Kathryn M. Ringrose, *The Perfect Servant: Eunuchs and the Social Construction of Gender in Byzantium* (University of Chicago Press, Chicago 2003); Shaun Tougher (ed.), *Eunuchs in Antiquity and Beyond* (Classical Press of Wales, Swansea 2002); Shaun Tougher, *The Eunuch in Byzantine History*

and Society (Routledge, Oxford 2008); Shaun Tougher, *Roman Castrati: Eunuchs in the Roman Empire* (Continuum, London 2015 [*forthcoming*]); Shih-Shan Henry Tsai, *The Eunuchs in the Ming Dynasty* (State University of New York Press, Albany 1996); Taisuke Mitamura, *Chinese Eunuchs: Structure of Intimate Politics* (trans. Charles A. Pomeroy; Tuttle Publishing, North Clarendon 1992); Piotr O. Scholz, *Eunuchs and Castrati: A Cultural History* (trans. John A. Broadwin & Shelly L. Frisch; Markus Wiener Publishers, Princeton 2001 [1999]).

305. Hathaway, *supra* n. 234, p. 8.

306. *Ibid*, pp. 8–14. See also Black, *supra* n. 24, p. 195. The studies focusing on the *khuddam/aghawat* in Muslim polities include Marmon, *supra* n. 30; Hathaway, *supra* n. 234; and Ayalon, *supra* n. 236.

307. Hathaway, *supra* n. 234, p. 9.

308. In the Mughal court, for example, a subjectivity known as *khwajasara* encompassed both castrated individuals and those seen as unable to procreate. This subjectivity is still present in today's Pakistan and it is discussed comprehensively in Chapter 5 of this book.

309. Marmon, *supra* n. 30, p. ix. Shaun Marmon argues that the 'obscure founders' of the Medinan society of *khudam/aghawat* were Salah al-Din, who established the 'Ayyubid dynasty in Egypt and famously restored Jerusalem to Muslim rule, and Nur al-Din Zangi, a Zangid dynasty ruler of Palestine and Syria (r. 1146/541 – 1174/569 CE/AH). See *ibid*, pp. 31–45.

310. 'In 1990 [CE] the Saudi magazine *al-Yamama* published an interview with Salim Farid, the official in charge of the "affairs of the *aghawat*" of Mecca. According to this interview, fourteen eunuchs [*sic*] still served at the sanctuary of Mecca and seventeen at the sanctuary in Medina. [Also] [a]ccording to this interview, the Saudi monarchy has repeatedly confirmed the independence of the eunuchs [*sic*] of Mecca in the exercise of "their customs and traditions" and in their rights to their considerable income from centuries of endowments. Little mention is made of the eunuchs [*sic*] of Medina except for the observation that, unlike the eunuchs [*sic*] of Mecca, they control their own funds and have no separate official in charge of their affairs'; *ibid*, p. 111.

311. *Ibid*, p. ix. The Mughal/Pakistani *khwajasara*, as we shall see in Chapter 5, were/are similarly associated with the sanctuaries of Sufi saints.

312. See generally Hathaway, *supra* n. 234. See also Hamza 'Abd al-Aziz Badr & Daniel Crecelius, 'The *Awqaf* of al-Hajj Bashir Agha in Cairo' (1993) 27 *Annales islamologiques* 291; Hamza 'Abd al-Aziz Badr & Daniel Crecelius, 'The Wealth and Influence of an Exiled Ottoman Eunuch in Egypt: The *Waqf* Inventory of Abbas Agha' (1994) 37(4) *Journal of the Economic and Social History of the Orient* 293; Jane Hathaway, 'The Role of the *Kızlar Ağası* in 17th–18th Century Ottoman Egypt' (1992) 75 *Studia Islamica* 141.

313. See Marmon, *supra* n. 30, pp. 55–61.

314. See generally Hathaway, *supra* n. 234. See also Badr & Crecelius, 'The *Awqaf* of al-Hajj Bashir Agha in Cairo', *supra* n 312.

315. 'Even so, there are accounts of castrations performed within [the Ottoman sultans'] Topkapı Palace itself'; Hathaway, *supra* n. 234, p. 19.

316. See Paula Sanders, 'Gendering the Ungendered Body: Hermaphrodites in Medieval Islamic Law' in Nikki R. Keddie & Beth Baron (eds), *Women in Middle Eastern History: Shifting Boundaries in Sex and Gender* (Yale University Press, New Heaven 1991), pp. 74–95.

317. *Ibid.* See also Mohammad Hashim Kamali, 'Transgenders, from Islam's Perspective', *New Straits Times*, Kuala Lumpur, 29 December 2009, available at http://leonalo.wordpress.com/2009/12/ (accessed 28 July 2014).

318. See, for example, Taj al-Din 'Abd al-Wahhab ibn 'Abd Allah al-Subki, *Kitab mu'id al-ni'am wa-mubid al-niqam* (ed. David W. Myhrman; London 1906 [*c.*1360]), also discussed in Marmon, *supra* n. 30, pp. 61–63.

319. See generally Hathaway, *supra* n. 234. See also Badr & Crecelius, 'The *Awqaf* of al-Hajj Bashir Agha in Cairo', *supra* n. 312.

320. Some Medinan *aghawat*, apparently, did have wives; *ibid*, p. 54. That was, however, an exception.

321. Genital difference, caused by castration, was not the only bodily consequence of that act: 'If the eunuch [*sic*] were castrated before puberty, as most eunuchs [*sic*] in court service were, he [*sic*] would probably suffer from osteoporosis in later life, since his [*sic*] bones would not have undergone the development and strengthening typically brought on by surging testosterone levels at puberty. On the other hand, his [*sic*] arms and hands would grow disproportionately long relative to his [*sic*] torso [...]. As a result of hormonal deficiencies, eunuchs [*sic*] were either prone to obesity or, on the other hand, remained underweight and therefore appeared unusually slender and delicate [...]. For the same reason, their skin would wrinkle prematurely, creating an odd [*sic*] contrast to their beardless faces; meanwhile, their faces were often disproportionately large. The eunuch's [*sic*] voice never broke, remaining relatively high-pitched throughout his [*sic*] life. By the time he [*sic*] reached old age [...] his [*sic*] voice could resemble what Chinese sources describe as that of a shrieking old woman'; *ibid*, p. 21.

322. See *ibid*, pp. 26, 29.

323. There are, however, some scant reports of voluntary castrations. Jane Hathaway, for example, mentions one Gazanfer Ağa, a 'close confidant' of the future Sultan Selim II, who voluntarily underwent castration in order to 'retain intimacy' with Selim when he took the throne; *ibid*, p. 20.

324. For a similar conclusion in the context of the Byzantine Empire and its 'others', see generally Kuefler, *supra* n. 304.

325. Wael B. Hallaq thus concludes his voluminous study of 'the shari'a and its *fiqh*' with the following sentence: 'At the end of the day, the shari'a has ceased to be even an approximate reincarnation of its historical self'; Hallaq, *supra* n. 156, p. 550. See also *ibid*, pp. 543–550.

326. See Daniel R. Headrick, *The Tools of Empire: Technology and European Imperialism in the Nineteenth Century* (Oxford University Press, New York 1981), pp. 3–4.

327. See Peters, *supra* n. 263, p. 104.

328. See generally Hallaq, *supra* n. 156, pp. 357–370.

329. Warren Hastings (1732–1818 CE) was the first British Governor-General of India (then known as the Governor-General of the Presidency of Forth William, in Calcutta), from 1773 to 1785 CE.

330. Hallaq, *supra* n. 156, p. 372.

331. Or, in Warren Hastings' own interpretation: 'Every accumulation of knowledge and especially such as is obtained by social communication with people over whom we exercise dominion founded on the right of conquest, is useful to the [British] state [. . .]. [I]t attracts and conciliates distant affections; it lessens the weight of the chain by which the natives are held in subjection; and it imprints on the hearts of our countrymen the sense of obligation and benevolence'; quoted in Bernard S. Cohn, *Colonialism and Its Forms of Knowledge: The British in India* (Oxford University Press, Oxford 1997), p. 45.

332. Sir William Jones (1746–1794), one of the architects of Anglo-Muhammadan law, quoted in *ibid*, p. 68.

333. Peters, *supra* n. 263, p. 106.

334. This was, of course, a well-known British colonial tactic *everywhere*. Consider, for example, the infamous observation by Evelyn Baring, 1st Earl of Cromer, a Consul-General in Egypt under the British occupation (served from 1883 to 1907 CE): 'It is true that, prior to 1883, no system of justice existed in Egypt'; quoted in Shalakany, *supra* n. 16, p. 39.

335. Hallaq, *supra* n. 156, p. 376.

336. Who were, as put by a British colonial legist and poet, 'Indian in blood and colour, but English in taste, in opinions, in morals, and in intellect'; Thomas Babington Macaulay, 'Minute of 2 February 1835 on Indian Education' in G. M. Young (ed.), *Macaulay: Prose and Poetry* (Harvard University Press, Cambridge 1957), p. 729.

337. Peters, *supra* n. 263, p. 119. Rudolph Peters cites the following changes, within the sphere of Islamic criminal justice, instituted by Anglo-Muhammadan law between 1790 and 1807 CE: 'Private prosecution was replaced with prosecution by the state. Anybody who had committed an act of wilful homicide could be sentenced to death, regardless of the circumstances. The heirs of the victim in cases of homicide, and the victim himself [*sic*] in cases of wounding, could no longer claim bloodmoney. Culpable homicide and wounding would be punished with imprisonment, whereas in those cases where, under [*fiqh*], there was a liability for the bloodprice even though the killer had acted without fault, there would be neither compensation nor imprisonment. The penalties of amputation and stoning to death were abolished and the numerous defences in *hadd* cases, based on the strict rules of evidence and the notion of doubt (*shubha*), were repealed. [. . .] [Overall, the] criminal law applied in the Indian courts had entirely lost its Islamic character except in name'.

338. Hallaq, *supra* n. 156, p. 383.

339. In the Ottoman *millet* system, Muslim, Christian and Jewish communities – organised into 'nations' (*millet*) – 'enjoyed a semi-autonomous status within the empire and were to be guided, predominantly in family law and internal administrative matters, by their own religious laws'; Hamzić, *supra* n. 260, p. 192.
340. *Ibid*, pp. 193–194.
341. Remarkably, the *Mecelle* was used in Albania, Cyprus, Lebanon, Syria, Jordan, Palestine and Israel, Iraq and Kuwait. It is *still* in use in the Israeli-occupied territories of Palestine; see *ibid*, p. 194.
342. Exacerbated, of course, by the nationalist movements across the Empire and especially in the Balkans.
343. Peters, *supra* n. 263, p. 116.
344. Art. 188, Ottoman Penal Code 1858; quoted in Hamzić, *supra* n. 260, p. 194.
345. Art .462, Turkish Penal Code 1926; see also Hamzić, *supra* n. 260, pp. 201–202.
346. The Turkish Penal Code 2004 finally abrogated the defence of 'passion'. See generally *ibid*, pp. 194–209.
347. Jean Comaroff & John L. Comaroff, *Theory from the South: Or, How Euro-America is Evolving toward Africa* (Paradigm Publishers, Boulder 2012), p. 1.
348. *Ibid*, p. 9.
349. Cf. Michael Silverstein, 'Shifters, Linguistic Categories, and Cultural Description' in Keith H. Basso & Henry A. Selby (eds), *Meaning in Anthropology* (Harper & Row, New York 1976).
350. Comaroff & Comaroff, *supra* n. 347, p. 10.
351. Hallaq, *supra* n. 156, p. 359.
352. See generally *ibid*, pp. 357–370. Note, also, Wael B. Hallaq, *The Impossible State: Islam, Politics, and Modernity's Moral Predicament* (Columbia University Press, New York 2013).
353. *Stare decisis* (*et non quieta movere*; 'to stand by decisions and not disturb the undisturbed') is the common law principle of legal precedent, which obliges judges to respect the precedents established by prior decisions.
354. Abdullahi Ahmed An-Na'im, *Islam and the Secular State: Negotiating the Future of Shari'a* (Harvard University Press, Cambridge 2008), p. 7.
355. This brief overview of the Islamic modernist thought is by no means exhaustive. My intention is to review some of the central hypotheses of more notable theorists of Muslim modernity, and of the reactions they elicited from within their contemporary *umma*. For a more exhaustive analysis, see Mansoor Moaddel, *Islamic Modernism, Nationalism, and Fundamentalism: Episode and Discourse* (University of Chicago Press, Chicago 2005). See also Hallaq, *supra* n. 156, pp. 500–542.
356. Zubaida, *supra* n. 5, p. 142.
357. Which featured as one of the central tenets of the Mu'tazili philosophical thought, and, by extension, of the proto-Hanafi legal movement known as *ahl al-ra'y*, in the 'formative' period of Islamic law; see *supra* n. 105.

358. For a 'post-classical' treatise on the subject, see Takiyy al-Din Ahmad ibn Taymiyya, *Dar'a ta'arud al-'aql wal-naql* (ed. 'Abd al-Latif 'Abd al-Rahman; Dar al-kutub al-'ilmiyya, Beirut 1997 [*c.*1315]), 5 Vols.
359. Hallaq, *supra* n. 156, p. 503.
360. *Ibid.* (emphasis added).
361. Zubaida, *supra* n. 5, p. 143.
362. Cf. Hallaq, *supra* n. 156, p. 504.
363. *Ibid*, p. 507.
364. On the *maqasid* in 'classical' and 'post-classical' era of Islamic law, see, for example, Wael B. Hallaq, *A History of Islamic Legal Theories* (Cambridge University Press, Cambridge 1997), pp. 162–206.
365. Wael B. Hallaq thus maintains that, 'aside from matters of worship and religious ritual, which he insists are to remain within the parameters of revelation, Rida upholds a legal theory strictly anchored in natural law, where considerations of human need, interest and necessity would reign supreme in elaborating a legal corpus. Any revealed text, notwithstanding its epistemological strength, could be set aside if it were to contravene these considerations'; Hallaq, *supra* n. 156, p. 508.
366. See 'Abd al-Wahhab Khallaf, *Masadir al-tashri' al-islami fi-ma la nassa fih* (Dar al-kitab al-'arabi, Cairo 1955).
367. See Muhammad Sa'id Ramadan al-Buti, *Dawabit al-maslaha fi al-shari' a al-islamiyya* (al-Maktaba al-umawiyya, Damascus 1966).
368. *Ibid*, p. 59.
369. See generally Abdolkarim Soroush, *Reason, Freedom and Democracy in Islam* (trans./ed. M. Sadri & A. Sadri; Oxford University Press, Oxford 2000).
370. Usually by an oblique reference to the 'Islamic *shari'a*'. What is striking about such laws is that they are often introduced for purely political reasons, i.e. to increase the sway or in search for legitimacy of a political establishment. For a paradigmatic example of the political revival of *zina* laws in Indonesia, Iran, Nigeria and Pakistan, and – indirectly – in Turkey, see Hamzić & Mir-Hosseini, *supra* n. 28.
371. See generally Vanja Hamzić, 'Pakistan' in Vanja Hamzić & Ziba Mir-Hosseini, *Control and Sexuality: The Revival of Zina Laws in Muslim Contexts* (Women Living under Muslim Laws, London 2010), pp. 155–179. Pakistani legal system is assessed in some detail in Chapter 5 of this book.
372. See Ibn Taymiyya, *supra* n. 250.
373. Peters, *supra* n. 263, pp. 143, 149.
374. *Ibid*, p. 143.
375. Zubaida, *supra* n. 5, p. 156.
376. *Ibid*, p. 155.
377. Hamzić, *supra* n. 171, pp. 260–261.
378. For instance, same–sex relations were made illegal in 27 Muslim-majority nation states, usually by means of colonial, mostly British, nineteenth-century

CE legislation, while five of these countries also introduced the death penalty for *liwat*. See *ibid*, p. 261 *et passim*.

379. Abdelwahab Bouhdiba, *Sexuality in Islam* (trans. Alan Sheridan; Routledge, London 1985 [1975]), p. 30.

380. Foucault, *supra* n. 40, p. 43.

381. See, for example, Barlas, *supra* n. 65. For some current debates, see Anitta Kynsilehto (ed.), *Islamic Feminism: Current Perspectives* (Juvenes Print, Tampere 2008).

382. Ziba Mir-Hosseini, 'Classical *Fiqh*, Contemporary Ethics and Gender Justice' in Karl Vogt, Lena Larsen & Christian Moe (eds), *New Directions in Islamic Thought: Exploring Reform and Muslim Tradition* (I.B.Tauris, London 2009), p. 78.

383. 'To accept the authority of any group and then to resign oneself to its misreadings of Islam not only makes one complicit in the continued abuse of Islam and the abuse of women in the name of Islam, but it also means losing the battle over meaning without even fighting it'; Barlas, *supra* n. 65, p. xi.

384. See, for example, Ahmed, *supra* n. 232; Mir-Hosseini, *supra* n. 382; Wadud, *supra* n. 29. See also generally Lila Abu-Lughod (ed.), *Remaking Women: Feminism and Modernity in the Middle East* (Princeton University Press, Princeton 1998).

385. But, of course, even the notion of 'progress' can be reclaimed from its modernist usage, as attempted, for example, in Omid Safi (ed.), *Progressive Muslims: On justice, Gender, and Pluralism* (Oneworld, Oxford 2003).

386. Cf. Wadud, *supra* n. 29.

387. Cf. Robert H. Mnookin & Lewis Kornhauser, 'Bargaining in the Shadow of the Law: The Case of Divorce' (1979) 88(5) *Yale Law Journal* 950.

388. See *supra* n. 33.

389. Kugle, *supra* n. 33, p. 41.

390. *Ibid.*

391. See generally *ibid*, pp. 33–274.

392. See especially Habib, *Islam and Homosexuality*, *supra* n. 33, for a collection of essays from across sexual/gender-pluralist perspectives.

393. See *supra* n. 325.

394. The German exegetical phrase *Sitz im Leben* ('setting in life') here comes to mind, for the Seljuk interlude really provides a historical (social/political/ legal) *context* to the classical *fuqaha*'s theory of *liwat*.

395. Reading the *fuqaha*'s treatises, written in genre-specific, high literary style, Norman Calder poignantly concludes: 'This is art, and it reminds this reader of nothing so much as a medieval miniature'; Calder, *supra* n. 22, p. 94.

396. I.e. codified, 'transformed from a worldly institution and culture to a [mere] textuality'; Hallaq, *supra* n. 156, pp. 546–547. To be sure, some late-nineteenth-century CE attempts at the 'entextation' of Islamic law, as in the case of the *Mecelle*, promulgated in 1868 CE by the Ottoman state, were not, *sensu stricto*, directly imposed by the external (European imperial) forces, but were

still, without dobt, strongly influenced by them. See generally Messick, *supra* n. 4, Ch. 3, pp. 54–72.

397. Ahmad Atif Ahmad, *Structural Interrelations of Theory and Practice in Islamic Law: A Study of Six Works of Medieval Islamic Jurisprudence* (Brill, Leiden 2006), p. 23.

Chapter 4   Muslim Sexual and Gender Diversity in Contemporary Pakistan

1. It has been proposed that the foremost Mughal designation of *khwajasara* was, quite literally, the master (Persian: *khwaja*) of the palace (Persian: *sara* or *sarai*), who was castrated at an early age and sent/sold to the imperial service. See for, example, R. Nath, 'The Mughal Institution of Khwajasara' in R. Nath, *Medieval Indian History and Architecture* (APH Publishing Corporation, New Delhi 1995), pp. 13–22.

2. The neologism *ethnoscape* was introduced by the anthropologist Arjun Appadurai, who describes it as the globalised spatial diffusion and mobility of correlated people. This book, however, does not follow that definition. Instead, it endorses Anthony D. Smith's conceptualisation of ethnoscape, who understands it as 'the territorialisation of ethnic memory'; Conrad Schetter, 'Ethnoscapes, National Territorialisation, and the Afghan War' (2005) 10(1) *Geopolitics* 50, p. 51. See also Arjun Appadurai, *Modernity at Large: Cultural Dimensions of Globalization* (University of Minneapolis Press, Minneapolis 1996); Anthony D. Smith, 'Culture, Community and Territory: The Politics of Ethnicity and Nationalism' (1996) 72(3) *International Affairs* 445.

3. What I term here as Khwajasara Farsi is the common vernacular of the *khwajasara* subjectivity, not to be confused with the Persian language, which is *also* known as Farsi. Whenever mentioned in this book, 'Farsi' means the language of *khwajasara*, not Persian.

4. In a recent address to a New Delhi conference which I have attended as well, the veteran of radical international legal critique, B.S. Chimni, has summarised the elementary properties of *critical knowledge* in the following order: (a) it must contest all local and global structures of oppression; (b) it must provide for cognitive reciprocity – and cognitive justice – without essentialising any culture; (c) it must be rooted in *vernacular knowledge*, especially that of insurrectionary movements; (d) it must resist essentialising (any) knowledge, through historical re-readings; (e) every knowledge, after the collapse of socialism, must state its nominative preferences; and (f) in Marx's words, the point is not to create the world, but to change it.

5. Qur'an 55:19–21 ('God has let loosed the two seas, meeting together. Between them is a barrier (*barzakh*), which none of them can transgress. So which of the favours of your Sustainer (*Rabb*) would you deny?' (my translation)).

6. Bruce Riedel, 'Foreword' in Stephen P. Cohen (ed.), *The Future of Pakistan* (Brookings Institution Press, Washington 2011), p. viii.

7. Stephen P. Cohen, 'Preface' in Stephen P. Cohen (ed.), *The Future of Pakistan* (Brookings Institution Press, Washington 2011), p. xi.
8. Fawaz A. Gerges, 'Foreword' in James Wynbrandt, *A Brief History of Pakistan* (Facts on File, New York 2009), p. x.
9. The 2012 Failed States Index ranks Pakistan at the 'critical' 13th place, preceded, in the same analysts' coarse description, '[o]nly [by] the worst African hellholes, Afghanistan, Haiti, Yemen, and Iraq'; Robert D. Kaplan, 'What's Wrong with Pakistan?', *Foreign Policy*, July/August 2012, available at http://www.foreignpolicy.com/articles-/2012/06/18/whats_wrong_with_pakistan (accessed 20 August 2014); see also the 2012 Failed States Index, *Foreign Policy*, available at http://www.foreignpolicy.com/failed_states_index_2012_interactive (accessed 20 August 2014).
10. Louise Brown, *The Dancing Girls of Lahore: Selling Love and Saving Dreams in Pakistan's Ancient Pleasure District* (PerfectBound, New York 2005), p. 241
11. The name of the state is a portmanteau, arguably coined in the 1930s CE by Choudhry Rahmat Ali, while studying at the University of Cambridge, who dreamt of an independent country for 'thirty million Muslims [. . .] who live in the five Northern Units of British Raj', namely: Punjab, Afghania (today known as Khyber Pakhtunkhwa province), Kashmir, Sindh and Baluchistan; quoted in Stanley Wolpert, *Jinnah of Pakistan* (Oxford University Press, Oxford 1984), p. 131. 'Pak' also means 'pure' in Urdu, while 'stan' is the region's common term for 'land'.
12. Muhammad Ali Jinnah (in 1943 CE), quoted in Afzal Iqbal, *Islamisation of Pakistan* (Vanguard Books, Lahore 1986), p. 33. Jinnah was a (Shi'i) Muslim modernist, a London-educated lawyer and skilful politician, for whom 'Islamic renaissance' – if anything – was an idea compatible with that of 'modern nation state', based on common law.
13. Vanja Hamzić, 'Pakistan' in Vanja Hamzić & Ziba Mir-Hosseini, *Control and Sexuality: The Revival of* Zina *Laws in Muslim Contexts* (Women Living under Muslim Laws, London 2010), pp. 157–158.
14. James Wynbrandt, *A Brief History of Pakistan* (Facts on File, New York 2009), p. 160.
15. The five Hudood Ordinances 1979 were prepared by an *ad hoc* committee selected by Zia, with the assistance of the Arab jurist Ma'aroof al-Dawalibi. They were: the Offence against Property (Enforcement of Hudood) Ordinance; the Offence of Qazf (Enforcement of Hadd) Ordinance; the Offence of Zina (Enforcement of Hudood) Ordinance; the Prohibition (Enforcement of Hadd) Order; and the Execution and Punishment of Whipping Ordinance (IX/1979). Flogging, the amputation of limbs and stoning to death for the four *hudud* crimes (*zina*, *qazf* (*qadhf*) or false accusation of *zina*, theft and intoxication) were thus incorporated into Pakistani legal system.
16. Established by the Presidential Order I/1980 and incorporated in the Constitution of Pakistan 1973, under Chapter 3(A). See http://www.federalshariatcourt.gov.pk/ (accessed 21 August 2014).

17. *Hazoor Bakhsh* v *Federation of Pakistan*, PLD 1981 FSC 145.
18. *Federation of Pakistan* v *Hazoor Bakhsh*, PLD 1983 FSC 255. The phrase 'Injunctions of Islam', as we shall see, is one of the favourite concepts of Pakistan's legists. See also the Presidential Order V/1981 (Constitution (Amendment) Order), which empowered this court to review its prior decisions.
19. Created in 1956 CE, the 'Supreme Court of Pakistan is the highest appellate court of the country and court of last resort. It is the final arbiter of the law and the Constitution. Its orders/decisions are binding on all other courts in the country. All executive and judicial authorities are bound to act in aid of the Supreme Court. The Constitution contains elaborate provisions on the composition, jurisdiction, powers and functions of the Court'; 'History', *Supreme Court of Pakistan*, available at http://www.supremecourt.gov.pk/web/page.asp?id=113 (accessed 21 August 2014).
20. See generally Hamzić, *supra* n. 13, pp. 160–172.
21. Whether they spoke in Farsi, Punjabi or Urdu, my interlocutors, who otherwise had almost no knowledge of the English language, would *always* use English words to describe their law-related affairs (e.g. 'Supreme Court', 'judgment', 'application', 'request', 'letter', 'Chief Justice', 'ID card', 'demanding', 'election' and 'fight').
22. By way of example, Section 377 of the Penal Code 1860 of the Islamic Republic of Pakistan reads: 'Whoever voluntarily has carnal intercourse against the order of nature with any man, woman or animal, shall be punished with imprisonment for life, or with imprisonment of either description for a term which shall not be less than two years nor more than ten years, and shall also be liable to fine. Explanation: Penetration is sufficient to constitute the carnal intercourse necessary to the offense described in this section'. It is, of course, the 'domesticated'/post-independence version of the Act No 45 of the [all-British, colonial] Legislative Council for India of 6 October 1860. This section, in Pakistan, remains to date legally unchallenged.
23. The hierarchy of the formal judicial system is as follows: (1) Supreme Court; (2) high courts (one for each province and one in the federal capital – Islamabad); (3) district and sessions courts (one in each district); and (4) executive and judicial magistrate courts and courts of civil judge.
24. Hamzić, *supra* n. 13, p. 163.
25. See Martin Lau, 'Sharia and National Law in Pakistan' in Jan Michiel Otto (ed.), *Sharia Incorporated: A Comparative Overview of the Legal Systems of Twelve Muslim Countries in Past and Present* (Leiden University Press, Leiden 2010), p. 400.
26. Conversely, the Federal Sharia Court's decisions on any matters within its jurisdiction are binding on the high courts. To ensure the special status of this court, 'it was established that any appeal against the decisions of the Federal Shariat Court went to the Shariat Appellate Bench of the Supreme Court and two *ulama* appointed by the President'; Hamzić, *supra* n. 13, p. 163. But even

with such system in place, the Supreme Court was gradually able to assert its more independent supervision of the entire formal judicial system.

27. *Ibid*, p. 164. See also Niaz A. Shah, *Women, the Koran and International Human Rights Law: The Experience of Pakistan* (Martinus Nijhoff Publishers, Leiden 2006), p. 100.

28. See, for example, *Shirin Munir*, PLD 1990 SC 295; *Azizullah Memon*, PLD 1993 SC 341; *Ghulam Mustafa Ansari*, PLD 2004 SC 1903. See also Shah, *supra* n. 27, pp. 110–114.

29. 'Our Section 377 is not at all a *real* stumbling block. It's very much a symbolic thing for us [...]. Hardly ever has anybody actually been convicted or even charged under it [...]. For us, it's a non-issue'; my interview with a young Muslim female leader of an underground Lahore-based middle-class queer organisation, 6 October 2011.

30. This potentially has to do with the fact that the favoured school of *fiqh* amongst the Pakistani Sunni legal scholars is the Hanafi *madhhab*, which historically preferred not to associate *liwat* with the *hadd* offence of *zina*. This issue is discussed in some detail in Chapter 4 of this book.

31. Note that the Human Rights Constitutional Petition 63/2009, or Case 63/09, is mistakenly referred to as the Human Rights Constitutional Petition 43/2009, or Case 43/09, in some (but not all) related orders of the Supreme Court (and its chief justice).

32. My interview with Dr Muhammad Aslam Khaki, Islamabad, 9 October 2011. He is a professor of Islamic law who regularly litigates the cases before the Supreme Court of Pakistan and the Federal Shariat Court. He has represented *khwajasara* applicants in all human rights petitions/cases before the Supreme Court.

33. See Paula Sanders, 'Gendering the Ungendered Body: Hermaphrodites in Medieval Islamic Law' in Nikki R Keddie & Beth Baron (eds), *Women in Middle Eastern History: Shifting Boundaries in Sex and Gender* (Yale University Press, New Heaven 1991), pp. 74–95. See also Mohammad Hashim Kamali, 'Transgenders, from Islam's Perspective', *New Straits Times*, Kuala Lumpur, 29 December 2009, available at http://leonalo.wordpress.com/2009/12/ (accessed 22 August 2014). The concept in question is briefly discussed in Chapter 4 of this book.

34. Bobby, or Almas Shah, a *khwajasara* political and community leader, used to be a chairperson of the Association for She-Male Rights, based in Rawalpindi; see Claire Pamment, 'Hijraism: Jostling for a Third Space in Pakistani Politics' (2010) 54(2) *Drama Review* 29, p. 36. The political identity of *khwajasara*, as well as other identitary aspects of this subjectivity, are discussed later on in the present chapter.

35. Order of 20 November 2009 in Re Case 63/09 [misreported as Case 43/09] SC, p. 2.

36. Order of 14 July 2009 in Re Case 63/09 SC, p. 2.

37. *Ibid*, p. 1.

38. *Ibid*, p. 2.
39. Order of 4 November 2009 in Re Case 63/09 [misreported as Case 43/09] SC, p. 1.
40. Order of 17 August 2009 in Re Case 63/09 SC, p. 2.
41. Order of 22 March 2011 in Re Case 63/09 [misreported as Case 43/09] SC, p. 2.
42. *Ibid*.
43. '[T]he Government has already ensured [. . .] jobs to the disable persons[;] [a] similar policy can also be adopted for [the unix]'; Order of 20 November 2009 in Re Case 63/09 [misreported as Case 43/09] SC, p. 3.
44. Cf. Robert H. Mnookin & Lewis Kornhauser, 'Bargaining in the Shadow of the Law: The Case of Divorce' (1979) 88(5) *Yale Law Journal* 950.
45. Farina Mir, *The Social Space of Language: Vernacular Culture in British Colonial Punjab* (University of California Press, Berkeley 2010), p. 18. This is an excellent study of the Punjabi print culture and literature in 'Our Prussia', as the British colonisers used to call Punjab.
46. *Ibid*.
47. *Ibid*.
48. Practically at the same time, Bosnian Muslims, Jews, Catholic and Orthodox Christians were refashioned into separate *ethnic* communities, divided along the religious fault lines, under the influence of Austro-Hungarian, Serbian, Croatian, Ottoman and other *modernist* political agendas. See, for example, Noel Malcolm, *Bosnia: A Short History* (New York University Press, New York 1994).
49. The Mughal Empire is usually dated between 1526/932 CE/AH, when Babur, a descendant of both the Turkic conqueror Timur (or 'Tamerlane') and the Mongol emperor Genghis Khan, laid the basis for the Mughal dynasty in the Indian subcontinent, and 1862/1278 CE/AH, when the British deposed and exiled its last emperor, Bahadur Shah II. It was, however, an imperial power only until about 1757/1170 CE/AH.
50. Mir, *supra* n. 45, p. 4.
51. Saeed Bhutta, 'Kafi: A Genre of Punjabi Poetry' (2008) 23(2) *South Asian Studies* 223, p. 227.
52. For an assortment of recent references to Hafez-e Shirazi, Nizam al-Mulk Tusi, Akbar the Great, Jalaluddin Rumi and Abu Hamed Mohammad ibn Mohammad al-Ghazzali in the case law of the Supreme Court of Pakistan, see *Sindh High Court Bar Association* v *Federation of Pakistan*, PLD 2009 SC 879; *Mobashir Hassan* v *Federation of Pakistan*, PLD 2010 SC 265; Constitutional Petitions 10/2011 SC & 18/2011 SC, Judgment, 4 March 2011; *Federation of Pakistan* v *Munir Hussain Bhatti* et al, Judgment, 20 April 2011.
53. The official website for *Minhaj-ul-Qur'an* is http://www.minhaj.org/english/index.html (accessed 23 August 2014).
54. The examples include *The Inner Circle* in South Africa, led by a Pakistan-educated imam, Muhsin Hendricks; *Imaan* and *The Safra Project* in the United

Kingdom; *Salaam* in Canada; *Al-Fatiha* in the United States of America; and *HM2F* (*Collectif citoyen pour un Islam de France véritablement inclusif et une laïcité véritablement respectueuse de toutes les croyances*) in France. Similar collectives also exist under larger organisations, such as the *Catalan Islamic Council* in Spain; *Helem* and *Meem* in Lebanon; *Koalisi Perempuan Indonesia untuk Keadilan dan Demokrasi* (*Indonesian Women's Coalition for Justice and Democracy*) in Indonesia; and many others, which cannot be named here for the reasons of security.

55. 'Inclusive, progressive, reformist Muslims, supporters of a peaceful, egalitarian and non-sexist representation of Islam'; see L. Zahed & Amina Wadud, *Livre Blanc: 2012 retraite spirituelle et quête culturelle aux sources de l'islam* (n.p; Paris 2012), p. 2, available at http://www.calem.eu/Tawhid-Omrah_pelerinage-is lamique-Mecque-Madinah-Juin2012-Radjab1433_avec-Amina-Wadud-&-i nclusifs-progressistes-Musulman-es.html (accessed 24 August 2014).

56. 'An inclusive pilgrimage with the imam Amina Wadud, to Mecca and Medina'; *ibid.*

57. *Ibid*, pp. 36–37.

58. Ayesha explained: 'It is always religion mixed with other things that parents have particularly. So they always say: What Will people say about you? Will you ever have children? How could that happen? God hates you! All of that comes in one big horrible package'.

*. Some parts of the following sub-section in this chapter are based on Vanja Hamzić, 'The (Un)Conscious Pariah: Canine and Gender Outcasts of the British Raj' (2015) 40(2) *Australian Feminist Law Journal* 185.

59. There is a wealth of literature on *hijre* of India, of which the most relevant for the present study are the following two ethnographies: Gayatri Reddy, *With Respect to Sex: Negotiating Hijra Identity in South India* (University of Chicago Press, Chicago 2005); Serena Nanda, *Neither Man nor Woman: The Hijras of India* (Wadsworth, New York 1990). Also, for a resourceful socio-historical analysis of *hijre* in the colonial time, see Shane Patrick Gannon, 'Translating the *Hijra*: The Symbolic Reconstruction of the British Empire in India', a PhD thesis submitted in Fall 2009, Department of Sociology, University of Alberta.

60. One of the popular androgynous forms of the Hindu god Śiva, for example, is Ardhanārīśvara, usually depicted as a half-male and half-female. The heroes of *Mahābhārata* and *Ramayana* occasionally change their sex/gender, and even marry a member of their own sex/gender (e.g. the Princess Sikhandni), which is why the contemporary Indian gender-variant and sexually diverse subjectivities sometimes locate their aetiological roots in these epics. Furthermore, the subjectivities from the ancient Hindu law books – such as *śandha*, *klība*, *pandaka* and *napumsaka* – are often associated with *hijre*. See, for example, Ruth Vanita & Saleem Kidwai (eds), *Same-Sex Love in India: Readings from Literature and History* (Palgrave, New York 2001 [2000]); Shane Gannon, 'Exclusion as Language and the Language of Exclusion: Tracing Regimes of Gender through Linguistic Representations of the "Eunuch"' (2011) 20(1) *Journal of the History of Sexuality* 1.

61. See *supra* n. 1.
62. A cursory inspection of historical resources reveals a number of Muslim dignitaries in the Indian subcontinent with the title of *khwajasara*, who were, *inter alia*, military leaders, architects, (Mughal) imperial advisors and poets. Some of the well-known *khwajasara* include: Jawahar Khan Khwajasara, Firoz Khan Khwajasara, I'timad Khan Khwajasara, I'tibar Khan Khwajasara, Abul Qasim Khwajasara, Khush Nazar 'Ali Khan Khwajasara, Yaqut Khan Khwajasara, Mehrban Agha Khwajasara, Shihab Khwajasara, Bakhtawar Khan Khwajasara, Miyan Almus 'Ali Khan Khwajasara, Agha Khan Khwajasara, Shamshir Singh Khan Khwajasara, Bashir Sultani Khwajasara, Arif 'Ali Khan Khwajasara, Mahbub 'Ali Khwajasara and Hidayatu'llah Khwajasara.
63. Not the Mughal imperial throne, though, but that of a sultanate. One such *khwajasara* was Sultan Shahzade, the ruler of Bengal, who assumed the title of Barbak Shah in 1487/892 CE/AH. See Gavin Hambly, 'A Note on the Trade in Eunuchs in Mughal Bengal' (1974) 94(1) *Journal of the American Oriental Society* 125, p. 127.
64. For the reasons of clarity, when referring to a place, the term 'zenana' is not italicised in this book; when referring to subjectivity, it is.
65. Syed Ahmed [Khan Bahadur], 'Legislation against Eunuchs', letter to John Strachey, 14 April 1870, quoted in Gannon, *supra* n. 59, p. 188.
66. *Ibid*. It is worth comparing this statement with that in Order of 14 July 2009 in Re Case 63/09 SC, p. 1, which intimates that 'the she-males are compelled to live an immoral life including offering themselves for dancing etc'.
67. Syed Ahmed Khan Bahadur, *c.* 1870 CE, quoted in Gannon, *supra* n. 59, p. 232.
68. Criminal Tribes Act 1871 (Act XXVII of 1871), Part 2, §24.
69. Gannon, *supra* n. 59, pp. 347–348 (emphasis in original).
70. As soon as the Criminal Tribes Act 1871 was passed, the Governor General of India clarified that it was his duty to 'take care that no persons came upon the register to whom the Act was not intended to apply. Domestic servants, for instance, in Muhammadan families of rank would not be registered'; the Governor General of India, 'Proceedings from November 1871 on the Criminal Tribes Act, 1871', quoted in Gannon, *supra* n. 59, p. 188.
71. *Ibid*, p. 155.
72. *Ibid*.
73. See Anuja Agrawal, 'Gendered Bodies: The Case of the "Third Gender" in India' (1997) 31 *Contributions to Indian Sociology* 273, p. 282. The colonial censuses generally tended to construe *hijre* as a caste, composed of both male and female members.
74. Gannon, *supra* n. 59, p. 358.
75. *Ibid*, p. 278. The connection between the Punjabi *mukhannas* and the Arabic *mukhannath* ('male-born effeminate') is all too obvious. The latter represents an elusive subjectivity from the Prophet Muhammad time's Medina, mentioned, *inter alia*, in the *hadith* literature. See generally Everett K. Rowson, 'The

Effeminates of Early Medina' (1991) 111(4) *Journal of the American Oriental Society* 671.

76. An anonymous *hijra*, Lahore, 1910 CE; quoted in D.C.J Ibbetson, M.E. MacLagen & H.A. Rose, *A Glossary of the Tribes of and Castes of the Punjab and North-West Frontier Province* (Civil and Military Gazette, Lahore 1911), Vol. 2, p. 331.

77. Morris E. Opler, 'The Hijarā (Hermaphrodites) of India and Indian National Character: A Rejoinder' (1960) 62 *American Anthropologist* 505.

78. James M. Freeman, 'Transvestites and Prostitutes, 1969–72' in James M. Freeman, *Untouchable: An Indian Life History* (Stanford University Press, Stanford 1979); Laurence W. Preston, 'A Right to Exist: Eunuchs and the State in Nineteenth-Century India' (1987) 21(2) *Modern Asian Studies* 371.

79. George Morrison Carstairs, 'Hinjra and Jiryan: Two Derivatives of Hindu Attitudes to Sexuality' (1956) 29 *British Journal of Medical Psychology* 128.

80. *Ibid.*

81. Malavika Sanghvi, 'Walking the Wild Side', *Illustrated Weekly of India*, 11 March 1984, pp. 25–28.

82. I. Bhooshana Rao, 'Male Homosexual Transvestism: A Social Menace' (1955) 52 *Antiseptic* 519.

83. A.P. Sinha, 'Procreation among the Eunuchs' (1967) 20(2) *Eastern Anthropologist* 168.

84. *Ibid.*

85. George Morrison Carstairs, *The Twice Born: A Study of a Community of High Caste Hindus* (Hogarth Press, London 1957).

86. K. Lakshmi Raghuramaiah, *Night Birds: Indian Prostitutes from Devadasis to Call Girls* (Chanakya, New Delhi 1991).

87. Satish Kumar Sharma, *Hijras: The Labelled Deviants* (Gian, New Delhi 1989).

88. A.M. Shah, 'A Note on the Hijadas of Gujarat' (1961) 63(6) *American Anthropologist* 1325, p 1329. See also Nanda, *supra* n. 59.

89. Sekh Rahim Mondal, 'The Eunuchs: Some Observations' (1989) 24 *Journal of Indian Anthropology and Sociology* 244. I am indebted to Kira Hall's excellent chapter for pointing out to some of the above mentioned descriptions of *hijre* in the post-1950s CE (mainly anthropological) scholarship; Kira Hall, '"Go Suck Your Husband's Sugarcane!": Hijras and the Use of Sexual Insult' in Anna Livia & Kira Hall (eds), *Queerly Phrased: Language, Lender, and Sexuality* (Oxford University Press, New York 1997), pp. 430–460.

90. Nanda, *supra* n. 59; Serena Nanda, 'Hijras: An Alternative Sex and Gender Role in India' in Gilbert Herdt (ed.), *Third Sex, Third Gender: Beyond Dimorphism in Culture and History* (Zone Books, New York), pp. 373–417.

91. Vinay Lal, 'Not This, Not That: The Hijras of India and the Culture Politics of Sexuality' (1999) 61 *Social Text* 119, pp. 130–131. For an alternative critique of the 'third gender' and 'third sex' approaches, see Reddy, *supra* n. 59, pp. 30–34.

92. Pamment, *supra* n. 34, p. 48.

93. My interview with Professor Claire Pamment, Beaconhouse National University, Lahore, 26 September 2011.

94. My interview with Bindiya Rana, Lahore, 30 September 2011.

95. 'In Mughal times, *khwajasara* used to serve at the imperial courts, to educate people, to give them good manners, to teach them how to be well-behaved. That used to be their job. [...] Back in the day, only *khwajasara* knew what it meant to have good manners. They used to teach people how to greet others, how to invite them over, how to speak to them. Unfortunately, nowadays, *khwajasara* are ill mannered. They can barely help themselves, let alone teach the others'; my interview with Saima, the head of a low-class *khwajasara* household (*dera*), Lahore, 30 September 2011.

96. My interview with Bindiya Rana, Lahore, 30 September 2011.

97. Based on the individual and group interviews I had with Bindiya Rana, Chalu, Chandhi, Gangha, Hashu, Jala, Jelek, Kajol, Nariman, Neeli and Saima. *Khwajasara* names usually do not include a surname. Most of these individuals are, however, *also* known by *other* names in non-*khwajasara* social environments.

98. As Kajol confidently avered: 'There is no much difference between the Pakistani and the Indian *khwajasara*'.

99. The majority of the Indian *hijre* consider the Hindu goddess Bahuchara Mata (or Bedhraj Mata) as their patroness and the 'first *hijra*'; see, for example, Reddy, *supra* n. 59, pp. 2, 57, 90, 97–98, 100, 108 & 113.

100. Madayantī is mentioned in *Mahābhārata* as the name of the beautiful wife of King Saudasa, and, also, as the name of the favourite wife of King Mitrasaha; see *Mahābhārata*, 1.122.6555, 1.122.6556, 12.233.14490, 13.137.11354, 14.57.2592, 14.58.2611, 14.58.2623 & 14.58.2648. However, in this epic, no gender-variant characteristics had been attributed to either of those women. In *Kāmasūtra*, 2.42, *madayantī* is the term used for the Arabian jasmine (Latin: *jasminum sambac*; other Sanskrit names: *malati, mallika*), which *reverses* the effect of the following recommended beauty regime: 'Take the sweat from the testicles of a white horse and dilute in seven volumes of yellow arsenic (*alakta*). Applied to white lips, this mixture makes them become red'; *Kāmasūtra*, 2.41. Besides, in *Pādatāditaka,* a classical Sanskrit *bhana* (the literary sub-genre of short comical-dramatical essays), the character Madayantī is 'the chowrie-bearer of Gangā and Yamuna, the reciter of scriptures'; *Pādatāditaka*, 1.214. I could, therefore, establish no viable connection between this data and the Punjabi *khwajasara* originative narrative.

101. This is how Kajol and Neeli, among others, would pronounce her name.

102. My interview with Kajol, Lahore, 26 September 2011.

103. Kajol told me: 'There is a *guru*; her name is Jiju. She often goes to India. She has told us this story'.

104. Other versions of the story that I have heard are more detailed, but the central plot remains the same.

105. For a candid description of *nirban* amongst the group of Pakistani *zenana*, see Tahir Khilji, 'The World of Zenanas' (2008) 3 *In Plainspeak* 13.
106. They are *all* part of various *khwajasara* collectives. For some, though, their '*zenana*-hood' is *also* an important part of their selfhood, to the effect that any distinction between those two subjectivities is effectively blurred. This may be an idiosyncratic element of *khwajasara/zenana* gender-variance in Punjab, since, for example, in southern India, the boundaries between the *hijra* and *zenana* subject positions appear to be more solid; see generally Reddy, *supra* n. 59. Note that in this part of the present chapter I interrogate only the *khwajasara/hijra/zenana* tropes; some *other* forms of gender-variance in Punjab/ Pakistan are discussed later on.
107. Saima told me: 'I knew from my childhood that this was inside of me [...]. Other kinds around me, of my age or older, used to tease me because of how I was [...]. I am *khwajasara* by birth'. Kajol elaborated: 'If certain matters in the mother's womb are mixed in a particular way, there comes a girl; with some other mixtures, a boy comes out. And with another special mixture, in which a spirit is involved, *khwajasara* emerges'.
108. Said Kajol: 'When I was six, my sister used to dress me up as a girl and I used to feel very, very well that way'. Chalu added: 'When I was a kid, people in the neighbourhood used to make fun of me. They used to call me *zenana*. I've found acceptance from *khwajasara*; not so much from anyone else'.
109. Jelek's story is as follows: 'I entered a *khwajasara* household when I was eleven. I went to a *mela* [a local festival; plural: *mailay*]. At *mailay*, there are always many *khwajasara*, who go there and dance. I used to dance with them. Eventually, they enticed me to go and live with them. So I did. Through them, I got in touch with my *guru*. My family is rather open-minded, so when I was young they already knew I was *khwajasara*. They also knew I was a good dancer'.
110. Saima explained: 'When I was a kid, I'd see all these *khwajasara* being invited by other people to their homes when child was born, to give blessings. And, if a baby happened to be a *khusra*, they would take it away. They wouldn't let the baby stay in the house'. Curiously, she has not been taken away, despite being a *khusra* herself.
111. Bindiya Rana informed me that some of these *bare-bare guru* are between 105 and 120 years of age. 'One of the responsibilities of the big *guru* would be, if somebody dies, to go and sit at their grave for ten days', she said. 'Or, when it's somebody's birthday, to go and celebrate it for many, many days with that person'.
112. 'Sex work' and 'sex worker' are precisely the terms used in the Khwajasara Farsi language in Lahore, having the same meaning as their English cognates.
113. 'I used to dance at the festival some four years ago', said Gangha. 'I fell in love with a boy there, in Gujranwala, but my affection was unrequited. I used to love him more than he used to love me. Look, I even carved his name into my arm!' Hashu's love story is different. 'My lover used to keep me away all the time. But now that I am *nirban*, we went to a Sufi shrine [*dergah*] and he made

promises there that he will stay with me'. Nariman used to be married to an
Arab businessman in Dubai. 'He knew that I was *khwajasara*', she told me.
'But my in-laws didn't know that'.

114. Cf. the excellent study of sex workers in Sonagachi, a red-light district in
Kolkata, and in Tirupati, a temple-town in southern India; Prabha
Kotiswaran, *Dangerous Sex, Invisible Labor: Sex Work and the Law in India*
(Princeton University Press, Princeton 2011). For an ethnography of Lahore's
Heera Mandi, see Brown, *supra* n. 10.

115. The Christian missionary work in the early twentieth century CE Punjab was
particularly intense among the caste of 'untouchables' (*churha*; 'sweepers').
'During Partition in 1947, the Christian sweepers of Lahore stayed on to
become part of the new Muslim state of Pakistan'; *ibid*, p. 78. Many
khwajasara Christians hail from the *churha* caste.

116. The Persian term *pir* signifies a 'wise old person' and is used interchangeably to
describe both ancient and living Sufi masters and teachers, as well as wise
(Muslim) elders more generally.

117. *Zikr* ('remembrance') is a Muslim meditative act, practiced mainly amongst
the Sufis, typically involving the recitation of the Names of God, and of
supplications taken from Qur'anic verses and other devotional literature.

118. In Sufi cosmology, the term *murid* denotes a disciple of a Sufi teacher. For
khwajasara, however, *murid* is a spirit, sent onto them directly by God or
through a *pir*'s intercession, which *makes* them *who they are*.

119. The Muslim prayer practice, usually performed five times a day, in mosque or
elsewhere.

120. 'Only in the community with others', said Saima, 'one can hope to earn respect
in this life and also in the afterlife'.

121. A congregational *salat* that Muslims hold every Friday, just after noon. Most
Sunni Muslim men in Pakistan perform the *jum'ua* together, in a mosque or in
its inner courtyard.

122. *Hafiz* (masc. sing.) or *hafiza* (fem. sing.), in the contemporary Muslim
contexts, is an honorific for someone who has completely memorised the
Qur'an.

123. In post-colonial India, they were allowed to vote as 'women' in 1994 CE; see
Gannon, *supra* n. 59, pp. 7–8. In 1952 and 1977 CE, *hijre* were allowed to run
for local political office as 'women' in India; see Hall, *supra* n. 89, p. 431.

124. See Pamment, *supra* n. 34, pp. 41–42. See also Nauman Naqvi & Hasan
Mujtaba, 'Two Balochi *Buggas*, a Sindhi *Zenana*, and the Status of *Hijras* in
Contemporary Pakistan' in Stephen O. Murray & Will Roscoe, *Islamic
Homosexualities: Culture, History, and Literature* (New York University Press,
New York 1997), p. 266.

125. Pamment, *supra* n. 34, p. 41.

126. *Ibid*, p. 42.

127. In this section, I rely primarily on my recorded conversations with Adeel,
Ayesha, Fauzia, Jamila, Nawaz and Waheed (some real names; some

pseudonyms; each of them self-identify as Muslims), who are all members of various underground sexually diverse collectives, from the loose spirituality/sociality-based working-class networks to the middle-class support groups and activist organisations.

128. Waheed dubbed the HIV/AIDS prevention networks the 'HIV industry' and recalled a moment when one of its local male representatives proposed at a Baluchistan-based strategic planning session: 'Let's assemble a group of *hijre* and call it a CBO!'

129. 'Major Objectives of MQI', *Minhaj-ul-Qur'an International*, official website, available at http://www.minhaj.org/-english/tid/1799/Minhaj-ul-Quran-International.html (accessed 29 August 2014) (emphasis added).

130. My interview with Adeel, Lahore, 30 September 2011.

131. This parallel with the Protestant Reformation and the Catholic Revival (or the Counter-Reformation) is, indeed, salient in the present case. Not only did Akbar's reforms occur just a few decades after Martin Luther famously posted *The Ninety-Five Theses* on the door of the Castle Church in Wittenberg, but their contents, and the reactions thereupon, were of a comparable nature. A comprehensive comparative analysis of these phenomena is, however, outside the purview of this book.

132. My interview with Adeel, Lahore, 30 September 2011.

133. Adeel told me: 'There are periods of retreat in mosque, which are called *i'tiqaf*. You go and sit in a mosque for, say, ten days, in seclusion. There are curtains around you. I've met one of my boyfriends there. He was in the curtained area right next to me. When, after ten days, we came out of the mosque, our relationship grew more and more and we became sexually intimate as well. So, things like that can also start in mosque'.

134. *Niyana* (pl. *niyanay*) means 'woman' in Khwajasara Farsi and 'young child' in Punjabi. Obviously, in the present case, it denotes a woman.

135. My interview with Fauzia, Lahore, 6 October 2011.

136. See *Naz Foundation v Government of NCT of Delhi & Others*, 2009 (160) DLT 277. As noted earlier in this book, on 11 December 2013 CE, the Supreme Court of India's two-member bench (Justices G.S. Singhvi and S.J. Mukhopadhaya) overturned the decision of the High Court of Delhi as 'constitutionally unsustainable', reportedly due to Parliament's sole prerogative to change a law, which cannot be assumed by courts.

137. Fauzia elaborated: 'You can talk, as a group, of Asians trying to share an Asian identity while acknowledging that you are *a diversity of people* over a humongous landmass, and not even one landmass. You can acknowledge that the Asian ethea are *different* from the European ones. And, broadly speaking, that is correct. But, there is *also* an East Asian ethos that is *different* from South Asian and that is just as correct. And, they are not *subsets*. It doesn't work like that'.

138. My interview with Jamila, Lahore, 6 October 2011.

139. Guy Debord, *The Society of the Spectacle* (trans. Donald Nicholson-Smith; Zone Books, Cambridge 1994), available at http://www.cddc.vt.edu/sionline/si/ts ots01.html (accessed 31 August 2014).

140. See generally Hadi Hussain, 'US Embassy's Pride Celebrations in Islamabad: More Damage than Support', *Gaylaxy*, 24 August 2011, available at http://www.gaylaxymag.com/blog/index.php/2011/08/us-embassys-pride-celebrati ons-in-islamabad-more-damage-than-support/ (accessed 31 August 2014).

141. Hamzić, *supra* n. 13, p. 156.

142. The Act removed, *inter alia*, the offence of rape (*zina-bil-jabr* or '*zina* by force') from the Ordinance and made it prosecutable, instead, under the Penal Code 1860. It also made the offence of *zina* inconvertible to *zina-bil-jabr*, and *vice versa*. Prior to this reform, under the Offence of Zina (Enforcement of Hudood) Ordinance 1979, a woman alleging rape could end up being charged with *zina* herself. See generally *ibid*, pp. 155–179.

143. I.e. non-interventionalist, non-spectacular.

144. For a seminal work on class-consciousness, see Georg Lukács, *Geschichte und Klassenbewußtsein: Studien über marxistische Dialektik* (Malik-Verlag, Berlin 1923).

145. For an example of a failed foreign missionary project, angrily pointed out to me by one of my interlocutors who had been directly involved in it, see Babar Mirza, 'Discontents of ICJ Mission', *Dawn*, 29 September 2011, available at http://dawn.com/2011/09/29/discontents-of-icj-mission/ (accessed 1 August 2014).

146. The OIC international political strategies are discussed in Chapter 3 of this book, including with a reference to Pakistan's representatives to this theopolitical bloc. The OIC official views can be studied at http://www.oic-oci. org/ (accessed 1 August 2014).

147. The Yogyakarta Principles are available at http://www.yogyakartaprinciples. org (accessed 1 August 2014). They are discussed in Chapter 3 of this book.

148. The 1979 Convention on the Elimination of All Forms of Discrimination against Women (CEDAW), 1249 UNTS 13, entered into force 3 September 1981.

149. For an excellent study of this issue, see Sundhya Pahuja, *Decolonising International Law: Development, Economic Growth and the Politics of Universality* (Cambridge Studies in International and Comparative Law Series, Cambridge University Press, Cambridge 2011).

150. I refer, of course, to the critical scholarship produced under the banner of the Third World Approaches to International Law (TWAIL) stream. For an introductory article, see Antony Anghie & B.S. Chimni, 'Third World Approaches to International Law and Individual Responsibility in Internal Conflicts' (2003) 2(1) *Chinese Journal of International Law* 77.

151. To paraphrase Georg Wilhelm Friedrich Hegel's well-known concept. Hegel describes a sophisticated primeval type of law as 'the law of every heart [...] for this means nothing else than that individuality becomes an object to itself in the form of [relational] universality'; Georg Wilhelm Friedrich Hegel, *Phenomenology of Spirit* (Clarendon Press, Oxford 1977 [1807]), pp. 224–225.

152. Wael B. Hallaq, *Shari'a: Theory, Practice, Transformations* (Cambridge University Press, Cambridge 2009), p. 547.
153. Cf. Walter Benjamin, 'The Storyteller' in Walter Benjamin, *Illuminations* (Cape, London 1970), p. 75.

Conclusion

1. Cf. Julie F. Codell (ed.), *Imperial Co-Histories: National Identities and the British and Colonial Press* (Fairleigh Dickinson University Press, Madison 2013).
2. 'Vernacularization as an idea originally sought to explain how national languages developed and challenged in nineteenth century Europe, as elites moved from Latin to colloquian Castilian or everyday Danish'; Richard Ashby Wilson, 'Tyrannosaurus Lex: The Anthropology of Human Rights and Transnational Law' in Mark Goodale & Sally Engle Merry (eds), *The Practice of Human Rights: Tracking Law between the Global and the Local* (Cambridge University Press, Cambridge 2007), p. 357.
3. Sally Engle Merry, 'Transnational Human Rights and Local Activism: Mapping the Middle' (2006) 108(1) *American Anthropologist* 38, p. 39.
4. *Ibid*, p. 44.
5. Wilson, *supra* n. 2, p. 357.
6. Merry, *supra* n. 3, p. 39.
7. *Ibid*, p. 41.
8. Merry suggests, apropos, that '[t]ranslators can produce a dramatic shift in subjectivity, analogous to conversion'; *ibid*, p. 43.
9. *Ibid*, p. 42.
10. *Ibid*, p. 39.
11. Mark Goodale, 'Locating Rights, Envisioning Law between the Global and the Local' in Mark Goodale & Sally Engle Merry (eds), *The Practice of Human Rights: Tracking Law between the Global and the Local* (Cambridge University Press, Cambridge 2007), p. 30.
12. *Ibid*.
13. Sara Ahmed, *The Promise of Happiness* (Duke University Press, Durham 2010).
14. *Ibid*, p. 13.
15. *Ibid*.
16. *Ibid*, p. 218.
17. *Ibid*, p. 168.
18. Lila Abu-Lughod, 'The Active Social Life of "Muslim Women's Rights"' in Dorothy L. Hodgson (ed.), *Gender and Culture at the Limit of Rights* (University of Pennsylvania Press, Philadelphia 2011), p. 118.
19. *Ibid*.

BIBLIOGRAPHY

International Human Rights Instruments

African [Banjul] Charter on Human and Peoples' Rights, adopted on 27 June 1981, OAU Doc CAB/LEG/67/3 rev 5, 21 ILM 58 (1982), entered into force on 21 October 1986

American Convention on Human Rights, OAS Treaty Series No. 36, 1144 UNTS 123, entered into force on 18 July 1978

Arab Charter of Human rights, adopted by League of Arab States, September 1994

Cairo Declaration on Human Rights in Islam, adopted by the 19[th]Islamic Conference of Foreign Ministers, July/August 1990

Charter of Fundamental Rights of the European Union, not yet in force, 'solemnly proclaimed' on 7 December 2000 and adapted on 12 December 2007

Charter on Sexual and Reproductive Rights, the International Planned Parenthood Federation, 1995

Convention on the Elimination of All Forms of Discrimination against Women, UN General Assembly Res 34/180, 34 UN GAOR Supp (No. 46), p. 193 (1979), UN Doc A/34/46, entered into force on 3 September 1981

Convention for the Protection of Human Rights and Fundamental Freedoms[European Convention on Human Rights], ETS 5, 4 November 1950, entered into force on 3 September 1953

Convention on the Rights of the Child, UN General Assembly Res 44/25, Annex, 44 UN GAOR Supp (No. 49), p. 167, UN Doc A/44/49 (1989), entered into force on 2 September 1990

Declaration on the Elimination of All Forms of Intolerance and of Discrimination Based on Religion or Belief, AG/RES 36/55 of 25 November 1981, 36 UN GAOR Supp (No. 51), p. 171, UN Doc A/36/684 (1981)

Inter-American Convention against All Forms of Discrimination and Intolerance, adopted by the General Assembly of the Organisation of American States on 5 June 2013, not yet in force

International Convention on the Elimination of All Forms of Racial Discrimination, UN General Assembly Res 2106 (XX), Annex, 20 UN GAOR Supp (No. 14), p. 47, UN Doc A/6014 (1966), 660 UNTS 195, entered into force on 4 January 1969

International Covenant on Civil and Political Rights (ICCPR), UN General Assembly Res 2200A (XXI), 21 UN GAOR Supp (No. 16), p. 52, UN Doc A/6316 (1966), 993 UNTS 3, entered into force on 23 March 1976

International Covenant on Economic, Social and Cultural Rights (ICESCR), UN General Assembly Res 2200A (XXI), 21 UN GAOR Supp (No 16), p 49, UN Doc A/6316 (1966), 993 UNTS 3, entered into force on 3 January 1976

Principles and Best Practices on the Protection of Persons Deprived of Liberty in the Americas, adopted by the Inter-American Commission on Human Rights during its 131st regular period of sessions, 3-14 March 2008, available at www.cidh.org (accessed in 2 August 2014)

Resolution 17/19 on Human Rights, Sexual Orientation and Gender Identity, UN Doc A/HRC/RES/17/19, adopted at the 34thSession of the UN Human Rights Council in Geneva, 17 June 2011

Resolution on Human Rights, Sexual Orientation and Gender Identity, General Assembly of the Organisation of American States, AG/RES 2435 (XXXVIII-O/08), adopted at the 4th plenary session, Medellin, Colombia, 3 June 2008

Resolution on Human Rights, Sexual Orientation and Gender Identity, General Assembly of the Organisation of American States, AG/RES 2504 (XXXIX-O/09), adopted at the 4th plenary session, San Pedro Sula, Honduras, 4 June 2009

Resolution on Human Rights, Sexual Orientation and Gender Identity, General Assembly of the Organisation of American States, 4 June 2009, GA Res 2435 (XXXVIII-O/08)

Resolution on Human Rights, Sexual Orientation and Gender Identity, General Assembly of the Organisation of American States, 4 June 2009, GA Res 2504 (XXXIX-O/09)

Rome Statute of the International Criminal Court, adopted on 17 July 1998, entered into force on 1 July 2002

Statement on Human Rights, Sexual Orientation and Gender Identity, on behalf of 66 States, under Agenda Item 64(b), UN General Assembly, 63rdsession, New York, 18 December 2008, UN Doc A/63/635

Tehran Declaration on the Role of Women in Islamic Societies, adopted by the Symposium of Experts on the Role of Women in the Development of Islamic Society, Organisation of Islamic Conference [Co-operation], April 1995

Universal Declaration of Human Rights, UN General Assembly Res 217A (III), UN Doc A/810 (1948)

Universal Islamic Declaration of Human Rights (UDIHR), adopted by the Islamic Council in Paris on 19 September 1981

Yogyakarta Principles on the Application of International Human Rights Law in relation to Sexual Orientation and Gender Identity, available at www.yogyakartaprinciples.org (accessed 31 July 2014)

Selected National Statutes

France

Code Napoléon [Code civil des français], 1804, 1810
Code penal, 1791

India

Indian Penal Code, 1860 [Act No. 45 of 1860 of the Legislative Council for India]

Pakistan

Constitution of Pakistan 1973
Criminal Law Amendment (Protection of Women) Act 2006
Execution and Punishment of Whipping Ordinance (IX/1979)
Muslim Family Laws Ordinance 1961
Offence against Property (Enforcement of Hudood) Ordinance 1979
Offence of Qazf (Enforcement of Hadd) Ordinance 1979
Offence of Zina (Enforcement of Hudood) Ordinance 1979
Penal Code 1860
Presidential Order I/1980
Prohibition (Enforcement of Hadd) Order 1979
Qanun-e-Shahadat Order 1984

Russian Federation

Закон Рязанской области о защите нравственности и здоровья детей в Рязанской области, Управление Внутренних Дел по Рязанской области, No. 41-ОЗ, 3 April 2006
Закон Санкт-Петербурга о внесении измененй в Закон Санкт-Петербурга об административных правонарушениях в Санкт-Петербурге, 7 March 2012

Turkey

Ottoman Penal Code 1858
Turkish Penal Code 1926
Turkish Penal Code 2004

United Kingdom

Act Concerning Ecclesiastical Appointments and Absolute Restraint of Annates; 25 Henry VIII c. 20 (1533)
Act Concerning Peter's Pence and Dispensations; 25 Henry VIII c. 21 (1533)
Act of Conditional Restraints of Annates; 23 Henry VIII c. 20 (1532)
Act for Consolidating and Amending the Statutes in England relative to Offences against the Person; 9 George IV c. 31 (1828)
Act for the Dissolution of the Greater Monasteries; 31 Henry VIII c. 13 (1539)
Act Extinguishing the Authority of the Bishop of Rome; 28 Henry VIII c. 10 (1536)
Act for the Punishment of the Vice of Buggery; 25 Henry VIII c. 6 (1533); made permanent by 32 Henry VIII c. 3 (1540)
Act for the Punishment of the Vice of Buggery; 5 Elizabeth I c. 17 (1563)
Act Restoring to the Crown the Ancient Jurisdiction over the State Ecclesiastical and Spiritual and Abolishing All Foreign Power Repugnant to the Same; 26 Henry VIII c. 1 (1534)
Act for the Suppression of the Lesser Monasteries; 27 Henry VIII c. 28 (1536)
Criminal Justice and Public Order Act, 1994, c. 33
Criminal Law Amendment Act, 1885 (*An Act to Make Further Provision for the Protection of Women and Girls, the Suppression of Brothels and Other Purposes*); 48-49 Victoria c. 69 (1885)

BIBLIOGRAPHY 289

Criminal Tribes Act, 1871 (Act **XXVII** of 1871)
Ecclesiastical Appeals Act (or the *Statute in Restraint of Appeals*); 24 Henry VIII c. 12 (1532);
Offences against the Person Act; 24 & 25 Victoria c. 100 (1861)
Sexual Offences Act, 1956, c. 60
Sexual Offences Act, 1967, c. 60
Sexual Offences Act, 2003, c. 42
Sexual Offences (Amendment) Act, 2000, c. 44
Succession to the Crown Act; 25 Henry VIII c. 22 (1533)
Succession to the Crown Act; 26 Henry VIII c. 2 (1534)
Succession to the Crown Act; 28 Henry VIII c. 7 (1536)
Treasons Act; 26 Henry VIII c. 13 (1534)

Cases

European Court of Human Rights

Ahmet Arslan et al Turkey, Application No. 41135/98, Judgment, 23 February 2010
Alexeyev v Russia, Applications Nos 4916/07, 25924/08 & 14599/09, Judgment, 21 October 2010
B v France, Application No. 13343/87, Judgment, 25 March 1992
Bayatyan v Armenia, Application No. 23459/03, Judgment, 7 July 2011
Bęczkowski et al v Poland, Application No. 1543/06, Judgment, 3 May 2007
Cossey v United Kingdom, Application No. 10843/84, Judgment, 27 September 1990
Dudgeon v United Kingdom, A 45 (1981); (1982) 4 EHRR 149
EB v France, Application No 43546/02, Judgment, 22 January 2008
Goodwin v United Kingdom, Application No. 28957/95, Judgment, 11 July 2002
Handyside v United Kingdom A 24 (1976); 1 EHRR 737
I v United Kingdom, Application No. 25680/94, Judgment, 11 July 2002
Karner v Austria, 2003-IX 199; (2003) 38 EHRR 24
Kokkinakis v Greece, Application No.14307/88, Judgment, 25 May 1993
L v Lithuania, Application No. 27527/03, Judgment, 11 September 2007
L and V v Austria, 2003-I 29; (2003) 36 EHRR 55
Lustig-Prean and Beckett v United Kingdom, (1999) 29 EHRR 548
Masaev v Moldova, Application No. 6303/05, Judgment, 12 August 2009
Modinos v Cyprus, A 259 (1993); (1993) 16 EHRR 485
Norris v Ireland, A 142 (1988); (1988) 13 EHRR 186
Rees v United Kingdom, Application No. 9532/81, Judgment, 17 October 1986
Salgueiro da Silva Mouta v Portugal, 1999-IX 309; (1999) 31 EHRR 1055
Schalk and Kopf v Austria, Application No. 30141/04, Judgment, 24 June 2010
SL v Austria, 2003-I 71; (2003) 37 EHRR 39
Smith and Grady v United Kingdom, 1999-VI 45; (1999) 29 EHRR 493
Sutherland v United Kingdom, Application No. 25186/94, report of 1 July 1997
Thlimmenos v Greece, Application No. 34369/97, Judgment, 6 April 2000
Van Kück v Germany, 2003-VII 1; (2003) 37 EHRR 51
Van Oosterwijck v Belgium, Application No. 7654/76, Judgment, 6 November 1980

Inter-American Commission on Human Rights

AIDS-Free World (on behalf of two petitioners) v *Jamaica*; submission of petition announced on 26 October 2011
Marta Lucía Álvarez Giraldo v *Colombia*, Case No 11.656, Report No. 71/99 (Admissibility), 4 May 1999

Inter-American Court for Human Rights

Advisory Opinion OC-18/03, *Juridical Condition and Rights of the Undocumented Migrants*, 17 September 2003, Series A No. 18
Atala Riffo y Niñas v *Chile*, Judgment, 24 February 2012

International Criminal Tribunal for the Former Yugoslavia

Prosecutor v *Kunarac* etal, Judgment, Case No. IT-96-23 (Trial Chamber, 22 February 2001), Judgment (Appeals Chamber, 12 June 2002)

United Nations Human Rights Committee

Toonen v *Australia*, (488/1992), CCPR/C/50/D/488/1992 (1994); 1-3 IHHR 97 (1994)
X v *Colombia*, (1361/2005), CCPR/C/89/D/1361/2005 (2007)
Young v *Australia*, (941/2000), CCPR/C/78/D/941/2000 (2003)

India

Naz Foundation v *Government of NCT of Delhi and Others*, 2009 (160) DLT 277

Pakistan

Abdul Waheed v *Asma Jehangir*, PLD 2004 SC 219
Alladad v *Mukhtar*, 1992 SCMR 1273
Constitutional Petitions 10/2011 SC & 18/2011 SC, Judgment, 4 March 2011
Federation of Pakistan v *Hazoor Bakhsh*, PLD 1983 FSC 255
Federation of Pakistan v *Munir Hussain Bhatti et al*, Judgment, 20 April 2011
Ghulam Mustafa Ansari v *Government of Punjab*, PLD 2004 SC 1903
Government of Baluchistan v *Azizullah Memon,* PLD 1993 SC 341
Hazoor Bakhsh v *Federation of Pakistan*, PLD 1981 FSC 145
Human Rights Constitutional Petition 63/2009 [Case 63/09] SC
    Order of 14 July 2009 in Re Case 63/09 SC
    Order of 17 August 2009 in Re Case 63/09 SC
    Order of 4 November 2009 in Re Case 63/09 [misreported as Case 43/09] SC
    Order of 20 November 2009 in Re Case 63/09 [misreported as Case 43/09] SC
    Order of 22 March 2011 in Re Case 63/09 [misreported as Case 43/09] SC
Malik Javed v *Abdul Kadir*, 1987 SCMR 518
Mobashir Hassan v *Federation of Pakistan*, PLD 2010 SC 265
Shirin Munir v *Government of Punjab*, PLD 1990 SC 295
Sindh High Court Bar Association v *Federation of Pakistan*, PLD 2009 SC 879

Books, Manuscripts, Chapters, Articles and Reports

Abraham, Ibrahim, '"Out to Get Us": Queer Muslims and the Clash of Sexual Civilisations in Australia', *Contemporary Islam* 3(2009), p. 79.

——, '"Everywhere You Turn You Have to Jump into Another Closet": Hegemony, Hybridity, and Queer Australian Muslims' in Samar Habib (ed.), *Islam and Homosexuality* (Praeger, Santa Barbara, 2010).

Abu Dawud Sulayman, al-Sijistani, *Kitab al-sunan* (Thesaurus Islamicus Foundation, Liechtenstein, 2000 [c.847-888]).

Abu-Lughod, Lila (ed.), *Remaking Women: Feminism and Modernity in the Middle East* (Princeton University Press, Princeton, 1998).

——, 'The Active Social Life of "Muslim Women's Rights"' in Dorothy L. Hodgson (ed.), *Gender and Culture at the Limit of Rights* (University of Pennsylvania Press, Philadelphia, 2011).

Abu-Odeh, Lama, 'Modernizing Muslim Family Law: The Case of Egypt', *Vanderbilt Journal of Transnational Law* 37(2004), p.1043.

AbuKhalil, As'ad, 'A Note on the Study of Homosexuality in the Arab/Islamic Civilization', *Arab Studies Journal* 32(1993), p. 48.

Agrawal, Anuja, 'Gendered Bodies: The Case of the "Third Gender" in India', *Contributions to Indian Sociology* 31 (1997), p.273

Ahmad, Ahmad Atif, *Structural Interrelations of Theory and Practice in Islamic Law: A Study of Six Works of Medieval Islamic Jurisprudence* (Brill, Leiden, 2006).

Ahmed, Leila, *Women and Gender in Islam: Historical Roots of a Modern Debate* (Yale University Press, New Haven, 1992).

Ahmed, Sara, *Queer Phenomenology: Orientations, Objects, Others* (Duke University Press, Durham, 2006).

——, *The Promise of Happiness* (Duke University Press, Durham, 2010).

Akeel, Maha, 'First Session of IPHRC: OIC Human Rights Body Identifies Women's Rights, Education, Development and Research as Priority', *OIC Journal* 20 (2012), pp. 28–29, available at http://www.oic-oci.org/journal.asp (accessed 30 April 2014).

Akram, Zamir, 'Letter to HE Ms Laura Dupuy Lasserre, President of the Human Rights Council, from Zamir Akram, Ambassador and Permanent Representative of the Permanent Mission of Pakistan to the United Nations and Other International Organisations', Geneva, 14 February 2012, available at http://blog.unwatch.org/index.php/2012/02/17/letter-from-uns-islamic-group-to-unhrc-president-opposing-panel-on-violence-against-gays/#more-1760 (accessed 30 April 2014)

al-Asimi, 'Abd al-Rahman ibn Qasim (ed.), *Majmu' fatawa shaykh al-islam Ahmad ibn Taymiyya* (Matabi' al-Riyad, Riyadh, 1962 [c.1320]).

al-Bukhari, Muhammad ibn Isma'il, *al-Jami' al-sahih* (Thesaurus Islamicus Foundation, Liechtenstein, 2000 [c.842-869]).

al-Buti, Muhammad Sa'id Ramadan, *Dawabit al-maslaha fi al-shari'a al-islamiyya* (al-Maktaba al-umawiyya, Damascus, 1966).

al-Fadli, 'Abd al-Hadi, *Introduction to Hadith*, translated by Nazmina Virjee (ICAS Press, London, 2002).

al-Farabi, Abu Nasr, *as-Siyasa al-madaniya al-mulaqqab bi-mabadi' al-mawjudat*, (ed.) F. Najjar (Imprimerie Catholique, Beirut, 1964).

————, *Mabadi' ara' ahl al-madinat al-fadilah* / *On the Perfect State*, translated by/ (ed.) Richard Walzer (Kazi Publications, Chicago, 1998).

al-Farghani, Siraj al-Din 'Ali ibn 'Uthman Ushi, *Al-Fatawa al-sirajiyya* (Calcutta, 1827 [*c.*1190]).

al-Harawi, 'Ali ibn Sultan al-Qari', *al-Masnu' fi ma'rifat al-hadith al-mawdu'*, (ed.) 'Abd al-Fattah Abu Ghudda (2ⁿᵈ edn; Mu'assasat al-risala, Beirut, 1978 [*c.*1598]).

————, *Fath bab al-'inayah bi-sharh al-niqayah*, (eds)M.N. Tamim and H.N. Tamim (Beirut, 1997 [*c.*1601]), Vol. 3.

al-Isfahani, Adib al-Raghib, *Muhadarat al-udaba' wa muhawarat al-shu'ara' wa al-bulagha'*, (ed.) 'Umar Taba' (Dar al-arqam bin abi arqam, Beirut, 1999 [*c.*982]).

al-Jabri, Mohammed Abed, *Democracy, Human Rights and Law in Islamic Thought* (I.B.Tauris, London, 2009).

al-Jazari, Muhammad, *Ghayat al-nihaya fi tabaqat al-qura'* (G. Bergstäßer, Cairo, 1932), Vol. 1.

al-Kasani, 'Ala' al-Din Abu Bakr ibn Mas'ud, *Bada'i' al-sana'i' fi tartib al-shara'i'* (Al-Matba'a al-jamaliyya, Cairo, 1910 [*c.*1180]), 7 Vols.

al-Maqrizi, Taqi al-Din, *Mukhtasar al-kamil fi al-du'afa wa 'ilal al-hadith by Ibn 'Adi* (Dar al-jil, Beirut, 2001).

al-Marghinani, Burhan al-Din 'Ali ibn Abi Bakr ibn 'Abd al-Jalil, *Bidayat al-mubtadi* (Maktabat wa-matba'at Muhammad 'Ali Subh, Cairo, 1969 [*c.*1188]).

————, *al-Hidaya sharh al-bidaya* (Mustafa al-Babi al-Halabi, Cairo, 1975 [*c.*1138]), 2 Vols.

al-Ramli, Shams al-Din Muhammad, *Nihayat al-muhtaj bi-sharh al-minhaj* (Cairo, 1969 [*c.*1590]) Vol. 8.

al-Samarqandi, 'Ala al-Din Muhammad ibn Ahmad, *Tuhfat al-fuqaha'* (Dar al-kutub al-'ilmiyya, Beirut, 1984 [*c.*1140]).

al-Sarakhsi, Muhammad ibn Ahmad, *Le grand livre de la conduite de l'état* [*Sharh al-siyar al-kabir*], translated by Muhammed Hamidullah (Türkiye Diyanet Vakfı, Ankara, 1989 [*c.*1070]).

————, *al-Kitab al-mabsut* (Dar al-ma'rifa, Beirut, 1993 [*c.*1080]), 9 Vols.

al-Sayyad, Ayisha A, '"You're What?": Engaging Narratives from Diasporic Muslim Women on Identity and Gay Liberation' in Samar Habib (ed.), *Islam and Homosexuality* (Praeger, Santa Barbara, 2010).

al-Shirazi, Abu Ishaq Ibrahim ibn 'Ali ibn Yusuf al-Firuzabadi, *al-Muhadhdhab fi fiqh al-imam al-Shafi'i* (Dar al-fikr, Beirut, 1980 [*c.*1080]), Vol. 2.

al-Subki, Taj al-Din 'Abd al-Wahhab ibn 'Abd Allah, *Kitab mu'id al-ni'am wa-mubid al-niqam*, (ed.)David W. Myhrman (London, 1906 [*c.*1360])

al-Sughdi, Abu'l-Hasan 'Ali, *al-Fatawa* (2ⁿᵈ edn; Dar al-furqan, Amman 1984 [*c.*1065]), Vol. 2.

al-Zurqani, 'Abd al-Baqi, *Sharh mukhtasar Khalil* (Cairo 1890 [*c.*1680]), Vol. 7.

Ali, Kecia, *Sexual Ethics & Islam: Feminist Reflections on Qur'an, Hadith, and Jurisprudence* (Oneworld Publications, Oxford, 2007).

Altman, Dennis, 'Rupture or Continuity?: The Internationalization of Gay Identities', *Social Text* 48 (1996), p. 77.

————, *Global Sex* (Allen and Unwin, Crows Nest, 2001).

Amer, Sahar, *Crossing Borders: Love Between Women in Medieval French and Arabic Literatures* (University of Pennsylvania Press, Philadelphia 2008).

————, 'Medieval Arab Lesbians and Lesbian-Like Women', *Journal of the History of Sexuality* 18/2 (2009), p. 215.

American Psychological Association, *Resolution on Appropriate Affirmative Responses to Sexual Orientation Distress and Change Efforts* (2008), available at www.apa.org/about/governance/council/policy/sexual-orientation.aspx (accessed 14 January 2010).

Amit, Vered (ed.), *Constructing the Field, Ethnographic Fieldwork in the Contemporary World* (Routledge, London, 2000).

Amitai, Reuven and Amalia Levanoni (eds), *The Mamluk Sultanate in Egypt and Syria: Aspects of a Medieval Muslim State* (Ashgate, Surrey [*forthcoming*]).

Andrews, Walter G. and Mehmet Kalpaklı, *The Age of Beloveds: Love and the Beloved in Early-Modern Ottoman and European Culture and Society* (Duke University Press, Durham, 2005).

An-Na'im, Abdullahi Ahmed, *Toward an Islamic Reformation: Civil Liberties, Human Rights, and International Law* (Syracuse University Press, Syracuse 1990).

———— (ed.), *Human Rights in Cross-Cultural Perspectives: A Quest for Consensus* (University of Pennsylvania Press, Philadelphia, 1992).

————, *Islam and the Secular State: Negotiating the Future of Shari'a* (Harvard University Press, Cambridge, 2008).

Anghie, Antony, *Imperialism, Sovereignty and the Making of International Law* (Cambridge University Press, Cambridge, 2004).

Anghie, Antony and B.S. Chimni, 'Third World Approaches to International Law and Individual Responsibility in Internal Conflicts', *Chinese Journal of International Law* 2/1 (2003) p. 77.

Anvari, Awhad al-Din Muhammad ibn Muhammad, *Diwan* (Bungah-i Tarjama u Nashr-i Kitab, Tehran, 1959-1961 [*c.*1180]).

Appadurai, Arjun, *Modernity at Large: Cultural Dimensions of Globalization* (University of Minneapolis Press, Minneapolis, 1996).

Appiah, K. Anthony, 'Identity, Authenticity, Survival: Multicultural Societies and Social Reproduction' in Amy Guttmann (ed.), *Multiculturalism: Examining the Politics of Recognition* (Princeton University Press, Princeton, 1994).

ARC International, *UN General Assembly Joint Statement on Sexual Orientation & Gender Identity: Building on the Past, Looking to the Future* (ARC International, Geneva 2009).

————, 'UN Human Rights Council: Landmark Report and Panel on Sexual Orientation and Gender Identity', ARC International, Press Release, 7 March 2012, available at http://arc-international.net/global-advocacy/human-rights-council/hrc19/press-release (accessed 24 April 2014).

Arendt, Hannah, *The Origins of Totalitarianism* (Harcourt Brace & Co, San Diego, 1979 [1951]).

Asad, Talal, *The Idea of an Anthropology of Islam* (Georgetown University Center for Contemporary Arab Studies, Washington, 1996 [1986]).

Augustine of Hippo, *De civitate Dei*, translated by R.W. Dyson (Cambridge University Press, Cambridge, 1998).

Aull Davies, Charlotte, *Reflexive Ethnographies: A Guide to Researching Selves and Others* (Routledge, London, 2002 [1999]).

Ayalon, David, 'Mamlukiyat', *Jerusalem Studies in Arabic and Islam* 2(1980 [1950]), p. 321.

————, *Eunuchs, Caliphs and Sultans: A Study in Power Relationships* (Magnes Press, Tel Aviv, 1999).

Azikiwe, Abayomi, 'Non-Aligned Movement Calls for "New Economic Order"', *WorkersWorld*, 27 July 2009, available at http://www.workers.org/2009/world/nonaligned_0730/ (accessed 8 April 2014).

Bacchetta, Paola, 'Rescaling Transnational "Queerdom": Lesbian and "Lesbian" Identitary-Positionalities in Delhi in the 1980s', *Antipode: A Radical Journal of Geography* 34 (2002), p. 947.

Baderin, Mashood A, *International Human Rights Law and Islamic Law* (Oxford University Press, Oxford, 2003).

Badr, Hamza 'Abd al-Aziz & Daniel Crecelius, 'The *Awqaf* of al-Hajj Bashir Agha in Cairo', *Annales islamologiques* 27 (1993), p. 291.

————, 'The Wealth and Influence of an Exiled Ottoman Eunuch in Egypt: The *Waqf* Inventory of Abbas Agha', *Journal of the Economic and Social History of the Orient* 37/4 (1994), p. 293.

Bailey, Derrick Sherwin, *Homosexuality and the Western Christian Tradition* (Longmans/Green, London, 1955).

Baldwin, John, *The Language of Sex* (University of Chicago Press, Chicago 1994).

Barlas, Asma, *'Believing Women' in Islam: Unreading Patriarchal Interpretations of the Qur'an* (University of Texas Press, Austin, 2002).

Barlow, Frank, *William Rufus* (University of California Press, Berkeley, 1983).

Barrett, Michele and Anne Phillips (eds), *Destabilizing Theory: Contemporary Feminist Debates* (Polity Press, Cambridge, 1992).

Bauden, Frédéric, 'Maqriziana IX: Should al-Maqrizi Be Thrown Out with the Bath Water?: The Question of His Plagiarism of al-Awhadi's *Khitat* and the Documentary Evidence', *Mamluk Studies Review* 14 (2010), p. 159.

————, 'Maqriziana VII: Al-Maqrizi and the *Yasa*: New Evidence of His Intellectual Dishonesty' in Reuven Amitai and Amalia Levanoni (eds), *The Mamluk Sultanate in Egypt and Syria: Aspects of a Medieval Muslim State* (Ashgate, Surrey [*forthcoming*]).

BBC News, 'Cameron Threat to Dock Some UK Aid to Anti-Gay Nations', BBC News UK, 30 October 2011, available at http://www.bbc.co.uk/news/uk-15511081 (accessed 3 May 2014).

Bearman, Peri, Wolfhart Heinrichs and Bernard G. Weiss (eds), *The Law Applied: Contextualizing the Islamic Shari'a* (I.B.Tauris, London, 2008).

Beck, Ulrich, *Der kosmopolitische Blick oder: Krieg ist Frieden* (Suhrkamp Verlag K.G, Frankfurt am Mein, 2004).

Bell, David and Jon Binnie, *The Sexual Citizen: Queer Politics and Beyond* (Polity Press, Oxford, 2000).

Benhabib, Seyla, Ian Shapiro and Danilo Petranović (eds), *Identities, Affiliations, and Allegiances* (Cambridge University Press, Cambridge, 2007).

Benjamin, Walter, 'The Storyteller' in Walter Benjamin (ed.), *Illuminations* (Cape, London, 1970).

Bercher, Léon, *Les délits et les peines du droit commun prévu par le Coran* (Société anonyme de l'imprimerie rapide, Tunis, 1926).

Bereket, Tarik and Barry D. Adam, 'Navigating Islam and Same-Sex Liaisons among Men in Turkey', *Journal of Homosexuality* 55 (2008), p. 204.

Berkey, Jonathan, *The Formation of Islam: Religion and Society in the Near East, 600-1800* (Cambridge University Press, Cambridge, 2003).

Bernard, Russel H, *Research Methods in Anthropology: Qualitative and Quantitative Approaches* (Altamira Press, Oxford, 2006 [1988]).

Besen, Wayne R, *Anything but Straight: Unmasking the Scandals and Lies behind the Ex-Gay Myth* (Harrington Park Press, Binghamton, 2003).

Besson, Samantha and John Tasioulas (eds), *The Philosophy of International Law* (Oxford University Press, Oxford, 2010).

Bhabha, Homi K, *The Location of Culture* (Routledge Classics, London, 2004 [1994]).

Bhutta, Saeed, 'Kafi: A Genre of Punjabi Poetry', *South Asian Studies* 23/2 (2008), p. 223.

Binder, Guyora, 'Cultural Relativism and Cultural Imperialism in Human Rights Law', *Buffalo Human Rights Law Review* 5 (1999), p. 211.

Black, Antony, *The History of Islamic Political Thought: From the Prophet to the Present* (2nd edn; Edinburgh University Press, Edinburgh, 2011 [2001]).

Blackwood, Evelyn and Saskia E. Wieringa (eds), *Female Desires: Same Sex Relations and Transgender Practices across Cultures* (Columbia University Press, New York, 1999).

Bloch, Maurice E.F, *How We Think They Think: Anthropological Studies in Cognition, Memory and Literacy* (Westview Press, Boulder, 1998).

Boellstorff, Tom, 'Between Religion and Desire: Being Muslim and Gay in Indonesia', *American Anthropologist* 107 (2005), p. 575.

———, *The Gay Archipelago: Sexuality and Nation in Indonesia* (Princeton University Press, Princeton, 2005).

Bohan, Janis S, *Psychology and Sexual Orientation: Coming to Terms* (Routledge, New York, 1996).

Boone, Joseph A, 'Modernist Re-Orientations: Imagining Homoerotic Desire in "Nearly" Middle East', *Modernism/Modernity* 17/3 (2010), p. 561.

Boswell, John, *Christianity, Social Tolerance and Homosexuality: Gay People in Western Europe from the Beginning of the Christian Era to the Fourteenth Century* (University of Chicago Press, Chicago, 1980).

Bosworth, Clifford E, *The Ghaznavids: Their Empire in Afghanistan and Eastern Iran, 994-1040* (Edinburgh University Press, Edinburgh, 1963).

———, 'The Political and Dynastic History of the Iranian World (AD 1000-1217)' in John A. Boyle (ed.), *The Cambridge History of Iran* (Cambridge University Press, Cambridge, 1968), Vol. 5.

Bouhdiba, Abdelwahab, *Sexuality in Islam*, translated by Alan Sheridan (Routledge, London, 1985 [1975]).

Bourdieu, Pierre, *Esquisse d'une théorie de la pratique, précédé de trois études d'ethnologie kabyle* (Droz, Genève, 1972).

Boutry, Monique (ed.), *Petri Cantoris Parisiensis, Verbum abbreviatum: Textus conflatus* (Corpus Christianorum: Continuatio Mediæualis, Vol. 196; Brepols, Turnhout, 2004).

Boyle, John A. (ed.), *The Cambridge History of Iran* (Cambridge University Press, Cambridge, 1968).

Braudel, Fernand, *Écrits sur l'histoire* (Flammarion, Paris, 1969).

———, *La Méditerranée et le monde méditerranéen à l'époque de Philippe II* (Armand Colin, Paris, 1990 [1949]), Vol. 1.

Brewer, John, *Ethnography* (Open University Press, Buckingham, 2000).

Briffault, Robert, *Sin and Sex* (Allen & Unwin, London, 1931).

Broadie, Sarah and Christopher Rowe (eds), *Aristotle, Nicomachean Ethics: Translation, Introduction and Commentary* (Oxford University Press, Oxford, 2002).

Brölmann, Catherine, René Lefeber and Marjoleine Zieck (eds), *Peoples and Minorities in International Law* (Martinus Nijhoff Publishers, Dordrecht, 1993).

Brown, Jonathan A.C, *Hadith: Muhammad's Legacy in the Medieval and Modern World* (Oneworld, Oxford, 2009).

Brown, Louise, *The Dancing Girls of Lahore: Selling Love and Saving Dreams in Pakistan's Ancient Pleasure District* (PerfectBound, New York, 2005).

Brown, Wendy, *States of Injury: Power and Freedom in Late Modernity* (Princeton University Press, Princeton, 1995).

Brown, Wendy and Janet Halley, 'Introduction' in Wendy Brown and Janet Halley (eds), *Left Legalism / Left Critique* (Duke University Press, Durham, 2002).

Browne, Kath, Jason Lim and Gavin Brown (eds), *Geographies of Sexualities: Theory, Practices and Politics* (Ashgate, Surrey, 2007).

Browne, Thomas, 'Religio medici' in William Swann Sonnenschein (ed.): *Thomas Browne: Works* (George Routledge & Sons, London, 1884).

Brundage, James A, *Law, Sex, and Christian Society in Medieval Europe* (University of Chicago Press, Chicago, 1987)

Bugge, John, *Virginitas: An Essay in the History of a Medieval Ideal* (Martinus Nijhoff, The Hague, 1975).

Burak, Guy, 'The Second Formation of Islamic Law: The Post-Mongol Context of the Ottoman Adoption of a School of Law', *Comparative Studies of Society and History* 55/3 (2013), p. 579.

Burchard of Worms, 'Decretum' in Jacques-Paul Migne (ed.), *Patrologiæ cursus completus... Series Latina* (Imprimerie Catholique, Paris, *c.*1850), Vol 140.

Bureau of Investigative Journalism, 'Covert War on Terror: The Data', the Bureau of Investigative Journalism, available at http://www.thebureauinvestigates.com/category/projects/drone-data/ (accessed 3 May 2014).

Burgwinkle, William, *Sodomy, Masculinity, and Law in Medieval Literature: France and England, 1050–1230* (Cambridge University Press, Cambridge, 2004).

Buss, Doris E, 'Queering International Legal Authority', *American Society of International Law Proceedings* 101 (2007), p.122.

Butler, Judith, 'Imitation and Gender Insubordination' in D. Fuss (ed.), *Inside/Out: Lesbian Theories, Gay Theories* (Routledge, New York, 1991).

———, *Bodies that Matter: On the Discursive Limits of 'Sex'* (Routledge, New York, 1993).

———, *Gender Trouble: Feminism and the Subversion of Identity* (4th edn; Routledge, London, 1999 [1990]).

———, *Undoing Gender* (Routledge, New York, 2004).

Cæsarius of Arles, *Serm. 142.2* (Corpus christianorum, Continuatio mediævalis; Brépols, Turnhout, 1958), Vol. 103.

Calder, Norman, *Studies in Early Islamic Jurisprudence* (Clarendon Press, Oxford, 1993).

———, 'Law' in Seyyed Hossein Nasr and Oliver Leaman (eds), *History of Islamic Philosophy* (Routledge, London, 1996), Vol. 2.

———, *Islamic Jurisprudence in the Classical Era*, (ed.) (Colin Imber Cambridge University Press, Cambridge, 2010).

Cantarella, Eva, 'Gender, Sexuality, and Law' in Michael Gagarin and David Cohen (eds), *The Cambridge Companion to Ancient Greek Law* (Cambridge University Press, Cambridge, 2005), available at http://cco.cambridge.org/extract?id=ccol05218 18400_CCOL0521818400A017 (accessed 30 June 2014).

Carey, Henry F, 'The Postcolonial State and the Protection of Human Rights', *Comparative Studies of South Asia, Africa and the Middle East* 22 (2002), p. 59.

Carstairs, George Morrison, 'Hinjra and Jiryan: Two Derivatives of Hindu Attitudes to Sexuality', *British Journal of Medical Psychology* 29 (1956), p. 128.

————, *The Twice Born: A Study of a Community of High Caste Hindus* (Hogarth Press, London 1957).

Carty, Anthony, *Philosophy of International Law* (Edinburgh University Press, Edinburgh 2007).

Castronovo, Russ and Dana D. Nelson, (eds), *Materializing Democracy: Toward a Revitalized Cultural Politics* (Duke University Press, Durham, 2002).

Cavaliero, Roderick, *Ottomania: The Romantics and the Myth of the Islamic Orient* (I.B.Tauris, London 2010).

Charlesworth, Hilary and Christine Chinkin, *The Boundaries of International Law: A Feminist Analysis* (Manchester University Press, Manchester, 2000).

Cheema, Moeen H, 'Cases and Controversies: Pregnancy as Proof of Guilt Under Pakistan's Hudood Laws', *Brooklyn Journal of International Law* 32 (2006), p. 121.

Cheema, Moeen H. and Abdul-Rahman Mustafa, 'From the Hudood Ordinances to the Protection of Women Act: Islamic Critiques of the Hudood Laws of Pakistan', *UCLA Journal of Islamic and Near Eastern Law* 1 (2008-2009), p.1.

Chibnall, Marjorie (ed./trans.), *The Ecclesiastical History of Ordericus Vitalis* (Clarendon Press, Oxford, 1969-80), 6 Vols.

Chimni, B.S, *International Law and World Order: A Critique of Contemporary Approaches* (Sage, New Delhi, 1993).

Chowdhry, Geeta and Sheila Nair (eds), *Power, Postcolonialism and International Relations: Reading Race, Gender and Class* (Routledge, London, 2002).

Clavier, Sophie M, 'Objection Overruled: The Binding Nature of the International Norm Prohibiting Discrimination against Homosexual and Transgendered Individuals', *Fordham International Law Journal* 35 (2012), p. 385.

Cleveland, William L, *A History of the Modern Middle East* (3rd edn; Westview Press, Boulder, 2004).

Clinton, Hillary Rodham, 'Free and Equal in Dignity and Rights', Human Rights Day speech, Palais des Nations, Geneva, Switzerland, 6 December 2011, transcript available at http://www.humanrights.gov/2011/12/06/remarks-in-recognition-of-international-human-rights-day/ (accessed 3 May 2014).

Codell, Julie F. (ed.), *Imperial Co-Histories: National Identities and the British and Colonial Press* (Fairleigh Dickinson University Press, Madison, 2013).

Cohen, Stanley, *Folk Devils and Moral Panics* (Paladin, St Albans, 1973).

Cohen, Stephen P, 'Preface' in Stephen P. Cohen (ed.), *The Future of Pakistan* (Brookings Institution Press, Washington, 2011).

Cohn, Bernard S, *Colonialism and Its Forms of Knowledge: The British in India* (Oxford University Press, Oxford, 1997).

Comaroff, Jean and John L. Comaroff, *Theory from the South: Or, How Euro-America is Evolving toward Africa* (Paradigm Publishers, Boulder, 2012).

Comaroff, John, 'Notes on Anthropological Method, Mainly in the Key of E', presented at *Workshop on Interdisciplinary Standards for Systematic Qualitative Research,* National Science Foundation, 19-20 May 2005, Washington, DC, USA, available at http://www.wjh.harvard.edu/nsfqual/Comaroff%20Paper.pdf (accessed 1 September 2014).

Cook, Michael, *Commanding Right and Forbidding Wrong in Islamic Thought* (Cambridge University Press, Cambridge, 2004 [2001]).

Cook, Nancy, *Gender, Identity, and Imperialism: Women Development Workers in Pakistan* (Palgrave Macmillan, New York, 2007).

Corrêa, Sonia, 'From Reproductive Health to Sexual Rights: Achievements and Future Challenges', *Reproductive Health Matters* 5 (1997), p.107.

Corrêa, Sonia, Richard Parker and Rosalind Petchesky (eds), *Sexuality, Health and Human Rights* (Routledge, London, 2008).

Cossman, Brenda, 'Sexuality, Queer Theory, and "Feminism After": Reading and Rereading the Sexual Subject', *McGill Law Journal* 49 (2004), p.847.

Coulson, Noel J, *A History of Islamic Law* (Edinburgh University Press, Edinburgh, 1964).

Cowan, Jane K, Marie-Bénédicte Dembour and Richard A. Wilson, 'Introduction' in Jane K. Cowan, Marie-Bénédicte Dembour and Richard A. Wilson (eds), *Culture and Rights: Anthropological Perspectives* (Cambridge University Press, Cambridge, 2001).

Crompton, Louis, 'Male Love and Islamic Law in Arab Spain' in Stephen O. Murray and Will Roscoe (eds), *Islamic Homosexualities: Culture, History, and Literature* (New York University Press, New York, 1997).

———, *Homosexuality & Civilization* (Harvard University Press, Cambridge, 2003).

Cruz, David B, 'Disestablishing Sex and Gender' *California Law Review* 90 (2002), p. 997.

Cruz-Malavé, Arnaldo and Martin F. Manalansan IV (eds), *Queer Globalizations: Citizenship and the Afterlife of Colonialism* (New York University Press, New York, 2002).

Currah, Paisley, Richard M. Juang and Shannon Price Minter (eds), *Transgender Rights* (University of Minnesota Press, Minneapolis, 2006).

D'Amato, Anthony, *International Law Studies: Collected Papers* (The Hague: Martinus Nijhoff Publishers, 1997), Vol. 2.

D'Emilio, John, *Sexual Politics, Sexual Communities: The Making of a Homosexual Minority in the United States, 1940-1970* (University of Chicago Press, Chicago, 1983).

Dalacoura, Katerina, *Islam, Liberalism and Human Rights: Implications for International Relations* (rev. edn; I.B.Tauris, London, 2003).

Dawson, Catherine, *Practical Research Methods: A User-friendly Guide to Mastering Research Techniques and Projects* (How To Books Ltd, Oxford, 2002).

De Vitriacus, Jacobus, *Historia Hierosolymitana*, (ed.) Bongars ([Free Library of Philadelphia, Rare Book Department]; Paris 1459 [c.1224]), Vol. 1.

Debord, Guy, *The Society of the Spectacle*, translated by Donald Nicholson-Smith (Zone Books, Cambridge, 1994), available at http://www.cddc.vt.edu/sionline/si/tsots01.html (accessed 31 August 2014).

DeLamater, John D.and Janet Shibley Hyde, 'Essentialism vs. Social Construction-ism in the Study of Human Sexuality: The Use of Theory in Research and Scholarship on Sexuality', *Journal of Sex Research* 35 (1998), p.10.

Delphy, Christine, 'Rethinking Sex and Gender', *Women's Studies International Forum* 16 (1993), p. 1.

Dembour, Marie-Bénédicte, 'Following the Movement of a Pendulum: Between Universalism and Relativism' in Jane K. Cowan, Marie-Bénédicte Dembour and Richard A. Wilson (eds), *Culture and Rights: Anthropological Perspectives* (Cambridge University Press, Cambridge, 2001).

Denzin, Norman K, *The Research Act: A Theoretical Introduction to Sociological Methods* (McGraw-Hill, New York, 1978).

Derichs, Claudia and Andrea Fleschenberg (eds), *Religious Fundamentalisms and Their Gendered Impacts in Asia* (Friedrich-Ebert-Stiftung, Berlin, 2010).

Derrida, Jacques, 'A propos de Cogito et histoire de la folie', *Revue de Metaphysique et de Morale* 4 (1963), p. 460.

———, 'Choreographies', *Diacritics* 12 (1982), p. 66.

Donnelly, Jack, *Universal Human Rights in Theory and Practice* (Cornell University Press, Ithaca, 1989).

———, 'Third Generation Rights' in Catherine Brölmann, René Lefeber and Marjoleine Zieck (eds), *Peoples and Minorities in International Law* (Martinus Nijhoff Publishers, Dordrecht, 1993).

Dowsett, Gary, Jeffrey Grierson and Stephen McNally, *A Review of Knowledge about the Sexual Networks and Behaviours of Men Who Have Sex with Men in Asia* (Australian Research Centre in Sex, Health and Society, Melbourne, 2006).

Drucker, Peter, '"In the Tropics There Is No Sin": Sexuality and Gay-Lesbian Movements in the Third World', *New Left Review* 218 (1996), p.75.

Duggan, Lisa, 'The New Homonormativity: The Sexual Politics of Neoliberalism', in Russ Castronovo and Dana D. Nelson, (eds), *Materializing Democracy: Toward a Revitalized Cultural Politics* (Duke University Press, Durham, 2002).

El-Azhary Sonbol, Amira, 'Class and Violence in Nineteenth-century Egypt', in Peri Bearman, Wolfhart Heinrichs and Bernard G. Weiss (eds), *The Law Applied: Contextualizing the Islamic Shari'a* (I.B.Tauris, London, 2008).

El Fadl, Khaled M. Abou (2009), 'The Human Rights Commitment in Modern Islam', in Zainah Anwar (ed.), *Wanted: Equality and Justice in the Muslim Family* (Musawah, Kuala Lumpur, 2009).

———, *The Great Theft: Wrestling Islam from the Extremists* (HarperCollins, New York, 2007 [2005]).

El-Rouayheb, Khaled, *Before Homosexuality in the Arab-Islamic World, 1500-1800* (University of Chicago Press, Chicago, 2005).

Ellis, Mark S, Anver M. Emon and Benjamin Glahn (eds), *Islamic Law and International Human Rights Law: Searching for Common Ground?* (Oxford University Press, New York, 2012).

Emon, Anver M, *Islamic Natural Law Theories* (Oxford University Press, Oxford, 2010).

Epstein, Julia and Kristina Straub (eds), *Bodyguards: The Cultural Politics of Gender Ambiguity* (Routledge, New York, 1991).

Errante, Antoinette, 'But Sometimes You're Not Part of the Story: Oral Histories and Ways of Remembering and Telling', *Educational Researcher* 29/16 (2000), p.16.

Failed States Index 2012, *Foreign Policy*, available at http://www.foreignpolicy.com/failed_states_index_2012_interactive (accessed 20 August 2014).

Fausto-Sterling, Anne, *Myths of Gender: Biological Theories about Women and Men* (Basic Books, New York, 1992).

———, *Sexing the Body: Gender Politics and the Construction of Sexuality* (Basic Books, New York, 2000).

Feinberg, Leslie, *Transgender Warriors: Making History from Joan of Arc to Dennis Rodman* (Beacon Press, Boston, 1996).

Ferguson, Kathy, *The Man Question: Visions of Subjectivity in Feminist Theory* (University of California Press, Berkeley, 1993).

Fillieule, Olivier and Jan Willem Duyvendak, 'Gay and Lesbian Activism in France: Between Integration and Community-Oriented Movements' in Barry D. Adam, Jan Willem Duyvendak and André Krouwel (eds), *The Global Emergence of Gay and Lesbian Politics: National Imprints of a Worldwide Movement* (Temple University Press, Philadelphia, 1999).

Fisher, William, 'Karl Llewellyn' in David Kennedy and William W. Fisher III (eds), *The Canon of American Legal Thought* (Princeton University Press, Princeton, 2006).

Foster, Jonathan K, *Memory: A Very Short Introduction* (Oxford University Press, Oxford, 2009).

Foucault, Michel, *Dits et Ecrits* (Gallimard, Paris, 1971), Vols 1-2.

——, *The Order of Things: An Archaeology of the Human Sciences* (Pantheon Books, New York, 1972 [1966]).

——, *Histoire de la sexualité: La volonté de savoir* (Gallimard, Paris, 1976), Vol. 1.

——, *The History of Sexuality* (Penguin, London, 1978), Vol. 1.

Freeman, James M, 'Transvestites and Prostitutes, 1969-72' in James M. Freeman (ed.), *Untouchable: An Indian Life History* (Stanford University Press, Stanford, 1979).

Fuchs, Eric, *Sexual Desire and Love: Origins and History of the Christian Ethic of Sexuality and Marriage*, translated by Marsha Daigle (Seabury Press, New York, 1983).

Gagarin, Michael and David Cohen (eds), *The Cambridge Companion to Ancient Greek Law* (Cambridge University Press, Cambridge, 2005).

Gannon, Shane Patrick, '*Translating the Hijra: The Symbolic Reconstruction of the British Empire in India*'. PhD thesis, Department of Sociology, University of Alberta (2009)

——, 'Exclusion as Language and the Language of Exclusion: Tracing Regimes of Gender through Linguistic Representations of the "Eunuch"', *Journal of the History of Sexuality* 20/1 (2011), p.1.

Gaudemet, Jean, 'Le célibat ecclésiastique: le droit et la pratique du XIe au XIIe siècle', *Zeitschrift der Savigny-Stiftung für Rechtsgeschichte: Kanonistische Abteilung* 68 (1982), p.10.

GayRussia, 'Санкт-Петербург стал четвертым российским регионом, запретившим гей-пропаганду', *GayRussia* (по материалам РИА *Новости*), 11 March 2012, available at http://www.gayrussia.eu/russia/3883/ (accessed 23 April 2014).

Geertz, Clifford, *Islam Observed: Religious Development in Morocco and Indonesia* (University of Chicago Press, Chicago, 1971 [1968]).

——, *Local Knowledge: Further Essays in Interpretive Anthropology* (Basic Books Inc, New York, 1983).

Gerges, Fawaz A, 'Foreword' in James Wynbrandt (ed.), *A Brief History of Pakistan* (Facts on File, New York, 2009).

Ghazali, Abdus Sattar, *Islamic Pakistan: Illusions and Reality* (National Book Club, Islamabad, 1996).

Girard, Françoise, 'Negotiating Sexual Rights and Sexual Orientation at the UN' in Richard Parker, Rosalind Petchesky and Robert Sember (eds), *Sex Politics: Reports from the Front Lines* (Sexuality Policy Watch, Rio de Janeiro, 2007).

Girshick, Lori B, *Transgender Voices: Beyond Women and Men* (University Press of New England, Lebanon, 2008).

Gleave, Robert, 'The Qadi and the Mufti in Akhbari Shi'i Jurisprudence' in Peri Bearman, Wolfhart Heinrichs and Bernard G. Weiss (eds), *The Law Applied: Contextualizing the Islamic Shari'a* (I.B.Tauris, London, 2008).

———, 'Introduction' in Norman Calder (ed.), *Islamic Jurisprudence in the Classical Era* (Colin Imber (ed.); Cambridge University Press, Cambridge, 2010).

Global Equality Today, 'LGBT Activists from Around the World React to Secretary Clinton's Speech', *Global Equality Today*, the Council for Global Equality Blog, 9 December 2012, available at http://globalequality.wordpress.com/2011/12/07/lgbt-activists-from-around-the-world-react-to-secretary-clintons-speech/# (accessed 3 May 2014).

Global Rights, *Demanding Credibility and Sustaining Activism: A Guide to Sexuality-based Advocacy* (Global Rights, Washington, 2008).

Goodale, Mark, 'Locating Rights, Envisioning Law between the Global and the Local' in Mark Goodale and Sally Engle Merry (eds), *The Practice of Human Rights: Tracking Law between the Global and the Local* (Cambridge University Press, Cambridge, 2007).

Goodale, Mark and Sally Engle Merry (eds), *The Practice of Human Rights: Tracking Law between the Global and the Local* (Cambridge University Press, Cambridge, 2007).

Goodich, Michael, 'Sodomy in Medieval Secular Law', *Journal of Homosexuality* 1 (1976), p. 295.

Goodman, Ryan, 'Beyond the Enforcement Principle: Sodomy Laws, Social Norms, and Social Panoptics', *California Law Review* 89 (2001), p. 643.

Graham Davies, Sharyn, *Gender Diversity in Indonesia: Sexuality, Islam and Queer Selves* (Routledge, London, 2010).

Gray, John, *Liberalism* (Oxford University Press, Oxford, 1986).

Green, Arnold H, *In Quest of an Islamic Humanism: Arabic and Islamic Studies in Memory of Mohamed al-Nowaihi* (American University in Cairo Press, Cairo, 1984).

Green, Penny, 'Criminal Justice and Democratisation in Turkey: The Paradox of Transition' in Penny Green and Andrew Rutherford (eds), *Criminal Policy in Transition* (Hart Publishing, Oxford, 2000).

Green, Penny and Tony Ward, *State Crime: Governments, Violence and Corruption* (Pluto Press, London, 2004).

Greenwald, Glenn, 'Obama Escalates in Yemen – Again', *Salon*, 26 April 2012, available at http://www.salon.com/2012/04/26/obama_escalates_in_yemen/ (accessed 3 May 2014).

Griffin, James, *On Human Rights* (Oxford University Press, Oxford, 2008).

Gross, Aeyal M, 'Sex, Love, and Marriage: Questioning Gender and Sexuality Rights in International Law', *Leiden Journal of International Law* 21 (2008), p. 235, p. 251.

Gross, Daniel R, 'Time Allocation: A Tool For the Study of Cultural Behavior', *Annual Review of Anthropology* 13 (1984), p.519.

Grosz, Elizabeth, 'Identity and Difference: A Response' in Paul James (ed.), *Critical Politics: From the Personal to the Global* (Arena Publications, Melbourne, 1994).

Guillaume, Alfred, *The Life of Muhammad* (Oxford University Press, Oxford, 2003 [1955]).

Gulick, John, 'Village and City Field Work in Lebanon' in Morris Freilich (ed.), *Marginal Natives: Anthropologists at Work* (Harper & Row, New York, 1970).

Gupta, Alok, *This Alien Legacy: The Origins of 'Sodomy' Laws in British Colonialism* (Human Rights Watch, New York, 2008).

Guthrie, Donald, *New Testament: Introduction* (InterVarsity Press, Downers Grove, 1990).

Guttmann, Amy (ed.), *Multiculturalism: Examining the Politics of Recognition* (Princeton University Press, Princeton, 1994).

Haas, Michael, *International Human Rights: A Comprehensive Introduction* (Routledge, London, 2008).

Habib, Samar (ed.), *Female Homosexuality in the Middle East: Histories and Representations* (Routledge, New York, 2007).

———, 'Reading the Familiarity of the Past: An Introduction to Medieval Arabic Literature on Female Homosexuality' (2007) 7(2) *EnterText* 162, available at http://arts.brunel.ac.uk/gate/entertext/home.htm (accessed 13 January 2014).

———, *Islam and Homosexuality* (Praeger, Santa Barbara, 2010), 2 Vols.

———, 'Introduction' in Samar Habib (ed.), *Islam and Homosexuality* (Praeger, Santa Barbara, 2010), Vol. 1.

Hall, Kira, '"Go Suck Your Husband's Sugarcane!": Hijras and the Use of Sexual Insult' in Anna Livia and Kira Hall (eds), *Queerly Phrased: Language, Lender, and Sexuality* (Oxford University Press, New York, 1997).

Hall, Stuart, 'Introduction: Who Needs "Identity"?' in Stuart Hall and Paul Du Gay (eds), *Questions of Cultural Identity* (Sage, London, 1996).

Hallaq, Wael B, 'From *Fatwa*s to *Furu'*', *Islamic Law and Society* 1/1 (1994), p. 29.

———, 'Was the Gate of *Ijtihad* Closed?', *International Journal of Middle East Studies* 16 (1984), p. 3.

———, *A History of Islamic Legal Theories* (Cambridge University Press, Cambridge, 1997).

———, *Authority, Continuity, and Change in Islamic Law* (Cambridge University Press, Cambridge, 2004).

———, *The Origins and Evolution of Islamic Law* (Cambridge University Press, Cambridge, 2004).

———, *Shari'a: Theory, Practice, Transformations* (Cambridge University Press, Cambridge, 2009).

———, *The Impossible State: Islam, Politics, and Modernity's Moral Predicament* (Columbia University Press, New York, 2013).

Halley, Janet, 'Gay Rights and Identity Imitation: Issues in the Ethics of Representation' in David Kairys (ed.), *The Politics of Law* (3rd edn; Basic Books, New York, 1998 [1982]).

———, *Split Decisions: How and Why to Take a Break from Feminism* (Princeton University Press, Princeton, 2006).

Halley, Janet and Andrew Parker (eds), *After Sex? On Writing since Queer Theory* (Duke University Press, Durham, 2011).

Halley, Janet and Kerry Rittich, 'Critical Directions in Comparative Family Law: Genealogies and Contemporary Studies of Family Law Exceptionalism', *American Journal of Comparative Law* 58 (2010), p. 753.

Halley, Janet, Prabha Kotiswaran, Hila Shamir and Chantal Thomas, 'From the International to the Local in Feminist Legal Responses to Rape, Prostitution/Sex Work, and Sex Trafficking: Four Studies in Contemporary Governance Feminism', *Harvard Journal of Law and Gender* 29 (2006), p.335.

Halliday, Fred, 'Relativism and Universalism in Human Rights: The Case of the Islamic Middle East' in David Beetham (ed.), *Politics and Human Rights* (Blackwell, Oxford, 1995).

Halper, Louise, '"Legal Realism" in Tehran: Gender Law and the Transformative State' in Peri Bearman, Wolfhart Heinrichs and Bernard G Weiss (eds), *The Law Applied: Contextualizing the Islamic Shari'a* (I.B.Tauris, London, 2008).

Hambly, Gavin, 'A Note on the Trade in Eunuchs in Mughal Bengal', *Journal of the American Oriental Society* 94/1 (1974), p.125.

Hammurabi, *Code*, translated by G.R. Driver and John C Miles (Clarendon Press, Oxford, 1960 [1952]), Vol. 2.

Hamzić, Vanja, 'Introduction' in Vanja Hamzić and Ziba Mir-Hosseini (eds), *Control and Sexuality: The Revival of Zina Laws in Muslim Contexts* (Women Living under Muslim Laws, London, 2010).

———, 'Pakistan' in Vanja Hamzić and Ziba Mir-Hosseini (eds), *Control and Sexuality: The Revival of Zina Laws in Muslim Contexts* (Women Living under Muslim Laws, London, 2010).

———, 'Turkey' in Vanja Hamzić andZiba Mir-Hosseini (eds), *Control and Sexuality: The Revival of Zina Laws in Muslim Contexts* (Women Living under Muslim Laws, London, 2010).

———, 'The Case of "Queer Muslims": Sexual Orientation and Gender Identity in International Human Rights Law and Muslim Legal and Social Ethos', *Human Rights Law Review* 11/2 (2011), p. 237.

———, 'The Resistance from an Alterspace: Pakistani and Indonesian Muslims beyond the Dominant Sexual and Gender Norms' in A. Kam-Tuck Yip and P. Nynäs (eds), *Religion, Gender and Sexuality in Everyday Life* (Ashgate, Surrey, 2012).

———, 'Unlearning Human Rights and False Grand Dichotomies: Indonesian Archipelagic Selves Beyond Sexual/Gender Universality', *Jindal Global Law Review* 4/1 (2012), p.157.

———, 'The (Un)Conscious Pariah: Canine and Gender Outcasts of the British Raj', *Australian Feminist Law Journal* 40/2 (2015), p. 185.

Hamzić, Vanja and Ziba Mir-Hosseini, *Control and Sexuality: The Revival of Zina Laws in Muslim Contexts* (Women Living under Muslim Laws, London, 2010).

Hanawalt, Barbara A, *'Of Good and Ill Repute': Gender and Social Control in Medieval England* (Oxford University Press, New York, 1998).

Haqq, Irshad A, 'Homosexuality and Islam in America', *Journal of Islamic Law & Culture* 5 (2000), p.87.

Har-El, Shai, *Struggle for Domination in the Middle East: The Ottoman-Mamluk War, 1485-1491* (Brill, Leiden, 1995).

Haritaworn, Jin, Tamsila Tauqir and Esra Erdem, 'Gay Imperialism: Gender and Sexuality Discourse in the "War on Terror"' in Adi Kuntsman and Esperanza Miyake (eds), *Out of Place: Interrogating Silences in Queerness/Raciality* (Raw Nerve Books, York, 2008).

Harris, Marvin, *Cultural Materialism: The Struggle for a Science of Culture* (Random House, New York, 1979).

Haskins, Charles Homer, *The Renaissance of the Twelfth Century* (Harvard University Press, Cambridge, 1927).

Hathaway, Jane, 'The Role of the *Kızlar Ağası* in 17th-18th Century Ottoman Egypt', *Studia Islamica* 75 (1992), p. 141.

———, *Beshir Aga: Chief Eunuch of the Ottoman Imperial Harem* (Oneworld, Oxford, 2005).

Headrick, Daniel R, *The Tools of Empire: Technology and European Imperialism in the Nineteenth Century* (Oxford University Press, New York, 1981).

304 Sexual and Gender Diversity in the Muslim World

Hefner, Robert W. (ed.), *Remaking Muslim Politics: Pluralism, Contestation, Democratization* (Princeton University Press, Princeton, 2005).

Hegel, Georg Wilhelm Friedrich, *Phenomenology of Spirit* (Clarendon Press, Oxford, 1977 [1807]).

Heinze, Eric, *Sexual Orientation: A Human Right* (Martinus Nijhoff Publishers, Dordrecht, 1995).

Henkin, Louis, *The Age of Rights* (Columbia University Press, New York, 1990).

Herek, Gregory M, *Stigma and Sexual Orientation: Understanding Prejudice against Lesbians, Gay Men and Bisexuals* (Sage, London, 1998).

Heyd, Uriel, *Studies in Old Ottoman Criminal Law*, (ed.) V.L. Ménage (Clarendon Press, Oxford, 1973).

Hilli, Muhaqqiq Najm al-Din Ja'far ibn Hasan, *Shara'i' al-islam fi masa'il al-halal wal-haram* (Dar al-Qari', Beirut, 2004), Vol. 4.

Hines, Sally, *TransForming Gender: Transgender Practices of Identity, Intimacy and Care* (Policy Press, Bristol, 2007).

Hodgson, Dorothy L. (ed.), *Gender and Culture at the Limit of Rights* (University of Pennsylvania Press, Philadelphia, 2011).

Hodgson, Marshall G.S, *The Venture of Islam: Conscience and History in a World Civilization* (University of Chicago Press, Chicago, 1974), Vol. 2.

Hodson, Loveday, 'A Marriage by Any Other Name? *Schalk and Kopf v Austria*', *Human Rights Law Review* 11 (2011), p. 170.

Hoffmann, Richard C, Nancy Langston, James C. McCann, Peter C. Perdue and Lise Sedrez, 'AHR Conversation: Environmental Historians and Environmental Crisis', *American Historical Review* 113/5 (2008), p. 1431.

Holbraad, Martin. 2007. 'The Power of Powder: Multiplicity and Motion in the Divinatory Cosmology of Cuban Ifá (or Mana Again)' in Amiria Henare, Martin Holbraad and Sari Wastell (eds), *Thinking through Things: Theorising Artefacts Ethnographically* (Routledge, London, 2007).

Holmes Jr, Oliver Wendell, 'The Path of Law' in David Kennedy and William W. Fisher III (eds), *The Canon of American Legal Thought* (Princeton University Press, Princeton, 2006 [reproduced from (1897) 10 *Harvard Law Review* 457]).

———, *The Common Law* (Little, Brown, Boston, 1963 [1881]).

Human Dignity Trust, 'The Human Dignity Trust: Legally Challenging the Illegality of Homosexuality', Human Dignity Trust, available at http://www.humandignitytrust.org/pages/ABOUT%20US (accessed 3 May 2014).

Hume, Lynne and Jane Mulcock (eds), *Anthropologists in the Field, Cases of Participant Observation* (Columbia University Press, New York, 2004).

Hunt, Paul, *Report of the Special Rapporteur on the Right to Health* (United Nations Office of the High Commissioner for Human Rights, Geneva 2004), UN Doc E/CN.4/2004/49.

Hussain, Hadi, 'US Embassy's Pride Celebrations in Islamabad: More Damage than Support', *Gaylaxy*, 24 August 2011, available at http://www.gaylaxymag.com/blog/index.php/2011/08/us-embassys-pride-celebrations-in-islamabad-more-damage-than-support/ (accessed 4 May 2014).

Hutton, Patrick H, *History as an Art of Memory* (University Press of New England, Hanover, 1993).

Ibbetson, DCJ, M.E. MacLagen and H.A. Rose, *A Glossary of the Tribes of and Castes of the Punjab and North-West Frontier Province* (Civil and Military Gazette, Lahore, 1911), Vol. 2.

Ibn 'Abd al-Barr, *al-Intiqa' fi fada'il al-thalathah al-a'imma* (al-Qudsi, Cairo, 1931).

Ibn 'Abidin, Muhammad Amin, *Radd al-muhtar 'ala al-durr al-mukhtar* (Bulaq, 1856 [1830]), Vol. 3.

Ibn 'Allan, Muhammad 'Ali, *Dalil al-falihin li-turuq Riyad al-salihin* (Cairo, 1938), Vol. 3.

Ibn Abi Ya'la', *Tabaqat al-hanabilah*, (ed.) Muhammad Hamid al-Fiqi (Matba'at al-sunna al-Muhammadiya, Cairo 1952 [*c*.1130]), Vol. 1.

Ibn Ahmad, 'Abdullah, *Kitab al-Sunna*, (ed.) Muhammad ibn Sa'id ibn Salim al-Qahtani (Dar Ibn al-Qayyim, Dammam, 1986 [*c*.893]).

Ibn al-Jawzi, Abu'l-Faraj 'Abd al-Rahman ibn 'Ali, *al-Muntazam fi tarikh al-umam wa-l-muluk* (Dar al-kutub al-'ilmiyya, 1992 [*c*.1190]), Vol. 18.

Ibn Hajar, *Tahdib 'al-tahdib'* (Majlis Da'irat al-Ma'arif al-Nizamiya, Hyderabad, 1909 [*c*.1425]), Vol. 10.

———, *Lisan 'al-mizan'* (Matba'at Majlis Da'irat al-Ma'arif, Hyderabad, 1912 [*c*.1420]), Vol. 6.

Ibn Hazm al-Andalusi, *Asma' al-sahabat al-ruwat wa ma li-kulli wahid min al-'adad*, (ed.) Sayyid Kurdi Hasan (Dar al-kutub al-'ilmiyya, Beirut, 1992 [*c*.1040]).

Ibn Jama'a, Badr al-Din, *Tahrir al-ahkam fi'l-tadbir ahl al-islam*, (ed.) Fu'ad 'Abdul-Mun'im Ahmad (Dar al-thaqafa, Qatar, 1988 [*c*.1300]).

Ibn Khaldun [Abu Zayd 'Abdurrahman ibn Muhammad ibn Khaldun al-Hadrami], *The Muqaddimah: An Introduction to History*, translated by Franz Rosenthal (2nd edn; Princeton University Press, Princeton, 1967), 3 Vols.

———, *Muqaddimat Ibn Khaldun*, (ed.) E.M. Quatremere (Maktabat Lubnan, Beirut, 1970 [1858]), 3 Vols.

Ibn Nujayam, Zayn al-'Abidin, *al-Bahr al-ra'iq sharh kanz al-daqa'iq* (Cairo, 1894 [*c*.1560]), Vol. 5.

Ibn Taymiyya, Takiyy al-Din Ahmad, *al-Siyasa al-shar'iyya fi islah al-ra'i wa l-ra'iyya* (translated as *Le Traité de droit public d'Ibn Taymiyya*), translated by/(ed.) Henri Laoust (Institut français de Damas, Beirut, 1948 [*c*.1309-1312]).

———, *Dar'a ta'arud al-'aql wal-naql* (ed.) 'Abd al-Latif 'Abd al-Rahman; Dar al-kutub al-'ilmiyya, Beirut, 1997 [*c*.1315]), 5 Vols.

ILGA-LAC, *A 40 Años de Stonewall Inn: Transfobia, Lesbofobia, Homofobia, Bifobia en Latinoamérica y El Caribe* (ILGA-LAC, 2009), available at http://www.clam.org.br (accessed 15 January 2014).

İlkkaracan, Pınar, 'Introduction: Sexuality as a Contested Political Domain in the Middle East' in Pınar İlkkaracan (ed.), *Deconstructing Sexuality in the Middle East* (Ashgate Publishing, Burlington, 2008).

Imber, Colin, *Ebu's-su'ud: The Islamic Legal Tradition* (Stanford University Press, Stanford, 1997).

İnalcık, Halil, *The Ottoman Empire: The Classical Age, 1300-1600* (Wiedenfeld & Nicolson, London, 1973).

Ingber, Stanley, 'Religion or Ideology: A Needed Clarification of the Religion Clauses', *Stanford Law Review* 41 (1989), p. 233.

Ingold, Tim, 'The Temporality of the Landscape', *World Archaeology* 25/2 (1993), p. 152.

International Council on Human Rights Policy, *Sexuality and Human Rights: Discussion Paper* (International Council on Human Rights Policy, Versoix, 2009).

Iqbal, Afzal, *Islamisation of Pakistan* (Vanguard Books, Lahore, 1986).

ISHR, 'Ground-Breaking Statement on Sexual Orientation and Gender Identity by Record Number of 85 States', International Service for Human Rights (ISHR),

Press Release, 24 March 2011, available at http://www.ishr.ch/council/1033-ground-breaking-statement-on-sexual-orientation-and-gender-identity-by-record-number-of-85-states (accessed 24 April 2014).

Izutsu, Toshihiko, *God and Man in the Koran: Semantics of the Koranic Weltanschauung* (Keiō Institute of Cultural and Linguistic Studies, Tokyo, 1964).

Jackson, Peter A. (2009), 'Capitalism and Global Queering National Markets, Parallels Among Sexual Cultures, and Multiple Queer Modernities', *Journal of Lesbian and Gay Studies* 15/3 (2009), p. 357.

Jackson, Sherman A, 'Fiction and Formalism: Toward a Functional Analysis of *Usul al-Fiqh*' in Bernard G. Weiss (ed.), *Studies in Islamic Legal Theory* (Brill, Leiden, 2002).

Jackson, Stevi and Sue Scott, 'Sexual Skirmishes and Feminist Factions' in Stevi Jackson and Sue Scott (eds), *Feminism and Sexuality: A Reader* (Edinburgh University Press, Edinburgh, 1996).

Jamal, Amreen, 'The Story of Lot and the Qur'an's Perception of the Morality of Same-Sex Sexuality', *Journal of Homosexuality* 41/1 (2001), p. 1.

James, Stephen A, 'Reconciling International Human Rights and Cultural Relativism: The Case of Female Circumcision', *Bioethics* 8 (1994), p. 1.

Jameson, Fredric, *The Political Unconscious: Narrative as a Socially Symbolic Act* (Routledge Classics, London, 2002 [1981]).

———, *Archaeologies of the Future: The Desire Called Utopia and Other Science Fictions* (Verso, London, 2005).

Johansen, Baber, 'Eigentum, Familie und Obrigkeit im hanafitischen Strafrecht', *Die Welt des Islams* 19 (1979), p. 1.

———, *The Islamic Law on Land Tax and rent:The Peasant's Loss of Property Rights as Interpreted in the Hanafite Legal Literature of the Mamluk and Ottoman Periods* (Croom Helm, London, 1988).

———, 'Legal Literature and the Problem of Change: The Case of the Land Rent' in Chibli Mallat (ed.), *Islam and Public Law: Classical and Contemporary Studies* (Graham and Trotman, London, 1993).

———, 'Signs as Evidence: The Doctrine of Ibn Taymiyya (1263-1328) and Ibn Qayyim Al-Jawziyya (d. 1351) on Proof', *Islamic Law and Society* 9 (2002), p. 168.

———, 'A Perfect Law in an Imperfect Society: Ibn Taymiyya's Concept of "Governance in the Name of the Sacred Law"' inPeri Bearman, Wolfhart Heinrichs and Bernard G Weiss (eds), *The Law Applied: Contextualizing the Islamic Shari'a* (I.B.Tauris, London, 2008).

Jones-Pauly, Chris, 'Use of the Qur'an in Key Pakistani Court Decisions on *zina* and *qadf*', *Arabica* 47/3 (2000), p.539

Justinian, 'Novellæ constitutiones' in Justinian (ed.), *Institutes*, translated by J.B. Moyle (Oxford University Press, Oxford 1911).

———, *Corpus iuris civilis: Novellæ* (eds) Wilhelm Kroll and Rudolf Schoell (4th edn; Apud Weidmannos, Berlin, 1912), Vol. 3.

Juynboll, Gautier H.A, *The Authenticity of the Tradition Literature: Discussions in Modern Egypt* (Brill, Leiden, 1969).

Kain, Philip J, *Hegel and the Other: A Study of the Phenomenology of Spirit* (State University of New York Press, New York, 2005).

Kairys, David (ed.), *The Politics of Law* (3rd edn; Basic Books, New York, 1998 [1982]).

Kamali, Mohammad Hashim, *Principles of Islamic Jurisprudence* (Islamic Texts Society, Cambridge, 1991).

———, *Shari'ah Law: An Introduction* (Oneworld, Oxford, 2008).

———, 'Transgenders, from Islam's Perspective', *New Straits Times*, Kuala Lumpur, 29 December 2009, available at http://leonalo.wordpress.com/2009/12/ (accessed 28 July 2014).

Kantola, Johanna and Hanne Marlene Dahl, 'Gender and the State: from Differences between to Differences within', *International Feminist Journal of Politics* 7 (2005), p. 49.

Kaplan, Robert D, 'What's Wrong with Pakistan?', *Foreign Policy*, July/August 2012, available at http://www.foreignpolicy.com/articles-/2012/06/18/whats_wrong_with_pakistan (accessed 20 August 2014).

Katyal, Sonia, 'Exploring Identity', *Yale Journal of Law and Feminism* 14 (2002), p. 97.

Kennedy, David and William W. Fisher III (eds), *The Canon of American Legal Thought* (Princeton University Press, Princeton, 2006).

Kertelge, Karl (ed.), *Paulus in den neutestamentlichen Spätschriften* (Herderg, Freiburg, 1981).

Khallaf, 'Abd al-Wahhab, *Masadir al-tashri' al-islami fi-ma la nassa fih* (Dar al-kitab al-'arabi, Cairo, 1955).

Khan, Shahnaz, '"Zina" and the Moral Regulation of Pakistani Women', *Feminist Review* 75 (2003), p. 75.

———, 'Locating the Feminist Voice: The Debate on the Zina Ordinance', *Feminist Studies* 30/3 (2004), p.660.

———, *Zina, Transnational Feminism, and the Moral Regulation of Pakistani Women* (University of British Columbia Press, Vancouver, 2007).

Khilji, Tahir, 'The World of Zenanas', *In Plainspeak* 3 (2008), p. 13.

Khir, Bustami Mohamed, 'The Islamic Quest for Sociopolitical Justice' in Peter Scott and William T. Cavanaugh (eds), *The Blackwell Companion to Political Theology* (Blackwell Publishing, Malden, 2004).

Knowles, David Dom, *The Religious Orders in England: The Tudor Age* (Cambridge University Press, Cambridge, 1959), Vol. 3.

Kohen, Ari, *In Defense of Human Rights: A Non-Religious Grounding in a Pluralist World* (Routledge, London, 2007).

Kollman, Kelly and Matthew Waites, 'The Global Politics of Lesbian, Gay, Bisexual and Transgender Human Rights: An Introduction', *Contemporary Politics* 15 (2009), p.1.

Kornfeld, Walter, 'L'adultère dans l'Orient antique', *Revue biblique* 57 (1970), pp. 96–104.

Koskenniemi, Martti, *The Gentle Civilizer of Nations: The Rise and Fall of International Law, 1870-1960* (Cambridge University Press, Cambridge, 2004 [2001]).

———, 'What Should International Lawyers Learn from Karl Marx?' in Susan Marks (ed.), *International Law on the Left: Re-examining Marxist Legacies* (Cambridge University Press, Cambridge, 2008).

Kotiswaran, Prabha, *Dangerous Sex, Invisible Labor: Sex Work and the Law in India* (Princeton University Press, Princeton, 2011).

Kuefler, Mathew, *The Manly Eunuch: Masculinity, Gender Ambiguity and Christian Ideology in Late Antiquity* (University of Chicago Press, Chicago, 2001).

Kugle, Scot Siraj al-Haqq, 'Sexuality, Diversity, and Ethics in the Agenda of Progressive Muslims' in Omid Safi (ed.), *Progressive Muslims: On Justice, Gender, and Pluralism* (Oneworld, Oxford, 2003).

——, *Homosexuality in Islam: Critical Reflection on Gay, Lesbian, and Transgender Muslims* (Oneworld, Oxford, 2010).

Kumar, P. Pratap and Knut A. Jacobsen (eds), *South Asians in the Diaspora: Histories and Religious Traditions* (EJ Brill, Leiden, 2004).

Kuntsman, Adi and Esperanza Miyake, *Out of Place: Interrogating Silences in Queerness/Raciality* (Raw Nerve Books, York, 2008).

Kuttner, Stephen, 'The Revival of Jurisprudence' in Robert L Benson and Giles Constable (eds), *Renaissance and Renewal in the Twelfth Century* (Harvard University Press, Cambridge, 1982).

Kynsilehto, Anitta (ed.), *Islamic Feminism: Current Perspectives* (Juvenes Print, Tampere, 2008).

Lal, Vinay, 'Not This, Not That: The Hijras of India and the Culture Politics of Sexuality', *Social Text* 61 (1999), p.119.

Lambton, Ann K.S, 'The Administration of Sanjar's Empire as Illustrated in the '*Atabat al-kataba*', *Bulletin of the School of Oriental and African Studies* 20 (1957), p. 367.

——, 'Changing Concepts of Justice and Injustice from the 5th/11th Century to the 8th/14th Century in Persia: The Saljuq Empire and the Ilkhanate', *Studia Islamica* 68 (1988), p. 27.

Lange, Christian, *Justice, Punishment, and the Medieval Muslim Imagination* (Cambridge University Press, Cambridge, 2008).

Lau, Martin, 'Sharia and National Law in Pakistan' in Jan Michiel Otto (ed.), *Sharia Incorporated: A Comparative Overview of the Legal Systems of Twelve Muslim Countries in Past and Present* (Leiden University Press, Leiden, 2010).

Lauterpacht, Hersch, *International Law and Human Rights* (Stevens, London, 1950).

Lawrence-Berg, Bruce, *Qualitative Research Methods for the Social Sciences* (Allyn and Bacon, London, 2001).

Lerner, Ralph and Muhsin Mahdi (eds), *Medieval Political Philosophy: a Sourcebook* (Free Press of Glencoe, Toronto, 1963).

Lerner, Robert E, *The Heresy of the Free Spirit in the Later Middle Ages* (University of California Press, Berkeley, 1972).

Lever, Maurice, *Les Bûchers de Sodome: Histoire des «infâmes»* (Fayard, Paris, 1985).

Lewis, Bernard, 'Siyasa' in Arnold H. Green (ed.), *In Quest of an Islamic Humanism: Arabic and Islamic Studies in Memory of Mohamed al-Nowaihi* (American University in Cairo Press, Cairo, 1984).

Libson, Gideon, 'On the Development of Custom as a Source of Law in Islamic Law', *Islamic Law and Society* 1/1 (1994), p.131.

Lindgren Alves, José A, 'The Declaration of Human Rights in Postmodernity', *Human Rights Quarterly* 22 (2000), p.478.

Llewellyn, Karl, 'Some Realism about Realism: Responding to Dean Pound' in David Kennedy and William W. Fisher III (eds), *The Canon of American Legal Thought* (Princeton University Press, Princeton, 2006 [reproduced from (1931) 44 *Harvard Law Review* 1222]).

Long, Scott, 'Unbearable Witness: How Western Activists (Mis)Recognize Sexuality in Iran', *Contemporary Politics* 15 (2009), p.119.

Lovell, Nadia (ed.),*Locality and Belonging* (Routledge, London, 1998).

Low, Setha M. and Denise Lawrence-Zúñiga (eds), *The Anthropology of Space and Place: Locating Culture* (Blackwell, Malden, 2003).

Lukács, Georg, *Geschichte und Klassenbewußtsein: Studien über marxistische Dialektik* (Malik-Verlag, Berlin, 1923).

Lybyer, Albert H, *The Government of the Ottoman Empire in the time of Suleiman the Magnificent* (Harvard University Press, Cambridge, 1913).

Maalouf, Amin, *In the Name of Identity: Violence and the Need to Belong*, translated by Barbara Bray (Penguin Books, New York, 2003 [1996]).

Macaulay, Thomas Babington, 'Minute of 2 February 1835 on Indian Education' in G.M. Young (ed.), *Macaulay: Prose and Poetry* (Harvard University Press, Cambridge, 1957).

Maghen, Ze'ev, *Virtues of the Flesh: Passion and Purity in Early Islamic Jurisprudence* (Brill, Leiden, 2005).

Mahmood, Saba, *Politics of Piety: The Islamic Revival and the Feminist Subject* (Princeton University Press, Princeton, 2005).

Makdisi, George, 'The Guilds of Law in Medieval Legal History: An Inquiry Into the Origins of the Inns of Court', *Zeitschrift für Geschichte der arabisch-islamischen Wissenschaften* 1 (1984), p. 233.

———, 'La Corporation à l'époque classique de l'Islam' in Daniel Massignon (ed.), *Présence de Louis Massignon: hommages et témoignages* (Maisonneuve et Larose, Paris, 1987).

———, *The Rise of Humanism in Classical Islam and the Christian West: With Special Reference to Scholasticism* (Edinburgh University Press, Edinburgh, 1990).

———, 'Tabaqat–Biography: Law and Orthodoxy in Classical Islam', *Islamic Studies* 32 (1993), p.371.

Malcolm, Noel, *Bosnia: A Short History* (New York University Press, New York, 1994).

Malik, Iftikhar H, *The History of Pakistan* (Greenwood Press, Westport, 2008).

Malinowski, Bronisław, *Agronauts of the Western Pacific* (Routledge, London, 2002 [1922]).

Manderson, Lenore and Margaret Jolly (eds), *Sites of Desires, Economies of Pleasure: Sexualities in Asia and the Pacific* (University of Chicago Press, Chicago, 1997).

Mann, Benjamin, 'Vatican Official: UN Gay "Rights" Agenda Endangers Church's Freedom', Catholic News Agency, 8 July 2011, available at http://www.catholicnewsagency.com/news/vatican-official-says-un-gay-rights-agenda-endangers-churchs-freedom/ (accessed 1 May 2014).

Marks, Susan (ed.), *International Law on the Left: Re-examining Marxist Legacies* (Cambridge University Press, Cambridge, 2008).

———, 'Human Rights and Root Causes', *Modern Law Review* 74/1 (2011), p. 57.

Marmon, Shaun, *Eunuchs and Sacred Boundaries in Islamic Society* (Oxford University Press, New York, 1995).

Marshal, M.N, 'The Key Informant Techniques', *Family Practice* 13 (1996), p. 92.

Massad, Joseph A, *Desiring Arabs* (University of Chicago Press, Chicago, 2007).

Masud, Muhammad Khalid, Brinkley Messick and David S. Powers (eds), *Islamic Legal Interpretation: Muftis and Their Fatwas* (Harvard University Press, Cambridge, 1996).

———, 'A Study of Waki's (d. 306/917) Akhbar al-Qudat' in Peri Bearman, Wolfhart Heinrichs and Bernard G. Weiss (eds), *The Law Applied: Contextualizing the Islamic Shari'a* (I.B.Tauris, London, 2008).

Matthews Sanford, Eva, 'The Verbum Abbreviatum of Petrus Cantor', *Transactions and Proceedings of the American Philological Association* 74 (1943), p.33.

Maudoodi, Sayyid Abul A'la, *Purdah and the Status of Women in Islam* (Islamic Publications Ltd, Lahore, 1967).

Mayer, Ann Elizabeth, *Islam and Human Rights: Tradition and Politics* (3rd edn; Westview Press, Boulder, 1999).

Mayer, Tamar (ed.), *Gender Ironies of Nationalism: Sexing the Nation* (Routledge, London, 2000).

McCorquodale, Robert, 'The Individual and the International Legal System' in Malcolm D. Evans (ed.), *International Law* (2nd edn, Oxford University Press, Oxford, 2006).

McGinn, Thomas A.J, *Prostitution, Sexuality, and the Law in Ancient Rome* (Oxford University Press, New York, 1998).

McNamara, Jo-Ann, 'Muffled Voices: The Lives of Consecrated Women in the Fourth Century' in John A Nichols and Lillian Thomas Shank (eds), *Medieval Religious Women: Distant Echoes* (Cistercian Publications, Kalamazoo, 1984).

McNamara, Jo Ann and Suzanne Wemple, 'The Power of Women through the Family in Medieval Europe, 500-1100', *Feminist Studies* 1 (1973), p. 126.

McNeill, John T, *A History of the Cure of Souls* (Harper Brothers, New York, 1951).

Melchert, Christopher, *The Formation of the Sunni Schools of Law, 9th-10th Centuries C. E.* (Brill, Leiden, 1997).

Ménage, V.L, 'Devshirme' in B. Lewis, Ch. Pellat and J. Schacht (eds), *Encyclopædia of Islam* (2nd edn; Brill, Leiden, 1965), Vol. 2.

————, 'Some Notes on the Devshirme', *Bulletin of the School of Oriental and African Studies* 29 (1966), p.64.

Menski, Werner F, 'South Asian Muslim Law Today: An Overview', *Sharqiyyat* 9/1 (1997), p. 16.

Mernissi, Fatima, *Beyond the Veil: Male-Female Dynamics in a Muslim Society* (Saqi Books, London, 2011 [1975, 1985]).

Merry, Sally Engle, *Colonizing Hawai'i: The Cultural Power of Law* (Princeton University Press, Princeton, 2000).

————, 'Rights Talk and the Experience of Law: Implementing Women's Human Rights to Protection from Violence', *Human Rights Quarterly* 25/2 (2003), p. 343.

————, *Human Rights and Gender Violence: Translating International Law into Local Justice* (University of Chicago Press, Chicago, 2006).

————, 'New Legal Realism and the Ethnography of Transnational Law', *Law & Social Inquiry* 31/4 (2006), p. 975.

————, 'Transnational Human Rights and Local Activism: Mapping the Middle', *American Anthropologist* 108/1 (2006), p. 38.

Messick, Brinkley, *The Calligraphic State: Textual Domination and History in a Muslim Society* (University of California Press, Berkeley, 1993).

Miéville, China, 'The Commodity-Form Theory of International Law' in Susan Marks (ed.), *International Law on the Left: Re-examining Marxist Legacies* (Cambridge University Press, Cambridge, 2008).

Migne, Jacques-Paul (ed.), *Patrologiæ cursus completus... Series Græca* (Imprimerie Catholique, Paris, 1857), 165 Vols.

———— (ed.), *Patrologiæ cursus completus...Series Latina* (Imprimerie Catholique, Paris, 1858), 221 Vols.

Miller, Alice M, 'Human Rights and Sexuality: First Steps Toward Articulating a Rights Based Framework for Claims to Sexual Rights and Freedoms', *American Society of International Law Proceedings* 93 (1999), p. 288.

Miller, Alice M.and Carole S. Vance, 'Sexuality, Human Rights, and Health', *Health and Human Rights* 7 (2004), p. 5.

Miller, Daniel (ed.), *Materiality* (Duke University Press, Durham, 2005).

Minwalla, Omar, B.R. Simon Rosser, Jamie Feldman and Christine Varga, 'Identity Experience among Progressive Gay Muslims in North America: A Qualitative Study within Al-Fatiha', *Culture, Health & Sexuality* 7 (2005), p.113.

Mir, Farina, *The Social Space of Language: Vernacular Culture in British Colonial Punjab* (University of California Press, Berkeley, 2010).

Mir-Hosseini, Ziba, 'Classical *Fiqh*, Contemporary Ethics and Gender Justice' in Karl Vogt, Lena Larsen and Christian Moe (eds), *New Directions in Islamic Thought: Exploring Reform and Muslim Tradition* (I.B.Tauris, London, 2009).

Mirza, Babar, 'Discontents of ICJ Mission', *Dawn*, 29 September 2011, available at http://dawn.com/2011/09/29/discontents-of-icj-mission/ (accessed 1 August 2014).

Mitamura, Taisuke, *Chinese Eunuchs: Structure of Intimate Politics*, translated by Charles A. Pomeroy (Tuttle Publishing, North Clarendon, 1992).

Mitchell, Timothy, *Colonising Egypt* (Cambridge University Press, Cambridge, 1988).

Mnookin, Robert H.and Lewis Kornhauser, 'Bargaining in the Shadow of the Law: The Case of Divorce', *Yale Law Journal* 88/5 (1979), p. 950.

Moaddel, Mansoor, *Islamic Modernism, Nationalism, and Fundamentalism: Episode and Discourse* (University of Chicago Press, Chicago, 2005).

Mondal, Sekh Rahim, 'The Eunuchs: Some Observations', *Journal of Indian Anthropology and Sociology* 24 (1989), p.244.

Monro, Surya, 'Transgender: Destabilising Feminisms?' in Vanessa E. Munro and Carl F. Stychin (eds), *Sexuality and the Law: Feminist Engagements* (Routledge-Cavendish, New York, 2007).

Monroe, James T, 'The Striptease that was Blamed on Abu Bakr's Naughty Son: Was Father Being Shamed, or was the Poet Having Fun? (Ibn Quzman's Zajal No. 133)' in Jerry W Wright Jr.and Everett K. Rowson (eds), *Homoeroticism in Classical Arabic Literature* (Columbia University Press, New York, 1997).

Monshipouri, Mahmood, *Islamism, Secularism, and Human Rights in the Middle East* (Lynne Rienner Publishers, Boulder, 1998).

Montgomery Hyde, Hartford, *The Love that Dared Not Speak Its Name: A Candid History of Homosexuality in Britain* (Little/Brown, Boston, 1970).

Morgan, Wayne, 'Queering International Human Rights Law' in Carl Stychin and Didi Herman (eds), *Law and Sexuality: the Global Arena* (University of Minnesota Press, Minneapolis, 2001 [2000]).

Mortimer, Edward, 'Islam and Human Rights', *Index on Censorship* 12 (1983), p. 5.

Morton, A.Q.and James McLeman, *Paul, the Man and the Myth: A Study in the Authorship of Greek Prose* (Hodder & Stoughton, London, 1966).

Motzki, Harald, *The Origins of Islamic Jurisprudence: Meccan Fiqh before the Classical Schools* (Brill, Leiden, 2002).

Mullally, Siobhán, *Gender, Culture and Human Rights: Reclaiming Universalism* (Hart Publishing, Oxford, 2006).

Müller, Michael, *Die Lehre des hl. Augustinus von der Paradiesesehe und ihre Auswirkung in der Sexualethik des 12. und 13. Jahrhunderts bis Thomas von Aquin* (Friedrich Pustet, Regensburg, 1954).

Murray, Stephen O, 'Homosexuality among Slave Elites in Ottoman Turkey' in Stephen O. Murray and Will Roscoe (eds), *Islamic Homosexualities: Culture, History, and Literature* (New York University Press, New York, 1997).

———, 'Male Homosexuality, Inheritance Rules, and the Status of Women in Medieval Egypt: The Case of the Mamluks' in Stephen O. Murray and Will Roscoe (eds), *Islamic Homosexualities: Culture, History, and Literature* (New York University Press, New York, 1997).

———, 'The Sohari *Khanith*' in Stephen O. Murray and Will Roscoe (eds), *Islamic Homosexualities: Culture, History, and Literature* (New York University Press, New York, 1997).

Murray, Stephen O.and Will Roscoe, *Islamic Homosexualities: Culture, History, and Literature* (New York University Press, New York, 1997).

Musić, Rusmir, 'Queer Visions of Islam' in Samar Habib (ed.), *Islam and Homosexuality* (Praeger, Santa Barbara, 2010), Vol. 2.

Najmabadi, Afsaneh, *Women with Mustaches and Men without Beards: Gender and Sexual Anxieties of Iranian Modernity* (University of California Press, Berkeley, 2005).

Nanda, Serena, *Neither Man nor Woman: The Hijras of India* (Wadsworth, New York, 1990).

———, 'Hijras: An Alternative Sex and Gender Role in India' in Gilbert Herdt (ed.), *Third Sex, Third Gender: Beyond Dimorphism in Culture and History* (Zone Books, New York, 1996).

Naqvi, Nauman and Hasan Mujtaba, 'Two Balochi *Buggas*, a Sindhi *Zenana*, and the Status of *Hijras* in Contemporary Pakistan' in Stephen O. Murray and Will Roscoe (eds), *Islamic Homosexualities: Culture, History, and Literature* (New York University Press, New York, 1997).

Narrain, Arvind, 'The Articulation of Rights around Sexuality and Health: Subaltern Queer Cultures in India in the Era of Hindutva', *Health and Human Rights* 7 (2004), p.142.

Nasr, Seyyed Hossein and Oliver Leaman (eds), *History of Islamic Philosophy* (Routledge, London, 1996).

Nath, R, 'The Mughal Institution of Khwajasara' in R. Nath (ed.), *Medieval Indian History and Architecture* (APH Publishing Corporation, New Delhi, 1995).

Negri, Antonio and Michael Hardt, *Empire* (Harvard University Press, Cambridge, 2000).

Nichols, John A.and Lillian Thomas Shank (eds), *Medieval Religious Women: Distant Echoes* (Cistercian Publications, Kalamazoo, 1984).

Nietzsche, Friedrich, *Zur Genealogie der Moral: Eine Streitschrift* (Reclam, Ditzingen, 1988 [1887]).

Noiriel, Gérard, '"L'éthique de la discussion": A propos de deux conférences sur l'histoire (1903-1906)' in Lucien Gillard and Michel Rosier (eds), *François Simiand (1873-1935): sociologie, histoire, économie* (Editions des archives contemporaines, Paris, 1996).

Nörr, Knut Wolfgang, 'The Institutional Foundations of the New Jurisprudence' in Robert L. Benson and Giles Constable (eds), *Renaissance and Renewal in the Twelfth Century* (Harvard University Press, Cambridge, 1982).

Norton, Rictor, 'A Critique of Social Constructionism and Queer Theory', published on-line (2002, 2008) at http://rictornorton.co.uk/extracts.htm (accessed 13 January 2014).

O'Connor, Noreen and Joanna Ryan, *Wild Desires and Mistaken Identities: Lesbianism and Psychoanalysis* (Virago, London, 1993).

O'Flaherty, Michael and Gwyneth Williams, 'Jurisprudential Annotations to the Yogyakarta Principles', Human Rights Law Centre, University of Nottingham, November 2007, available at http://www.yogyakartaprinciples.org/-yogyakarta-principles-jurisprudential-annotations.pdf (accessed 24 April 2014).

O'Flaherty, Michael and John Fisher, 'Sexual Orientation, Gender Identity and International Human Rights Law: Contextualising the Yogyakarta Principles', *Human Rights Law Review* 8 (2008), p. 207.

Oberhelman, Steven M, 'Hierarchies of Gender, Ideology, and Power in Ancient and Medieval Greek and Arabic Dream Literature' in Jerry W. Wright Jr.and Everett K. Rowson (eds), *Homoeroticism in Classical Arabic Literature* (Columbia University Press, New York, 1997).

Offord, Baden and Leon Cantrell, 'Unfixed in a Fixated World: Identity, Sexuality, Race and Culture' in Peter A. Jackson and Gerard Sullivan (eds), *Multicultural Queer: Australian Narratives* (Harrington Park Press, Binghamton, 1999).

OHCHR, 'Ending Violence and Criminal Sanctions on the Basis of Sexual Orientation and Gender Identity', United Nations, Office of the High Commissioner for Human Rights (OHCHR), 23 September 2010, available at http://www.ohchr.org/EN/NewsEvents/Pages/GenderIdentity.aspx (accessed 21 April 2014).

Ohlson, Winfred E, 'Adultery: A Review', *Boston University Law Review* 17 (1937), p. 330.

Opler, Morris E, 'The Hijarā (Hermaphrodites) of India and Indian National Character: A Rejoinder', *American Anthropologist* 62 (1960), p. 505.

Origen, 'In Genesim homiliæ' in Jacques-Paul Migne (ed.), *Patrologiæ cursus completus... Series Græca* (Imprimerie Catholique, Paris, 1857), Vol. 12.

Otiz, Fernando, *Cuban Counterpoint: Tobacco and Sugar* (Duke University Press, Durham, 1995 [1940]).

Packer, John and Murtaza Shaikh, 'OIC Independent Permanent Human Rights Commission: A Key Step towards Implementation' (2012) 20 *OIC Journal* 68, available at http://www.oic-oci.org/journal.asp (accessed 30 April 2014).

Pagden, Anthony, 'Human Rights, Natural Rights, and Europe's Imperial Legacy', *Political Theory* 31 (2003), p. 2.

Pahuja, Sundhya, *Decolonising International Law: Development, Economic Growth and the Politics of Universality* (Cambridge Studies in International and Comparative Law Series, Cambridge University Press, Cambridge, 2011).

Pal, Izzud-Din, 'Women and Islam in Pakistan', *Middle Eastern Studies* 26/4 (1990), p.449

Pamment, Claire, 'Hijraism: Jostling for a Third Space in Pakistani Politics', *Drama Review* 54/2 (2010), p. 29 .

Parker, Holt N, 'The Myth of the Heterosexual: Anthropology and Sexuality for Classicists', *Arethusa* 34/3 (2001), p.313.

Parker, Richard, Regina Maria Barbosa and Peter Aggleton (eds), *Framing the Sexual Subject: the Politics of Gender, Sexuality and Power* (University of California Press, Berkeley, 2000).

Peirce, Leslie, 'Writing Histories of Sexuality in the Middle East', *American Historical Review* 114/5 (2009), p. 1325.

Pelras, Christian, *The Bugis* (Blackwell, Oxford, 1996).

Permanent Mission of Pakistan to the United Nations in Geneva, 'Aide Memoire on behalf of the OIC', distributed to the delegates of the 59th session of the United Nations Commission on Human Rights, 17 March – 24 April 2003, in response to the draft resolution E/CN.4/2003/L.92 entitled 'Human Rights and Sexual Orientation'.

Permanent Mission of Syria to the United Nations, *Response to Statement on Human Rights and the So-Called Notions of 'Sexual Orientation' and 'Gender Identity'*, UN General Assembly, 63rd Session, New York, 18 December 2008, available in audio-visual form at www.un.org/webcast/ga2008.html (accessed 7 January 2014), transcript on file with author.

Perry, Michael J, *The Idea of Human Rights: Four Inquiries* (Oxford University Press, Oxford, 1998).

Petchesky, Rosalind, 'Sexual Rights: Inventing a Concept. Mapping an International Practice' in Richard Parker, Regina Maria Barbosa and Peter Aggleton (eds), *Framing the Sexual Subject: the Politics of Gender, Sexuality and Power* (University of California Press, Berkeley, 2000).

——, 'Sexual Rights Policies across Countries and Cultures: Conceptual Frameworks and Minefields' in Richard Parker, Rosalind Petchesky and Robert Sember (eds), *Sex Politics: Reports from the Front-lines* (Sexuality Policy Watch, Rio de Janeiro, 2007).

Peters, Rudolph, *Crime and Punishment in Islamic Law: Theory and Practice from the Sixteenth to the Twenty-first Century* (Cambridge University Press, Cambridge, 2005).

Peters, Ruud, 'Islamic Law and Human Rights: A Contribution to an Ongoing Debate', *Islam and Christian-Muslim Relations* 10/1 (1999), p. 5.

Petersen, Marie Juul, *Islamic or Universal Human Rights? The OIC's Independent Permanent human Rights Commission*, DIIS Report 2012:03 (Danish Institute for International Studies, Copenhagen, 2012).

Philipp, Thomas and Ulrich Haarmann (eds), *The Mamluks in Egyptian Politics and Society* (Cambridge University Press, Cambridge, 1998).

Pillay, Navanethem, *High Commissioner's Report to the Human Rights Council on Violence and Discrimination based on Sexual Orientation and Gender Identity*, 15 December 2011, UN Doc A/HRC/19/41, available at http://www.ohchr.org/EN/Issues/Discrimination/Pages/LGBTUNReports.aspx (accessed 24 April 2014).

Pinckney Stetkevych, Suzanne, 'Intoxication and Immorality: Wine and Associated Imagery in al-Ma'arri's Garden' in Fedwa Malti-Douglas (ed.), *Critical Pilgrimages: Studies in the Arabic Literary Tradition* (spec.edn. of *Literature East and West*; Department of Oriental and African Languages and Literatures, University of Texas at Austin, Austin, 1989).

Plummer, Ken (ed.), *The Making of Modern Homosexual* (Hutchinson, London, 1981).

——, *Intimate Citizenship: Private Decisions and Public and Public Dialogues* (University of Washington Press, Seattle, 2003).

Pohier, Jacques Marie, *Le Chrétien, le plaisir et la sexualité* (Editions du Cerf, Paris, 1974).

Popescu-Judetz, Eugenia, 'Köçek and Çengi in Turkish Culture', *Dance Studies* 6 (1982), p. 53.

Pottage, Alain, 'Persons and Things: An Ethnographic Analogy', *Economy and Society* 30/1 (2010), p. 112.

Pound, Roscoe, 'Law in Books and Law in Action', *American Law Review* 44 (1910), p. 12.

Powell, Kimberly, 'Making Sense of Place: Mapping as a Multisensory Research Method', *Qualitative Inquiry* 16 (2010), p. 539.

Powers, David S, *Law, Society, and Culture in the Maghrib, 1300-1500* (Cambridge University Press, Cambridge, 2002).

Preston, Laurence W, 'A Right to Exist: Eunuchs and the State in Nineteenth-Century India', *Modern Asian Studies* 21/2 (1987), p. 371.

Prumiensis, Regino, *Libri duo de synodalibus causis et disciplinis ecclesiasticis* (ed.)FGA Wasserschleben (G Engelmann, Lipsiæ, 1840).

Puar, Jasbir K, *Terrorist Assemblages: Homonationalism in Queer Times* (Duke University Press, Durham, 2007).

Qadikhan, al-Hasan ibn Manzur al-Uzjandi al-Farghani, *al-Fatawa* (Dar al-ma'rifa, Beirut, 1973 [c.1189]).

Raghuramaiah, K Lakshmi, *Night Birds: Indian Prostitutes from Devadasis to Call Girls* (Chanakya, New Delhi, 1991).

Rahman, Fazlur, *Major Themes of the Quran* (Bibliotheca Islamica, Minneapolis, 1980).

Rahman, Momin, *Sexuality and Democracy: Identities and Strategies in Lesbian and Gay Politics* (Edinburgh University Press, Edinburgh, 2000).

————, 'In Search of My Mother's Garden: Reflections on Migration, Sexuality and Muslim Identity', *Nebula* 5/4 (2008), p. 1.

Rajagopal, Balakrishnan, 'Introduction: Encountering Ambivalence' in Mark Goodale and Sally Engle Merry (eds), *The Practice of Human Rights: Tracking Law between the Global and the Local* (Cambridge University Press, Cambridge, 2007).

Rao, I. Bhooshana, 'Male Homosexual Transvestism: A Social Menace', *Antiseptic* 52 (1955), p. 519

Rao, Rahul, *Third World Protest: Between Home and the World* (Oxford University Press, Oxford, 2010).

Redding, Jeffrey A, 'Human Rights and Homo-sectuals: The International Politics of Sexuality, Religion, and Law', *Northwestern Journal of International Human Rights* 4 (2005-2006), p. 436.

Reddy, Gayatri, *With Respect to Sex: Negotiating Hijra Identity in South India* (University of Chicago Press, Chicago, 2005).

Rehman, Javaid and Susan C Breau (eds), *Religion, Human Rights and International Law: A Critical Examination of Islamic State Practices* (Martinus Nijhoff Publishers, Leiden, 2007).

Reinhart, A. Kevin, 'Transcendence and Social Practice: Muftis and Qadis as Religious Interpreters', *Annales islamologiques* 27 (1993), p. 5.

Reus-Smit, Christian (ed.), *The Politics of International Law* (Cambridge University Press, Cambridge, 2004).

Rich, Adrienne, 'Compulsory Heterosexuality and Lesbian Existence' in Henry Abelove, Michele Aina Barale and David M Halperin (eds), *The Lesbian and Gay Studies Reader* (Routledge, New York, 1993).

Richardson, Diane, 'Heterosexuality and Social Theory' in Diane Richardson (ed.), *Theorising Heterosexuality* (Open University Press, Milton Keynes, 1996).

————, 'Constructing Sexual Citizenship: Theorizing Sexual Rights', *Critical Social Policy* 20 (2000), p. 105.

————, *Rethinking Sexuality* (Sage, London, 2000).

Riedel, Bruce, 'Foreword' in Stephen P. Cohen (ed.), *The Future of Pakistan* (Brookings Institution Press, Washington, 2011).

Riley-Smith, Jonathan, *The Oxford History of the Crusades* (Oxford University Press, New York, 1999).

Ringrose, Kathryn M, *The Perfect Servant: Eunuchs and the Social Construction of Gender in Byzantium* (University of Chicago Press, Chicago, 2003).

Rist, John M, *Stoic Philosophy* (Cambridge University Press, Cambridge, 1977).

Robinson, Colin, 'Decolonising Sexual Citizenship: Who Will Effect Change in the South of the Commonwealth?', *Opinions*, April 2012, the Commonwealth Advisory Bureau, p 6, available at http://www.commonwealthadvisorybureau. org-/fileadmin/CPSU/documents/Publications/April_Opinion.pdf (accessed 3 May 2014).

Rosenthal, Franz, 'Ar-Razi on the Hidden Illness', *Bulletin of the History of Medicine* 52 (1978), p.45.

———, 'Male and Female: Described and Compared' in Jerry W. Wright Jr.and Everett K. Rowson (eds), *Homoeroticism in Classical Arabic Literature* (Columbia University Press, New York, 1997).

Rowson, Everett K, 'The Categorization of Gender and Sexual Irregularity in Medieval Arabic Vice Lists' in Julia Epstein and Kristina Straub (eds), *Bodyguards: The Cultural Politics of Gender Ambiguity* (Routledge, New York, 1991).

———, 'The Effeminates of Early Medina', *Journal of the American Oriental Society* 111/4 (1991), p.671.

———, 'The Homoerotic Narratives from Mamluk Literature: al-Safadi's *Law'at al-shaki* and Ibn Daniyal's *al-Mutayyam*' in Jerry W. Wright Jr.and Everett K. Rowson (eds), *Homoeroticism in Classical Arabic Literature* (Columbia University Press, New York, 1997).

Rydström, Jens and Kati Mustola (eds), *Criminally Queer: Homosexuality and Criminal Law in Scandinavia, 1842–1999* (Aksant, Amsterdam, 2007).

Safi, Omid (ed.), *Progressive Muslims: On justice, Gender, and Pluralism* (Oneworld, Oxford, 2003).

Said, Abdul Aziz, Mohammed Abu-Nimer and Meena Sharify-Funk (eds), *Contemporary Islam: Dynamic, not Static* (Routledge, London, 2006).

Said, Edward W, *Orientalism* (Penguin Books, London, 2003 [1978, 1995, 2003]).

Sanders, Paula, 'Gendering the Ungendered Body: Hermaphrodites in Medieval Islamic Law' in Nikki R. Keddie and Beth Baron (eds), *Women in Middle Eastern History: Shifting Boundaries in Sex and Gender* (Yale University Press, New Heaven, 1991).

Sandland, Ralph, 'Crossing and Not Crossing: Gender, Sexuality and Melancholy in the European Court of Human Rights (*Christine Goodwin* v. *United Kingdom* [. . .], *I* v. *United Kingdom* [. . .])', *Feminist Legal Studies* 11/2 (2003), p. 191.

———, 'Feminism and the Gender Recognition Act 2004', *Feminist Legal Studies* 13/1 (2005), p.43.

Sanghvi, Malavika, 'Walking the Wild Side', *Illustrated Weekly of India*, 11 March 1984, pp. 25-28.

Sanyal, Usha, *Devotional Islam and Politics in British India: Ahmad Riza Khan Barelwi and His Movement, 1870-1920* (Oxford University Press, Delhi, 1996).

Sardar Ali, Shaheen, 'The Twain Doth Meet! A Preliminary Exploration of the Theory and Practice of *as-Siyar* and International Law in the Contemporary World' in Javaild Rehman and Susan C Breau (eds), *Religion, Human Rights and International Law: A Critical Examination of Islamic State Practices* (Martinus Nijhoff Publishers, Leiden, 2007).

Schacht, Joseph, *Introduction to Islamic Law* (Oxford University Press, London, 1964).

Schetter, Conrad, 'Ethnoscapes, National Territorialisation, and the Afghan War', *Geopolitics* 10/1 (2005), p. 50.

Schimmel, Annemarie, 'Eros – Heavenly and Not So Heavenly – in Sufi Literature and Life' in Afaf Lutfi as-Sayyid Marsot (ed.), *Society and the Sexes in Medieval Islam* (Undena Publications, Malibu, 1979).

Scholz, Piotr O, *Eunuchs and Castrati: A Cultural History*, translated by John A. Broadwin and Shelly L. Frisch (Markus Wiener Publishers, Princeton, 2001 [1999]).

Scott, Joan, 'Deconstructing Equality-Versus-Difference: Or, the Uses of Poststructuralist Theory for Feminism' in Diana Tietjens Meyers (ed.), *Feminist Social Thought: A Reader* (Routledge, New York, 1997).

Seale, Patrick, *The Struggle for Arab Independence: Riad el-Solh and the Makers of the Modern Middle East* (Cambridge University Press, Cambridge, 2009).

Sedgwick, Eve Kosofsky, *The Epistemology of the Closet* (University of California Press, Berkeley, 1990).

———, *Tendencies* (Routledge, London, 1994).

———, 'Melanie Klein and the Difference Affect Makes' in Janet Halley and Andrew Parker (eds), *After Sex? On Writing since Queer Theory* (Duke University Press, Durham, 2011).

Segesvary, Victor, 'Group Rights: The Definition of Group Rights in the Contemporary Legal Debate based on Socio-Cultural Analysis', *International Journal on Group Rights* 3 (1995), p. 89.

Seidman, Steven (ed.), *Queer Theory/Sociology* (Blackwell, Oxford, 1996).

Seneca, Lucius Annæus, *De vita beata*, translated by Russell Halderman Wagner (Cornell University Press, Ithaca, 1923).

———, *De beneficiis*, (ed.) William Hardy Alexander (University of California Press, Berkeley, 1950).

———, *L Annæi Senecæ ad Lucilium epistolæ selectæ* (University of Michigan Library, Ann Arbor, 2009).

Shah, A.M, 'A Note on the Hijadas of Gujarat', *American Anthropologist* 63/6 (1961), p. 1325.

Shah, Niaz A, *Women, the Koran and International Human Rights Law: The Experience of Pakistan* (Martinus Nijhoff Publishers, Leiden, 2006).

Shaheed, Farida, 'The Women's Movement in Pakistan: Challenges and Achievements' in Amrita Basu (ed.), *Women's Movements in the Global Era: The Power of Local Feminisms* (Westview Press, Boulder, 2010).

Shalakany, Amr, 'Islamic Legal Histories', *Berkeley Journal of Middle Eastern and Islamic Law* 1 (2008), p. 1.

Sharma, Satish Kumar, *Hijras: The Labelled Deviants* (Gian, New Delhi, 1989).

Shaw, Stanford, *History of the Ottoman Empire and Modern Turkey* (Cambridge University Press, Cambridge, 1976), Vol. 1.

Sheill, Kate, 'Loosing Out in the Intersections: Lesbians, Human Rights, Law and Activism', *Contemporary Politics* 15 (2009), p. 55.

Sibalis, Michael David, 'The Regulation of Homosexuality in Revolutionary and Napoleonic France' in Jeffrey Merrick and Bryant T. Ragan (eds), *Homosexuality in Modern France* (Oxford University Press, Oxford, 1996).

Silverstein, Michael, 'Shifters, Linguistic Categories, and Cultural Description' in Keith H Basso and Henry A Selby (eds), *Meaning in Anthropology* (Harper & Row, New York, 1976).

Sinha, A.P, 'Procreation among the Eunuchs', *Eastern Anthropologist* 20/2 (1967), p. 168.

Slater, Sharon, 'UN Delegates Honored for Standing for the Family', the Family Watch International, 18 November 2010, available at http://www.family watchinternational.org/fwi/newsletter/0485.cfm (accessed 30 April 2014).

Smart, Carol, 'The Woman of Legal Discourse', *Social and Legal Studies* 1 (1992), p. 29.

Smith, Anthony D, 'Culture, Community and Territory: The Politics of Ethnicity and Nationalism', *International Affairs* 72/3 (1996), p. 445.

Soroush, Abdolkarim, *Reason, Freedom and Democracy in Islam*, translated by/(ed.) M Sadri and A Sadri (Oxford University Press, Oxford, 2000).

Sousa Santos, Boaventura de, *Toward a New Legal Common Sense: Law, Globalization, and Emancipation* (2nd edn; Butterworths, London, 2002).

———, *Another Production is Possible: Beyond the Capitalist Canon* (Verso, London, 2006), Vol. 2.

———, *Another Production is Possible: Beyond Northern Epistemologies* (Verso, London 2006), Vol. 3.

———, 'The World Social Forum and the Global Left', *Politics and Society* 36/2 (2008), p. 247.

Spivak, Gayatri Chakravorty, 'Can the Subaltern Speak?' in Cary Nelson and Lawrence Grossberg (eds), *Marxism and the Interpretation of Culture* (University of Illinois Press, Urbana, 1988).

———, *The Post-Colonial Critic: Interviews, Strategies, Dialogues* (Routledge, New York, 1990).

———, 'Righting Wrongs', *South Atlantic Quarterly* 103 (2004), p. 523.

Squires, Judith, *The New Politics of Gender Equality* (Palgrave Macmillan, Basingstoke, 2007).

Statement on Human Rights, Sexual Orientation and Gender Identity, on behalf of 66 States, under Agenda Item 64(b), UN General Assembly, 63rd session, New York, 18 December 2008, UN Doc A/63/635.

Statement by the Permanent Observer Mission of the Holy See to the United Nations, 63rd session of the United Nations General Assembly, Item 64(b); available at http://www.holyseemission.org/statements/statement.aspx?id=112 (accessed 21 April 2014).

Sterns, Indrikis, 'Crime and Punishment among the Teutonic Knights', *Speculum* 57 (1982), p. 91.

Stilt, Kristen, 'Price Setting and Hoarding in Mamluk Egypt: The Lessons of Legal Realism for Islamic Legal Studies' in Peri Bearman, Wolfhart Heinrichs and Bernard G. Weiss (eds), *The Law Applied: Contextualizing the Islamic Shari'a* (I.B.Tauris, London, 2008).

Stoller, Robert, *Sex and Gender: On the Development of Masculinity and Femininity* (Science House, New York, 1968).

Stryker, Susan, 'Transgender Studies: Queer Theory's Evil Twin', *Journal of Lesbian and Gay Studies* 10/2 (2004), p. 212.

Stryker, Susan and Stephen Whittle (eds), *The Transgender Studies Reader* (Routledge, London, 2006).

Stryker, Susan, Paisley Currah and Lisa Jean Moore, 'Introduction: Trans-, Trans, or Transgender?', *Women's Studies Quarterly* 36/3-4 (2008), p. 11.

Stubbs, William and Helen J. Nicholson, *Chronicle of the Third Crusade: A Translation of the Itinerarium peregrinorum et gesta Regis Ricardi* (Ashgate, Aldershot, 201).

Stychin, Carl and Didi Herman (eds), *Law and Sexuality: the Global Arena* (University of Minnesota Press, Minneapolis, 2001 [2000]).

Swiebel, Joke, 'Lesbian, Gay, Bisexual and Transgender Human rights: The Search for an International Strategy', *Contemporary Politics* 15 (2009), p. 19.

Tatchell, Peter, 'David Cameron Urged: Apologise for Anti-Gay Laws Imposed by UK', Peter Tatchell Foundation, 27 October 2011, available at http://www.petertatchellfoundation.org/commonwealth/david-cameron-urged-apologise-anti-gay-laws-imposed-uk (accessed 3 May 2014).

Teh, Yik Koon, '*Mak Nyahs* (Male Transsexuals) in Malaysia: The Influence of Culture and Religion on Their Identity' (2001) 5 *International Journal of Transgenderism*, on-line edition, available at http://www.symposion.com/ijt (accessed 16 January 2010).

Thapar, Romila, *Aśoka and the Decline of the Mauryas* (rev. edn; Oxford University Press, New York 1998 [1961]).

The Wolfenden Report: Report of the Committee on Homosexual Offences and Prostitution (Stein and Day; New York 1963 [1957]).

Thomas, J.A.C, 'Accusatio adulterii', *Iura* 12 (1961), p.65.

Tor, Deborah G, 'Sanjar, Ahmad b Malekšah' in *Encyclopaedia Iranica* (online edn.), available at http://www.iranicaonline.org/articles/sanjar (accessed 17 July 2014).

Tougher, Shaun (ed.), *Eunuchs in Antiquity and Beyond* (Classical Press of Wales, Swansea, 2002).

——, *The Eunuch in Byzantine History and Society* (Routledge, Oxford, 2008).

——, *Roman Castrati: Eunuchs in the Roman Empire* (Continuum, London, 2015 [*forthcoming*]).

Tsai, Shih-Shan Henry, *The Eunuchs in the Ming Dynasty* (State University of New York Press, Albany, 1996).

Tsevat, Matitiahu, 'The Husband Veils a Wife (Hittite Laws, §§197-98)', *Journal of Cuneiform Studies* 27 (1975), p. 235.

Turner, Victor, *The Ritual Process: Structure and Anti-structure* (Cornell University Press, New York, 1991 [1969]).

UNHCR, *Handbook for the Protection of Women and Girls* (Office of the UN High Commissioner for Refugees (UNHCR), Geneva, 2008).

Vakulenko, Anastasia, '*Islamic Dress in Human Rights Jurisprudence and the Surrounding Debate: A Critical Feminist Analysis*'. PhD in Laws thesis submitted to the University of Nottingham (University of Nottingham School of Law, Nottingham, 2008), on file with author.

Valentine, David, *Imagining Transgender: An Ethnography of a Category* (Duke University Press, Durham, 2007).

Valocchi, Stephen, 'Not Yet Queer Enough: The Lessons of Queer Theory for the Sociology of Gender and Sexuality', *Gender and Society* 19/6 (2005), p. 750.

Van Dobben, Danielle J, '*Dancing Modernity: Gender, Sexuality and the State in the Late Ottoman Empire and Early Turkish Republic*' MA thesis, Department of Near Eastern Studies, University of Arizona (2008).

Van Hoecke, Willy and Andries Welkenhuysen (eds), *Love and Marriage in the Twelfth Century* (Leuven University Press, Leuven, 1981).

Vanita, Ruth and Saleem Kidwai (eds), *Same-Sex Love in India: Readings from Literature and History* (Palgrave, New York, 2001 [2000]).

Varisco, Daniel Martin, *Islam Obscured: The Rhetoric of Anthropological Representation* (Palgrave Macmillan, New York, 2005).

Vines, Gail, *Raging Hormones: Do They Rule Our Lives?* (Virago, London, 1993).

Voltaire, François Marie Arouet de, *Oeuvres completes de Voltaire*, (ed.) L.E.D. Moland (Garnier Frères, Paris, 1877-1885), 52 Vols.

Wadud, Amina, *Inside the Gender Jihad: Women's Reform in Islam* (Oneworld, Oxford, 2007 [2006]).

Waites, Matthew, 'Critique of "Sexual Orientation" and "Gender Identity" in Human Rights Discourse: Global Queer Politics beyond the Yogyakarta Principles', *Contemporary Politics* 15 (2009), p. 137.

Watkins, Oscar D, *A History of Penance* (Longmans, Green & Co, London, 1920), 2 Vols.

Weber, Max, *Max Weber on Law in Economy and Society*, translated by Edward Shils and Max Rheinstein; (ed.) Max Rheinstein (Simon and Schuster, New York, 1954).

Weinthal, Benjamin, 'Iran Reportedly Hangs Gay Man', the *Jerusalem Post*, 29 April 2012, available at http://www.jpost.com/MiddleEast/Article.aspx?id=267868 (accessed 4 May 2014).

Weiss, Bernard G. (ed.), *Studies in Islamic Legal Theory* (Brill, Leiden, 2002).

———, 'Text and Application: Hermeneutical Reflections on Islamic Legal Interpretation' in Peri Bearman, Wolfhart Heinrichs and Bernard G. Weiss (eds), *The Law Applied: Contextualizing the Islamic Shari'a* (I.B.Tauris, London, 2008).

Whittle, Stephen, *Respect and Equality: Transsexual and Transgender Rights* (Cavendish Publishing, London, 2002).

Wiedemann, Hans-Georg, *Homosexuelle Liebe: Für eine Neuorientirung in der christlichen Ethik* (Kreuz, Stuttgart, 1982).

Wieringa, Saskia Eleonora, 'Postcolonial Amnesia: Sexual Moral Panics, Memory, and Imperial Power' in Gilbert H. Herdt (ed.), *Moral Panics, Sex Panics: Fear and the Fight over Sexual Rights* (New York University Press, New York, 2009).

Wilcke, Claus, 'Der Kodex Urnamma (CU): Versuch einer Rekonstruktion' in Zvi Abusch (ed.), *Riches Hidden in Secret Places: Ancient Near Eastern Studies in Memory of Thorkild Jacobson* (Eisenbrauns, Winona Lake, 2002).

Williams, Zoe, 'Gay Rights: A World of Inequality', *Guardian*, 13 September 2011, available at http://www.guardian.co.uk/world/2011/sep/13/gay-rights-world-of-inequality (accessed 3 May 2014).

Wilson, Angelia R, 'The "Neat Concept" of Sexual Citizenship: A Cautionary Tale for Human Rights Discourse', *Contemporary Politics* 15 (2009), p. 73.

Wilson, Richard Ashby, 'Tyrannosaurus Lex: The Anthropology of Human Rights and Transnational Law' in Mark Goodale and Sally Engle Merry (eds), *The Practice of Human Rights: Tracking Law between the Global and the Local* (Cambridge University Press, Cambridge, 2007).

Wink, André, *Al-Hind: The Making of the Indo-Islamic World* (Brill, Leiden, 2004), Vol. 3.

Wintemute, Robert, *Sexual Orientation and Human Rights: The United States Constitution, the European Convention, and the Canadian Charter* (Clarendon Press, Oxford, 1995).

———, 'De l'égalité des orientations sexuelles à la liberté sexuelle: Jurisprudence européenne et comparée' in Daniel Borrillo and Danièle Lochak (eds), *La liberté sexuelle* (Presses Universitaires de France, Paris, 2005).

———, 'Same-Sex Love and Indian Penal Code §377: An Important Human Rights Issue for India', *National University of Juridical Sciences Law Review* 4 (2011), p. 31.

Wintemute, Robert and Mads Andenæs (eds), *Legal Recognition of Same-Sex Partnerships: A Study of National, European and International Law* (Hart Publishing, Oxford, 2001).

Wolpert, Stanley, *Jinnah of Pakistan* (Oxford University Press, Oxford, 1984).

Woodward, Kathryn (ed.), *Identity and Difference* (Sage, London, 1997).

Wright Jr, Jerry W. and Everett K. Rowson (eds), *Homoeroticism in Classical Arabic Literature* (Columbia University Press, New York, 1997).

Wynbrandt, James, *A Brief History of Pakistan* (Facts on File, New York, 2009).

Yaron, Reuven, *The Laws of Eshnunna* (2nd rev. edn, Magnes Press, Jerusalem, 1988 [1969]).

Yip, Andrew Kam-Tuck, 'The Quest for Intimate/Sexual Citizenship: Lived Experiences of Lesbian and Bisexual Muslim Women', *Contemporary Islam* 2 (2008), p. 99.

Yoshino, Kenji, 'Covering', *The Yale Law Journal* 111 (2002), p. 769.

Zahed, L. and Amina Wadud, *Livre Blanc: 2012 retraite spirituelle et quête culturelle aux sources de l'islam* (n.p; Paris 2012), available at http://www.calem.eu/Tawhid-Omrah_pelerinage-islamique-Mecque-Madinah-Juin2012-Radjab1433_avec-Amina-Wadud-&-inclusifs-progressistes-Musulman-es.html (accessed 24 August 2014).

Zayyat, Habib, 'al-Mar'a al-ghulamiyya fi al-Islam', *al-Machriq* 50 (1956), p. 15.

Ze'evi, Dror, *Producing Desire: Changing Sexual Discourse in the Ottoman Middle East, 1500-1900* (University of California Press, Berkeley, 2006).

Zeidan, Sami, 'The Limits of Queer Theory in LGBT Litigation and the International Human Rights Discourse', *Willamette Journal of International Law and Dispute Resolution* 14 (2006), p. 73.

Zilfi, Madeline C, 'The Ottoman *Ulema*' in Suraiya N. Faroqhi (ed.), *The Cambridge History of Turkey: The Latter Ottoman Empire 1603-1893* (Cambridge University Press, Cambridge, 2006), Vol. 3.

———, *Women and Slavery in the Late Ottoman Empire: The Design of Difference* (Cambridge University Press, Cambridge, 2010).

Zubaida, Sami, *Law and Power in the Islamic World* (I.B.Tauris, London, 2005 [2003]).

INDEX

'Abbasids, 89, 94, 96, 97, 102–3, 110, 112, 115, 121, 138, 249n.92, 254n.154

Abbottabad, 145, 166

'Abduh, Muhammad, 130–1, 249n.97

Abraham, see Prophet Abraham

Abu Bakr, 88, 245n.46

Abu Hanifa, 95, 98, 101, 102, 250n.111, 250–1n.113, 253n.144, 254n.146, 258n.200, 262n.263

Abu Nuwas, 134, 258n.204

Abu Yusuf, 105, 262n.263

Abu-Lughod, Lila, 197

Abyssinia, 121–2, 156
  see also habshi

Act of Dissolution, the second, 50

Act of Supremacy, the first, 49

adab, 97

'adaletname, 117

'adl, 100

adulterium, 41

adultery, 37, 41, 46, 89, 100, 128, 217n.41, 218n.46, 243n.27
  see also fornication

Afghanistan, 35, 273n.9

ağa, see khuddam

agha, see khuddam

aghawat, see khuddam

'ahadith, see hadith

ahl al-hadith, traditionalists, 95–9, 138-9, 250n.105, 253n.139

ahl al-kalam, 95, 250n.105

ahl al-ra'y, rationalists, 95–9, 139, 250n.105, 254n.147, 269n.357

Ahmed, Sara, 13, 28, 195–6

Akbar the Great, Mughal emperor, 141, 172, 243–4n.27, 276n.52, 283n.131

al-Andalus (Andalusia), 89, 101, 246n.51, 259n.221

Alfonso the Wise, king of Castile, 47

'Ali b. Abi Talib, 88, 245n.46, 245n.47

'alim, see ulama

Alvaro of Urgel, Count, 47

'amal qawm Lut, 90, 91
  see also Prophet Lot

American Convention of Human Rights, 62

Anglo-Muhammadan law, 124–6, 128, 132, 138, 268n.332

'aqida, 197

Arabian Nights, The, 134

ARC International, 59, 62, 229n.143

Aristotle, 15

Armenia, 88

Asad, Talal, 16

askeri, 115–16, 119–20, 262n.260

Aslam, Mohammad, *khwajasara*
    activist, 166
Aśoka the Great, 15
'asr al-sa'ada, 88
Augustine of Hippo, St, 41, 216n.27,
    218n.50
Augustus, first Roman emperor, 41
Aurangzeb, Mughal emperor, 172
awlad al-nas, 110, 112
    see also Mamluks
awqaf, 260–1n.238
a'yan, 103
'Ayyubids, 266n.309

Baghdad, 7, 89, 103, 164, 250n.105,
    256n.185, 258n.213
Ban Ki-moon, 64
Bangladesh, 31, 146, 224–5n108
Barlas, Asma, 91–2
Baybars, Mamluk sultan, 110, 112–13
beau vice, 51
Beijing Platform for Action, 57
beloveds, 97, 98, 118, 252–3n.131
Beşir, Ottoman *kızlar ağası*, 122
Bhutto, Benazir, 144
Bible, 39, 41, 90, 216n.21
    see also Old Testament;
    New Testament; Gospels
Boleyn, Anne, 49
Boniface VIII, Pope, 47
Bosnia and Herzegovina, 10, 63, 119,
    142, 145, 151, 232n.178,
    264n.291, 276n.48
Bouhdiba, Abdelwahab, 134
Braudel, Fernand, 86, 245n.36
Britain, *see* United Kingdom
British Raj, 54, 273n.11
Brown, Louise, 145,
Brown, Wendy, 17
Browne, Sir Thomas, 39
bûcheres de Sodome, 51, 78, 107, 191
Buddhism, 15, 37, 109
Buggery Act, 48–50
Bulleh Shah, 152–3

Buti, Muhammad Sa'id, 132
Butler, Judith, 17, 212n.135
Byzantium, 47, 115, 117, 121,
    267n.324

Cæsarius of Arles, St, 41
Cairo, 7, 110, 112, 113, 121–2,
    259n.218
Calder, Norman, 80, 243n.22,
    251n.119, 271n.395
caliph, 88, 93, 95, 102, 104, 112,
    114, 115, 116, 120, 138, 192,
    203–4n.23, 246n.51, 249n.92,
    249n.94, 249n.98, 250n.111,
    250–1n.113, 255n.168
    see also khulafa' al-rashidun
caliphate, 15, 88, 89, 95, 112, 115,
    121, 128, 129, 138
    the first Muslim, 15, 203–4n.23,
    259n.221
capitalism, 31, 124, 128, 142, 180, 191
Case 63/09, 148–51, 166, 168, 169,
    177–8, 183, 188, 275n.31
Charter on Sexual and Reproductive
    Rights, 20
Chaudhry, Iftikhar Muhammad, 147,
    149, 168
China, 37, 223n.103
Christianity, 37–47, 52–3, 68, 78, 85,
    102, 113, 115, 119, 141,
    144, 151, 155, 164, 190–1,
    213–14n.153, 215n.14, 216n.27,
    216–17n.33, 217n.39, 217n.45,
    234n.205, 253n.132, 264n.291,
    269n.339, 276n48, 282n.115
class, 15, 22, 38, 41, 46, 48, 51, 78, 83,
    89, 97, 98, 103, 107, 108, 110,
    111, 112, 115–16, 119–20, 136,
    140, 143, 144, 145, 153,
    155, 156, 157, 161, 163, 164,
    169–174, 176, 179, 181,
    183, 186, 189, 191, 194, 198n.1,
    200–1n.27, 260n.233, 260n.237,
    260–1n.238, 262n.260,

264n.291, 275n.29, 280n.95, 282–3n.127
Code pénal de la Révolution, 51
colonialism, 7, 9, 12, 15, 32, 37–8, 53–5, 62, 68, 70, 75–9, 84–5, 94, 123–6, 129, 130, 132, 134, 135, 137, 138, 140, 145, 146, 147–8, 149, 151, 153, 156, 157, 159, 160, 166, 172, 182–6, 191, 202n.5, 223–4n.104, 224n.107, 224–5n.108, 225n.109, 226–7n.117, 231n.171, 240n.247, 241n.151, 244n.29, 244n.32, 268n.334, 268n.336, 270–1n.378, 274n.22, 276n.45, 277n.59, 278n.73, 282n.123
Commission on Human Rights, the former United Nations', 59, 62, 198n.2
commodification, 77, 179, 186
common law, English, 48, 147, 148, 269n.353, 273n.12
Comperta, 49
Condorcet, Nicolas de, 51
Constantine the Great, Roman emperor, 41
Constantinople, 109, 115, 117
   see also Istanbul
Constitution of Medina, 203n.22
constructionism, 12, 26–7, 30, 202n.2, 212n.133
Convention on the Elimination of all Forms of Discrimination Against Women, 185
Corpus iuris civilis, 43
Coulson, Noel J., 83, 249n.95, 242n.16, 252n.123
Council of Europe, 57–8, 60, 61, 71, 198–9n.6, 226n.114
crime passionnel, 128
Criminal Tribes Act, 157, 278n.70
critical legal studies, 13
Cromwell, Thomas, 49, 50, 221n.81
Crusades, 45, 78, 110, 192, 220n.67

cultural relativism, 11–12, 14, 15–16, 74, 77, 79, 202n.1

Damascus, 6, 88, 113, 133
dar'a ta'arud al-'aql wal-naql, 130
darura, 131
Declaration on the Elimination of All Forms of Intolerance and of Discrimination Based on Religion or Belief, 22
dera, see deray
deray, khwajasara households, 162, 163, 280n.95
devşirme, 119–20, 139, 264n.289, 264n.291, 264n.292
dhikr, 164, 282n.117
Diwan, 134
Diwan-i 'Amm, 141
diyya, 100, 254n.156, 255n.157

East India Company, 125
Ebussu'ud Efendi, 117
Egypt, 71, 88, 109, 110, 130, 131, 242n.18, 246n.51, 249n.97, 259–60n.224, 266n.309, 268n.334
El-Rouayheb, Khaled, 119
Elizabeth I, queen of England, 50
English law, 45–52, 53–5, 126, 147, 200n.18, 222n.94, 224–5n.108
   see also common law
Enlightenment, 51, 129, 131, 140
Eshnunna, 37
essentialism, 12, 26–7, 29, 59, 86, 137, 170, 202n.2, 211n.113
étatism, 35, 116, 130, 132
ethnography, 2, 6, 8–9, 142, 155, 188, 201n.37, 277n.59, 282n.114
ethnoscape, 142, 154, 155, 188, 272n.2
eunuchs, 54, 87, 150, 157, 244n.30, 266n.310, 267n.321
European Convention on Human Rights, 57–8, 60, 61, 79, 198n.6, 223n.102, 226n.114

European Court of Human Rights, 3, 57–8, 60–1, 65, 71, 198n.6, 223n.102, 233n.194

fahisha, 89–90, 105, 246n.59
faqih, see fuqaha'
farj, 105–6
fatawa, 96, 99, 104, 107, 117, 243n.22, 251n.119
Fatimids, 121, 246n.51
fatwa, see fatawa
Federal Shariat Court, of Pakistan, 146, 148, 274–5n.26
feminism, 7, 17, 22, 27, 45, 85, 91, 134–7, 138, 140, 149, 176
see also Islamic feminism
ferman, 116, 117
fiqh, 68, 80–5, 87–140, 147, 171, 172, 191, 192, 196, 197, 241–2n.7, 243n.22, 243–4n.27, 251–2n.121, 253n.141, 254n.155, 258n.208, 267n.325, 268n.337, 275n.30
fornication, 40, 41, 89, 100, 243n.27
Foucault, Michel, 18, 86, 206n.51
France, 12, 51, 52, 53, 54, 55, 78, 86, 107, 124, 127, 128, 226n.114, 245n.36, 264n.286, 276–7n.54
Fuero Real, 47
fuqaha', 81–2, 84, 87, 89, 93, 96, 99, 101–5, 108, 113, 122–4, 133, 136, 139, 140, 149, 192, 241n.7, 250n.111, 255n.162, 256n.179, 258n.204, 262n.263, 271n.394, 271n.395
furu' al-fiqh, 81, 83, 104, 243n.22, 257–8n.197, 258n.199

Geertz, Clifford, 9
gender identity, 2, 11, 12, 19, 23–31, 36, 38, 52, 53, 56–70, 73, 74, 77, 79, 85, 97, 185, 193, 209–10n.99, 228n.138, 229n.143, 233n.189, 236n.228, 237n.230
gender *jihad*, 136

Ghazan Khan, chief of the Mongol Ilkan clan, 110
ghulamiyyat, 97
ghusul, 122
giriya, 161, 163
Goodale, Mark, 195
Gospels, 40
Great Britain, *see* United Kingdom
Greece, ancient, 37, 39–41, 78, 95, 194, 215n.14
Guichard of Troyes, Bishop, 47
guru/chela relationship, 161–3

haba'ib, see beloveds
habashi, see habshi
habshi, 156
see also Abbyssinia
hadd, as Qur'anic punishment, *see hudud*
hadith, 92–6, 98, 99, 105, 137, 139, 171, 241n.6, 246n.63, 247n.76, 247n.79, 247–8n80, 248n.85, 248n.86, 248–9n.91, 249n.92, 250n.109, 251n.117, 251–2n.121
Hallaq, Wael B., 83, 94, 243n.22, 249n.92, 267n.325, 270n.365
Hammurabi, 37
hamzan, 173
Hanafis, 98, 101–2, 104–8, 116, 120, 122, 127, 139, 250n.106, 254n.147, 254n.152, 255n.162, 258n.200, 258n.207, 262n.263, 269n.357, 275n.30
Hanbalis, 102, 113–14, 133, 250n.106, 256n.179
haram, 106
Hastings, Warren, 126, 268n.329, 268n.331
hayba, 103
Heera Mandi, 141, 145
Henry VIII, king of England, 48, 49
hermeneutics, Islamic, 4, 32–3, 82, 85, 93, 99, 104, 125, 134–40, 244–5n.33

heteronormativity, 4, 30–2, 54, 59, 61,
68, 75, 78–9, 102, 139, 142,
212n.140, 241n.251, 244n.32
Hijaz, 6, 200n.22, 259n.221
hijre, see khwajasara
Hinduism, 126, 141, 145, 146, 151,
155, 165, 277n.60, 280n.99
hiraba, 100, 243n.27
histoire événementielle, 86–7, 245n.36
Hittites, 37
Holy See, 68, 73, 228n.138
homonationalism, 76, 211n.117
homonormativity, 30, 76, 241n.251
Hudood Ordinances, 146, 149, 183,
273n.15, 284n.142
hudud, 83, 85, 89, 100–1, 105–8, 112,
117–18, 120, 127, 128, 132, 133,
138, 140, 146, 191, 243–4n.27,
246n.64, 254n.155, 254–5n.156,
255n.163, 258n.200, 258n.208,
263n.274, 268n.337, 273n.15,
275n.30
hukm, 105
Human Rights Committee, the United
Nations', 58, 65, 79
Human Rights Council, the United
Nations', 59, 63, 64, 69, 198n.2,
239n.243
human rights wars, 35
Hunt, Paul, 18
huriya', 97, 252n.124
hybridisation, 124, 125, 130, 132, 140,
147, 153, 182, 187, 193

'ibadat, 131
Ibn Hanbal, Ahmad, 95, 98, 253n.144
Ibn Hazm, Muhammad, 101
Ibn Ishaq b. Yasar, Muhammad,
203n.22
Ibn Khaldun, 'Abd al-Rahman,
110, 113, 153, 247n.77,
253n.139
Ibn Taymiyya, Takiyy al-Din, 113–14,
133, 140

iç oğlanları, Ottoman sultan's personal
pages, 119, 120
ijma', 94, 105, 249n.94
ijtihad, 94, 98, 99, 131, 249n.96,
249n.98, 254n.147, 254n.152
ikhtilaf, 91, 102, 139
ilaj, 100, 105–6
ilmiye, 119
imperialism, 15, 16, 35, 38, 41, 45, 53,
74–5, 77, 78, 84, 85, 88, 121,
125, 126, 139, 156, 178, 191–2,
195, 211n.117, 213–14n.153,
214n.8, 218n.48, 223n.103,
224n.105, 225n.109,
226–7n.117, 239n.242,
240n.247, 265n.298,
271–2n.396, 272n.1, 276n.49,
277–8n.62, 280n.95
imponderabilia, 7, 11, 187, 200n.23
imtiyazat, Ottoman capitualtions, 126
Independent Permanent Human Rights
Commission, of the Organisation
of Islamic Cooperation, 70–1, 73
India, 7, 15, 31, 54, 121, 124–6, 138,
141, 145–6, 151, 155–60, 162,
166, 176–7, 223–4n.104,
224n.107, 237n.233, 268n.329,
268n.336, 268n.337, 274n.22,
276n.49, 277n.59, 277n.60,
277n.62, 278n.70, 280n.98,
280n.99, 280n.103, 281n.106,
282n.114, 282n.123
Indian Penal Code, §377, 158, 176,
222n.94, 283n.136
Indonesia, 31, 64, 213n.145, 233n.187,
262n.261, 270n.370, 276–7n.54
Inter-American Commission on Human
Rights, 62, 71
Inter-American Convention against All
Forms of Discrimination, 61
Inter-American Court of Human
Rights, 62, 71
International Covenant on Civil and
Political Rights, 22, 58

interruption, 6, 7–8, 86–7, 108, 121, 129, 137, 197
interventionism, 56, 75, 79, 145, 180–2, 238–9n.241
iqrar, 100
Iran, 76, 110, 238–9n.241, 259n.221, 270n.370
see also Persia
Iraq, 35, 102–3, 269n.341, 273n.9
irtidad, see ridda
ırz, 128
'ishq, 187
Islamabad, 145, 180, 181, 200n.27, 239n.242, 274n.23
Islamic feminism, 85, 91–2, 134–40
Istanbul, 7, 115, 116, 265n.298
see also Constantinople
izzat, 156, 162, 164, 168, 181

James II, king of Aragon, 47
Janissaries, see yeniçeri
Japan, 37, 239–40n.243, 259n.221
Jawziyya, Ibn Qayyim, 114
Jerome, St, 44, 216n.27, 220n.62
Jerusalem, 121, 220n.67, 266n.309
Jesus Christ, see Prophet Jesus
jharoka, 141
Jinnah, Muhammad Ali, 145–6, 273n.12
Judaism, 39, 78, 255n.168, 264n.291, 269n.339, 276n.48
Justinian I, Byzantine emperor, 41–4, 47, 218n.46, 218n.48

kadı, see qadi
kadınlar saltanatı, the sultanate of women, 265
kanun, 115–18, 120, 139, 243–4n.27, 263n.274, 263n.275
Kanun-i Osmani, 117–18, 120
kanunname, 116–17, 263n.275
Karachi, 166, 168
Kasani, 'Ala' al-Din Abu Bakr, 105

Kashmir, 146, 273n.11
Kemal Atatürk, Mustafa, 127–8, 259n.219
khadim, see khuddam
Khaki, Muhammad Aslam, 149, 275n.32
khalifa, see caliph
Khallaf, 'Abd al-Wahhab, 131
Khan Bahadur, Syud Ahmed, 156–7
Khan, Mohammed Ayub, 146, 166
khanith, 31
khojay, see khwajasara
khuddam, 84, 109, 111–12, 120–3, 138–40, 162, 244n.30, 260n.233, 261n.239, 266n.309, 266n.310, 267n.320
khulafa' al-rashidun, 88, 93, 138, 203–4n.23, 248n.85
see also caliph
khuntha
    ghayr mushkil, 122
    mushkil, 122, 149
khusre, see khwajasara
khwajasara, 1, 31, 141, 143, 144, 149–51, 155–69, 170, 174, 177, 179, 181, 184, 186, 188, 198n.1, 213n.148, 224n.105, 266n.308, 266n.311, 272n.1, 275n.32, 275n.34, 277–8n.62, 280n.95, 280n.97–9, 280n.100, 281n.106–10, 281–2n.113, 282n.115, 282n.118
Khwajasara Farsi, language, 143, 272n.3, 281n.112, 283n.134
kızlar ağası, 122
see also khuddam
köçekler, 120, 265n.300
Kufa, 95, 98
Kugle, Scott Siraj al-Haqq, 136–7

Lahore, 1, 6, 7, 8, 141–2, 145, 148, 154, 160, 163–4, 169, 170, 174, 176, 188

Lange, Christian, 107, 254n.154, 258n.199
Lateran councils, 43–4, 46, 219n.58
Lauterpacht, Sir Hersch, 34
lavat, see liwat
Lawyers' Movement, 147
legal historiography, 6, 77, 80–2, 86, 104, 109, 241–2n.7, 249n.96
see also new historians; scripturalism
legal Positivism, 98, 99
legal Realism, 5, 7, 56, 81, 104, 108, 136, 142, 227n.118
see also proto-Realism
Levant, 220n.67
lex Iulia de adulteriis coercendis, 41, 218n.46, 218n.48
LGBT, 31, 56, 61, 66, 74–6, 155, 173, 178, 180, 229n.143, 237n.233, 239n.242
Liber Gomorrhianus, 44
livata, see liwat
liwat, 84, 91, 99, 100–8, 118, 138, 139, 149, 171, 191, 252n.130, 258n.204, 258–9n.213, 262n.263, 271n.394, 275n.30
al-akbar, grand *liwat,* 101, 106
al-asghar, petty *liwat,* 101, 106
Lot, *see* Prophet Lot

ma'an/dhi relationship, 161, 163
Maalouf, Amin, 12
madaris, 113
Madayantī, *see* Mainandi
madhahib, 95–6, 98–9, 101–2, 104, 107, 116, 250n.106, 251n.117, 251n.119, 254n.147–8, 254n.152, 256n.176, 275n.30
madhhab, see madhahib
Mainandi, 1–2, 160–1, 280n.100
Majalla, see Mecelle
mak nyah, 31
Malaysia, 31, 224–5n.108

Malik b. Anas, 95, 98, 253n.139
Malikis, 101, 250n.106, 254n.152, 255n.162
Mamluks, 108–15, 120–2, 138, 139, 259n.218, 259–60n.224, 260n.225, 260n.233, 260–1n.238
maqasid, 131
Marxism, 7, 272n.4
Mary, queen of Scots, 50
maslaha, 93, 131, 132
Masud, Muhammad Khalid, 82
Mauryas, 15
mazalim, 115
Mecca, 88, 121, 154, 200n.22, 266n.310
Mecelle, 127–8, 269n.341, 271–2n.396
Medina, 80, 88, 89, 93, 98, 121–2, 154, 200n.22, 203n.22, 266n.309–10, 267n.320, 278n.75
Mehmed II, Ottoman sultan, 117
Merry, Sally Engle, 193–4
Miller, Alice M., 22
millet, 127, 269n.339
Mongols, 89, 103, 109–10, 113, 115, 259n.221, 276n.49
Mosaic law, 39, 255n.168
see also Judaism
mu'amalat, 131
mufti, 99, 115, 116, 126, 243n.22
müftü, see mufti
Mughals, 1, 7, 119, 121, 141, 151, 156, 159, 162, 172, 187, 224n.105, 243–4n.27, 266n.308, 266n.311, 272n.1, 276n.49, 277–8n.62, 278n.63, 280n.95
muhaddithun, 95, 247n.76
Muhammad, *see* Prophet Muhammad
muhtasib, 104, 113
mujtahid, see mujtahidun
mujtahidun, 98, 99
mujun, 97

mukhannasat, 158
   see also mukhannathun
mukhannath, see mukhannathun
mukhannathun, 94, 97, 278n.75
mulk, 88, 203–4n.23
Muqaddima, 153, 247n.77, 253n.139
murid, 156, 161, 164, 282n.118
Musharraf, Pervez, 147
Muslim modernism, 32, 129–32,
   134–5, 138, 193, 196, 249n.97,
   269n.355
Muslims
   Shi'a, 88, 101, 109, 113, 122,
   245n.47, 246n.50–1, 247n.76,
   254n.152, 255n.162, 255n.165,
   273n.12
   Sunni, 88, 95, 98, 103, 109,
   110, 112–13, 118, 120, 122, 133,
   147, 203–4n.23, 246n.50–1,
   247n.76, 248n.85, 248–9n.91,
   250n.106, 254n.147, 256n.176,
   256n.185, 262n.263, 275n.30,
   282n.121
mutakhannathin min al-rijal, 94
mutarajjulat min al-nisa', 94

nafs, 91, 137
Napoleon Bonaparte, 51, 54, 110,
Napoleonic Code, 51
Nasim, Ifti, 175
nation state, 53, 125, 129, 133, 138,
   140, 153, 192, 196, 273n.12
nationalism, 32, 84, 85, 128, 151, 160,
   205n.39, 269n.342
nazar ila al-amrad jamil, 98
   see also beloveds
neo-liberalism, 14, 18, 21, 30, 53, 73,
   76, 77, 79, 128, 146, 170, 180,
   186, 195
new historians, 82–3, 242n.18,
   243n.23
New Testament, 216n.21, 216n.28
Nietzsche, Friedrich, 17
Nigeria, 63, 224n.108, 270n.370

nirban, 160–1, 280n.105, 281n.113
nisa' mudhakkarat, 97
niyana, 172, 283n.134
niyyat, 176, 178
nizam, 133
Non-Aligned Movement, 56,
   226–7n.117
Normans, 45

O'Flaherty, Michael, 66
Old Testament, 39, 216n.21
Oman, 31
ordre public, 52
Organisation of American States, 61–2,
   71, 230–1n.167
Organisation of Islamic Co-operation,
   38, 62–3, 68 –73, 77, 79, 184,
   185, 226n.112, 231n.173,
   232n.178, 232n.180, 236n.225,
   284n.146
Orientalism, 12, 32, 76, 86, 135, 192,
   202n.5, 240n.247, 241n.251,
   264n.286
Origen, 39, 216n.27
Osman I, founder of the Ottoman
   Empire, 115, 259n.219
Osman III, Ottoman sultan, 265n.298
Ottoman Penal Code, 117, 127, 128
Ottomans, 108–10, 115–22, 125–8,
   138–9, 243–4n.27, 259n.219,
   260n.233, 262n.259–61,
   262n.264, 263n.275, 264n.286,
   264n.291–2, 267n.315,
   269n.339, 271n.396, 276n.48

pak nyah, 31
Pakistan, 2, 6, 7, 8, 9, 31, 38, 54, 63,
   69, 76, 132, 141–89, 192, 193,
   195, 196, 197
Pakistani law
   constitutional, 147, 148–51, 166,
   183, 186, 274n.19, 275n.31
   criminal, 132, 146–8, 149, 176–7,
   183, 223–4n.104, 224n.107

vernacular, 143, 151–3, 155,
182–3, 186–9, 192–3
Palestine, 184, 266n.309, 269n.341
Pamment, Claire, 158
panchayat, 153
patristics, 40, 41, 215n.14, 216n.27
Paul the Apostle, St, 40–3, 216n.28,
217n.39
peccatum mutum, 44, 51
pèlerinage inclusif, 153–4, 182
Pentateuch, 39
Persia, 88, 89, 102, 103, 121, 151, 156,
246n.50, 256n.185, 257n.189,
264n.292, 272n.1, 272n.3,
282n.116
see also Iran
Peter Cantor of Paris, 44
Peter Damian, St, 44–5, 221n.74
Peters, Rudolph, 118, 242n.18,
263n.285, 268n.337
Pillay, Navanethem, 59, 64
Plato, 15
post-coloniality, 7, 12, 15, 53, 55, 68,
70, 77–8, 84–5, 123, 134–5, 145,
147, 185–6, 241n.251, 282n.123
praxis, 93, 97, 155, 174, 190, 194–7,
241n.6, 254n.149, 255n.168
Prophet Abraham, 121
Prophet Jesus, 'Isa b. Maryam, Jesus
Christ, 40, 44, 164
Prophet Lot, 90–1, 93, 246n.55,
246n.58–60, 246n.62, 248n.86,
252n.130
Prophet Muhammad, 15, 32, 45, 72, 80,
82, 88, 89, 91–5, 99, 102, 105,
121, 196, 203n.22, 241n.6,
247n.79–80, 248n.85, 248–9n.91,
249n.92, 249n.99, 254n.149,
278n.75
proto-Realism, 82, 93, 97
see also legal Realism
Puar, Jasbir K., 76
Punjab, 6, 8, 141–5, 151–5, 156, 158,
160, 164, 165, 169–72, 174,

187–9, 201–2n.27, 273n.11,
274n.21, 276n.45, 278n.75,
280n.100, 281n.106, 282n.115,
283n.134

qadhf, 100, 243–4n.27, 273n.15
qadi, 81, 82, 88, 96, 97, 99–101,
103–4, 113–15, 117, 118, 126,
133, 139, 250n.111, 250–1n.113,
251n.117, 255n.163
qanun, see kanun
qat' al-tariq, see hiraba
qisas, 100, 254–5n.156
qisse, 152
qiyas, 94, 95, 99, 249n.95, 250–1n.113,
258n.200
qubl, 106
quda', see qadi
queer, 16, 26, 29, 31, 66, 76, 145,
155, 170, 173, 174, 240n.246,
244–5n.33, 275n.29
Qur'an, 32–3, 72, 80, 89–95, 97,
100, 105–6, 124, 131,
135–9, 143, 175, 243–4n.27,
246n.55, 249n.98, 250n.105,
252n.124, 252n.126, 253n.134,
254n.155, 255n.168, 282n.117,
282n.122

ra'y, 94, 95, 249n.95, 250n.105,
254n.146
Rabb, 91, 92, 272n.5
Rahman, Fazlur, 91
raison d'état, 83
rajm, 146–7
Rana, Bindiya, *khwajasara* activist, 150,
159, 162, 164, 166–8, 184, 186,
281n.111
Rao, Rahul, 76
rationalists, *see ahl al-ra'y*
reaya, 120, 262n.260
Reformation and Counter-Reformation,
78, 172, 187, 283n.131
Renaissance, 47, 48

renaissance of the twelfth century, 42, 47
renovatio imperii, 43
ressentiment, 17, 18
ri'asa, 83
Rida, Muhammad Rashid, 131,
    270n.365
ridda, 100, 243–4n.27
Robinson, Mary, 64,
Roman law, 37, 39, 41, 43, 95
Rome, ancient, 37, 39, 41, 43, 78, 95,
    121, 215n.14, 218n.48
Russia, 61, 222n.95, 223n.103,
    237n.233

Sa'ud, 'Abd al-Aziz, founder of Saudi
    Arabia, 132
ṣabb-ı emred, see beloveds
Safavids, 121
saff al-khuddam, 122
    see also khuddam
sahaba, 88, 105, 247–8n.80, 248n.85,
    249n.99, 254n.149
Salah al-Din Yusuf b. Ayyub, 121,
    266n.309
Sanjar, Seljuk sultan, 107
saqaliba, 121
Sarakhsi, Muhammad b. Ahmad, 106,
    258n.204
sariqa, 100, 243–4n.27
satr, 101, 118
Saudi Arabia, 85, 124, 125, 132–3,
    134, 200n.22, 266n.310
Schacht, Joseph, 83, 87–8, 242n.16,
    249n.96, 255n.163, 255n.168
scripturalism, 82–4, 87, 104,
    242n.16–17, 249n.92, 249n.96
Selim II, Ottoman sultan, 267n.323
Seljuks, 100, 102–4, 106–8, 119,
    121, 138–9, 246n.50, 254n.154,
    256–7n.185, 257–8n.197,
    259n.219, 271n.394
Seneca, 40, 217n.41
şeriat, see shari'a
Sexual Offences Act, 50

sexual orientation, 2, 11, 12, 19,
    20, 23–30, 36, 38, 52, 53, 56,
    58–70, 73, 77, 85, 102, 185, 193,
    209n.89, 209–10n.99, 211n.129,
    212n.134, 212n.136, 226n.113,
    227n.122, 228n.138, 229n.143,
    233n.188, 236n.228, 237n.230,
    238n.241
şeyhülislam, 116, 117,
Shafi'i, 'Abdullah ibn Idris, 95, 98, 99,
    253n.144, 254n.151,
Shafi'is, 102, 250n.106, 254n.151–2,
    254n.156, 256n.179
Shah, Almas (Bobby), *khwajasara*
    activist, 149, 166, 275n.34
Shalakany, Amr, 82–3, 242n.16,
    242n.18
shari'a, 68, 80–1, 83, 104, 116, 118,
    124, 132, 137, 197, 241–2n.7,
    242n.17, 252n.123, 261n.251,
    267n.325, 270n.370
Shaybani, Muhammad, 105, 262n.263
shaykh al-islam, see şeyhülislam
Shirazi, Abu Ishaq, 104
shubha, 100, 255n.162, 268n.337
shudhudh jinsi, 134
shurta, 104
Sikhism, 151, 155, 165
Sindh, 159, 168, 273n.11
sirat, 203n.22
siyar, 71–3, 79, 235n.219
siyasa, 82–3, 93, 102, 103–4, 107,
    109, 113, 118, 120, 133, 138,
    242n.15, 242n.17
siyasa shar'iyya, 114, 115, 133, 140,
    261n.251
social Darwinism, 15, 204n.25
Socrates, 15
Sodom, 41, 47, 51, 78, 107, 191,
    218n.50, 220n.63
sodomy, 44–8, 50–2, 54–5, 57,
    62, 75, 78, 102, 158, 191,
    220–1n.69, 221n.76, 222n.95,
    223n.98, 225n.109, 264n.286

Soroush, Abdolkarim, 132
Sousa Santos, Boaventura de, 9
Special Procedures, 59, 64, 66
spectacle, 154, 180–2
Spivak, Gayatri Chakravorty, 15, 204n.25
stare decisis, 130, 269n.353
Stoicism, 38, 40–1, 43, 217n.38
stoning to death, see *rajm*
stuprum, 41
subaltern, 15, 30, 204n.27
subjectivity, 4, 66, 77, 79, 85, 109, 111, 120, 122, 142, 144, 149, 150, 154, 155, 156, 162, 198n.1, 209–10n.99, 213n.148, 224n.105, 260n.233, 266n.308, 272n.3, 275n.34, 278n.64, 278n.75, 285n.8
Sufism, 98, 109, 113, 153, 164, 171, 266n.311, 281n.113, 282n.116–18
Sughdi, Abu'l-Hasan, 104
Süleyman I, Ottoman sultan, 117
sunna, 72, 92–5, 99, 131, 138, 196, 241n.6, 249n.92, 249n.98–9
  madiya, 95
  see also Prophet Muhammad
Supreme Court of Pakistan, 147–53, 166–8, 177–8, 182, 188, 274n.19, 274n.23, 274–5, n. 26, 275n.32–3, 276n.52
Synod of Gangra, 41
Syria, 63, 88, 109, 110, 132, 266n.309, 269n.341

ta'zir, 100–1, 103–5, 107, 118, 133, 255n.158, 256n.181
tamasha, see spectacle
Tanzimat, 109, 120, 125, 126–7, 265n.302
taqlid, 98, 254n.147
tashri', 131
Templars, the Knights, 47

temps géographique, 86–7
temps individuel, 86–7
temps social, 86
theopolitics, 45, 68, 114, 125, 132, 146, 153, 182, 183, 184, 284n.146
traditionalists, see *ahl al-hadith*
transculturation, 77, 241n.250
translation, socio-cultural process, 143, 183, 188, 193–4, 196, 197, 213n.145, 218n.46, 246n.55, 252n.124, 261n.251
Turkey, 63, 115, 127–8, 226n.114, 270n.370

ulama, 95, 103, 112, 113, 119, 133, 172, 175, 262n.260, 274–5n.26
ulema, see ulama
'Umar b. al-Khattab, 88, 245n.46, 249n.98
Umayyads, 88, 121, 138, 249n.92
umma, 32, 33, 70, 80–1, 84, 87, 92–4, 97, 123, 125, 131, 135, 137, 139, 154–5, 159, 175, 182, 192, 269n.355
'Uthman b. 'Affan, 88, 245n.46
United Kingdom, 52–5, 73, 75, 78, 124, 125–6, 132, 138, 146, 147, 151, 153, 156–7, 159, 191, 223–4n.104, 224n.107–8, 224–5n.108, 225n.109, 226n.114, 231n.171, 239–40n.243, 268n.329, 268n.331, 268n.334, 268n.336, 270–1n.378, 273n.11, 274n.22, 276n.45, 276n.49
United Nations, 18, 35, 53, 55, 57–9, 62–6, 68–71, 74, 76, 79, 184
United States of America, 15, 35, 56, 71, 73, 74, 76, 133, 144, 180, 208n.77, 209n.89, 211n.129, 232n.178, 233–4n.195, 236n.228, 237n.230, 239n.242, 276–7n54

Universal Declaration of Human Rights, 69, 71, 72
Universal Islamic Declaration of Human Rights, 71, 72
universalism, 11, 14–16, 30, 56, 84, 86
Ur-Nammu, 15
usul al-fiqh, 81, 83, 92, 94

Verbum abbreviatum, 44
vernacular knowledge, 143, 153, 160, 175, 183, 188, 189, 193, 194, 272n.4
insurectionary, 190, 193
vice ultramountain, 51, 223n.98
vitium nefandum, 45, 52
Vitry, Cardinal Jacques de, 45

Wadud, Amina, 154
Wahhabism, 131, 133
waqf, see awqaf
waria, 31, 213n.146
Waris Shah, 152, 153
Wars of *Ridda*, 88
Weber, Max, 81
wilayat, 114
wildan al-mukhalladun, 97
William II, king of England, 45, 46
William of Malmesbury, Benedictine historian, 46, 221n.71
William of Nogaret, councillor to Philip IV of France, 47

Wolfenden Committee, 50,
world conferences on women, 57

yasa
Mamluk, 115, 259–60n.
Mongol, 110, 115
yeniçeri, the Janissaries, 119–20
Yogyakarta Principles, 12, 24–9, 59, 64–7, 185

Zahiris, 101, 256n.176
zajr, 102
Zangi, Nur al-Din, 266n.309
Zardari, Asif Ali, 147
zat, 161
zawaj, 91–2
Ze'evi, Dror, 119
zenana
subjectivity, 1–2, 31, 141, 155, 157–61, 166, 198n.1, 278n.64, 280n.105, 281n.106, 281n.108
women's quarters, 141, 156–7, 278n.64
Zia-ul-Haq, Muhammad, 146–8, 273n.15
zikr, see dhikr
zina, 89, 91, 100–2, 104–6, 108, 118, 127, 140, 147, 149, 183, 191, 243–4n.27, 246n.64, 255n.162–3, 258n.204, 262n.263, 270n.370, 273n.15, 275n.30, 284n.142

www.ingramcontent.com/pod-product-compliance
Lightning Source LLC
Chambersburg PA
CBHW060142280326
41932CB00012B/1604